Liberal Modernism
and Democratic Individuality

Liberal Modernism
and Democratic Individuality

GEORGE KATEB

AND THE PRACTICES OF POLITICS

EDITED BY
AUSTIN SARAT
AND
DANA R. VILLA

PRINCETON UNIVERSITY PRESS

PRINCETON, NEW JERSEY

Library of Congress Cataloging-in-Publication Data

Liberal modernism and democratic individuality : George Kateb and
the practices of politics /edited by Austin Sarat and Dana R. Villa.
p.   cm.
Includes index.
ISBN 0-691-02596-7 (alk. paper)
1. Individualism.   2. Liberalism   3. Democracy   4. Kateb, George—Contributions in
political science.   I. Sarat, Austin.   II. Villa, Dana Richard.
JC571.L5294   1996   320.5'12—dc20   96-16565

This book has been composed in Sabon

Princeton University Press books are printed on acid-free paper and meet the guidelines for
permanence and durability of the Committee on Production Guidelines for Book
Longevity of the Council on Library Resources

Printed in the United States of America
by Princeton Academic Press

1   3   5   7   9   10   8   6   4   2

1   3   5   7   9   10   8   6   4   2
(pbk)

• CONTENTS •

• A C K N O W L E D G M E N T S •

WE ARE GRATEFUL to the friends, former students, and colleagues of George Kateb whose work is contained in this volume for their enthusiastic response to our invitation to write about George, his scholarship, and his passionate commitment to the life of the mind. George sets an example for all of us, an example of what it means to be a democratic individual, an inspiring teacher, and a humane person. His writings provide a rich legacy of engagement with the most important issues of our times. We are grateful to him for that legacy, but most of all for his inspiring example and his steadfast friendship.

We also would like to acknowledge the generous support of Amherst College and express our thanks to Peter Pouncey and Lisa Raskin for their help.

We are grateful for permission to reprint the following as chapters in this book:

> Jeffrey Abramson's essay on "Juries and Local Justice" is reprinted with minor changes and a new conclusion from Chapter 1 of his book, *We, The Jury: The Jury System and the Ideal of Democracy* (Basic Books, 1994). Permission to reprint granted by the author and publisher.
>
> David Bromwich, "Mary Wollstonecraft as a Critic of Burke," from *Political Theory* 23 (1995): 617–634. Reprinted by permission of Sage Publications.
>
> Austin Sarat, "Doing Death: Violence, Responsibility, and the Role of the Jury in Capital Trials," from *Indiana Law Journal* 70 (1995): 1103–35. Reprinted by permission of Indiana Law Journal.
>
> George Shulman, "American Political Culture, Prophetic Narration, and Toni Morrison's *Beloved*," from Shulman, "Narrative, Political Culture, and American Politics," *Political Theory* (forthcoming). Reprinted by permission of Sage Publications.
>
> Kim Townsend, "William James's Rugged Individualism." Adapted from Kim Townsend's *Manhood at Harvard*, New York, W. W. Norton, 1996. Reprinted by permission of the publisher.

Unpublished letters of William James and unpublished typescript of Henry James III excerpted by permission of the Houghton Library, Harvard University.

"A Cabin in the Clearing," from *In the Clearing* by Robert Frost. Copyright 1942, 1948, 1950, 1951, 1952, 1953, 1954 © 1955, 1956, 1958, 1959, 1960, 1961, 1962 by Robert Frost. Reprinted by permission of Henry Holt and Co., Inc.

JEFFREY ABRAMSON is Louis Stulberg Professor of Law and Politics at Brandeis University.

BENJAMIN R. BARBER is Professor of Political Science and Director of the Walt Whitman Center at Rutgers University.

DAVID BROMWICH is Professor of English at Yale University.

WILLIAM E. CONNOLLY is Professor of Political Science at Johns Hopkins University.

THOMAS L. DUMM is Associate Professor of Political Science at Amherst College.

AMY GUTMANN is Professor of Political Science and Dean of the Faculty at Princeton University.

JOHN HOLLANDER is the A. Barlett Giamatti Professor of English at Yale University.

HELENE KEYSSAR is Professor of Communication at the University of California, San Diego.

AUSTIN SARAT is the William Nelson Cromwell Professor of Jurisprudence and Political Science at Amherst College.

JUDITH SHKLAR was the John Vowles Professor of Government at Harvard University.

GEORGE SHULMAN is Assistant Professor of Political Science at New York University.

TRACY B. STRONG is Professor of Political Science at the University of California, San Diego.

LESLIE PAUL THIELE is Assistant Professor of Political Science at the University of Florida.

KIM TOWNSEND is Professor of English at Amherst College.

DANA R. VILLA is Assistant Professor of Political Science at Amherst College.

CORNEL WEST is Professor of African-American Studies at Harvard University.

Liberal Modernism
and Democratic Individuality

Liberalism, Modernism, and the Political Theory of George Kateb: An Introduction

DANA R. VILLA AND AUSTIN SARAT

WHAT IS democratic individuality, and what are its prospects in the modern age? Is democratic individuality a normatively desirable political position, or does it do violence to the appropriate claims of group identity and community life? How, if at all, does it differ from traditional liberal individualism? What sort of self is appropriate for a democratic individual, and how is that self revealed in the cultural projects and civic engagements of constitutional democracy? These are the central questions taken up by LIBERAL MODERNISM AND DEMOCRATIC INDIVIDUALITY: GEORGE KATEB AND THE PRACTICES OF POLITICS.

While the essays assembled here cross disciplinary divides separating political theory, literary studies, and the humanistic analysis of culture, they are brought together by a shared interest in exploring the significance of democratic individuality and by a shared desire to honor George Kateb, whose distinguished career as a teacher and scholar at Amherst College and Princeton University has been marked by a passionate devotion to that idea. They are written by his former students, by his colleagues from Amherst and Princeton, and by scholars from further afield who engage Kateb's passion for political theory as well as his distinctive arguments about the nature and desirability of democratic individuality. These essays are by no means merely celebratory; they honor Kateb through the intellectual work they do and through their cumulative contribution to the effort to understand the fate of democratic individuality in the modern age.

•

For over thirty years, George Kateb—along with John Rawls, the late Judith Shklar, and Sir Isaiah Berlin—has been one of liberal political theory's most distinctive voices. An eloquent spokesman for the moral dimensions of individual rights and constitutional democracy, he is a fierce critic of statism and communitarianism, a staunch advocate of individualism in the struggle against all forms of paternalism, conformity, and groupthink. He is, in short, a "liberal's liberal." This characterization, however, is somewhat misleading; and as the essays in this volume demonstrate, it ultimately conceals more than it reveals.

Approached simply as "liberal political theory," the import of Kateb's work seems plain: we believe we can grasp it, so to speak, *avant la lettre*. After all, what political philosophy is more familiar than liberalism? What regime is more familiar than constitutional democracy? And what "ideology" is more firmly entrenched than individualism? Confronted by a theorist who, like Kateb, advocates individualism as the moral center of our culture and who seeks to "justify" constitutional democracy in terms of this moral center, one is prepared to encounter an edifying banality, a moralizing platitude.[1]

Of course, as anyone who knows or reads Kateb can attest, he has little tolerance for banality. Indeed, his work represents a sustained protest against the banality that liberalism (or, more accurately, liberal individualism) has become. Thus, while Kateb begins with the most familiar of themes—the dignity of the individual, the theory of rights, constitutionalism—his trajectory is always toward the unfamiliar, toward the forgotten or previously unarticulated. He is, like Walter Benjamin, a kind of "pearl fisher": he has the uncanny ability to take the most familiar fragments of our culture and render them "rich and strange."[2] Thus liberal political philosophy, is, in Kateb's account, intimately tied to the "death of God" and the legitimacy of the modern age; democratic individuality expands the existential possibilities hinted at by Nietzsche and Heidegger, and the theory of rights becomes a prolegomenon to a new moral-aesthetic attitude toward existence as such.[3] Liberalism is more than a narrow, political doctrine. It is, and invites, a way of being in the world that defies conventional understandings. For Kateb, the radiating effects of life in a constitutional democracy spread throughout the culture and challenge each individual to be civically engaged in a way that avoids both self-interest and self-righteousness.

As a political theorist, Kateb's broad concern has been to unveil the cultural, moral, and existential dimensions of our liberal, constitutionalist, and American heritage that have been obscured by "piety, cynicism, boredom, and familiarity."[4] His scholarship suggests that we have grasped only the surface of the doctrines, institutions, and cultural innovations we claim to know so well: their real significance—their moral and existential significance—remains unexplored. Kateb invites his readers to go beneath the surface by surfacing taken-for-granted aspects of our political life. His political theory is edifying; it broadens our understanding of both the vocation of political theory and the nature of politics itself. And he is no respecter of boundaries: his work knits together philosophical, political, cultural, and literary perspectives to provoke a reexamination of liberalism in the modern era.

Kateb is, moreover, painfully aware of the role that liberal theory itself has played in inhibiting such a reexamination. Hence his fight is not only with the usual critics of liberalism, but with liberal theory itself, at least with its ascendent (Kantian, utilitarian) modes. The theoretical discourse of liberalism tends either to falsely describe autonomy or to undermine it. The result is a radically foreshortened individualism, one subject to deontological or teleological constraints, an individualism cut off from its most profound cultural resonances. In this way, liberal theory blocks our ability to appreciate the new mode of being-in-the-world made possible by liberal democratic culture. Following the Emersonians, Kateb calls this new mode of existence democratic individuality.[5]

For Kateb, democratic individuality denotes a revolutionary conception of experience and selfhood, one implicit in rights-based individualism and constitutional democracy.[6] Its original articulators were Emerson, Whitman and Thoreau, voices largely ignored by liberal theory.[7] Kateb seeks to repair this disregard, to tease out the cultural, moral, and existential dimensions of this new notion of self by developing the suggestions of the Emersonians. But while the Emersonians are crucial to understanding the contribution democratic culture makes to fostering this mode of individuality, they are ultimately insufficient.[8] To supplement, correct, and (if possible) deepen their insights, Kateb calls upon not only liberal writers, such as Mill and Tocqueville, but antiliberal ones as well: Arendt, Foucault, Nietzsche, and Heidegger. The theme of democratic individualism, as conceived by Kateb, is too large for liberalism; it is even, strange to say, too large for Emerson, Whitman, and Thoreau.

The reason for this should be clear. In Kateb's view, democratic individuality is something more than the culmination of liberalism or the distinctive American contribution to liberalism. Democratic individuality stands for a genuinely modern form of selfhood, a self capable not merely of choosing itself, of transcending role and convention, but also of periodically transcending its own drive to self-creation and redefinition. Democratic individuality feeds on modernity's Faustian and Promethean energies, but it also purges these energies of resentment and the will to power. It fosters an attitude toward the given that is at once affirming and transformative. The democratic individual is aware of evil in its distinctly modern forms, but is not paralyzed by it. Democratic individuals thrive on a life with others, but will not live for others, or as others live. They take themselves both seriously and playfully; they are as Kateb says, both in and out of the game. Thus, the theme of democratic individuality implicates, at its deepest level, the question of modernity.

The power of Kateb's writing flows, at least in part, from his refusal to separate the theme of democratic individuality from the question of modernity. To do so would be to promote yet another version of American exceptionalism. It is because the question of modernity—its nature, prospects, and pathologies—forms the ever present backdrop to his work that Kateb is able to avoid this trap and do so much to enrich liberal theory. Modernity is a "symbol of ultimate concern" in Kateb's work. In this concern, Kateb seeks to understand the conditions of democratic politics and the culture it fosters. We can trace the thematic development of his oeuvre in light of this overarching concern. Let us begin with *Utopia and Its Enemies* (1963).

A reader familiar only with Kateb's later work will be startled by his first book, a passionate defense of *modern* utopian aspirations in the face of powerful and corrosive criticism born not only of the cold war and the "end of ideology" but of the technological age itself. Kateb's consideration of the range of modern antiutopian argument contrasts significantly with Shklar's *After Utopia* (1957).[9] The latter skeptically surveys the romantic critique of the Enlightenment's social and political hopes, showing how this critique is developed in a number of directions by twentieth century thought. Shklar's approach to modern antiutopianism is, broadly, Hegelian: she historicizes it as a mode of "unhappy consciousness," which arose in response to the French Revolution. Kateb, in contrast, takes a detour off the Hegelian "highway of despair." What concerns him is not so much the "spirit of the age" as the surprising growth in antiutopian thought at the historical moment when the traditional goals of utopian aspiration—peace, abundance, leisure, equality, and "untroubled virtue"[10]—appear, technologically speaking, attainable. It is at this moment, over a hundred years *after* the French Revolution, that modern antiutopian thought really comes into its own, offering damning critiques not only of the instrumentalities necessary to attain and maintain utopia, but—most surprisingly—of utopian goals themselves. With high modernity comes the paradoxical demand that we repudiate what has been, in Kateb's words, "the moral prepossession of our race"—utopian aspiration—*for moral reasons*.[11]

Utopia and Its Enemies thoroughly canvasses the strongest arguments of modern antiutopianism, heaping difficulty upon difficulty for the utopian apologist (Kateb). No argument—and Kateb surveys nineteenth- and twentieth-century philosophy, literature, and political and social theory—is left unanswered. Moreover, he goes out of his way to register the most telling objections, the better to refine and clarify utopian hopes in the present. This respect for, and engagement with, the best arguments one's opponents have to offer is an instruction in the proper vocation of political theory. Taking on such arguments, Kateb demonstrates how those who would reject utopian politics on the ground that it leads to "dirty hands" preach an absolutism likely to lead to bloody consequences in the political realm.[12]

Like Weber, Kateb insists that the appropriate ethic in the political sphere is not complete abstention from violence, but the ethic of the lesser evil. Only the latter ethic avoids enabling truly radical evil. Kateb further shows how those, like Popper, who argue that the scale of radical or revolutionary change necessarily creates greater evil succumb to the very same myth of historical inevitability they detect in their Marxian-Hegelian opponents.[13] The fallacy is to think that radical political change—the revolution, if you will—is always already immoral, incapable of turning rotten because it already was, in its essence, a moral and political disaster.

Despite the pause given us by the fate of the Russian Revolution, Kateb reminds us that there is no *necessary* link between radical political change and increased state domination. Indeed, in certain circumstances, radical political change is the only moral alternative. Finally, Kateb demonstrates how the technological and political means necessary for maintaining utopia need not result in a static society or the reintroduction of the distinction between rulers and ruled, as some antiutopians fear.[14]

So much for the antiutopian critique of utopian means. The real moral energy animating *Utopia and Its Enemies* is apparent in Kateb's discussion of the antiutopian critique of utopian ends—perpetual peace, guaranteed abundance, and "conditioned" virtue. Crudely put, the argument against these ends boils down to the assertion that a society characterized by peace and abundance, whose members have been educated, or "conditioned," to virtue, is a society bereft of human difference, depth, and genuine aspiration. One way or another, it will resemble Plato's "city of pigs"; it will be devoid of all genuine wisdom, art, effort, and culture. Ironically, the very idea of utopia is seen as depriving humanity of its dignity.

That Kateb finds much in the antiutopian argument compelling ought not to be surprising given his subsequent development of the theory of democratic individuality and his call for "moderate alienation." Ultimately, however, he sees the antiutopian argument as motivated by either a kitschy aestheticism—a willingness to promote human division and suffering for the sake of aesthetic delectation—or by a residual religious desire to be overwhelmed by unfathomable powers (the "mysteries" of the human soul). Why not, for example, promote the behavioral and psychological sciences in the quest to create a better society, since to eschew their aid is finally to prefer the domination of fatelike forces? This is the context for Kateb's surprising defense of B. F. Skinner, a defense totally in the spirit of the Enlightenment.

What is at stake for Kateb in answering the arguments of modern antiutopians? To let their objections stand, to be persuaded by their arguments, would be to repudiate what Kateb considers an essential part—perhaps *the* essential part—of the moral legacy of the West. To regard utopian aspiration and exertion simply as a mistake (or a disguised will to power) is to bury, once and for all, the source of moral energy that informs the most admirable human action and achievement throughout history. And as Kateb reminds us throughout his work, action and achievement are an important expression of human freedom. To criticize utopian aspiration and exertion is to give in to the Christian, premodern idea that to be human is, necessarily, to suffer. It is to think, most intolerably, that people must be left to suffer. In sum, to give way before the modern antiutopians is to give up on the modern project. This is something Kateb steadfastly refuses to do. Here, as in his later work, Kateb seeks to take advantage of the opportunities that modernity makes available for the development of a richer, more complete individualism.

Kateb's *Political Theory: Its Nature and Uses* (1968) is a different sort of book, a sophisticated introduction to the vocation of political theory. At first, the connections between it and *Utopia and Its Enemies*, let alone the larger theme of modernity, are hard to discern. But just as *Utopia and Its*

Enemies sought to preserve the moral core of utopian aspiration from the pessimism engendered by technological expansion and ubiquitous rationalization, *Political Theory* asserts the integrity of its subject as a species of moral philosophy in an age of specialized scholarship, or *Wissenschaft*. The overview Kateb provides of the field, and particularly his defense of the works that make up the "great tradition," is a direct response to those inclined to measure the worth and maturity of a discipline according to standards of agreement and accumulation of knowledge.

In the face of the prejudices of what Kuhn calls "normal science," Kateb sets out to revalue moral and political disagreement. His goal, however, is not merely to pose political theory's plurality of discordant voices as a kind of aesthetic counterweight to the steady, lockstep advance of social science. Rather, it is to focus attention on the common questions and commitments that inform the diverse writings that make up the canon of political theory. The hope is that once we appreciate the nature of the questions and the shared quality of the commitments, we will cease viewing political theory as either an immature form of science or a clumsy approximation of truth. Political theory is, rather, a kind of questioning that human beings, so long as they remain political animals, can never really escape. It is a questioning concerning the moral role of politics and the impact of civic engagement on the lives of citizens and on the cultural forms in which it is embedded.

Like the defenses of political theory put forth by Strauss in *What Is Political Philosophy?* and Voegelin in *The New Science of Politics*, Kateb's discussion stands in the formidable shadow of Max Weber.[15] The ascetic legislating voice of Weber's *Vocation* lectures serves as Kateb's silent partner in dialogue as he attempts to mark out the boundaries of a field that, according to Weber, is an anachronism, the plaything of some "big children" in the universities.[16] Kateb's description of political theory as writing that treats politics from "a broadly moral point of view" and is driven by the "fundamental" question of "What ends or purposes should government serve?" is no quaint Aristotelianism.[17] Rather, it should be read as a vehement rejection of the Weberian claim that the historical plurality of purposes pursued by political societies renders any attempt to delimit the state—or more broadly, the political—in terms of ends both arbitrary and incoherent.[18] By thematizing the question of ends as the fundamental question of political theory, Kateb distances himself from both the Weberian rejection of its normative dimension (accomplished by the call to focus on the instrumentalities rather than the purposes of the political association) and, more sweepingly, social science's claim to have replaced political theory. The standard by which Weber judges the question of ends to be meaningless or subjective— the fact that it does not permit of a single defining (and definitive) answer—is itself rejected as an inherited prejudice of metaphysics.

Disagreement—the conflicting array of answers to the "fundamental" question—is, then, the stuff of political theory, as it is the stuff of politics, for Kateb. Implicit in this recognizably liberal stance is a rejection of Strauss's

Platonist assumption that the goal of the political theorist is to replace opinion about moral and political matters with knowledge.[19] However, contrary to expectation, Kateb's rejection of the "dogmatic" stance does not lead him to endorse a Millian eclecticism that recognizes the presence of partial truths in each of the great political theorists. Nor does the essential fact of disagreement lead him to flirt with a historicizing relativism that explains the variation in answers by appeal to historical context (e.g., Skinner, Pocock). Kateb rejects these and other stances toward the disagreement that itself constitutes political theory, faulting all of them for failing to acknowledge the very thing that underlies political theory's lack of consensus, namely, a continuous commitment on the part of the great political theorists to the idea of the common good.[20] The more we overlook this commitment, the more inclined we will be to turn the tradition into a receptacle for timeless truth or to see its diversity as a prefiguration of Weber's "warring gods."[21] As he thinks about the vocation of political theory, Kateb steers a middle course between those who would reify political theory as a set of eternal answers to eternal questions and those who, like the postmodern inheritors of Weber, would deny the "language game" of normative political theory any integrity whatsoever. This middle course is not an attempt at mediation or synthesis, but a resolutely modernist attempt to avoid both dogmatism and relativism while eschewing the comforts of consensus.[22]

Kateb's strong emphasis upon disagreement informed by common commitment resonates with Hannah Arendt's vision of a genuine politics. The similarities, however, are more than balanced by Kateb's aversion to her idea that the game of politics is worth playing for its own sake, that the political should be granted a certain relative autonomy from the moral.[23] It is easy to see why Arendt, the "great anti-modernist," would exert a special fascination for Kateb, a fascination that culminates in his admiring yet tenaciously critical study, *Hannah Arendt: Politics, Conscience, Evil* (1984).

Kateb describes Arendt as a thinker whose "intellectual passion is devoted to distilling the meaning of modernity, of the new."[24] The characterization is an apt one; it captures not only Arendt's spirit, but Kateb's as well. But while both Arendt and Kateb are engaged in the project of "distilling the meaning of modernity," the meanings they extract are radically at odds. Following Nietzsche and Heidegger, Arendt views modernity as the age in which "resentment of the human condition" (i.e., resentment of the limits that condition and, to that extent, define human existence) reaches its apogee. The results of modernity's Faustian, extremist exertion are radical estrangement and horror. Our rejection of limits, our espousal of the belief that everything is possible, yields barbarism on an unprecedented scale.[25] Worse—and there is worse—such rejection effectively destroys the possibility of our ever being at home in the world. Kateb views modernist extremist exertion in an entirely different (and much more favorable) light. He acknowledges that the drive to overcome limitation may produce horror, yet also produces more than horror. Moreover, by fostering what Kateb calls a moderate (or everyday) alienation, modernity promotes a restless and improvisational attachment to existence.[26] Such attachment cultivates the ability to be at home in *not* being at home.[27] One becomes free for a creative self-fashioning when one knows no telos. This creative self-fashioning occurs, under the pressures of modernity, in the cultural and political realms. Cultural and civic engagements become more complex and problematic even as they provide an expanded arena for individualism, correctly understood.

Arendt's nostalgia for being at home—a nostalgia that she, like Novalis, recognized as a kind of *déformation professionalle* of the philosopher[28]—transforms political theory into the search for avenues of reconciliation. The avenue favored by the "Greek" Arendt—political action—is, as Kateb emphasizes, a surprising and paradoxical one.[29] For Arendt, no human activity surpasses genuine political action in existential significance. Action is, indeed, a kind of miracle, the miracle that "saves the world." Unlike all other forms of extremist exertion, political action mobilizes our agonistic and initiatory energies in a way that strengthens, rather than undermines, our commitment to the world. Action situates the self *in* a world; it provides the self with a public arena in which it can achieve a distinct identity through words and deeds; it creates meaning within a bounded whole, and thereby defeats the tragic wisdom of Silenus.[30] Modernity's greatest sin is to destroy this boundedness, thus rendering reconciliation with existence infinitely problematic. The "moral" of Arendt's critique of modernity is to counsel the repudiation of extremist exertion and acceptance of the limits intrinsic to the human condition.[31] Acceptance is the antidote to existential resentment, to Nietzsche's spirit of revenge; it is also the first step toward recovery of a public world and the meaning such a world makes possible.

Kateb recounts Arendt's critique with detachment and a certain sympathy. He counsels us, however, to beware the impulse to turn political theory into a vehicle that promotes reconciliation, that encourages acceptance. If we are to appreciate the existential possibilities opened by modernity, Kateb argues, it is precisely the "religious" temptation to valorize limitation as good and extremist exertion as evil that we must resist.[32] Here he returns to the subject of his critique in *Utopia and Its Enemies*. We must stop thinking of ourselves as exiles from a homeland: the idea of a homeland dies with God. We must also be attuned to the bad faith of all forms of *Gelassenheit*—even those that, like Arendt's, give a privileged place to action as "the true road to acceptance."[33] We must find another, completely secular way of expressing "thankfulness for being."

According to Arendt, the modern project can be seen, *à la* Marx and Hegel, as an attempt to completely humanize the world. For Marx and Hegel, the success of this project signals the end of alienation. For Arendt, as Kateb notes, this putative end of alienation is, in fact, its most extreme form: "The extreme of the human is . . . unnatural; the abolition of otherness in its otherness . . . is the *triumph* of alienation."[34] Human mastery of the world and of nature creates the kind of ontological homogenization Heidegger conveys with the notion of "standing-reserve": our world is characterized by the loss of all objective reality.[35] Not the will to mastery, but resentment of the human condition is to blame for this state of affairs. Resentment leads to extremism, and thence to alienation.[36] In Arendt's view, this alienation can only increase so long as contempt for the given remains an integral component of modernist dynamism.[37]

Contempt can be expunged only by gratitude for being, by wonder at the fact that there is something rather than nothing.[38] Such wonder is the basis of an attachment to existence characterized by grateful acceptance. For Arendt, only such an attachment overcomes world and earth alienation, enabling us to be free for the world, to be worldly once again. Insofar as the modern project is driven by existential resentment, by the extremist aspiration to remake the world in accordance with our needs, Arendt is at war with it.[39]

Kateb's response to Arendt is remarkable for its lack of bad faith. Unlike the liberal believer in progress, he makes no attempt to deny resentment and alienation as the hallmarks of modernity: Arendt's analysis is correct in this regard. Kateb's strategy is to suggest, via Emerson, a transformative revaluation of these distinctively modern phenomena. The essence of modernist resentment is not resentment of the human condition per se, but of human imperfection.[40] This Emersonian thought transforms our perspective on resentment: it appears now not as rancor but rather as mobility, as a kind of restless, antiteleological perfectionism. Antiteleological perfectionism—Emersonian perfectionism—enables us to affirm existence as we "work very hard to keep from feeling gratitude."[41] Indeed, Kateb goes so far as to suggest that the kind of extremist exertion favored by Emerson— the relentless quest to transcend all self-given boundaries—issues in a deeper form of thankfulness for being than the finitude-fixated thought of Arendt or Heidegger.

We have already noted how Kateb suggests a similar revaluation of alienation, one directed against the Arendtian ideal of being at home in the world. Such a revaluation of alienation is possible once we stop viewing individualism as a symptom of the pathological subjectivism of modernity. For Arendt, all forms of individualism (with the sole exception of agonistic citizenship) serve to further alienate us from the world. Yet this way of seeing things, Kateb suggests, blinds us to the positive value of alienation, its beneficial effects vis-à-vis the individual. The force of Arendt's "love of world" prevents her from seeing that "the true beneficiary of all the dislocations and uncertainties of modernity is the democratic individual living in a culture of moderate alienation and himself sharing in that alienation."[42] Thus, while Arendt is "probably right to see individualism as a symptom and expression of alienation," the theory of democratic individuality implicitly contained in the work of Emerson, Whitman, and Thoreau shows us how to convert this "distress and loss" into a "great good."[43] As Kateb puts it, "[E]ach individual becomes individual because the general condition of moderate alienation provides the opening."[44] Modernity turns out to be a great opportunity and resource for democratic individuality. The need is for cultural and political forms to respond to the restless energy of the democratic individual.

The perspective of democratic individuality, then, enables the transvaluation of the pathologies of modernity into great existential possibilities. Another way of putting this is to say that the redemption of modernity hinges upon the possibility of democratic individuality. Indeed, for Kateb, democratic individuality is the only thing that could genuinely redeem modernity and its horrors: "To wrest something fine from modernity requires sympathy to the ideal of democratic individuality."[45] It is democratic individuality, and not any presumed amelioration of the conditions of human existence, which allows us to be modernists in good faith.

While Kateb's *Hannah Arendt* ends with the evocation of Emerson, Whitman, and Thoreau, the essays collected in *The Inner Ocean* (1992) are entirely animated by their presence. It is in these essays that Kateb most fully develops his unique brand of Emersonian liberalism, a liberalism that focuses on the culture of democracy and the moral and existential attachments it makes possible.

The Inner Ocean, then, is Kateb's most fully Emersonian book, which is to say, his most American. This is readily apparent on a number of levels, beginning with the strong libertarian streak in Kateb's argument and his vigorous defense of constitutional representative democracy as the best regime. But while the primary ground of this defense, or "justification," is explicitly moral (viz., constitutional democracy's aspiration to "preserve rights and honor human dignity"), the real force of the argument aims at the moral-existential. Constitutional democracy has inestimable moral worth because it is predicated upon the defense of rights; yet it also has an equal moral-existential worth as the "indispensable provocation to a new way of life."[46] The rights-based individualism of constitutional democracy has profound (yet indirect) moral effects; through these effects it gives rise to a distinctive democratic culture:

> The combined effects, over time, of living with rights against government and also experiencing its form and routine workings are a potent force for revising human self-conception and all human relations. The meanings of rights are spread everywhere into society, in all the rest of life apart from government. As everyday life is revised, it shows more and more evidences of democratic individuality, which is a cultural, indeed a spiritual outgrowth and elaboration of rights-based individualism in a constitutional democracy.[47]

The greater part of *The Inner Ocean* is devoted to examining the nature and meaning of this "outgrowth." In this book, Kateb brings together his thinking about culture, meaning, and civic engagement in the modern era. It is Kateb's contention that constitutional democracy foments a "radical alteration of culture," one that creates a radically new kind of individualism and—it hardly need be said—a radically new kind of individual. This is an important point, since Kateb wishes to distinguish democratic individualism from competing (possessive or aristocratic) forms. Indeed, he goes so far as to characterize the Emersonian tradition as "an attempt to sever democratic individuality from all the other individualisms that resemble but reject or betray it, or that developed with it but then swerve and become narrowly extreme."[48]

What aspects define democratic individuality at this cultural level? Recalling the analyses of Plato and Tocqueville, Kateb picks out positive, negative, and "impersonal" aspects of democratic individuality. The culture produces human beings who "think of themselves as equal individuals and who therefore intermittently abandon ascribed identities and exchange roles."[49] Democratic individuals are characterized by mobility, restlessness, and experimentation; they strive to escape "the immemorial association of ordinariness with plainness or even ugliness"; they are driven to work on themselves.[50] Negatively, they are disposed to actively resist victimization or stigmatization. They demand not only the recognition of rights but, as members of marginal groups, speak and act on behalf of "a reconstruction of everyday life."[51] Finally, at the impersonal level, the culturally democratic individual is characterized by an "almost promiscuous acceptance of one thing after another, almost no matter what."[52]

So much for individualism at the "normal level of democratic culture." While appreciative of the many virtues it displays, this level does not attract the most intense attention of the Emersonians or, for that matter, of Kateb. The writings of the Emersonians address what Kateb calls the "higher levels of democratic individuality," its *extraordinary* "moments, moods, and episodes."[53] Extraordinary democratic individuality is manifest in "occasions of individual thinking, newly innocent perception, self-expressive activity, unexpected creativity,"[54] whether they are revealed in political engagement or in aesthetic production. What lies at the root of such disparate moments is "release from convention," a release sponsored by "all the conventions of democracy." Seen from the perspective of democratic extraordinariness, these conventions have their raison d'être in the "bursts" of self-reliance they make possible. It is the nature of democratic conventions to call attention to their conventionality, to undermine both the mystique of authority and the apparent naturalness of the social. In this way they help to encourage episodes of individual transcendence of convention through self-reliance.[55] Thus, at the "extraordinary" level, democratic individuality manifests itself in an existential intensity and honesty, in a fierce resistance to the self-loss encouraged by routine or everyday existence (what Heidegger calls "fallenness").[56]

Like the "normal level of democratic culture," the extraordinary level described by the Emersonians has negative and impersonal aspects as well. As with the positive aspects, these elements of extraordinary democratic individuality are intensifications of tendencies present in democratic culture at large. They include, negatively, episodes of public citizenship in which "some people whose rights are protected initiate resistance in behalf of others who are denied their rights, or join them in common struggle."[57] Extraordinary democratic individuality is manifest in an impersonal mode in those moments where "one labors to bestow sympathy abundantly, especially on what seems most to discourage or repel it."[58] In such efforts one finds "a belief in radical equality made aesthetic." Finally, over and above the various positive, negative, and impersonal manifestations of democratic extraordinariness there are those "moments, moods, and episodes" in which "one experiences a democratized understanding of all reality, an understanding which goes beyond self and society but does not (necessarily) aspire to the supernatural or more than human."[59] This is the highest level of extraordinary democratic individuality, an ecstatic mode rendered by the Emersonians, which Kateb calls "democratic transcendence."[60]

This summary of what Kateb has to say about democratic individuality in its "normal" and "extraordinary" modes only hints at the richness of his account. The bulk of *The Inner Ocean* is devoted to the elaboration of the idea of democratic individuality in its various aspects, from the mundane to the transcendent. And it is only in the course of this elaboration that we begin to appreciate the grounds for Kateb's astonishing claim that democratic individuality, more than any other phenomenon, redeems modernity.

Democratic individuality is invaluable because it transforms our relationship to others and to the world. Indeed, contra Arendt, genuine worldliness is achieved only through the pursuit of individualism in the Emersonian sense. In its more mundane, cultural form, democratic individuality denotes the possibility of an unashamed life, that is, a life uncorrupted by structural hierarchy. The theory of rights and constitutional government provide a moral horizon within which the treatment of people as mere means is no longer tolerated. The wonder of democratic individuality is that it transforms this Kantian dictum into the cultural a priori of all citizens: it is no longer an "ought," but the fundamental background assumption of everyone. It is the assumption that governs our relations to others, to ourselves, and to government. At the extraordinary level, democratic individuality sponsors a way of being-in-the-world that is (potentially) free of all conventional limits. In undemocratic thinkers (e.g., Nietzsche and Heidegger), this aspiration tends to promote the aristocratism of a caste (the "noble") or splits existence in two (the authentic vs. the unauthentic or everyday). Extraordinary democratic individuality does neither. The egalitarian nature of democratic culture makes the moments, moods, and episodes of transcendence available to all. Similarly, democratic individuality permits a poeticizing of the world that is inclusive in nature, not exclusive: the everyday becomes poetic.

It is fitting that Kateb's most recent work is dedicated to teasing out this highest mode of democratic individuality through an interpretation of its foremost theorist. *Emerson and Self-Reliance* (1995) focuses on the extraordinary democratic individualism displayed by Emerson's very mode of thought and perception. Indeed, according to Kateb, self-reliance is to be understood primarily as a *method* of thought, one that proceeds by the individual's taking up phenomena, experiences, and ideas in all their diversity and seeing their antagonism as a source of truth and beauty. Thus, in his essays, Emerson "impersonates" ideas, exaggerating their significance in order to "reinflate something to its real size and show how large or great it really is."[61] In this way self-reliant thinking enacts an expansive receptivity toward the world, a receptivity that is contemplative but not ascetic. It is a seeing, a mode of perception, that attempts to "stare the world into beauty," to do justice to everything that is.[62] Such thinking affirms life in its contradictoriness and multiplicity; it aims at a "Platonism of the visible world."

Why view Emersonian self-reliance as a method of thought expressing a detached, contemplative attitude toward existence, rather than as a mode of active engagement with the world? After all, wasn't Emerson concerned above all with the "conduct of life," with *active* self-reliance? Kateb does not deny that this was a dimension of Emerson's thought, but he makes the strongest possible case for the priority of thinking over doing—not only in Emerson, but in democratic individuality as such. No doubt, many will see this as a cause for disappointment. The new moral-existential possibility opened by the culture of representative democracy seems depressingly familiar: democracy is the best regime because it makes the life of thought, of contemplation, possible. With Kateb's interpretation of Emersonian self-reliance, we seem to return to the verities of the tradition, to the unquestionable superiority accorded the philosophical life by Plato and Aristotle.

Is this what Emerson is about? Is it what the culture of democratic individuality is, or should be, about? Kateb's answer is yes, but with an important qualification. The Emersonian celebration of the life of the mind is, paradoxically, devoid of the elitism that had been the hallmark of the tradition. As Kateb puts it, "everyone's vocation is to philosophize."[63] What does this mean? First, that individuals realize their individuality by thinking and saying their own thoughts, freed from the constraints of creedal thinking. Second, that thinking one's own thoughts is never easy, since it presupposes distinguishing one's own "opening to the world" from the various worldviews society makes available. Third, that the individual's reception of the world is intimately bound up with the development of their powers of articulation, with their capacity to produce sentences that are uniquely their own. In Kateb's words (glossing Emerson):

> Individual uniqueness is one's special power to see and to say; it is a power of observation and distillation. It is as if true expressiveness could only be mental, and what one expresses is not oneself but the world in which one finds oneself. We exist to produce the best possible sentences, to say the world as unegoistically or impersonally as possible; yet inevitably, and desirably, each one of us

says something different because each one of us is new and meets the new. What we express comes out as a perspective. Each one of us has "some incommunicable sagacity."[64]

The Emersonian/Katebian conviction that the "soil and fruit and flower of modern democracy" is to be found in the self-reliant thinking of individuals expressing their own unique and impersonal perspective on the world resonates with the thought of both Nietzsche and Arendt.[65] However, as noted above, Nietzsche reserves this "artist's" perception of the world for the few, the noble, the unherdlike, while Arendt insists that such expression is possible only in the active life of the public realm, in *political* words and deeds. Kateb's "Nietzschean" reading of Emerson reminds us that, while the tendency towards massification is constant and must always be combated, thinking and saying one's own thoughts is not a matter of "rank" or types: all can poeticize, if they have courage, energy, and a sense of vocation. His reading also reminds us that (contra Arendt) constant civic engagement and a life continuously devoted to moral or political activism never truly elicits the particular perspective of the individual. What Arendt called the individual's "natality" finds expression not in activities that demand solidarity and a self-effacing discipline to the cause, but in "thinking one's thoughts and thinking them through."[66]

To champion individualism, then, is to champion the life of the mind, while never forgetting that some evils demand that self-reliant individuals cease the mental affirmation of the world and contribute their best energies to its reform. But the cause of reform is double-edged, and can, with its focus on the unquestionable evils in our world, strip us of the distance, the detachment, that democratic culture makes available to all. Emersonian liberalism—Kateb's liberalism—is defeated if we let the historical fact of radical evil destroy our capacity as individuals to affirm the world, existence, life.[67] With this Nietzschean thought, Kateb concludes his study of what democratic individuality meant to Emerson, and what it can mean to us.

These claims about democratic individuality animate the essays collected in this volume. Some take them up by exploring the Emersonian contribution to democracy; others, by exploring the challenge an Emersonian sensibility poses to political theory itself. Some take them up by revisiting the question of modernity in its tragic and transformative dimensions; others, by exploring the cultural life of democratic politics. Still others take them up by considering the relationship of democratic individuality and political practice as well as the nature of the civic engagement it fosters.

LIBERAL MODERNISM AND DEMOCRATIC INDIVIDUALITY begins with two tributes to George Kateb; both explore the possibilities and pitfalls of the life of the democratic individual. The first, John Hollander's "An Epistle to Doctor Kateb," muses about the relationship between the poetic and the political under the harsh gaze of modernity. Hollander's ode suggests that political theory must always reengage the question of how best to live and of how we can live at our best when so much seems to conspire against us. Like Kateb, Hollander sees a looming threat in the push for a "uniform diversity that makes personal selves into puddings of group or sect." And like Kateb, Hollander celebrates the life of the intellectual as a way of engaging the question of how to live as our best selves in the face of such a threat. However, even as it celebrates the daily achievements of "legal observance," "decent civility," and "civic engagement," Hollander's ode notes that the poet and political theorist, like true democratic individuals, are "both in and out of the game and wondering at it."

Cornel West's "George Kateb—The Last Emersonian?" rejects this posture and calls for a more fully engaged political theory. West notes that Kateb, like Emerson, has a poetic understanding of the possibilities of democracy and that both Emerson and Kateb help us see that "everyday events have their own kind of beauty and tragedy, sublimity and comedy." West worries, however, that democratic individuality and the political theory it nurtures is "relatively alien to much of American life," and that it plays "primarily a negative role."

West sees in Kateb's democratic individuality the claim that life itself is the highest art and notes that Kateb's way of doing political theory brings literary flare to a deeply moral problematic, namely, resistance to "any form of political oppression and social degradation." But for West, it is not enough for the intellectual to be "in and out of the game and wondering at it." Thus he calls on his readers to go beyond Kateb's democratic individuality. Political theory must imagine, West contends, "forms of political solidarity and communal loyalty" that teach us "how to reform and remake our society as citizens."

Exploring the meaning of democratic individuality in relation to the competing claims of the detached intellectual versus the fully engaged, reform-minded citizen is the work done by the three essays in Part One, "Political Theory and the Claims of Democratic Individuality." Dana Villa's "Socrates, Lessing, and Thoreau: the Image of Alienated Citizenship in Hannah Arendt" begins this exploration by examining the central place occupied by themes of conscience, independent thought, and judgment in Hannah Arendt's political theory. Villa argues that there are surprising affinities between Kateb's ideal of democratic individuality and Arendt's writing about Socrates, Lessing, and Thoreau. Such affinities are all the more unexpected given the usual assimilation of Arendt to a communitarian or civic republican position. Against such readings—and, indeed, against Kateb's own interpretation of Arendt—Villa suggests that we should view in Arendt's political theory a celebration of politicized, yet detached and impersonal, individualism.

The late Judith Shklar takes up the question of democratic individuality and detachment by revisiting Emerson's essay "The American Scholar." By posing the question "Can We Be American Scholars?", Shklar invites us to inquire about the adequacy of Emerson's view of the vocation of the detached intellectual for the modern era. Her answer is mixed. While she continues to see great power in Emerson's "commitment to the democracy of daily relationships" and in his commitment to the progress of knowledge, she argues that, faced with the problems and possibilities of the modern age, we should not accept Emerson's "vision of an American scholar as our own." Shklar worries that Emerson's American scholar was both too nationalistic and too certain that learning was a morally enhancing activity.

In our era, nationalism seems too closed and, in its closure, too dangerous, and we are less confident about the simple virtue of learning. "In the end," Shklar argues, "the American scholar will be liberated. 'We will walk on our own feet: we will work with our own hands: we will speak our own minds.' Brave words and directed at both foreign domination and domestic dereliction." But for Shklar, Emerson's American scholar was too dependent on both "religious enthusiasm . . . and rampant sentimentality" to be an entirely useful guide to the vocation of political theory in our times. That vocation must never provide an excuse for the individual to feel detached from, and superior to, the groups of which he or she is a member, and it must always remind us that "America is just like the rest of he world, different, not better, not an eternal hope."

Thomas Dumm's "Spare Parts: Political Theory as Compensation" focuses on this rejection of "eternal hope" and what it means for political action and for political theory. Dumm argues that "the death of god is the historical event that gives rise to the possibility of political theory as compensation." Dumm treats Kafka's *The Penal Colony* as a meditation on the importance of "spare parts" and as a bridge to a reading of Emerson's essay "Compensation." Spare parts, Dumm claims, function like an insurance policy to alleviate anxiety, but once engaged, can no longer serve that function. "They then might be said," Dumm writes, "to exist in a gap between the actual and the potential, between the present operation of the apparatus and its moment of breakdown."

From this perspective Dumm tries to read Emerson against Emerson's own religiosity, and, in so doing, to rescue Emerson's insights for the modern era. Thus Dumm asks, "[C]an God be considered just another spare part?" His answer is suggested in his argument that the work of political theory should be to help us turn away from "the project of guilt and justice" that God and religiosity foster, and to promote an appreciation of "our existence precisely for what it lacks."

The essays in Part Two, "Democratic Individuality and the Politics of Identity," take up Shklar and Dumm's problematic, namely, How relevant are Emerson and the Emersonians in the modern age, an age characterized by an intensification of identity politics? They seek to understand how democratic individuality and the possibility of living as a poet of the everyday are transformed by the conditions of modernity, especially contemporary identity politics. For each of these authors, there is something distinctive in the late twentieth century that poses special challenges to the project of self-fashioning that Kateb has so richly described.

Tracy Strong's "Politics and Transparency" takes up the problem of democratic individuality in the age of identity politics by asking, following Kateb, "What if the self were not 'thin,' in Rawls's words, but transparent, no thing?" The idea that the democratic individual should be "transparent" suggests that there is "nothing any human being has become or done that I could not have become or done," and that there is no need for an "other" to define the self. In this view, identity need not take shape in the face of difference. Strong then compares the writings of Hawthorne and Emerson to explore "the difference between those who formulate individuality in a world filled with others and those who formulate it in thought with themselves." In his view, Hawthorne rejects the Emersonian notion of the self as a project, seeing it instead as "the affirmation of accidents." Strong concludes that Kateb, like Emerson, sees the self revealed in thought alone, and he mounts a friendly critique of the aspiration to make the self transparent in the modern era. As he sees it, "[T]he transparency of the democratic self has transmogrified into the kneejerk valetudinarianism of 'I can be anything I want to be'."

William Connolly's "Evil and the Imagination of Wholeness" criticizes Kateb's idea of democratic individuality for creating an "artificial dualism between the natural individual and the invented group" and for narrowing exploration of ways to combat political evil in the modern world to a mere celebration of individual rights. He argues that the "self is implicated from the start in the social world that constitutes it," and following Rene Girard, warns of the dangers that attach to the imagination of a self that "possesses wholeness of being." Such a self inevitably produces scapegoats to ensure its wholeness and thus contributes mightily to evil. Connolly notes that the imagination of wholeness "flows freely into political forms" and in so doing spawns violence.

In contrast to the imagination of wholeness, Connolly suggests that evil in modern politics can be resisted only by acknowledging, "Identity requires difference to be, that is, it requires difference to provide it with the contrast enabling it to be." But whenever the imagination of wholeness "captures an identity, some of the very differences that enable it also jeopardize its experience of self-security and wholeness." Thus the modern era requires recognition of the "ambiguity of identity," which is at odds with the self-confident assertions of the democratic individual. For Connolly, if there it is a barrier to political evil, it is found in the empathy that a recognition of the ambiguity of identity spawns.

This concern with cultivating empathy in the face of identity/difference relations is also in play in Benjamin Barber's "Multiculturalism between Individuality and Community: Chasm or Bridge?" For Barber, the challenge of the modern era is to be found in the confrontation between the demands of individuality on the one hand and those of multiculturalism on the other. It is the "tribe" rather than the nation that claims attention in our era, and the claims of difference that animate contemporary political life. Rather than wish tribalism and the politics of difference away in the reassertion of a faith in democratic individuality, Barber explores the way constitutional democracy transforms the politics of multiculturalism.

Just as for Kateb constitutional democracy has a transformative effect on individualism, Barber claims that democracy provides a distinctive frame for multiculturalism. It helps to create, Barber claims, "a civil religion of reciprocal rights and mutual respect," which is lived in democratic institutions. In this context, difference is not a formula for separation, but is instead a "claim to common membership." And democratic institutions "put flesh on the bones of civic identity and give to individualism something more than the sterility of abstract personhood." In so doing, democracy, while enlivened by ethnicity and other expressions of group identity, disciplines and domesticates them.

The last essay in this part, Leslie Paul Thiele's "Walden Three: Postmodern Ecology and Its Precursors," suggests that the claims of democratic individuality and the nature of modern identity can be understood only by reference to the way humans regard, and interact with, their natural environment. Thiele claims that environmentalism is not, as it has so often been portrayed, a threat to individualism. Instead, it provides the basis for a radical reconceptualization of the freedom so prized by liberal theorists. Drawing on Heidegger, Thiele claims that environmentalism fosters a "reconceptualization of human identity." This reconceptualization is designed to liberate humans from the equation of freedom, of being a self, with mastery over others, which, in Thiele's view, "sits at the center of the cultural and political drives that constitute modernism."

Here Thiele, like Connolly, implicitly criticizes Kateb's democratic individuality for failing to provide adequate resources to contend against modern forms of evil. Tutored by a heightened environmental consciousness, humankind, Thiele claims, "is to find its freedom not in limitless technological or economic growth, but in sustainable integration." The goal, he argues, "is to move beyond the mastery of beings . . . and toward an attunement to the being of all that is." In the end, Heidegger's "disclosive letting be" rather than Emerson's self-reliance is, in Thiele's view, "the measure that will best safeguard the earth's ecological diversity and health."

The essays in Part Three, "Culture, Sensibility, and the Self," take up Kateb's interest in the cultural dimensions of political life, the way political forms inform the literary and aesthetic sensibilities of an era. As Kateb put it, "If made real, democratic individuality produces a culture . . . that is the counterpart (replica and complement) of the political system of constitutional democracy."[68] The essays in this part explore a diverse group of thinkers, ranging from Mary Wollstonecraft to Edmund Burke and from William James to Toni Morrison, and a diverse array of cultural forms— pamphlets, biographies, novels, film. They focus on the historicity and contingency of democratic individuality and its complex intersections with the cultural construction of gender and subordination.

The first, David Bromwich's "Wollstonecraft as a Critic of Burke," explores Wollstonecraft's response to Burke's *Reflections on the Revolution in*

France as an example of an emerging democratic sensibility responding to an aristocratic appropriation of gender. Burke, on Bromwich's account, argued that the proper response to wicked deeds was to be found when "the feminine virtue of sensibility" informed judgment. This was, for Burke, part of a larger project to defend aristocratic privilege by associating it with "a specialized kind of feminine character." In response, Wollstonecraft denied that gender could provide the basis for a proper response to evil. For her, it was always wrong to assert the specialized virtue of either sex. Here, we can see how the cultural sensibility of democratic individuality is nurtured.

For Wollstonecraft, virtue is neither inbred nor assigned in different degrees to persons on the basis of gender or other ascriptive criteria. Virtue must be "acquired by struggle." For her, a society is good to the degree that its social and political arrangements permit "the development of the moral courage of individual minds." Anticipating Kateb, she suggested that the test of political arrangements is found in the moral and cultural opportunities and habits they provide. And only in a society that recognized the equal rights of all of its citizens, regardless of gender, could virtue flourish.

Whether the recognition of equal rights is sufficient to overcome gender divisions and whether democratic individuality is equally hospitable to men and women is the subject of Helene Keyssar's "As Time Goes By: Justice, Gender, Drama, and George." This essay reads *Casablanca*, which Keyssar contends is George Kateb's favorite film, by way of George Cukor's movie *Adam's Rib* and Aeschylus' *Oresteia*, both of which pose the question of justice as a question of gender. In the *Oresteia* a "jury" is torn between a case made for the superiority of men over women and a case for the equality of men and women. In *Adam's Rib* a similar question is posed. In the *Oresteia*, limits are placed on the "polyphony" of the democratic polis; in *Adam's Rib*, polyphony is celebrated.

Keyssar says that *Adam's Rib* establishes "complexities of gender, class and point of view" that demand discussion, and models the forms of participation made available in democratic culture. In this film, gender seems more resistant than class to transformation, yet the film itself does transform women into men and, in so doing, works, as Wollstonecraft tried to do 150 years earlier, to loosen its viewers' sense of the relevance of even seemingly intractable categories. Both the *Oresteia* and *Adam's Rib*, Keyssar argues, remind us that "women and theater have languages other than the verbal." Both remind us, however, that the place of women in a democracy, and the question of whether democratic individuality is available to women, remain unresolved.

In *Casablanca*, the message about gender is less subtle. There, through a series of displacements, *Casablanca* becomes "our Athens" and Rick's Cafe Americain "surely looks like a home for democratic individuals." Yet, while the film initially seems to encourage the polyphony that democratic individualism demands, Keyssar argues that "the authority of the dandy and the submission of the woman in *Casablanca* powerfully confirm the identity of the democratic individual as a man, whose single voice will suffice."

The centrality of gender to the development of self is also highlighted in Kim Townsend's "William James's Rugged Individualism." Townsend urges his readers to see through the heroic portrait of James that dominates thinking about him. James was, Townsend writes, "an important individual, but he was also another man struggling to be a man." As a result, there is much to be learned, Townsend believes, from his particular struggle about all such struggles.

Like Wollstonecraft, James did not believe that individuals were simply the captives of sentiments. Instead, James believed that action could influence or control sentiment. For James, then, individualism was found in the exercise of will, in, for example, willing oneself "to stay put in the face of danger" as a way of conquering fear. Yet, unlike Wollstonecraft, James, as Townsend presents him, did not believe that the struggle of the self toward its own realization could be loosened from the constraints of gender. Thus much of his writing was preoccupied with the question of how the institution of marriage could and would shape the social meaning of manliness. Throughout, as Townsend argues, James "would fashion woman in such a way as to bring himself into clear definition."

George Shulman's essay, "American Political Culture, Prophetic Narration, and Toni Morrison's *Beloved*," broadens the consideration of culture and its implications for the forging of democratic individuality by examining how narrative fashions political identities. "Politics," Shulman writes, "is cultural because it involves collective identities, which people build and enact through narratives." Our understanding of politics thus depends on an understanding of the narratives through which those identities are revealed. Shulman's essay focuses on what he calls "prophetic narrative" and argues that that narrative has framed both our understanding of liberal nationalism and the way its critics have proceeded.

Liberal norms, Shulman argues, drawing on Tocqueville's *Democracy in America* and Sacvan Bercovitch's *The American Jeremiad*, are sustained by "a redemptive narrative of captivity and deliverance." Shulman contends that "the narrative of captivity, legacy, corruption, and rebirth is a compulsively repeated form of self-understanding that generates both the logic of exclusion and the terms of reform and inclusion." This narrative shapes American politics because it appeals to both elites and those "outgroups" who embrace widely shared values not yet actualized. The danger in this embrace, as Shulman sees it, is that critical voices are wedded to the groups they wish to criticize by the very terms of the critique.

Shulman concludes his essay by examining Toni Morrison's *Beloved*, arguing that it is an effort to "identify, enter, and retell this compulsively repeated narrative, to depict its costs, subvert its power, elicit possibilities it has foreclosed, and yet also reconceive its promise." The novel serves to dramatize the dangers of narratives of redemption, and, in its ending, renounces that narrative "for the sake of . . . freedom." It suggests that "the conditions of freedom are learned and achieved by deliberating about the necessity and contingency, the causes and meaning, of suffering."

Finally, Part Four, "Democratic Individuality and Civic Action," moves from the level of culture back to a consideration of the question of civic engagement. As Kateb argues, the democratic individual may participate in political and civic affairs episodically, but always does so in a distinctive way. To be compatible with democratic individuality, civic engagement must be "impersonal." "The point of the encouragement of democratic individuality," Kateb writes, "is the transcendence not only of the social but even the individualistic, and the attainment of impersonality."[69]

But even when impersonality is attained, conflict, as Amy Gutmann writes, remains. Thus she begins her essay, "Democracy and Its Discontents," by asserting, "A representative democracy that succeeds in cultivating the independence of spirit that George Kateb so eloquently defends and evinces will also cultivate disagreement over matters of social justice." Such a democracy encourages a morally serious, yet contentious form of civic engagement by people "representing reasonable, yet conflicting moral positions." In the face of such contention, the question becomes, How should representative democracy respond?

For Gutmann the usual answers to this question, especially those that encourage mere tolerance, are insufficient. Democratic individuality requires more. As she argues, "Citizens owe something more than toleration to reasonable responses to controversial political issues." What they owe is an openness and receptivity compatible with what Gutmann calls deliberative democracy. Civic engagement in a deliberative democracy requires "the give and take of reasoned argument in a public forum with the aim of making a decision and justifying it." It "enjoins the respect that is due all reasonable opinions." Thus civic engagement, properly understood, is both rigorous and demanding.

Jeffrey Abramson's "Juries and Local Justice" examines our current understanding of the duties and qualifications of jurors to determine whether they are compatible with a rich notion of deliberation, like the one Gutmann advocates. He argues that in the way we think about jurors we want two incompatible things—impartiality, understood as the absence of prior knowledge or preconceptions, *and* a jury of peers, a jury representative of the community. The first imagines the jury to be an instrument of justice, abstractly understood; the second imagines it to be an instrument of democracy. How the balance between these two demands is struck is crucial in determining the nature of the civic engagement that jury service will represent.

Abramson presents a historical analysis of the place of juries in our legal system, demonstrating how in the original understanding jury service was a form of democratic, civic engagement. Quickly, however, the balance shifted in favor of the image of the jury as an instrument of abstract justice. In this image the ideal juror is, paradoxically, the least informed, least engaged member of the community. "A remarkable level of inattention and apathy," Abramson argues, "becomes the necessary condition for impartiality as a juror." This absurd situation strips civic engagement of its true democratic meaning in a way that Abramson contends demands redress and reform.

The last essay, Austin Sarat's "Doing Death: Violence, Responsibility, and the Role of the Jury in Capital Trials," presents a case study of jury deliberation in the context of a capital trial. The death penalty, Sarat argues, "is dangerous . . . to constitutional democracy because of its insidious impact on our political lives, our lives as citizens. Yet everyday citizens are put to death in and through legal rituals that enlist other citizens as authorizing agents." Sarat explores how citizens, in their role as jurors, allow themselves to participate in the capital punishment process. For him, more is at stake than the translation of abstract sentiments in favor of the death penalty into jury decisions. Like Kateb,[70] Sarat sees capital punishment as an unacceptable extension of state power, an extension incompatible with the survival and flourishing of democratic individuality.

Jurors in capital cases, in his view, are asked to endorse a form of statism that threatens to undermine the meaning of citizenship and civic engagement. That they do so seems to Sarat almost inexplicable. If there is an explanation, it is found in the peculiar dynamics of capital trials, which focus attention on the meaning and violence of the murder committed while making the meaning and violence of the death penalty invisible. If there is an explanation, it is found in the ways that capital trials focus the jurors' attention on their potential responsibility for any future harm caused by the murderer, while muting their responsibility for acts of state violence. In this way, civic engagement is enlisted in aid of, rather than in resistance to, the state's efforts to "own and control its own citizens."

From its consequences for the question of political engagement to its compatibility with capital punishment, the essays assembled here speak to the meaning and consequences of democratic individuality and to its possibility in the modern area. Each does so in its own distinctive voice. Yet, taken together, they provide an overview of the constituent elements of Kateb's liberal modernism. They are one vehicle for imagining the possibilities, as well as understanding the problems, of democratic individuality in the modern era.

NOTES

1. See George Kateb, Introduction to *The Inner Ocean* (Ithaca, N.Y.: Cornell University Press, 1992).

2. See Hannah Arendt's characterization of Walter Benjamin's approach in Arendt, *Men in Dark Times* (New York: Harcourt Brace Jovanovich, 1968), pp. 205–206.

3. See Kateb, *The Inner Ocean*, pp. 25–27, 127–151, 156–157, 162–171.

4. *Ibid.*, p. 42.

5. *Ibid.*, pp. 26–27.

6. *Ibid.*, pp. 36–56.

7. *Ibid.*, pp. 77–105.

8. *Ibid.*, pp. 166–171.

9. Judith Shklar, *After Utopia* (Princeton: Princeton University Press, 1957).

10. George Kateb, *Utopia and Its Enemies* (New York: Schocken Books, 1963), p. 83 and chs. 4–6.

11. *Ibid.*, p. 9.

12. *Ibid.*, pp. 31–32.

13. *Ibid.*, pp. 55–57.

14. *Ibid.*, pp. 88–112.

15. Leo Strauss, *What Is Political Philosophy? And Other Studies* (Chicago: University of Chicago Press, 1988); Eric Voegelin, *The New Science of Politics* (Chicago: University of Chicago Press, 1952).

16. Max Weber, "Science as a Vocation," reprinted in *From Max Weber*, ed. Hans Gerth and C. Wright Mills (New York: Oxford University Press, 1972), p. 143.

17. George Kateb, *Political Theory: Its Nature and Uses* (New York: St. Martin's Press, 1968), pp. 1, 9.

18. Max Weber, "Politics as a Vocation," reprinted in Gerth and Mills, *From Max Weber*, p. 77.

19. Strauss, *What Is Political Philosophy?* p. 15.

20. Kateb, *Political Theory*, pp. 15–20.

21. Weber, "Science as a Vocation," p. 153.

22. Compare this stance to that of Habermas's "modernism."

23. George Kateb, *Hannah Arendt: Politics, Conscience, Evil* (Totowa: Rowman and Allanheld, 1984), pp. 16–17.

24. *Ibid.*, p. 149

25. See Hannah Arendt, *The Origins of Totalitarianism* (New York: Harcourt Brace Jovanovich, 1973), pp. 347, 437.

26. Kateb, *Hannah Arendt*, pp. 158, 164.

27. Cf. Martin Heidegger, *Being and Time*, trans. John Macquarrie and Edward Robinson (New York: Harper and Row, 1962), p. 233.

28. Hannah Arendt, *The Life of the Mind* (New York: Harcourt Brace Jovanovich, 1978), vol. 2, p. 158.

29. Kateb, *Hannah Arendt*, p. 164.

30. *Ibid.*, p. 1. Cf. Hannah Arendt, *On Revolution* (New York: Penguin Books, 1977), p. 281.

31. *Ibid.*, pp. 164–172.

32. *Ibid.*, pp. 158, 172.

33. *Ibid.*, p. 167.

34. *Ibid.*, p. 161.

35. Martin Heidegger, *The Question Concerning Technology* (New York: Harper and Row, 1977), p. 27.

36. Kateb, *Hannah Arendt*, p. 163.

37. Hannah Arendt, *The Human Condition* (Chicago: University of Chicago Press, 1958), pp. 1–6.

38. Kateb, *Hannah Arendt*, p. 166.

39. *Ibid.*, p. 169.

40. *Ibid.*, p. 171.

41. *Ibid.*, p. 172.

42. *Ibid.*, p. 188.

43. *Ibid.*, p. 189.

44. *Ibid.*

45. *Ibid.*

46. Kateb, *Inner Ocean*, p. 26.

47. *Ibid.*

48. *Ibid.*, p. 28.

49. *Ibid.*

50. *Ibid.*

51. *Ibid.*

52. *Ibid.*

53. *Ibid.*, p. 32.

54. *Ibid.*, p. 33.

55. *Ibid.*, p. 83.

56. *Ibid.*, p. 84.

57. *Ibid.*, p. 33.

58. *Ibid.*, pp. 33–34.

59. *Ibid.*, p. 32.

60. *Ibid.*, pp. 32–35.

61. George Kateb, *Emerson and Self-Reliance* (Thousand Oaks, Calif.: Sage Publications, 1995), p. 13.

62. *Ibid.*, p. 52.

63. *Ibid.*, p. 170.

64. *Ibid.*

65. *Ibid.*, p. 202.

66. *Ibid.*, pp. 48, 167.

67. *Ibid.*, p. 200.

68. Kateb, *The Inner Ocean*, p. 27.

69. *Ibid.*, p. 165.

70. *Ibid.*, p. 192.

Prologue

An Epistle to Doctor Kateb

JOHN HOLLANDER

[Though the Muses, once fine sisters
   with smiles and curls,
Seem what Dr. Johnson called "wretched,
   unidea'd girls,"[1]

Yours, with her nods to the others,
   is never weary
(And which, by the way, is the Muse of
   Political Theory?)[2]

As still, in this stifling air of
   thick inanity
The body of thought inhales your
   mental sanity—

The best way of honoring which is
   with one's own work;
But we have to play at thinking
   when shadows lurk

Sometimes in professional corners;
   and I hope the gift
Of an unacademic performance
   which gives short shrift

To the prose of impassioned reason
   need not disgrace
Any inner ocean's surface
   If it replace

High, broad argument with these
   points that disperse,
Or sure steps of exposition
   with the hopping of verse.]

Pro patri mori dulce et
  decorum est?
But for both you and your country
  to live is best—

The schoolmaster John Owen
  wrote roughly that in
Around 1600 or so and in
  neo-Latin,[3]

Revising the end of a story
  by Horace begun,
Well said, but clearly easier
  said now, than done:

I mean, whether fighting or not, it's
  far better to live,
And clearly your life seems only
  yours to give,

Whether "for" or "to" your country,
  and yours to take;
But how best (again) to "live for" it?
  and thus, for the sake

Of argument thereby inquire
  how it could be
That the best of self might survive in
  community,

Rehearsing rather old questions
  that each new phase
Of our time feels need revision
  and paraphrase,

Whatever is new in the answers
  of which, isn't true,
And vice versa: whatever truth there
  is never new

—As Garrick said of some piece that
  was all the rage
In seventeen seventy-something
  on the London stage—[4]

But such are the risks of discourse
   the exploring don
And repetitive dean both contract for.
   I'll thus go on

In the rambling walking talk of
   a half-tired rover—
For the suddenly come-upon point, the
   design stumbled over:

To play well the part of a partner
   each must be whole,
To inhabit the politic body,
   each must be sole,

Quickened in self-possession
   with the joy of doubt
(As you have been recently writing
   so strongly about).

When the map of the *polis* fitted
   an inner state
Old harmonies sounded lovely
   to contemplate,

But cities seem like jungles,
   our talk is bereft
Of the Just—or the Gleaming—City: [5]
   what tropes have we left?

As the ungreening country
   gets more undergrown
With the various wastes of cities,
   can "*patria*," known

Long, in our tongue, by "our country"
   keep its faith?
Affirmation collapses
   with faltering breath;

And current *Fraternité*: is it
   to be a brother
Like Cain to Abel, or Jacob
   to Esau, that Other?

And Nationality, loud, but
  no longer with any
Loving strength to embrace as
  One, the Many,

E pluribus clamor, always
  shrill and yet dumb;
While, as if compensating,
  literal, glum,

Uniform "diversity"
  works to confect
Personal selves into puddings
  of group or sect.

As between mercy and truth,
  an unpleasant fuss
Disturbs the air between peace and
  righteousness—

Old foes still; nor can the *polis*
  itself police:
Seemingly only injustice
  can keep the peace.

Creeds unleashed lash out in
  bloodying hate
—The heat of liberty only;
  for its light, too late.

Polluted resources of language
  conspire to belie us
With newly-spawned euphemism,
  ugly and pious,

With the splendid play of nuances
  of tone unheard
And in the wake of Least Effort,[6]
  distinctions blurred;

With arts of the word near extinction
  and wit's decease
In the dark of the impolitest
  Thought Police.

It's the tone of the parabolic
   that hides in shame
The love of knowledge that dare now
   not speak its name.

No drama of moral thought, but
   trivial battle,
Gunslinger pitted against the
   baddie cattle

Rustlers, for few will have read now
   a better story:
Each virtue has its own weakness
   in allegory

And each vice its proper skill
   —no contradiction
In the strong personifications
   of moral fiction

—And I digress to observe that
   none have been denser
Than in stories of Justice contrived by
   Edmund Spenser:

An iron robot employed by his
   somewhat impliant
Patron of Justice dismembers a
   Rawlsian giant

Lusting for redistribution
   His only care
That hills are higher than valleys
   was quite unfair,[7]

And so the land must be leveled
   as if a height
Of mountain top were a thrust of
   tyrannic might,

As if valleys lay under oppression
   in need of redress
At the hands of this dangerous monster
   of literalness.

Yet the Knight has more complex fights (for
   political thought
This tale would be just kindergarten)
   yet to be fought.

And our quests and tasks? some orders
   seem Heaven-sent,
Mental fight needs no moral
   equivalent.

Our thought lay all before us
   when we were young
Offering so many prospects
   to move among.

But the future was so unrewarded
   and suffered such wrong,
from the claims of the insolent present
   and for so long,

Choking on too many passed, now
   inflated, bucks,
Chilled to a broken image
   of frozen flux,

So swilling our gratification
   that soon there will
Be nothing left that we'd care to
   defer it until.

The locus of worlds elsewhere
   becoming too quickly,
A grim, unpromising planet
   crowded and sickly

A now unmothering, monstrous
   (and what could requite
Past folly?) earth, and veiled in
   Unmöglichkeit,

Born of our later reason's
   unreasoning sleep
This slower human extinction
   now starts to creep

Up on our understanding
  tearing apart
More of too-rapidly aging
  Promise's heart.

Projected disasters of Then may
  infect the Now
Its imagination aghast, yet
  one might allow

That the two parties: Hopeful Memory,
  Memorious Hope,
Are always ready to manage
  (if only in trope),

Blazoned in what even springtime
  cannot quite bury—
The two-faced look of wintry
  January:

Prophecy telling its future
  truths that may last
Poetry telling its whitest
  lies of the past,

But even further than that, as
  some revelation
that dries into no revolution, a
  new relation,

Construed and constructed out of
  the truth told slant,
Lending itself to no Houses of
  Worship's cant.

(Yes, for social science a trope is
  rhetorical noise
Until institutionalized, but
  boys will be boys . . .)

Yet poems and democracies share the
  ghost of a thesis:
Selfstrong "representation"
  (for Greek *mimesis*

In our republic, now gets that
    nobler translation—
We no longer render it as
    low "imitation").

True individuation
    needs not to be
Stood for by dumbly mimetic
    metonymy—

What the handbooks always call "the
    part for the whole,"
A drop of the soup representing
    what's in the bowl—

But in the poetic republic,
    somehow far more
Humanely represented
    by metaphor,

The best of, and in, us figured
    by difference,
Not our shadows, taking umbrage,
    giving offense.

Generality fills our ears with
    its steady drumming
Yet all mere communal being
    is unbecoming.

Not in belabored community,
    though, we yet may
Become more of ourselves in
    the parts that we play.

Various, intricate, shifting
    American roles,
Ad hoc members of so many
    ad hoc wholes,

And thereby too might a nation
    become more and more
A new mode of institution
    worth living for:

Each act of legal observance
    then like a figure
Of a great dance, joyfully followed
    with lovely rigor;

Each small, decent civility
    we routinely do
Performed as if it had just been
    invented anew;

Each new civic engagement
    contrived but lately,
Met as if part of a ritual
    ancient and stately.

If not now, when? Why, whenever . . .
    Across the board,
The Freudians' "working through" is
    a working toward.

Toward some near and vivid future
    when all is said
And done, even given that darkened
    prospect ahead;

And *carpe diem?*—at least you
    can press its flower
In leaves of text that outlast more
    than just the hour.[8]

Finally then, with our palaver
    where do we stand?
Do we write with an acting or an
    applauding hand?

Spectators, agents, moving
    with mingled intent,
Yielding appropriate action,
    ennobled assent.

We stay here, you have suggested,
    as Whitman had it,
Both in and out of the game, and
    wondering at it.[9]

NOTES

1. Quoted by James Boswell, *Life of Johnson* (London and New York: Henry Frowde, 1904), vol. 1, p. 166.

2. One may well ask. An extended function of Clio, as Muse of history? Of Melpomene, as Muse of tragedy (she is shown by iconographers as a serious young woman, buskinned, holding a dagger in one hand and a scepter and crowns in another)? Of Polyhymnia, as patroness originally of mime, later of rhetoric, and the inventor of harmony? (The Muses were assigned generic roles only in Roman times.) (Even a letter in verse— / if it's given to quoting— / *Unwissenschaftlich*, may sink /for want of footnoting.)

3. "*Pro patria sit dulce mori licet, atque decorum;* / *Viuere pro patria dulcius esse puto.*" John Owen (1563?–1622), "Ad Philopatrium"; he echoes Horace's "*Dulce et decorum est pro patria mori*" (Ode III, ii, 13).

4. Or so I seem to recall reading that the celebrated eighteenth-century actor had said.

5. Gleaming city: "O beautiful for patriot dream / That sees beyond the years /Thine alabaster cities gleam / Undimmed by human tears." Katharine Lee Bates, "America the Beautiful." It may be observed that "gleam" is not in the present tense, but given a future aspect by the auxiliary phrase "sees [envisions] . . . beyond the years." Bates was not so fatuous as to believe that they could do so in anything but a prophetically envisioned future, "beyond the years." This point is usually lost when these lines are sung, given that the canonical musical setting tends to enforce a separation of the stanza into two independent sentences or clauses.

6. The phrase is from George Kingsley Zipf, *Human Behavior and the Principle of Least Effort* (Cambridge, Mass.: Addison-Wesley Press, 1949); I thought it a silly book.

7. Edmund Spenser, *The Faerie Queene*, Book V, Canto II, concerns a mad revolutionary giant, a communist of an Anabaptist sort (he represents distributive justice gone wild), and his undoing at the hands of Artegall, the patron and type of a Justice more retributive. Book V allegorizes the relations of Justice and Equity in general.

8. "*Carpe diem, quam minimum credula postero*" ["Pluck the day, not relying in the least on the future"]. Horace Ode I, xi, 7.

9. Walt Whitman, *Song of Myself*, 4: "Looking . . . at what will come next / Both in and out of the game and watching and wondering at it."

George Kateb—The Last Emersonian?

CORNEL WEST

GEORGE KATEB, my friend and colleague, is the most self-conscious Emersonian political theorist ever to emerge in the New World (or anywhere). This not only pits him against the grain of contemporary political thought. It also puts him outside of the dominant frameworks in which liberals, communitarians, conservatives, and civic republicans sharpen their rhetorical swords and do battle. It is no accident that Kateb's powerful and poignant works on Hannah Arendt, Walt Whitman, and Henry David Thoreau and his iconoclastic and idiosyncratic interventions regarding war, statecraft and resistance always seem far removed from the well-beaten paths of our day—as if they were written by one enchanted by the off-beat rhythms of a different drummer. In short, Kateb's intellectual vocation in the profession of political science is that of the Emersonian figure—thinking against the encrustations that diminish inwardness and discourage individuality. He is the last—that is, the first and only—thoroughgoing Emersonian in American political thought.

But what does it mean to be an Emersonian in political thought? Is it not to be misplaced, an oxymoronic hare chasing ecstatic states while running with hounds fixated on nation-states? Is there any space at the table of academic political philosophers for one who talks of the "sweet" (not good) life or the "lightness of being"? Is Kateb a creative preserver of "the love of letters amongst a people too busy to give to letters any more"?[1]—namely, an "American scholar," as defined by Emerson, suspicious of the conventions of scholarly pretensions that take us away from the risk and danger of honestly examining and expanding ourselves as selves?

Kateb's unique place in the history of American letters and political thought rests upon three basic pillars—his personality, his writing style, and his scholarship. Like his beloved Emerson—or the greatest Emersonian in American letters, William James—Kateb refuses to separate these three components of his dynamic self. And like Keats, what holds them together is a sheer energy that wards off despair, a willed buoyancy that holds misanthropy at arm's length. To put it bluntly, Kateb's grand contribution to political thought is a poetic reading of the multiform energies of receptive and responsive selves in perennial battle against institutional powers—powers that push these self-directed energies toward the herd, the tribe, the market, or the state. For Kateb, "all is ripeness" only when self-reliance avails, that is, only when the self is abandoned by undergoing metamorphosis, when new energies are released for self-creation and self-making. Kateb is a theorist of democracy (rather than a democratic theorist) precisely because Emersonian self-reliance is a democratic mode of being in the world that requires a rights-based individualism to flourish. Unlike democratic theorists who gloat on government, bureaucracy, and markets, Kateb delves into the existential and psychic dynamics of the raw stuff of democracy—namely, the kind of personalities, styles, and ideas of would-be citizens of a genuine democracy. In this sense, he is an utopian thinker preoccupied not with the ideal society but rather with the "new sense of life" made available to democratic individuals by the paths he opens—in the life of the mind and in life.

Like Nietzsche—that rare German who adored Emerson—Kateb believes one's distinctive perspective on life must be lived, that is, embodied in one's fundamental orientation and disposition toward life. Hence, philosophical reflections are inseparable from autobiographical grapplings with who one is and how one gets about. Kateb's personality—the flesh-and-blood George—is a grand example of the Socratic edict that the unexamined life is not worth living and the Emersonian follow-up that the examined life is painful, full of risk, vulnerability, yet also joy. The basic aim of life is neither noble service to a higher God, ideal, or power nor the cheap thrills of fame, prestige, sex, or status. Rather, the end of a democratic life is the treacherous, yet possible ecstatic joy of riding the roller coaster of life that makes available to us the ordinary things and everyday events that have their own kind of beauty and tragedy, sublimity and comedy. This "end" is not something one reaches; rather it is a perennial process in which one can revel— with all its dangers and opportunities—only if one can poetically read the world, that is, be a "complete lover" (Whitman's phrase for the greatest poet) with "a mobile and multiple perspectivism."[2]

Kateb's perspectivism, again like Nietzsche's, is not a sophomoric relativism. He does not believe that there are no standards or criteria by which to live so that anything goes or everything is permissible. Rather, he holds that our lives, our personalities, should be singularly our own, held fast by self-made standards and principles unique to our own flourishing. This is why Kateb's radical individualism is neither rugged nor ragged. It is not rugged individualism because it puts a low premium on pecuniary gain or stately honor. It is not ragged individualism because it shuns any leveling or conformity. The irony of Kateb's democratic individuality is that it is relatively alien to much of American life.

In this land of cultural hybridity and ethnic heterogeneity—with its deep tribal bonds and racial enclaves—Kateb affirms an Emersonian sensibility that shuns any group role-playing and mask-wearing that disempowers democratic individuality. His strong libertarian defense of the Bill of Rights is put forward not in order to safeguard primarily property, corporate rights, or parochial schools but rather to ensure that Emersonian selves can step out of any role, mask or ascribed identity based on one's filiative lineage. Kateb's nightmare—like that of any serious Emersonian—is the prison of imposed selves rooted in the past that freeze one's energies and thereby foreclose the metamorphosis of the self. Such an imposition results in hollow lives, shot through with the poisonous elements of the barbarous, infantile, and idolatrous.[3] Kateb abhors any straitjacketing or pigeonholing of life that locks us into mechanical motions, rehearsed reflections, and theatrical thoughts. Like Louie Armstrong—that Representative Man of the Emersonian art form—Kateb highlights "tentativeness, irony, distance, playfulness, uncertainty, awkwardness, looseness."[4] He calls his perspective "democratic aestheticism" that flows from democratic justice. It is aesthetic in that it claims that "[l]ife itself is the highest art. Life need not be beautiful to be beautiful."[5] It is just because it "is the constant disposition to give each person or creature or thing, just as it is, its due, its rights, in the fullest sense."[6] In other words, Kateb democratizes Plato's aesthetic conception of justice by wedding it to Emerson's effort to see the miraculous and sublime in the common, the quotidian, the everyday. Like Whitman, Kateb wants us to "bestow on every object its fit proportion neither more nor less."[7] Kateb's personality exemplifies this democratic aesthetic. His interactions with others and transactions with nature—space does not permit evidence to be marshaled to show this, though any of his friends and colleagues can testify to it—embody his unique perspective.

In addition to Kateb's personality, his writing style sets him apart from most of his colleagues in political science. His form of writing is an extension and expression of his personality. His prose does not simply incarnate a poetic reading of the self, society, and world; it also sounds like his voice in conversation. In stark contrast to most academicians, the sound, tone, and texture of his voice breaks through in his texts. This voice has the "tone of seeking" (as opposed to the "tone of having") that takes us beyond "low curiosity" and opens up new modalities of seeing and being.[8] In this regard, Kateb's style is closer to that of modern wisdom literature (as in the essays of Thomas Carlyle, George Eliot, Matthew Arnold, W.E.B. Du Bois, Lionel Trilling, or Richard Hofstadter) than to that of the treatises of modern political theory. His style attempts to not only instruct and inform, but also inspire. This inspiration has little to do with cheap enthusiasm or faddish cleverness. Rather, it provokes the reader and thereby awakens us from any dogmatic slumber. Kateb tries to get us interested, involved, and invested in who we are and what kind of life we're leading and why. In short, he wants to make arguments against the backdrop of a larger portrait of what it is to be human in order to touch our lives.

> There is no good life, only lives that are not bad. The mere absence of oppression and degradation is sweet. A person's equal acceptance by the rest removes the heavy weight of inferiority, contempt, invisibility. That too is sweet. The weakening of traditional enclosure in status, group, class, locality, ethnicity, race—the whole suffocating network of ascribed artificial, or biological but

culturally exaggerated, identity opens life up, at least a bit. The culture of individual rights has lightness of being; free being is light. It seems insubstantial and
lacking in positivity. Yet all its negativity, all its avoidances and absences and
abstentions, are a life, and a life that it takes patient eyes to see, and a new sense
of beauty to admire. The life that is not the good life is good in itself. However,
can something even richer come out of it?[9]

In this wisdom prose, note the creative tension between Kateb's affirmation of a liberated self (from filiation and affiliation) and his negation of an
utopian space (free of the need for the self's struggle). This fascinating blend
of a mobile and agile self forever battling against stultifying superegos and
a skeptical and suspicious self incessantly avoiding substantiality and positivity is a bench mark of his prosaic style—a style that echoes the poetic
practice of Wallace Stevens, the grand Emersonian bard of the twentieth
century:

> Under every no
> Lay a passion for yes that had never been broken.[10]

This prosaic tension is less a dialectical interplay than a diachronic flow
("The quality of the imagination is to flow," says Emerson) that aims to
"unlock our chains and admit us to a new scene."[11] In this sense, Kateb's style
puts a premium on heroic energies—on those courageous selves who are
willing to live dangerously so that they constitute a kind of Jeffersonian
"natural aristocracy" of the spirit. Ironically, such selves are the prime candidates for Whitman's "great composite democratic individual," since to
muster heroic energies and create multiple perspectives is to acknowledge
ambivalent relations with others and accent ambiguous possibilities for one's
self.[12] Kateb's prosaic tension—which undergirds the poetic living of democratic individuals—enacts the very process of self-overcoming that sits at the
center of his thought. This self-overcoming is quite different from that of
Nietzsche. For Kateb, Emersonian self-overcoming is a matter of relating to
and making connections with others by means of empathy and sympathy.
Nietzsche rejects this as a watered-down Protestant version of love and pity
and opts for an aristocratic perfectionist ideal of playful yet mean-spirited
toughness that spurns any moral link with others, especially ordinary people.

Kateb's swerve from Nietzsche is significant because though both focus
on self-overcoming, Kateb shuns any arrogant putdown of others or an "unnatural" aristocracy that shuts off prematurely the unrealized potentiality of
common folk. The major problematic of his scholarship is to reconcile
Emersonian self-overcoming (which seems to entail Nietzschean cruelty, ec-
centricity, and insularity) with moral resistance to any form of political oppression and social degradation (which puts him on the road to plebeian
revolution). His aim is to show that his allegiance to democratic individuality leads him to embrace a hatred of any form of collective subordination,
for example, that of nation, race, class, gender, region, or sexual orientation,

yet his deep commitment to resistance goes hand in hand with a profound suspicion of any public sphere linked to collective mind-sets. His love of and grapplings with the Levellers, especially Lilburne and Overton, as well as Hannah Arendt and the Emersonians (Emerson, Thoreau, and Whitman), bear the marks of this delicate tightrope walking.

From my own Emersonian vantage point, I think Kateb is, like most of us all, unable to stay on this slippery tightrope for long. This is, in part, because our postmodern condition—with its ubiquitous markets, gargantuan nation-states, and tribal mentalities—forces him to play primarily a negative role in reminding us what democratic individuality is not. This stance makes him downplay any positive content—regarding his fecund notions of responsiveness, empathy, sympathy, and connectedness—of democratic individuality. Like William James, Kateb is against bigness—big government, big business, big bureaucracy, and big lies. Yet to be a democrat in our time is to be preoccupied with massive poverty and social misery and to be bighearted enough and tough-minded enough to cast our lot with the big losers—the wretched of the earth. And, despite Kateb's profound existential ethic, which energizes heroic selves and galvanizes resistance to oppression, how can we democratize ourselves, our societies, and our world without forms of political solidarity and communal loyalty that go far beyond "mutual recognition" of our self-overcomings? Kateb's suspicion of such solidarity and loyalty is warranted. But if we democrats are to truly live dangerously we must do so not simply as individuals but also as members of communities. Like Ralph Ellison's Invisible Man, Kateb gives us wisdom as to how to live and rebel as selves, but he provides little or no *phronesis* as to how to reform and remake our society as citizens. If Kateb is the last Emersonian, then we must transcend the Emersonians in order to be true to the dynamic democratic spirit of those on whose shoulders we now stand.

Notes

1. Ralph Waldo Emerson, "The American Scholar," reprinted in *Ralph Waldo Emerson—Essays and Lectures* (New York: Viking Press, 1983), p. 53.

2. George Kateb, "Democratic Individuality and the Meaning of Rights," in *Liberalism and the Moral Life*, ed. Nancy L. Rosenblum (Cambridge: Harvard University Press, 1989), p. 197.

3. *Ibid.*, p. 202.

4. *Ibid.*, p. 199.

5. *Ibid.*, p. 197.

6. *Ibid.*

7. Walt Whitman, Preface 1855, reprinted in *Leaves of Grass and Selected Prose*, ed. John Kouwenhouen (New York: Modern Library, 1950), p. 444.

8. Ralph Waldo Emerson, "The Over-Soul," reprinted in *Ralph Waldo Emerson—Essays and Lectures* (New York, Viking Press, 1983), pp. 395, 394.

9. Kateb, "Democratic Individuality," pp. 188–189.

10. Wallace Stevens, "Esthetique du mal," reprinted in *Collected Poems* (New York: Vintage Press, 1988), p. 320.

11. Ralph Waldo Emerson, "The Poet," reprinted in *Ralph Waldo Emerson— Essays and Lectures* (New York, Viking Press, 1983), p. 463.

12. For Kateb's elaboration of this point, see his great essay, "Walt Whitman and the Culture of Democracy," the 1989 Whitman Lecture (Walt Whitman Center for the Culture and Politics of Democracy, April 24, 1989), pp. 3–42.

PART ONE

Political Theory and the Claims of Democratic Individuality

Socrates, Lessing, and Thoreau: The Image of Alienated Citizenship in Hannah Arendt

DANA R. VILLA

IN THE RECENT war between liberals and communitarians, the place of Hannah Arendt has never been seriously questioned. Communitarians of every stripe (especially neo-Aristotelians) routinely enlist her as an ally in their struggle against a debased and alienating liberal proceduralism. Thus, Arendt's view of life in the polis and her interpretation of the modern revolutionary tradition have provided grist for the antiliberal mills of such theorists as Charles Taylor, Benjamin Barber, Michael Sandel, and Ronald Beiner.[1] Arendt's notion of the public realm and her theory of political action provide these authors with a vision of that "good which we can know only in common" (Sandel), which is so conspicuously lacking in liberalism.[2] This good is that of the engaged and connected citizen, the community member who identifies strongly with the community's purposes, aspirations, and conception of justice. Such a citizen does not view him or herself as a "sovereign chooser" or as a member of a joint-stock company, but rather as deeply embedded in and defined by the historical and political traditions of the polity. The communitarians read Hannah Arendt's celebration of the *bios politikos* as a confirmation of everything they hold dear.

This picture of Arendt, while not exactly mistaken, is severely distorting in at least one crucial respect. The communitarians encourage us to read Arendt as a friend of the group and as an enemy of "excessive" individualism. On one level, this is fair enough: you can't have the kind of "public world" Arendt describes without a plurality of agents and a constitutional framework. The political way of life is, by definition, possible only through the existence of a community. Yet while Arendt's work focuses on such a public world and is permeated by a hostility toward romantic subjectivism, materialist egoism,[3] and a "worldless" care for one's soul, her political theory remains profoundly individualist in orientation.

Arendt's theory of political action is a case in point. Arendt looks to action in the public sphere as the medium for fully realized individuation.[4] The public realm presents a theatrical space, a "stage," which offers an escape from the darkness and determinism of the biological and psychological dimensions of human existence. Appearance on this stage enables an otherwise diffuse self to take on definite shape and color. Through public words and deeds we establish a persona that appears to all. Thus, the "unique distinctness" of every individual becomes tangible—and so achieves reality[5]—only through action in the public sphere. Political action, in Arendt's understanding, does not offer an escape from an anomic individualism to a robust sense of group membership; rather, it provides the vehicle to travel from a bogus and unworldly individualism to an authentic individuality. Bakunin's confessed wish, "I do not want to be *I*, I want to be *We*," is not Arendt's.[6]

The strong individualist strain in Arendt has not gone entirely unnoticed. It comes through loud and clear in the "Greek" theory of action found in *The Human Condition*, and has been roundly (and in my view, mistakenly) criticized for its "expressive" or "elitist" character.[7] A different but equally important dimension of her individualism—one that qualifies her more "heroic" formulations—is found in her reflections on the paradigmatic figures of Socrates, Lessing, and Thoreau. These reflections are not uniformly admiring: Arendt, like Nietzsche, is ambivalent about Socrates and overtly hostile to what might be called the Thoreau effect. Nevertheless, the essays "Philosophy and Politics," "On Humanity in Dark Times," "Civil Disobedience," and "Thinking and Moral Considerations" (along with material from the posthumously published *Lectures on Kant's Political Philosophy*) reveal surprising affinities between Arendt and these exemplars of what I shall call alienated citizenship.

The model of citizenship that emerges from these essays stands in sharp contrast to the republican model so often ascribed to Arendt.[8] Alienated citizenship—the kind of citizenship performed by Socrates, Lessing, and Thoreau—values distance, reflection, and resistance over patriotism, will, and duty; conscience and independent judgment over shared purposes; episodic intervention over constant engagement. Viewed from the standpoint of an Aristotle, Machiavelli, or Rousseau, the exemplars of this form of citizenship appear as apolitical pariahs. Yet, with the notable exception of Thoreau, Arendt frames them as supremely *political* actors.

My goal in considering Arendt's reflections on these figures is to help dispel the myth of her "republicanism," a myth which gives credence to the communitarian appropriation of Arendt. I contend that Arendt's ideal citizen combines emblematic qualities of Socrates, Lessing, and Thoreau, qualities that stand in sharp opposition to the ideal of "virtuous" citizenship as it has been articulated by Aristotle, Machiavelli, and Rousseau. Once the myth of Arendt's republicanism is laid to rest, we are in a better position to recover the peculiar brand of *political* individualism that inspires her work and makes it so distinct from both liberalism and communitarianism.

•

In her recent book Margaret Canovan argues that Arendt's political views are best understood "against the backcloth of the classical republican tradition."[9] Arendt's abiding concern with the *res publica*, combined with her "pessimistic outlook on the world of human affairs" and her sense that the "islands of freedom" in human history have been few and far between, indicate an underlying continuity with this tradition. However, even Canovan acknowledges that "Arendt's version of republicanism is significantly different from any of the models she inherited."[10]

The most significant difference resides in the role Arendt reserves for human plurality and the ongoing debate and deliberation that both manifests and enriches it. Her conviction that the essence of politics lies in debate among plural individuals (what Canovan somewhat blandly describes as "free discussion") radically displaces the traditional republican emphasis upon the virtues of the citizen-soldier.[11] According to Canovan, plurality "transforms" the classical republican elements in Arendt's thought. For this reason, she describes Arendt's political philosophy as a "new" republicanism.

I believe that the role of plurality in Arendt's thought is even more transformative than Canovan allows. Indeed, I want to demonstrate that Arendt's emphasis upon plurality—and her corresponding emphasis upon independent action and judgment—transcends the republican framework as we know it. It is not, in other words, a question of viewing Arendt's political theory as a modification of the classical republican tradition. What we are dealing with, rather, is a genuine *aufhebung*, one that negates as much as it preserves, while transforming all of the original elements. It is precisely in Arendt's readings of the "pariah" figures of Socrates, Lessing, and Thoreau that the transformative power of the concept of plurality is revealed, as well as the individualism that animates it.

Anyone familiar with Arendt's view of Socrates from either *The Human Condition* (1958) or the essay "Civil Disobedience" (1970) knows that she can be intensely critical of Plato's teacher. In the former work her anti-Platonism is so strong that it manages to engulf Socrates: the tradition of political thought born of Plato's antipolitical authoritarianism is dubbed "the Socratic tradition."[12] In the essay Socratic conscience is identified with a care for one's soul, and thus with a kind of self-interest. The Socratic injunction that it is better to suffer wrong than to do wrong is reduced to the seemingly unpolitical worry about having to live life with a wrongdoer, oneself.[13]

The image of Socrates that emerges from these two texts is that of an emblematic figure in the long struggle of philosophy against politics, a thinker whose moral absolutism demands nothing less than a withdrawal from the realm of human affairs. Arendt's approving citation of Machiavelli's *cri de coeur*—"I love my city more than my soul"—underlines the stakes of the opposition being constructed. On the one hand, we have the world of civic virtue, as represented by the Athenian demos; on the other, Socrates and his unrelenting quest for truth and moral knowledge, both of which are supremely important for the individual whose foremost concern is the state of his or her soul. Left at this, one half expects Arendt to endorse the verdict the demos rendered on Socrates: he *is* a corrupter of sorts, one who undermines care for this world and joy in action. Perhaps he got what he deserved.[14]

All the more reason, then, to be surprised by the treatment of Socrates in the 1954 essay "Philosophy and Politics."[15] Here, the operative distinction is not between Socrates and the polis but between Socrates and Plato. The former is presented as a political philosopher in an oddly literal sense, namely, as one who places his craft at the service of the polis. According to Arendt, Socrates, unlike Plato, did not want to educate the citizens of Athens by leading them to the acceptance of general truths. Rather, his concern was to remain entirely within the realm of opinion (*doxa*), where he could talk matters through with individual citizens.[16] The result of such "talking through" (*dialegesthai*) was not the destruction of opinion, but a slow and often painful drawing out of its truthfulness. As practiced by Socrates, *dialegesthai* aimed at making citizens more reflective and (thus) more fully aware of the specific truthfulness of their opinions, their perspective on the common world. This in turn made them better prepared to enter the public sphere, the political arena of speech and persuasion, for they were now attuned to the truthfulness of opinion as such, and more inclined to see at least partial truth where before they had only seen a competing interest or opinion. The crucial point is that for Socrates, it is not a question of transcending the order of *doxa* (the Platonic project), but of improving it, one viewpoint at a time.

We should note how Arendt's characterization of the Socratic project makes plurality the origin and goal of his "talking through." Socratic dialectic does not aim at moving from the many (opinion) to the one (truth), nor does it aim at synthesizing a more "complete" truth out of a plurality of "partially" true opinions, à la Mill. When Arendt says that Socrates "wanted to help others give birth to what they themselves thought anyhow, to find the truth in their *doxa*,"[17] she is claiming that what matters most to Socrates is the refinement of the individual citizen's "opening to the world": its specificity, its internal coherence, and the way it fits with the viewpoints of other citizens.

One's *doxa* ceases to be such an opening if it is so rigid, underdeveloped, or idiosyncratic that it effaces the common world on which all perspectives are perspectives. In the excessively agonistic atmosphere of Athenian politics, the urge to excel, to "show oneself the best of all," constantly threatened the very "commonness of the political world."[18] Where the political realm is simply an arena for competition, all *doxa* is devalued and deprived of its specific truthfulness. Socratic conversation attempted to promote a self-understanding, modesty, and distance that would enable the individual citizen to see "the truth inherent in the other's opinion."[19] This is the genuine meaning of civic friendship, Aristotle's *philia*: not the collapse of distance or eradication of perspective, but the assurance of a politically meaningful plurality.[20]

Arendt's claim that "politically speaking, Socrates tried to make friends out of Athens's citizenry" by promoting a kind of conversation about what individual citizens have in common appears to neutralize the Socratic threat to communitarianism.[21] This impression is reinforced by her invocation of the discussion of friendship in the *Nicomachean Ethics*: friendship, not justice, is the true bond holding communities together.[22] Yet it is precisely at this very communitarian moment that Arendt's essay takes a sharp and unexpected turn, moving without pause from a discussion of the Aristotelian idea of civic friendship to the Socratic theme of self-knowledge. Arendt's point is that the kind of understanding that makes civic friendship possible does not have the same basis for Socrates as for Aristotle (or, at least, for the Aristotle we have come to know from recent communitarian appropriaters). The ground of understanding teased out by Socratic dialectic is not one of shared purposes, virtues, or even character in the Aristotelian sense. Rather, Socratic "talking through" has the effect of throwing the conversational partner back upon his or her own internal dialogue, the dialogue of thought (what Arendt elsewhere refers to as the dialogue between me and myself).[23] Only those who have experienced their internal plurality, the "two-in-one" revealed in solitary thought, have the capacity for the kind of civic friendship Socrates and Arendt have in mind. As Arendt puts the Socratic point, "[O]nly someone who has had the experience of talking with himself is capable of being a friend, of acquiring another self."[24]

Why should this be so? How can the experience of thought, conscience, interiority be the sine qua non of authentic citizenship? The short answer is that only if I have learned how to live with myself, with my own internal plurality, can I affirm the plurality of the world. Otherwise, this plurality appears as an obstacle or a threat: we will want to strategically master it or reduce the "ever-increasing differentiation" it implies to a comforting sameness. The strong sense of group membership affirmed by classical republicanism, communitarianism, and many proponents of identity politics is, from this perspective, an attempt to escape the plurality we find ourselves delivered over to the moment we are alone. Only if we are at home with this plurality can we expect to embrace the worldly form: "living together with others begins with living together with oneself."[25]

The internal dialogue that Socrates wants to incite does not lead him to conflate politics with dialogue. On the contrary, Arendt emphasizes how the prompting provided by *dialegesthai* presumes the agonistic and theatrical dimensions of politics. It does not set out to destroy these dimensions (as does Platonic dialectic) but to alter their tonality. Thus, knowing how to live with oneself does not enable a civic friendship founded upon empathy (the Rousseau-inspired category mistake of much contemporary theory); rather, it enables a civic friendship founded upon the expectation of different "openings to the world." The experience of the "two-in-one" elicited by dialectic teaches the irreducibility of plurality. More important, it teaches that the one sphere in which agreement is crucial is not the public, political world (this world is defined by debate and disagreement) but the interior one—for, as Socrates never tired of stressing, "it is much better to be in disagreement with the whole world than being one to be in disagreement with myself."[26] This is the essence of the Socratic idea of a secular conscience, an idea rooted in the fear of having to live "in contradiction" with oneself—for example, of having to spend the rest of one's life in the company of a murderer, a collaborator, or even someone who "merely" acquiesced passively to horror.[27]

Socrates, in Arendt's reading, forces individual citizens to confront how they want to appear to *themselves*, for the rest of their lives. Conscience provides an internal audience of what we might call ideal peers. Thus, Socrates' advice to "be as you would like to appear to others" underlines not only the importance of individual conduct, but what it means to create a public persona. Conscience prevents this activity from devolving into mere playacting or other-directed conformity. One is what one does, in private as well as in public life. Performing in public (Arendt's characteristic description of political action) requires a consistency of style and a seriousness that can only be prepared for through the "theatrical" discipline of conscience—the discipline of not contradicting one's ideal appearance, of not disappointing one's internal audience.[28]

In Socrates the politics of conscience and performance are, paradoxically enough, reconciled. This reconciliation is manifest in Socrates' own activity, a point Arendt emphasizes in her Kant lectures:

> What he [Socrates] actually did was to make *public*, in discourse, the thinking process—the dialogue between me and myself; he *performed* in the marketplace the way the flute-player performed as a banquet. It is sheer performance, sheer activity. And just as the flute-player has to follow certain rules in order to perform well, Socrates discovered the only rule that holds sway over thinking—the rule of consistency.[29]

This rule determines acting as well as thinking, which leads Socrates not to escape the sentence imposed by the demos. For what is at stake in the *Crito* is less the binding nature of the obligation Socrates owes to the laws of Athens than the damage that would be done to the public persona, the moral exemplar, that he had striven to create over the years.[30] To take Crito up on his offer would be tantamount to revealing that the "gadfly" was in fact a hypocrite who did not take his appearance seriously. For Socrates, you are what you appear to be—to yourself and to others. Unlike Plato, Socrates does not attempt to degrade appearance, to make it superfluous to the "real" self; rather, he brings appearance and the plurality it implies into the theater of the self. In doing this, he makes us realize that choosing a public persona is no Deaveresque conjuror's trick, but a morally serious business of the first order. This is what makes Socrates, in Arendt's view, both a political moralist and a supreme individualist. The two are, for her, inseparable.

•

We know from *The Life of the Mind* that Arendt followed the tradition in sharply distinguishing between thinking and acting. The latter is our most worldly activity, according to Arendt, whereas the former is defined largely by its withdrawal from the world.[31] But we also know, from the Kant lectures and remarks scattered throughout her writings, that she considered our capacity for judgment as uniquely dependent upon a specific kind of thinking. The capacity for what Arendt calls representative thought is identified in "Philosophy and Politics" as "the political kind of insight *par excellence*."[32] This capacity is central to the process of opinion formation, a process Arendt describes in "Truth and Politics":

> Political thought is representative. I form an opinion by considering a given issue from different viewpoints, by making present to my mind the stand-points of those who are absent; that is, I represent them. This process of representation does not blindly adopt the actual views of those who stand somewhere else, and hence look upon the world from a different perspective; this is a question neither of empathy, as though I tried to be or feel like somebody else, nor of counting noses and joining a majority, but of being and thinking in my own identity where actually I am not. The more people's standpoints I have present in my mind while I am pondering a given issue, and the better I can imagine how I would feel and think if I were in their place, the stronger will be my capacity for representative thinking and the more valid my final conclusions, my opinion.[33]

Arendt links this ability with the Kantian notion of an "enlarged mentality," calling it the capacity which "enables men to judge."[34] It is precisely this capacity for representative thought that Arendt sees Socrates as cultivating with his "talking through." Such discourse introduces the reflective distance (or "disinterestedness," as Kant would say) necessary to move beyond the level of private or group interests. It is only with the creation of such distance that an opinion can hope to claim a potential validity for others.[35]

"Philosophy and Politics" is an important essay not merely for its positive depiction of Socrates but also for the continuity it establishes between this kind of thinking (which looks toward a potential agreement with others) and conscience (based on the imperative of agreement with myself). The two are obviously quite different. Nevertheless—and this is something overlooked by those who, like Seyla Benhabib, stress the Kantian dimension of Arendt over the Socratic—they crucially inform each other.

As interpreted by Benhabib, representative thought outlines a kind of decision procedure, one that substitutes the objectivity of Kant's universalizability criterion for the "intuitionism" of appeals to individual thought and conscience.[36] "Philosophy and Politics," along with "Thinking and Moral Considerations" (1971), tell a different story, however. Here, Arendt's emphasis is less on the elimination of subjective factors that present an obstacle to universal validity than on the role representative thought plays in enabling independent judgment. Like Kant in the *Critique of Judgment*, Arendt argues that the liberation from "subjective private conditions" is what enables an independent and communicable judgment in the first place.[37] In Kant, however, the imperative to "think for oneself" ("What is

Enlightenment?") is ultimately subsumed by the univeralizing machinery of the categorical imperative. The critical Kant—the Kant whom Arendt compares favorably to Socrates[38]—gives way to the dogmatic, absolutist Kant. Benhabib's anxiety about the firmness of the moral foundations of Arendt's thought leads her, like Kant, to sacrifice independence of judgment to the demand for universal validity (albeit one arrived at "intersubjectively," rather than deductively, as in Kant). Arendt, however, refuses to view representative thinking or the process of opinion formation in this light. Again, the point is to bring the truthfulness out of every *doxa* by pressing it to achieve impartiality—not to erect a standard by which they might all be rendered commensurable.

This point becomes somewhat clearer if we turn to Arendt's essay on Lessing. She presents Lessing as someone who "never felt at home in the world," who "experienced the world in anger and laughter," yet who nevertheless remained committed to it.[39] Lessing's detachment and irony yielded a relentlessly critical stance, but one that was the very opposite of dogmatic. Thus, his *Selbstdenken*, or "independent thinking for oneself," is marked by a peculiar sensitivity to context and a solicitude for "the relative rightness of opinions which for good reasons get the worst of it."[40] Thus, in the Enlightenment's defining dispute over the "truth" of Christianity, Lessing refused to take a fixed position. Dubious of those who would prove the "reasonableness" of Christianity, yet suspicious of those who would "trample it underfoot," he emphasized its position in the world rather than its truth or falseness. His defense of Christianity was informed by the anxiety that "it might again enforce its claim to dominance" and the fear that it "might vanish utterly."[41] This concern with the worldly configuration of forces at any given moment is the very opposite of all sectarian or ideological thinking. As Arendt puts it:

> Criticism, in Lessing's sense, is always taking sides for the world's sake, understanding and judging everything in terms of its position in the world at any given time. Such a mentality can never give rise to a definite world view which, once adopted, is immune to further experiences in the world because it has hitched itself firmly to one possible perspective.[42]

The worldliness and mobility of such a critical stance is the real fruit of "enlarged thinking." What Lessing teaches, and what is so hard for us to appreciate, is that "positionality," or perspectivism, is itself a form of absolutism, so long as it is uninformed by the relativity born of representative thinking. The worldly relativism of Lessing does not suspend judgment; rather, it is the presupposition of a critical intelligence whose discourse and argumentation humanizes the world instead of tearing it asunder. Lessing's thought, like that of Socrates, is dialogical. It is not, however, "the silent dialogue between me and myself, but an anticipated dialogue with others."[43] Benhabib invokes this phrase of Arendt's in order to demonstrate that enlarged thinking aims at consensus and commensurability. However, according to Arendt, it is precisely this "anticipated dialogue" with others that gives Lessing's thought its distinctively polemical character.[44]

Lessing presents us with the paradox of a polemicist who continually crossed and recrossed the ideological battle lines of his day, eshewing the coercive claims of moral or political "truth" in favor of the "fundamental relativity" of the realm of opinion. It was in this realm—the realm of *doxa*, of endless debate and argument—that he felt most at home, and could engage others in the distinctive friendship born of partnership in argument. This returns us to the theme of *philia*, which, in the Lessing essay, Arendt juxtaposes to both intimacy and fraternity. Only those who engage in endless talk and argument about the world, who hold different opinions, yet share a commitment to the world, are capable of "humanizing the world through discourse."[45] The dialogical spirit of Lessing's thought arises from his joy that, in the public realm at least, there is no such thing as moral or political truth:

> Lessing . . . rejoiced in the very thing that has ever—or at least since Parmenides and Plato—distressed philosophers: that the truth, as soon as it is uttered, is immediately transformed into one opinion among many, is contested, reformulated, reduced to one subject of discourse among others. Lessing's greatness does not merely consist in a theoretical insight that there cannot be one single truth within the human world but in his gladness that it does not exist and that, therefore, the unending discourse among men will never cease so long as there are men at all. A single absolute truth, could there have been one, would have been the death of all those disputes in which this ancestor and master of all polemicism in the German language was so much at home and always took sides with the utmost clarity and definiteness. And this would have spelled the end of humanity.[46]

In this respect, Lessing stands in the sharpest possible opposition to Kant, who deployed an absolute—the categorical imperative—precisely in order to escape the "fundamental relativity" of the realm of human affairs. Kant's attempt to "found truth on practical reason" aims at overcoming the effects born of human plurality and finitude in this realm: "[I]t is as though he who had so inexorably pointed out man's cognitive limits could not bear to think that in action, too, man cannot behave like a god."[47]

The example of Lessing demonstrates, contra Benhabib, that Arendt's appropriation of the Kantian idea of "enlarged thought" aims at escaping not only the monologism of the categorical imperative, but its universalizing machinery as well. As exemplified by Lessing's context-specific criticism, "enlarged thought" enables a mobile perspectivism, whose effect is to undermine hegemonic judgments from across the political spectrum. What makes Lessing a "completely political person" and a genuine inheritor of the Socratic idea of citizenship is his desire to see the "specific truthfulness" of minority or unpopular opinion preserved. This stance—the stance of *Selbstdenken*—demands a rejection of the Kantian/Habermasian idea that the "practical questions admit of truth."[48] Arendt's appreciation of Lessing shows that, for her, independent judgment, not agreement, is "an end in itself."[49]

To this it may be objected that the role of gadfly was suited to Lessing because the public-political world he inhabited was one that prohibited "participation in judgment and authority."[50] Independence of judgment is an end in itself so long as one is unburdened of the cares and responsibilities of genuinely democratic citizenship. Lessing's doggedly maintained independence—his refusal to toe anyone's ideological line—is defensible only in a context where action is out of the question. The "darkened" public world Lessing moved in was the same as that descibed by Kant in "What is Enlightenment?," a world summed up by Frederick's credo of enlightened despotism: "Argue as much as you like and about whatever you like, but obey!"[51] In such a world judgment is essentially the prerogative of a spectator. The actor, on the other hand, knows that representative thinking must be informed at every point by the anticipation of having to come to an agreement.[52] What matters, finally, is decision and the course of action chosen by the plural individuals who make up a political community.

This objection to the actual political quality of Lessing's *Selbstdenken* brings us to Arendt's reflections on Thoreau, whom she regarded as something less than a "completely political person." In "Civil Disobedience" Arendt contrasts Thoreau's refusal to pay a poll tax to a government that permitted slavery with more authentically political forms of resistance. The problem with Thoreau is that he "argued his case not on the ground of a *citizen's* moral relation to law, but on the ground of individual conscience and conscience's moral obligation." Citing a passage from "On the Duty of Civil Disobedience" in which Thoreau argues, "It is not a man's duty, as a matter of course, to devote himself to the eradication of any, even the most enormous, wrong; . . . but it is his duty, at least, to wash his hands of it, and . . . not to give it practically his support," Arendt attacks the inherent passivity of the conscientious objector.[53] As the example of Thoreau demonstrates, conscience is satisfied by avoiding complicity with evil; it does not demand action in order to *oppose* the evil in question. The good individual excuses him- or herself (and possibly spends a night in jail), whereas the good citizen embarks on a course of action designed to persuade his or her peers that the *polity* has contradicted itself by holding slavery consonant with human equality. Thus, the distinction between a Lincoln and a Thoreau is ultimately the distinction between an individual motivated by care for the world and one by care for his or her soul.

Conscience, then, expresses a kind of self-interest, the interest the moral individual has in avoiding "dirty hands." The demands of conscience require a withdrawal from the world, a denial of what Arendt in the Lessing essay calls our "obligation to the world." In the moral universe of Thoreau, the only obligation one has is to oneself. Tracing this unworldly concern back to Socrates, Arendt attacks the "subjectivism" of conscience:

> The counsels of conscience are not only unpolitical; they are always expressed in purely subjective statements. When Socrates stated that "it is better to suffer wrong than to do wrong," he clearly meant that it was better *for him*, just as it was better for him "to be in disagreement with multitudes than, being one, to be in disagreement with [himself]." Politically, on the contrary, what counts is that a wrong has been done; to the law it is irrelevant who is better off as a result—the doer or the sufferer.[54]

The rules of conscience are, moreover, "entirely negative": "They do not say what to do; they say what not to do. They do not spell out certain principles for taking action; they lay down boundaries no act should transgress."[55] The implicit message of all rules of conscience is "[B]eware of doing something that you will not be able to live with."[56] This is the essence of their "self-interested" character.

For Arendt, the "unpolitical" force of conscience can become politically significant only when there are numerous civil disobedients who are willing to "enter the market place and make their voices heard in public."[57] However, when this happens—as it did during the Vietnam War—a curious transformation takes place:

> [W]e are no longer dealing with individuals, or with a phenomenon whose criteria can be derived from Socrates or Thoreau. What had been decided *in foro conscientiae* has now become part of public opinion, and although this particular group of civil disobedients may still claim the initial validation—their consciences—they actually rely no longer on themselves alone. In the market place, the fate of conscience is not much different from the fate of the philosopher's truth: it becomes an opinion, indistinguishable from other opinions. And the strength of opinion does not depend on conscience, but on the number of those with whom it is associated. . . .[58]

Here, the inner plurality Arendt so appreciated in "Philosophy and Politics" is radically devalued. The realm of opinion, it seems, is no longer connected to the experience of "talking to oneself." What matters is not the quality of the dissident voice, but its volume. Speaking for themselves, Socrates and Thoreau are unpolitical.

The rest of "Civil Disobedience" aims at reframing contemporary civil disobedients as good citizens rather than good individuals. Arendt contends that civil disobedients are in fact nothing but the latest form of voluntary association, that is, a contemporary manifestation of that peculiar appetite for group action that so astonished Tocqueville in the early days of the republic.[59] She urges us to jettison the unpolitical and passivity-inducing vocabulary of conscience for a more activist grammar. As noted above, Arendt is at her most "republican" in these pages, almost to the point of implying that the only action or judgment that truly deserves the name is group action and judgment. The dissident individual is, politically speaking, nothing.

"Civil Disobedience" thus goes a long way toward taking back everything Arendt says in "Philosophy and Politics" and the Lessing essay. But this is not the end of the story, and it is not the place to render a final verdict on Arendt's individualism versus her communitarianism. A year after the essay on civil disobedience, Arendt returned to the theme of conscience and politics in "Thinking and Moral Considerations" (1971). The central figure is again Socrates, but with a decidedly different emphasis. The Socratic project is no longer presented as the attempt to "make friends" out of the citizens of the polis, nor is the Socratic dialectic seen as having the function of teasing out and preserving the "specific truthfulness" of every opinion. Instead, what Arendt now stresses is the destructive and resultless quality of Socrates' thinking.[60] The aporetic nature of the dialogues testifies to the fact that Socrates had no positive teaching he wished to impart. Rather, the goal of his "talking through" was to purge people of their unreflective opinions, to throw their everyday application of precepts and principles out of gear. It is not Socrates the gadfly who makes his appearance here, but Socrates the "electric ray," a fish that paralyzes and numbs by contact.[61] The nature of this paralysis is, according to Arendt, twofold:

> It is inherent in the *stop* and think, the interruption of all other activities, and it may have a paralyzing effect when you come out of it, no longer sure of what had seemed to you beyond doubt while you were unthinkingly engaged in whatever you were doing. If your action consisted in applying general rules of conduct to particular cases as they arise in ordinary life, then you will find yourself paralyzed because no such rules can withstand the wind of thought.[62]

The thinking with which the "electric ray" Socrates infects his conversational partners is intrinsically dangerous: it "inevitably has a destructive, undermining effect on all established criteria, values, measurements for good and evil, in short on those customs and rules of conduct we treat of in morals and ethics."[63] Thinking is "equally dangerous to all creeds and, by itself, does not bring forth any new creed."[64] It was to this apparently nihilistic quality of thought that the Athenians responded when they found Socrates guilty of corrupting the youth.

Arendt makes no attempt to mitigate the "nihilistic," destructive character of Socratic thought; on the contrary, she draws our attention to it again and again. But while thinking in the Socratic sense does not yield the truth of opinion or even a more reflective formulation of opinion, it stimulates the inner dialogue of consciousness, our inner plurality. And the by-product of this dialogue of the self is, as we might expect, conscience.

In "Thinking and Moral Considerations," Arendt accords a political role to dissolvant thought and the inner voice of conscience it stimulates. Her desire is to establish the strongest possible link between "the inability to think and a disastrous failure of what we commonly call conscience."[65] The hypothesis underlying this desire is that much of the radical evil encountered in the political history of the twentieth century was facilitated by "thoughtless" individuals like Eichmann, individuals bereft of evil motives and strong ideological convictions. Such individuals, Arendt argues, are immune to the claims of thinking and (thus) to the claims of conscience. It is only the individual who has experienced the "intercourse between me and myself" in thinking who will feel the weight of the Socratic claim that it is better "to be in disagreement with multitudes than, being one, to be in disagreement with [himself]." On the other hand, the thoughtless individual, who "does not know the intercourse between me and myself,"

> will not mind contradicting himself, and this means he will never be either able or willing to give account of what he says or does; nor will he mind committing any crime, since he can be sure that it will be forgotten the next moment.[66]

Such was the case with Eichmann, whose behavior was determined in accordance with the mechanical application of rules, and who had no difficulty in accepting the new set of rules offered by a criminal regime. It is the habitual, unthinking application of rules that destroys morality, that sets the stage for complicity with evil, from Cephalus in the *Republic* to totalitarianism. As Arendt put it in Toronto, at a conference on her work held in 1972:

> And if you go through such a situation [as totalitarianism] the first thing you know is the following: you *never* know how somebody will act. You have the surprise of your life! This goes throughout all layers of society and it goes throughout various distinctions between men. And if you want to make a generalization you could say that those who were still very firmly convinced of the so-called old values were the first to be ready to change their old values for a new set of values, *provided they were given one.* And I am afraid of this, because I think that the moment you give anybody a new set of values . . . you can immediately exchange it. And the only thing the guy gets used to is having a "bannister" and a set of values, no matter.[67]

The degeneration of ethics to a set of values or "language rules" paves the way to complicity in "infinite evil" by the "nonwicked everybody who has no special motives."[68]

It is in such a context that the power of thinking—of citizenship in the Socratic, alienated sense—reveals itself. The effect of Socrates, Lessing, and (indeed) Thoreau is to confront what Heidegger called the "they" (*das Mann*) with their fallenness, a real potential to do evil, which flows from the ready-to-hand character of their "values." The "stop and think" with which Socrates paralyzes his conversational partners is a genuine moment of anxiety, of *unheimlichkeit.* And, just as Heidegger argued in *Being and Time,* it is only with this uncanny dissolution of the grounds of everyday life that one is called back to oneself and hears, for the first time, the call of conscience.[69]

In "Thinking and Moral Cosiderations," Arendt limits the significance of this throwing out of gear: thinking and the experience of conscience remain "a marginal affair for society at large except in emergencies." Socratic citizenship proves its value only "in those rare moments in history when "Things fall apart; the centre cannot hold; / Mere anarchy is loosed upon the world."[70]

The political importance Arendt attributes to thinking and conscience— our inner plurality—moderates the fiercely republican stance of "Civil Disobedience." However, the limits she sets to this importance suggest an unresolved tension in her political theory as a whole. This tension is, as I suggested at the outset, between an individualist conception of reflective, distanced, and episodic citizenship and the more republican claims of "acting together." "Philosophy and Politics," the Lessing essay, and "Thinking and Moral Considerations" present us with variations on the theme of Socratic citizenship, and strong testimony to Arendt's discomfort with the claims of the group. While she abhors the unworldly and irresponsible withdrawal into the self born of Romanticism, she just as clearly refuses to be drawn into a conception of citizenship that has no place for the stubborn, dissenting individual.

From the perspective I have offered here, the civil disobedience essay represents an unfortunate lapse into a republicanisn akin to Machiavelli's, one in which care for the world and care for the self are dichotomized. Arendt falls prey to the tradition's distinction between the "good man" and the "good citizen." Offered the choice between these two, it is never in doubt which she will pick. There is, however, another alternative, the one she sketches in "Philosophy and Politics." In that essay she demonstrates that our inner plurality provides the basis for acting in the plural world. "Thinking and Moral Considerations" echoes this thought, although perhaps less forcefully than an individualist would like. The fact remains that Arendt, unlike her communitarian admirers, makes Socratic citizenship the other side of acting together. If she was finally unable to reconcile the two—if she sometimes allowed her commitment to the world to overwhelm her insight into the "two-in-one"—she at least was consistent in her appreciation of the value of stopping to think. The paradox of Arendt's thought flows from this effort: not a new or renewed republicanism, but a politicized individualism in which care for the "public thing" demands an unceasing suspicion of the seductions of tradition, the group, and the everyday.

NOTES

This essay was initially provoked by a dissatisfaction with the portrayal of Arendt found in George Kateb's *Hannah Arendt: Politics, Conscience, Evil* (Totowa: Rowman and Allanheld, 1983). In that book, Kateb presents an Arendt very much in line with the communitarian/civic republican account, although he negatively valorizes what the communitarians applaud. I should note, however, that Kateb modified his view of Arendt on the basis of a reading of the "Philosophy and Politics" manuscript. His appreciation of the individualist Arendt can be found in George Kateb, "Arendt and Individualism," *Social Research* 61 (1994): 765–794. My essay was written before Kateb's appeared.

1. See Charles Taylor, *Ethics of Authenticity* (Cambridge: Harvard University Press, 1991); Benjamin Barber, *Stong Democracy* (Berkeley: University of California Press, 1984); Michael Sandel, *Liberalism and the Limits of Justice* (New York: Cambridge University Press, 1982); and Ronald Beiner, *Political Judgment* (Chicago: University of Chicago Press, 1983) and *What's the Matter with Liberalism?* (Berkeley: University of California Press, 1992.

2. Sandel, *Liberalism and the Limits of Justice*, p. 183.

3. See, for example, the attacks on Rousseau in Hannah Arendt, *On Revolution* (New York: Penguin Books, 1962), and her biting comments about the bourgeoisie in Hannah Arendt, *The Origins of Totalitarianism* (New York: Harcourt Brace Jovanovich, 1966), ch. 5.

4. Hannah Arendt, *The Human Condition* (Chicago: University of Chicago Press, 1958), ch. 5.

5. For Arendt, that which appears to all is real. See Arendt, *Human Condition*, p. 50; see also Arendt, *On Revolution*, p. 98.

6. Bakunin, quoted in Arendt, *Origins of Totalitarianism*, p. 330.

7. See, among others, Hanna Fenichel Pitken, "Justice: On Relating Private and Public," *Political Theory* 9 (1981): 327–352; Barber, *Strong Democracy*; Sheldon Wolin, "Hannah Arendt: Democracy and the Political," *Salmagundi* 60 (1983): 3–19; and Martin Jay, "The Political Existentialism of Hannah Arendt," in Jay, *Permanent Exiles* (New York: Columbia University Press, 1985).

8. See, for example, Margaret Canovan's *Hannah Arendt: A Reinterpretation of Her Political Thought* (New York: Cambridge University Press, 1991); and Maurizio Passerin d'Entreves, *The Political Philosophy of Hannah Arendt* (New York: Routledge, 1990).

9. Canovan, *Hannah Arendt*, p. 204.

10. *Ibid.*, pp. 204–205.

11. Hannah Arendt, *Between Past and Future* (New York, Penguin Books, 1968), p. 241; Canovan, *Hannah Arendt*, p. 203. For a description of the transformation from a deliberative (Aristotelian) paradigm to the more militaristic idea of civic *virtu* one finds in Machiavelli and the Atlantic republican tradition generally, see J.G.A. Pocock, *The Machiavellian Moment* (Princeton: Princeton University Press, 1975).

12. Arendt, *Human Condition*, p. 37.

13. Hannah Arendt, *Crises of the Republic* (New York: Harcourt Brace Jovanovich, 1972), pp. 62–63.

14. A not–unheard of sentiment. See, for example, I. F. Stone's presentation of Socrates as the original antidemocrat in *The Trial of Socrates* (New York: Pantheon, 1988) and, less vulgar but just as vehement, Nietzsche's judgment in *Twilight of the Idols* (reprint, New York: Penguin Books, 1979), in the section entitled "The Problem of Socrates."

15. This essay was originally part of a lecture series given at Notre Dame and remained unpublished in Arendt's lifetime. It was finally published in 1990. Hannah Arendt, "Philosophy and Politics" [1954], *Social Research* 57, no. 1 (Spring, 1990): 72–103.

16. *Ibid.*, p. 81.

17. *Ibid.*

18. *Ibid.*, p. 82.

19. *Ibid.*, p. 83.

20. A non-Platonic reading of Thucydides would emphasize less the Athenians' lack of *sophrosyne* and concentrate more on the decline of such a plurality in an imperialist democracy. For a Platonic reading, see Leo Strauss, "On Thucydides' 'War of the Peloponnesians and the Athenians,'" in Strauss, *The City and Man* (Chicago: University of Chicago Press, 1964). For a more Arendtian view, see Peter Euben, "Creatures of a Day: Thought and Action in Thucydides," in *Theory and Practice: New Perspectives*, ed. Terrence Ball (Minneapolis: University of Minnesota Press, 1979).

21. *Ibid.*, p. 82.

22. Arendt, "Philosophy and Politics," p. 83. Cf. Ronald Beiner's discussion in his *Political Judgment*.

23. See Hannah Arendt, *The Life of the Mind* (New York: Harcourt Brace Jovanovich, 1978), pp. 179–193.

24. Arendt, "Philosophy and Politics," p. 85.

25. *Ibid.*, p. 86.

26. Plato, *Gorgias* 482C, in *Collected Dialogues*, ed. Edith Hamilton and Huntington Cairns (Princeton: Princeton University Press, 1982). Quoted by Arendt in "Philosophy and Politics," p. 84.

27. See Hannah Arendt, "Thinking and Moral Considerations," *Social Research* 51 (1984): 7–37. The closing discussion of *Richard III* is particularly relevant in this regard.

28. See, in this regard, Arendt's contrast between Socrates' "politics of appearance" and Machiavelli's in Arendt, *On Revolution*, pp. 101–102.

29. Hannah Arendt, *Lectures on Kant's Political Philosophy* (Chicago: University of Chicago Press, 1982), p. 37.

30. See Gregory Vlastos, "Socrates on Political Obedience and Disobedience," *Yale Review* 63 (1974): 517–534.

31. Arendt, *Life of the Mind*, vol. 1, pp. 69–92.

32. Arendt, "Philosophy and Politics," p. 84.

33. Arendt, *Between Past and Future*, p. 241.

34. *Ibid.*

35. Arendt, "Philosophy and Politics," p. 84; see also Hannah Arendt, "Truth and Politics," in Arendt, *Between Past and Future*, p. 242.

36. Seyla Benhabib, "Judgment and the Moral Foundations of Arendt's Political Thought," in Benhabib, *Situating the Self* (New York: Routledge, 1992).

37. See Immanuel Kant, *Critique Of Judgment* (reprint, New York: Hafner Press, 1951), sec. 40; cf. Hannah Arendt, "The Crisis in Culture," in Arendt, *Between Past and Future*, p. 220.

38. Arendt, *Lectures on Kant's Political Philosophy*, pp. 38–39.

39. Hannah Arendt, *Men in Dark Times* (New York: Harcourt Brace Jovanovich, 1968), pp. 5, 7.

40. *Ibid.*, p. 7.

41. *Ibid.*

42. *Ibid.*, p. 8.

43. *Ibid.*, p. 10.

44. *Ibid.*

45. *Ibid.*, p. 25.

46. *Ibid.*, p. 27.

47. *Ibid.*

48. See Jurgen Habermas, *Legitimation Crisis* (Boston: Beacon Press, 1978), p. 110.

49. See Jurgen Habermas, "Hannah Arendt on the Concept of Power," in Habermas, *Philosophical-Political Profiles* (Cambridge: MIT Press, 1983), p. 172.

50. Aristotle, *Politics*, trans. T. A. Sinclair (New York: Penguin Books, 1977), p. 169 (translation altered).

51. Kant, "What Is Enlightenment?" in *Political Writings*, ed. Hans Reiss (New York: Cambridge University Press, 1977), p. 59.

52. Hannah Arendt, "The Crisis in Culture," in Arendt, *Between Past and Future*, pp. 220–221.

53. "Argued his case": Hannah Arendt, "Civil Disobedience" in *Crises of the Republic*, p. 60. "It is not a man's duty": quoted *ibid.*, p. 60.

54. *Ibid.*, p. 62.

55. *Ibid.*, p. 63.

56. *Ibid.*, p. 64.

57. *Ibid.*, p. 67.

58. *Ibid.*, p. 68.

59. *Ibid.*, pp. 94–97.

60. Arendt, "Thinking and Moral Considerations," p. 25.

61. *Ibid.*, p. 22.

62. *Ibid.*, pp. 24–25 (my emphasis).

63. *Ibid.*, p. 24.

64. *Ibid.*, p. 26.

65. *Ibid.*, p. 8.

66. *Ibid.*, p. 35.

67. Hannah Arendt, "On Hannah Arendt," in *The Recovery of the Public World*, ed. Melvyn Hill (New York: St. Martin's Press, 1979), p. 314 (my emphasis).

68. Arendt, "Thinking and Moral Considerations," p. 36.

69. Martin Heidegger, *Being and Time*, trans. E. Robinson and J. Macquarrie (New York: Harper and Row, 1962), secs. 55–58.

70. W. B. Yeats, "The Second Coming," quoted in Arendt, "Thinking and Moral Considerations," p. 36.

Can We Be American Scholars?

JUDITH SHKLAR

EMERSON WAS AN INSPIRED teacher, and *The American Scholar*, addressed to a group of bright Harvard students, asks them the most fundamental questions one can put to such a group: What are you here for? What is the aim and the end of your education? Are you here entirely to develop your own personal faculties? Are you getting an education to enhance your own powers, to improve your skills and personality wholly for your own gratification and well-being, so that you may have a happier, fuller, and more prosperous life, or does the education impose a special duty upon you? He does not answer these or any other questions. By turns, hortatory, critical, upbeat, and dejected, he allows the students, and us, to choose. Can we, should we, be "American"?

I begin with Emerson as a teacher partly because *The American Scholar* was a Phi Beta Kappa speech and meant for young people, who, in fact, still respond to it at that age and in that place. Indeed, for many years I thought of it only as an offering to them, but that was a mistake. It is Emerson talking to himself, in doubt an inner dialogue, and therefore to other adults, like you and me. And so my main purpose in writing about it at all is to speak directly to you, to George Kateb. Not only because you are a remarkable teacher who has tactfully and generously moved generations of students to intellectual and moral maturity, but because your essays also tell us what it means to be an American scholar now.

Style is always important. Emerson never moves in a straight line. He circles around topics. And the circle was his favorite figure. To get to *The American Scholar* by way of *Circles* is not to take a detour, or one might say that, as in Montaigne, all roads are byways. "Around every circle another can be drawn." There is no limit to what we can achieve. To live in a circle is to be both enclosed and infinitely expansive. For "conversation is a game of circles" as every speaker liberates us from the opinions of his predecessor. (I shall say "he" and "man" throughout, because Emerson did so and I refuse either to falsify him or to reduce the distance between us.) In conversation, "we recover our rights," as we do in argument with what we read. As a man who moves in circles, Emerson knows that "no facts are sacred, none are profane; I simply experiment as an endless seeker with no past at my back." Surprises, novelty, the new truth that obliterates the old, forgetfulness and the drawing of new circles: these are the joys. Is he, "the circular philosopher," a fine Pyrrhonist? Not quite, for he cannot decide, and there is some declarative closing of the circle. He can, of course, go on to another, wider one, but not without having first affirmed that calamity does not signify, that there is an "eternal generator." He does not need to know where he is headed, but he has to believe that there is some great omniscient force out there. I cannot forgive him those gestures toward divinity and the metaphysical and moral optimism that they underwrite. That is the main reason why I do not think that we should simply accept his vision of an American scholar as our own.

Our historical calamities are such that they should not be forgotten. Evil is not, as he told another group of Harvard students, "merely private, not absolute." It may have been courageous at that moment to call on them to "love God without mediator or veil," but it was a failure of nerve, not to be able to draw his circles without that reassurance. Nor is it true that it will all turn out well, as he chose to believe. Emerson loved Montaigne, but far too gingerly, with all the sex laundered away, so that he lacked the old skeptic's worldly clarity. Instead, he tells Montaigne that "the appearance is immoral, the result moral." Who can now think that "the march of civilization is a train of felonies—yet, general ends are answered." And it is just silly to say that "the world spirit is a good swimmer" and will not drown. There is the Eternal to reassure us that circles of ever-deeper abysses are all for the best; all are contained in an enveloping positive divinity. Even Hegel did better than that. He may have identified God and history, but at least he did not pretty the story up.

Circles are Emerson's best and worst drawings, and *The American Scholar* contains them all. The expansiveness, the easy movement from doubt to doubt, from one level of discourse to another are dazzling, but then comes the descent to a center, to a fixed point of a trite moral deism: "The web of God is a circular power." Do we really need it? There may well be other lines less fluid than they should be. His America may be too fixed a point and as such no longer available to us. And to return to the end, to the beginning, Emerson may have endowed liberal education with moral qualities it simply does not have. About these matters there is for us much doubt.

What of America as a circle? It all depends on what we mean by "America." There is much in *The American Scholar* that sounds like the crudest chauvinism here: "We have listened too long to the courtly muses of Europe," and there is more in the same vein, of a need to cut the apron strings, to end our dependence upon European scholars. To be American is to be not-European. He does not, however, slight Europe. Indeed, Americans are called upon to be as creative and independent in their pursuit of knowledge as European scholars. Moreover, all his great men are European. Surely America is not a circle in the worst possible political sense, confining and xenophobic. In politics the circle is perhaps not the most liberal of symbols. It has a sinister implication. Are we to forget Rousseau's Genevan circles of gossipy citizens keeping a mean and censorious eye on their neighbors? Not all circles are composed of private friends. The political circle is the expelling and exiling political club. Yet all this is unfair. It would be utterly wrong to read Emerson as that sort of nationalist. He was, however, not immune to the opinions of the Jacksonians, for whom Europe stood for everything that was undemocratic, illiberal, and unjust. The Europe they knew was first ruled by Napoleon and then by Metternich, at the very time when America was becoming more democratic. Europe's agony was the fear of revolution; ours was slavery. Emerson's blast against Europe is a part of a decidedly democratic stance, and not-Europe can be taken as more free and more equal and becoming more so. "The spirit of the American freeman" shall not be "timid, imitative, tame." The call to stand on one's own feet was buckled to a reminder that there was much work to be done. It was just not Europe's work.

But what of America? It was surely not a closed social circle, but an expansive idea. America is always "our newfound land," not a place on the map, but the land that is to be discovered. It is an imagined continent, not a location. It is the name of worlds unknown, the creation of the mind. The American scholar is to embark upon an unending voyage of discovery. And as the world is a circle, he is to go round and round. Perhaps there is too much self-discovery in such a notion of scholarship, but it is hardly narrow or culturally exclusive. If America is the name of the exploration, then we can all be American scholars. The contrast with Europe has lost its interest. To alter Locke's haunting phrase, "all the world is America" now, and it is America that serves as a model, for good and ill. We do not envy European universities. Those circles do not help us define ourselves. It is only the distance between what we are and what we might be that can tell us the extent of our failures and achievements. If we want to be American scholars, we cannot invoke, as Emerson could, the specter of European cultural domination and an intellectual class that was content to passively consume the products of foreign capitals. When he scorns travel, he cannot, now at least, mean to tell us that a trip abroad will corrupt or impair the native intellect. I do not think that is what he actually had in mind. Without having the word, he was warning us not to become spiritual tourists. The casual museumgoers of the mind, who nibble at whatever is put before them, are Americans and very common, but they are not scholars, American or otherwise. They do occupy many university posts, and write for many journals, but we should not identify the scholar with the academic.

Almost none of Emerson's listeners at Harvard were going to become university teachers or professional scholars, though they were, of course, the best students in their class. Emerson knew that, but he was speaking to them in the hope that they would have active intellectual lives. Perhaps he only cared about the few who would follow him to Concord, not literally, but in the structure of their own lives. Perhaps he was not thinking about the boys in front of him at all, but conversing in an imaginary circle in which we might conceivably join. Certainly, we no longer teach groups such as the one he had in front of him in 1837. They were almost all from New England, and many had known one another since childhood. They were provincial, and Emerson tried to shake them out of their comfortable circle of conventions. There were no women in the room and, as far as we know, not one person of color. These young men could not yet imagine what the class of 1861 would face and the names, their own family names, that would grace the walls of Memorial Hall.

The lecture was a huge success. Some five hundred copies were sold as soon as it was printed. Can it still speak as directly to us, assuming that we are among those whom Emerson meant to reach? Can we be Emerson's American scholars who come from, and go to, places where people are un-imaginably different from those whom he knew and taught? Who could then have imagined what we know about their and our own century? These obstacles are not insuperable. After all, we do read Emerson and join him in the conversation of mankind, as he wanted his readers to do. His difficulty is not the burden of knowledge itself but its inevitable doubts and discouragements. What do we, what can we, still hope and expect education to achieve?

Emerson was very certain that learning for all as an activity was bound to be morally enhancing. Is it? Do we not know of cultivated mass murderers, of some of the places where and some of the people who played Beethoven very well, of science used and abused? Emerson had never read Primo Levi. We who have are not likely to see a liberal education as an open road to exalted virtues, personal or public. At a far less horrifying level, we may not know whether the education we offer our own perfectly decent students does them any good. They are certainly encouraged to take an extremely individualistic view of their education. It is theirs to do with as they choose. Some teachers have a great deal of confidence in the natural morality, even the purity, of the young and urge this doctrine of self-perfection and free choice upon them. So do those teachers who are inclined to see students as no better and no worse than their parents and the older members of the groups to which they adhere. These scholars do not expect to influence their students in any significant degree and think that they must be left free to build their own lives. Nevertheless, in a confused way, students and many young teachers also believe that the purpose of a higher education should be social. It should aim at making privileged young people the servants of society, trained to do the jobs that highly skilled and resourceful people can do best. Education should perhaps be reenvisioned as training for what Jefferson called the natural aristocracy. The most capable people should be prepared to do the difficult jobs of our society, because it is their duty as republican citizens and as scientifically educated persons to do them.

There is another idea of public education, public in being open, transparent, gracious, and not just useful. This is not a negligible thought. It was Emerson's view that this should be attempted. He certainly did believe that a liberal education was liberating and that it made better, more upright, and sincere men. If such optimism cannot for us be quite as evidently true as it seemed to him, neither is it obviously false. It is what one has to think about, back and forth. It depends on the meaning of America. If the American scholar is to receive an education in openness, it will be a totally new kind of learning. Such an American education may be potentially a scholar's paradise, in which social duty and personal development can be reconciled, certainly not easily, but at least as a plausible expectation. So let us say that it was his hope and not our fear, the two forces he so emphatically invokes in *The American Scholar*, that should decide what education might be and might achieve. In that case, education will make all of us more able to communicate with others and to speak justly and affectionately to them, so that in every language we will contribute something to the practice of justice and affection here and now. And by making affection and justice the ideals of human speech, Emerson managed to join the most personal and the most public of virtues. As a project it is surely the best we can imagine. And even the actual, not only the best, American scholar, needs some sort of aim.

How then does Emerson proceed? He begins with a declaration of independence from Europe, reminding us implicitly that the American Revolution has not fulfilled all its promises. The first and perhaps the foremost lack is human wholeness. The division of labor not as a way of dividing up work but as a social system, as a way of labeling people, is a scourge and a menace. Only society is taken to be a whole, while people are seen as bits and pieces of that grand unity. The individual is but the embodiment of his job, a slice of the social pie. We are cut-off limbs, not integrated bodies. Is this more an American or a universal state of affairs?

As an account of American manners this rings perfectly true. "What do you do?" and "Where are you from?" are the first questions we ask and are asked when we meet as strangers. It seems to be the essential information we need to begin a conversation at all. Does that really prevent us from being complete women and men? Only if we insist that being a farmer or a tradesman is all there is to a person. Emerson is accusing Americans of denying the essential, unique personality of every individual. He is also saying something about society. As in *Self-Reliance*, he is determined to recall that society is unreal, that only individuals palpably exist, as natural phenomena, self-created in their character and independent of any labeling that might be inflicted upon them. Nor is labeling the only wrong that the division of labor inflicts upon people. It also grades them. Americans do not do this with the brutality and finality of the English class system, but it is still done. The tinker, tailor, soldier, and sailor lose their self-esteem as they become their jobs and then are assigned its worth to society as their own value as human beings.

What America has forgotten or has failed to learn is that "[m]an is not a farmer, or a professor, or an engineer, but he is all. Man is one and present in each." The scholar is properly "Man Thinking." In "a degenerate state," he is just another victim of society, whose job it is to think, "or still worse the parrot of other man's thinking." If he is a true scholar he will be a representative man, a sharer, whom "the past instructs: the future invites."

Let there be no mistake about it—the division of labor is not just a metaphor for man's fallen state, his inability to be universal, as crafted by God. It is wrong because it means inequality, class division, the humiliation of those who work with their hands, and ultimately the reduction of human beings to their social function. Emerson has begun with an attack on all historically known society. But America was supposed to be better, to have begun anew, not settled down to this age-old system of degradation. There is, for us, something troubling here, and we cannot leave off where Emerson does.

How is the American scholar to learn his true vocation? Emerson begins with the lessons of nature, and they reveal Emerson at his worst, murky and religious. It is here that we must read those deplorable mystical rumblings about nature as "the inexplicable continuity of the web of God," which nevertheless resembles our own spirit, and is boundless. To study nature is to know thyself, a sort of free-floating divinity developed within and outside ourselves. In my view, miasma is the right word for this sort of talk, and it is also intellectual cowardice to resort to this sort of cover for an otherwise exemplary skepticism. If this is essential to being an American scholar, we should reject Emerson's invitation to become one and remain academic drudges, usefully employed and united to our fellow citizens by common sense, baseball, and fast food.

Fortunately we do not have to leave Emerson quite so abruptly. He recovers from his lapse into moonshine and goes on to say something very interesting. To know nature, he now argues, is the first step in the development of reason, and like a child, mankind progresses through the necessary stages of learning to know what knowing is. It is in a condensed way very close to Hegel's more elaborate account in the *Phenomenology*, a psychology of human knowledge.

We begin by seeing only individual irreducible objects, foreign and seemingly chaotic. To impose some order, to assimilate, we appropriate the elementary units of our experience; we classify them. Then we find that they have a law "which is also the law of the human mind." The scientist who finds them reduces the apparent disorder of nature to an organized whole. The laws of nature are his own creation; that is why there is such an identity between man and the nature he studies. But it cannot be said that Emerson went all the way with Hegel. It is not intersubjective communication that creates all our knowledge. To be consistent, Emerson would have to have followed Hegel. He would have had to recognize that science is not carried on by isolated individuals who can be understood in all languages; it is a lot more interactive than that. I expect that Emerson may have seen a danger to self-reliance and to the ideal of a society of self-generated individuals in the social theory of knowledge. He need not have hesitated, however, because the barriers to selfhood are built by illusion and conventionality, not by this or any other philosophy of knowledge. Perhaps he lacked Hegel's radical intellectual courage. In any event, Emerson was able to convince himself that by finding his own self in nature the young scholar will come to worship his own soul.

In that state of mind, the scholar is to turn next to the past. We have at last arrived at books, and it is reassuring to be told that "the theory of books is noble," but that they are also a dreadful threat to us. Emerson had, of course, read a good deal, and we now hear him speak in two voices, arguing with each other. This is Emerson at his best. "Man Thinking must not be subdued by his instrument." What is wrong with the instrument? Every book is the creature of a locality and a time, generally not the reader's own. It is burdened with irrelevant particularities. To be sure, the other voice says, books may "transmute life into truth," distilling something that speaks to the reader directly from whatever distant origins it may have come. There is, however, great mischief embedded in the written page. Thoughts are transferred to records, and these are apt to inspire reverence and a taste for listless consumption and submission to heroes, or to be exact, to the mere lifeless statue of the hero. Emerson's struggle with great men is once again uppermost in his mind. He has to protect the meek college student from the library of the great books, from becoming a mere bookworm, rather than Man Thinking. "Genius is always sufficiently the enemy of genius by overinfluence." Not a bad line. In fact it's terrific. He should have quit right there.

There is, however, a creative way of reading. Emerson's other self now reminds us that old poetry can inspire the young scholar with modern joy. Chaucer, Marvell, and Dryden are not only timeless, they fill us with the delight of surprise as we find ourselves in them, and their "authentic utterance" makes inventors of their readers, or at least the hardy ones among them. Every flame ignites another in a creative act of recognition as one reads the pages of the great books in a self-assertive spirit. So far, so good, but all is not well. "When we can read God directly, the hour is too precious to be wasted in other men's transcripts of their readings." Emerson does not stoop to saying that Shakespeare and Plato only left us their copybooks, but there is no hiding a certain malice here. Was it envy and resentment? Is God here an alibi for the fear of mediocrity? Is he saying, I may not be able to write *Hamlet*, but I can read God just as well as you could? It must be said that Nietzsche could smite the philistines without arousing such suspicions.

Emerson's being both for and against the past poses a challenge we do want to accept: scholars must not bow down before pages written long ago as if they were above questioning. Emerson is surely right about not simply swallowing every word of Cicero. It is a good example. We read him when we are too young and fail to see both what a dreadful man he was and how often he could be dazzlingly brilliant. He becomes a footnote, and we are treated to far too many footnotes that are to be taken as binding legal precedents, as thumping trumps in an argument, rather than as the mere references we might want to look at again. We should be able to say, Stuff Plato, though I am not in fact up to it. Yet I am not sold on the argument in *Crito*, and neither are you. But there are limits to the scorn we can heap on "those who were truly great." In any case, the problem for us as teachers is not there. Emerson has succeeded only too well among the poorly prepared adolescents who have been told to be "creative" since they left their cradles, and who do not read because they do not know how to sit still. They have been force-fed for too long. We cannot afford to scoff at these books. The college students we teach need a different example, not that of the spineless antiquarian, but also not that of the puffed-up illiterate who scorns the past because he has never met it eye to eye. May I remind you of your luminous essay on Thucydides? Where else than in his depths can we ever find a fuller sense of those moments when public and private evil meet? How else to grasp the true character of protracted war? I think that one of Emerson's voices knew perfectly well how liberating reading could be, but his self-reliant voice made too much of its stifling threats. It was hardly a warning needed in a culture already dedicated to being self-made. And it certainly was a false move to turn one's back upon the truth of tragedy, and it did not serve American scholars well.

The last step in the education of the American scholar, now that he knows about nature and books, is action. Scholars are not to be recluses, shut up in their rooms. They are not to be a protected class, sheltered from the tempest of history and its demands. Without action thought can never rise to truth. "Inaction is cowardice." Human action is first and foremost speaking. That is how action moves us from "the unconscious to the conscious." Does this sentence mean to Emerson what it so obviously implies to us post-Freudians, schooled also in the French elaborations of the frayed remnants of the truth of our age? I would like to think that it is so, however improbably. In any case, he goes on very persuasively. "Only so much do I know as I have lived." The deed we have not yet done lies deep in our unconscious life, where dormant is also childhood, now long past. It is not as inactive as Emerson thought (or did he know better?), but with that exception he is certainly subtle in speaking of life and action. Our "private history" becomes a public, visible, audible act, which can as a word fly across the globe. This is really fine, and one hopes that Emerson will go on to say more, but he veers off to a maddening aside as he meanders on about the activities of Dutchmen and Palestinian shepherds. Perhaps he wants to say something cosmopolitan, or he might just have been scared by the line of thinking on which he had embarked. To be sure, he must remember, as he did when he spoke of nature, that "[t]he world is that other me where I get to know myself."

The scholar's real action is speech, and it also is like the book, a resource, food for living. But this is not a call for green life such as Goethe's Mephisto gave the young scholar Faust. Instead of the tree of life, we get the sentiment, "Character is higher than intellect." This is merely upper-class chatter. If the scholar's vocabulary is to be devoted to justice and affection, he'll need a lot more than mindless chatter. Perhaps aware of the shallowness to which he has sunk, Emerson recoups. The active scholar should sacrifice nothing to popular opinion, and it might be a good idea to do some manual work. He rejoices in the greater awareness of "the dignity and necessity of labor to every citizen," whether scholarly or not. That is the true voice of democracy, and it is something an American scholar should not forget.

We have been moving in concentric circles. The transactions of the self with nature and the past are smaller in circumference than the circle of action as language. When we speak we transform ourselves from private into public persons. We transfigure our individual experiences and make them soar. We become visible, transparent to all. Our dictionary is life itself, for "only so much do I know as I have lived." When "life is our dictionary," we truly have something to say that others will welcome.

Is this call to live not a prelude to Nietzsche's *Use and Abuse of History*? Is not this the devil's seduction of the scholar, luring him to leave all learning behind him? No, but it is surely a call to put learning to the service of life, to make it the means to an expansive self-liberation. Life is both for the uninhibited expenditure of energy, physical and intellectual, upon what is eternally, inertly *there* and to move, transform, and create something that is not static. It is the widest of the circles we draw, as we remake ourselves in the act of creating the new. The great difference is, of course, that when Emerson speaks of public action he most decidedly means democratic politics. To live is to act justly and affectionately as one who works with his hands and his soul and does so to realize the promise of American *life*. As an erotic liberator Emerson was, indeed, Nietzsche's master, but in politics he traced a very different circle.

What is the mature scholar like, when he has learned to act, as well as to read nature and books and to use all for life, his own and that of America, his destination and his anchor? He is a scientist. It is one of Emerson's most attractive intellectual traits that, unlike European romantics, he did not scorn the natural sciences or, worse, turn to some Paracelsian ravings. The sciences did not scare him, nor did he think of them as an emotional desert. Sane in a deep way, he knew what we should all know, that natural science is the truth of the modern world, and that it is all our work. To shun it on some spurious excuse of its being alien to the higher spiritual qualities is to remain a hostage to mindless religiosity or, more significantly, to a romantic loathing for rationality. One might have thought that Emerson would have fallen victim to the latter, but he did not—quite on the contrary. That is why he is after all *the* American scholar, for what is American intellectual life without the natural sciences?

The greatest single contribution of the scientific spirit to moral life is that it inspires self-trust, and for Emerson that was indispensable. Without self-confidence, we cannot expect to have any sort of moral, intellectual, or social freedom, or, indeed, any creative life at all. Science enables us to distinguish the real from the apparent, illusion from experience, and the false from the genuine. The scientist knows "that a popgun is a popgun," though the ancient and honorable of the earth affirm that it is the crack of doom. It can tell us when the emperor has no clothes, when humbug is humbug and when hot air is just hot air. The learned ignorance, the fear of universally acclaimed reputations, the prestige of pretentious nonsense touted by the quality press and the educated public are not likely to impress him, because he relies on his own judgment. He is by far the most self-reliant member of the scholarly community. In short, "a popgun is popgun," no matter who says that it is a world-shaking explosion.

Self-assurance has its costs. The task of observation is unpaid and unhonored. Fame comes but to a few. For every Herschel there are many unheralded astronomers who can expect only poverty and obscurity, but there is, in spite of that, more to be gained than lost. "The world belongs to him who can see through its pretensions." Such men can alter the state of mind of their neighbors, and they are great whether they become Cuviers and Davys or remain in provincial America. Science says, So what? and Why? to custom and tradition, and the very question is a vote for life. However, "if in self-trust all virtue is comprehended" and the free man is free even to define freedom, then the scholar must surely be a political animal as well.

Here, with politics we again move back and forth. The political talk around him is not of enough consequence to distract the scientist, too pointless to matter to the man who seeks the truth and contemplates the harmony of the spheres. His impact on others is indirect, when his transforming news compels them to rethink their beliefs. But a few paragraphs later the scholar is summoned to do more than to say, "This is my music, this is myself," and so to arouse the dormant. It appears that as an American, the scholar has to do something quite directly to turn American society to a better future. To avoid politics is cowardly and even mindless. We have rounded back upon the circle of action. It is, for Emerson, always political, and courage is always social courage.

The circle of action is now historical, located in his and our own time and place. We have been reduced and allowed ourselves to become of no account. Men are called "the mass" and "the herd." They accept that demeaning station and let themselves worship a hero, who embodies all their unfulfilled possibilities: "He lives for us, and we live in him." This was, of course, Carlyle's doctrine. It is not entirely clear whether Emerson thinks that this is how we now live. He is not saying that we should not talk like that, though one might wish that he had said so, and said that it was wrong ever to call human beings "masses" and "herds." Unhappily, he does not say that. Fortunately, he does not say what his friend, Carlyle, said, that this is how it should be, that we are at our best when there are a few great men, surrounded by abject subjects, who find their fulfillment in them.

The alternative course for an American scholar is to create a revolution by "the domestication of the idea of Culture." This is not exactly a clear notion.

Emerson certainly did mean popular education. As a tireless public lecturer at endless lyceums, he did more than his share to enlighten and elevate his fellow citizens. Worthwhile and admirable as such service was and is, it can scarcely be called revolutionary. It does not transform. Outside the hall, audiences are not what they imagine themselves to be within its walls. Surely Emerson must have known that as well as Rousseau had? Or was he incapable of so high a level of self-understanding? His diaries, it seems to me, are utterly free of self-deception. Cultural transformation was not, therefore, to be the result of lecturing to the public. What were scholars to do?

Is the task of raising "the masses" to manhood to be political, then? After all, action is political. Here, he backtracks again. Emerson begins with telling young people to shun the normal prizes of politics. His Harvard students are to forgo power and money and to avoid politics as usual, especially the lure of "spoils" and "office." That is mere government, and is best left to clerks and drudges of that sort. In fact, Emerson does not seem to be able to come up with anything very concrete. He is certain of only one thing, that everyman must be made less timid, less given to admiring the great, and more conscious of his own portion of creative energy. This is not one of Emerson's better moments. He was never at his best when he talked about practicable reform. That is hardly surprising, since the private elevation he wanted to encourage could not, by definition, be brought about by public programs. That being the case, there was no reason to divert his privileged audience from doing the work of government. Why despise it without suggesting a new political spirit? The result is lamentable, then as now. Public service is envisioned by the young Emersonian scholar as private politics, private do-gooding, the shelter, the environment, the after-school program, instead of "We'll remember in November" and doing something about it. Surely, we should not encourage American scholars to listen to the siren voice of private edification posing as public action.

If Emerson is vague about the disaggregation of the masses into self-reliant men, he is not easily dismissed when he comes to "this country" at last. Perhaps there has never been a time in modern history when his brief and fleeting lesson of muted hope has sounded more authentic than it does now. It is only a paragraph, which is succeeded by a far less plausible trumpet of good cheer. It would, of course, be absurd to impose the post–hot and cold war consciousness upon Emerson, especially so many years before the Civil war. Nevertheless, when he says, "Our age is bewailed as an age of Introversion . . . must that needs be an evil?" he is one of us. It is a small circle after he has declared that all ages contain the same basic elements in any case, but he does now want to note a special modern mood amid the greater historical uniformities in which the classical, the romantic, and the reflective must all have their moment. The predominant sensibility he now sees is that of Hamlet, thoughtful and hesitant. Is there not much to be said for not being blind, and why should one long for the turbulence of revolution? The politics of unexalted and critical maturity have much to be said for them. Indeed, they may be even better than Emerson supposed. They are not the politics of great expectations, but they are also not the politics of ideological war. Was Emerson suggesting that America was better off than Europe in this respect as well? He does not say so directly, but as he is about to make his radical turn away from the Old World, one may at least suspect him of such a thought.

The calm of clear-sighted politics does not last. The joy of Romantic hope is too great to be resisted, and Emerson indulges in it to the full. He sees a new spirit in America, a new appreciation for modest daily "household life" and the "philosophy of the street." Surely he has America's glory in mind here, the democracy of everyday life. It is an incomparable cultural achievement, and there is no reason why he and we should not rejoice in it. "I embrace the common, explore and sit at the feet of the familiar, the low." If he made this a proclamation of what the new domestic culture was to be and what it meant in a call for the transformation of all values it would have enhanced his critical politics. That is not, however, quite what he does. It turns out that "the common" refers to the new romantic poetry of Goldsmith, Burns, Cowper, Goethe, Wordsworth, and Carlyle. What a mix! What did they share apart from being able to see beauty in the natural world we share? Is that "the common"? Lucy and Gretchen? Do we really have to call Pope, Johnson, and Gibbon "pedantic"? The near may be beautiful, but must we then scorn the distant? Do we really have to turn our back on Italy to appreciate the local daisies?

The final blow to intelligibility comes at the end, where Emerson enlists Goethe to prove to his own satisfaction that the poetry of the vulgar is a recreation of the wisdom of the ancients. This is the Hellenist side of the romantic spirit. Not, of course, Dionysian tragedy, but simplicity disguised as the minutiae of daily experience is now safely held up to us as our very own Greece—how well domesticated and assimilated it is to American life! This is what Matthew Arnold was to call "sweetness and light," and it is not exactly what we are likely to experience as we suffer with Hecuba and Oedipus. This is not our Greece, and it is not what we look for or what we find there. This is not the Emerson whom one can now follow. It may have been the classical spirit suitable for his America, but it is only an embarrassment to us, like all the fig leaves.

The paragraph following this disastrous venture into Hellenism is a tribute to Swedenborg. It is impossible to grasp what it was that drew so many Americans, including the elder Henry James, to this nut. After Kant's demolition job, it is difficult to understand what anyone could possibly find in those murky and completely unreadable pages. Let us make the best of things and say that it was not a form of Enlightenment-bashing, though that is what it may have been. Every great man is allowed a margin of folly, and Swedenborg was Emerson's. It is a consolation to know that the seer did not come off quite as well as Montaigne did in *Representative Men*.

Leaving this embarrassment behind us, we can find the Romantic Emerson, who does have something very immediate to say to America. He finds "the new importance given to the single person" a good sign of the times. The individual is surrounded by "natural respect," a "sovereign state" all by himself. With his inevitable irony, Emerson was elsewhere able to mock the little "empire of me," but he was the man who had constructed it, and it was no doubt his right to also dismiss it. Nevertheless, this is what the American scholar is finally being prepared to become, an utterly self-sufficient individual who will not even give alms to the poor unless they are *his* poor.

Having now moved over his three circles—reflective, classical, and romantic, the mature, the childlike, and the ever-youthful—Emerson again took up the offensive note. The most promising young Americans are discouraged by European models. It is not all Europe's fault. Our native avarice makes America a nation of complacent conformists. Where is the remedy? How are all these capable and energetic young men to become explorers? Emerson just keeps hoping. First there must be patience. Scholarship is demanding, and as we saw, it requires the tracing of many circles, historical and natural. In the end the American scholar will be liberated. "We will walk on our own feet; we will work with our own hands; we will speak our own minds." Brave words are directed at both foreign domination and domestic dereliction.

The sentiments are national, but not wholly so. Consider the last line of *The American Scholar*: "A nation of men will for the first time exist, because each believes himself inspired by the Divine Soul which also inspires all men." There is an excess of mystical feeling in that line, but these are not the words of a narrow-minded, abrasive nationalist. Emerson was not alone in hoping that America might be what it should and could be, the nation of the future, a beacon for all mankind, generous and adventurous and constantly improving itself, but he was not given to national self-congratulation.

To say that *The American Scholar* is a marvelous essay, that in its twenty-odd pages there is almost more feeling and thought than a reader can bear, is to be obvious. It is also not an answer to the question of whether we can still be American scholars in Emerson's sense. The most obvious distance between him and ourselves is that we do not and cannot feel inferior to contemporary Europe. All the great scientists are alive now, and they are Americans. Our university system is immeasurably superior in its versatility and virtuosity to any other. Our problem is not servility, but arrogance. We are not humbled by others, and there is no reason why we should be. As an academic culture, we follow Emerson in flailing ourselves for our failure to live up to our possibilities and hopes, and disdaining foreign examples. The heart of the matter is not these considerations. There is also no difficulty with Emerson's individualism and his commitment to the democracy of daily relationships in America. Above all, we ought to join him in his enthusiasm for the natural sciences as the great intellectual adventure and the model of truth in our time.

Why, then, must there be some uneasiness as we read this remarkable piece? First and foremost, there is the dependence on a divinity in Emerson and on the constant assertion that the direct vision of God is the ultimate proof of intellectual self-reliance and the aim of all our striving. The little church of me is better perhaps than a communal congregation, though it is not, as Emerson seemed to think, a mark of genuine independence. To be in bondage to a personal and universal divinity is no less fettering than to simply join a sect and perform the appropriate social gestures. The second hurdle is a rampant sentimentality. By "sentimentality" I mean false expressions of feeling. When the struggles of sex and power are the reality before us, it is tasteless, sentimental in short, to talk of classical light and ease. Greek tragedy is the truth of that very life that Emerson called the source and end of the scholar's vocation. Nietzsche understood what tragedy meant for life completely. Why did Emerson retreat? Why did he blush when he read Montaigne? Even Hawthorne made him uneasy. There is no evident answer, but it distances him from us irremediably. Religious enthusiasm and prudery are not insignificant intellectual flaws in an American scholar.

What of Emerson's romanticism? What of circles, that ascension of the spirit entirely on its internal energy? What of the dissociated self, fenced in to protect is uniqueness? We are free to choose. Politically romantic individuality can act as a fine basis for a radical theory of rights. Tempered by a democratic ethos and a self-generated sense of responsibility, it does not veer off into that Promethean exaggeration that has in our age lost its original innocence. There is nothing to fear in Emerson. There is no unacceptable outburst of contempt; the rebukes are fair and to the point. Perhaps there is too little bite, as an exasperated Thoreau came to think. If we do not choose to follow Emerson the Romantic, it is not necessarily because of some commitment to an unliberal ideology of solidarity, with all its dangers to freedom. The doubts he inspires arise from the reflective spirit that he could appreciate only to a degree. The resigned scholar does not think that the individual is superior to the groups of which he is a member, and, in the balance of good and evil, the contemporary scholar knows that America is just like the rest of the world, different, not better, not an eternal hope, but just home of many American scholars, old and young.

Note

Professor Shklar died before this essay could be revised. She left a typed draft with handwritten changes. We have tried to produce a faithful version.

Spare Parts:
Political Theory as Compensation

THOMAS L. DUMM

> Our institutions, though in coincidence with the
> spirit of the age, have not any exemption from the
> practical defects which have discredited other forms.
>
> —*Ralph Waldo Emerson, "Politics"*

> Is it not necessary, for the sake of preserving this
> tradition, to try even what might prove insufficient?
>
> —*Franz Kafka, "In the Penal Colony"*

WHAT WOULD it mean to say that there is a tradition of modern justice? And what would its insufficiencies be? I am led to these questions by both Emerson and Kafka, who I think are connected by a common response to both of these questions. Both Kafka and Emerson offer us ways to resist the idea of justice as the product of judgment. They do so by finding some of the ways in which justice is always slightly beyond the capacity of judgment to circumscribe it, even as judgment itself is composed of its deferments. They show us ways of being otherwise than we too often are, too fully determined by our endless determination to pursue justice. The resistance they represent to us is something familiar to many of us by now, but its increased importance is a result of its fittingness as a response to a century in which justice has been pursued with a vehemence that has been more intensely destructive of life than ever before. For me, the idea of resistance is created anew when I read their words. In response to the idea of modern justice as just deserts, Emerson gives us his idea of compensation, and in response to modern justice as law, Kafka gives us a new literature of delay and deferral. Even at the level of style they connect. Kafka is deeply connected to surface, as Emerson is superficially deep. Emerson gives us startling images presented as ideas, and Kafka gives us entire theories presented as images.

In this essay, I will focus on one such idea image held (almost) in common by Emerson and Kafka. I want to study the idea of spare parts as it operates in Kafka's story "In the Penal Colony" because Kafka presents it in a way that reflects an inclination toward compensation as a way of thinking about politics and shows the potential of compensation as a distinct political theory. I think that there is a resistance to the idea of politics as justice in Kafka that is something like that encouraged by Emerson's idea of compensation. I want to argue that a resistance to politics as justice is the distinguishing feature of whatever political theory emerges to endorse the idea of compensation.

For me, there is irony in thinking about the idea of compensation as a kind of political theory. My sense is that when we accept the idea of compensation, we also accept a diminution of the claims that we can make about ameliorating the pain caused by the imposition of force in the world. This sense of diminished possibility is to be distinguished from a simple resignation from the world, but it is often difficult to accept this distinction in the face of the atrocities that we see before us. Like others who want to be good citizens, I still seek to act, to resolve the problems that arise as a consequence of our political way of being. More particularly, as someone who has been inclined to the vocation of the study of political ideas, the desire to seek solutions that we might act upon to ease the ills constitutive of late modernity tempts me. But the idea of compensation cautions me against taking action quickly or lightly. It does not suggest that action is ineffectual, but rather the opposite, that acts are profoundly possible though always more or less beyond our control. But I think I find myself in a situation that is common for many of us who study political matters in this era. Those of us who think of political theory in vocational terms, which is to say, those of us who identify ourselves as political theorists, still feel at odds with the very idea of political theory even as we continue to need to theorize. The positions available to us to connect to the world of political affairs are too confining, so confining in fact that many of us are tempted to point to those connections as the primary source of our political maladies, and some of us have abandoned theory to operate as advocates for one or another position. Politics always seems to be threatened with reduction to a series of unacceptable alternatives. These alternatives are unacceptable regardless of the substantive outcomes they promise because they demand the sorts of endorsements that are antithetical to the possibility of recognizing the harm intrinsic to judgment. The project of judgment itself would condemn the objects of its power to pain or death and a diminished quality of life.

Emerson shows how we might evade the judgment that reduces to alternatives. And yet I also know that Emerson presents us with several traps. The ecstasy of his idea of self-reliance, which undergirds his confidence in compensation, also presents us with the temptation to political quiescence. Moreover, self-reliance is a godly doctrine, and godliness is vastly hollow at the end of the second millennium. So I begin this essay in an awkward position (and not for the first time). I find I must question the motives of Emerson even I try to think with him. This, too, is not such a new task for me. Having been introduced to Emerson's thought by a friend of both Emerson and me,

George Kateb, I feel at best as though I am representing a not so unfamiliar conversation to a larger audience. With the hidden aid of Kateb, the scribe of Emerson, and an unschooled reading of Kafka, the scribe of all Ks, I hope to think about the hollowness created in the wake of the death of God as something to celebrate. My task is threefold. I want to show the compensatory role of spare parts in Kafka's story. Such an understanding might aid me in understanding compensation as an idea, which in turn might lead me to make sense of how political theory could become a kind of compensation in Emerson's sense. Undoubtedly this task is obscure, in that I take as its end learning how to think through a singularly obscure version of contemporary Emersonianism, and how lessons derived from it might contribute to an understanding of politics that would better enable us to bear it than we now do. But unlike those who would want everything to be perfectly clear, I am almost happy to take on this task, because the risk of obscurity should, I think, always be welcome. Our difficulties more often begin when we are too easily understood.

KAFKA

I want to say that the story of "In the Penal Colony" is inexhaustible. But that is not quite right, because its indefinite finitude may be presumed, in one sense, simply by its closure as a narrative. It is a story with an ending, after all. But I am still tempted to say that it is inexhaustible because it represents such a range of possibilities that I find myself exhausted by reading the story. Maybe it is best to say simply that it is a story that is very rich in possibilities. Given its plentitude, I want to think through a version of it in which there is in the foreground a narrative about the breakdown of an apparatus designed to write sentences on the bodies of those convicted of crimes, the plot of the story. This version is in many ways the one most familiar to anyone who has ever read the story even casually. The familiarity provided by plot, though, as readers of Kafka come to know, is composed of fragments of the familiar reassembled to expose the familiar to the strangeness of experience. To say this more directly, Kafka is an uncanny writer.[1]

The plot is simple, the genre that of crime and punishment. The premise has to do with a form of punishment that is used at this penal colony. When a person is convicted of a crime, his sentence is to have a sentence inscribed on his body by a machine specifically designed for the purpose. This sentence is always a death sentence because the needles that inscribe the sentence dig deeper and deeper into the body until the person dies, but it is also rehabilitative, because the condemned man learns a valuable lesson before he dies, the substance of the sentence that is written on his body. He dies enlightened, realizing, for instance, that is it best to "HONOR THY SUPERIORS." The apparatus, designed and built by the former commandant of the colony, is itself close to perfect, maintained so as to run silently and automatically once it is set in motion. Yet it does have parts that wear out and must be replaced from time to time.

When there are spare parts available, the apparatus will be able to continue to function. But when the spare parts are no longer available, can it be said that the apparatus will cease to function? The lack of spare parts cannot be a cause of failure. Spare parts cease to be spare when used. How can the absence of something that is otherwise only in reserve, something not being used, be blamed for the failure of a machine? This incongruity is at the heart of the plot of "In the Penal Colony."

The officer in charge of the execution that is carried out in this story is the last follower of the old commandant. He expresses a deep ambivalence about spare parts, revealed during the course of his explanation of how the apparatus operates, which he presents to the explorer whom he wants to witness the execution. This indecisiveness is to be found in some of the side comments he makes concerning the value of the apparatus to the regime, especially when he harkens back to a time when the colony was under the control of the former commandant, and things operated as they were intended. In those days there were crowds at executions, and the commandant's ladies did not intrude in decisionmaking. There was a general appreciation of the aesthetics of the execution among the many inhabitants of the penal colony. They would watch carefully to be able to observe the face of the condemned at his moment of enlightenment. But the officer is harkening back to those days that are gone, and in the present tense he is very concerned about the details of the machinery itself.

In discussing the workings of the machinery, the officer says, "Up till now a few things had still to be set by hand, but from this moment it works all by itself." He then comments, "Things sometimes go wrong, of course; I hope nothing goes wrong today, but we have to allow for the possibility. The machinery should go on working continuously for twelve hours. But if anything goes wrong it will only be some small matter that can be set right at once."[2] Here we are presented with a subtle contradiction that later has larger consequences. If something goes wrong in an automatic mechanism intended to operate continuously for twelve hours, there would need to be a *resetting* of the machine before it could start after it was interrupted. The machinery is akin to a timepiece, in a sense.

This inconsistency is made clear when we see what happens when the apparatus does, in fact, break down. The first part the officer mentions that is worn out and in need of a replacement is a cogwheel in the "Designer," the part of the machine that sets the pattern to be inscribed on the body of the condemned. During the failure of the apparatus, the Designer spews cogwheel after cogwheel out of its lid:

> At that moment he heard a noise above him in the Designer. He looked up. Was that cogwheel going to make trouble after all? But it was something quite different. Slowly the lid of the Designer rose up and clicked wide open. The teeth of a cogwheel showed themselves and rose higher, soon the whole wheel was

visible, it was as if some enormous force was squeezing the Designer so that there was no longer room for the wheel, and the wheel moved up till it came to the very edge of the Designer, fell down, rolled along the sand a little on its rim and then lay flat. But a second wheel was already rising after it, followed by many others, large and small and indistinguishably minute, the same thing happened to all of them, at every moment one imagined the Designer must really be empty, but another complex of numerous wheels was already rising into sight, falling down, trundling along the sand and lying flat.[3]

We might well believe that the initial trouble started with that one worn-out wheel for which there is no spare part. The intricacy of the mechanism, the elaborate synchronization of the various parts (which presumably would make the breaking of a strap the first manifest failure of the machine, that is, the first failure to have an impact on its effectiveness), coupled with the idea that the old commandant who designed the machine was also the author of the total organization of the colony—all these details point toward a series of connections that lead back to the failure of a worn part, one that cannot be replaced for lack of a spare. Thus it seems that any minor failure must be disastrous to the entire operation of the apparatus, and that the role of spare parts to the adequate maintenance of the machine cannot be underestimated.

Spare parts also play a pivotal role in enabling us to establish a formula that would allow us to cling to the incommensurate order engendered in the (mal)functioning apparatus. The officer suggests, "This is a very complex machine, it can't be helped that things are breaking or giving way here and there; but one must not thereby allow oneself to be diverted in one's general judgment."[4] Yet if its parts continue to break down, how can the apparatus itself be said to work? Is it a machine we are being told about or is it something else? Can we render a general judgment about the machine on the basis of its utility, or is there some other appeal we need to know about? To do so, we must slip into the realm of metaphor. The machine would be a metaphor for the political order itself, and then we would need to ask what the standard is that we must employ if we are to determine the efficacy of an order that is always in (slight) disarray. Instead of asking if the machine is working properly, we might ask if there are spare parts available for it. The officer notes, "The resources for maintaining the machine are now very much reduced. Under the former Commandant I had free access to a sum of money set aside entirely for this purpose. There was a store, too, in which spare parts were kept for repairs of all kinds. I confess having been almost prodigal with them. . . ."[5] Later, the officer wistfully recalls life in the old regime, when "I got new parts for almost every execution."[6] The general judgment we are asked to make might concern the quality of a regime on the basis of how it underwrites its projects, not on the basis of how it completes them. Spare parts are a form of insurance.

As crucial as spare parts seem to be, though, the breakdown of the apparatus can never be attributed directly to a lack of them. The logic of breakdown is associative, not directly causal. The breakdown of the apparatus is caused not by the lack of spare parts, but by the failure of worn-out parts. Any part, no matter how worn, might hold up long enough for the apparatus to fulfill its twelve-hour function. In fact, we never know what causes the breakdown of the apparatus. In a larger sense, we do not know what it is that is breaking down. We might ask what it was that the old commandant had established that was breaking down, and plausibly guess many things, at least at the level of symbolic order—patriarchy, bureaucratic order, theocratic rule, a liberal colonial order based upon enlightenment. I think the role that is played by spare parts directly addresses the anxiety of the officer. We might note that spare parts themselves are technically useless as long as they remain unused. But the point is that their role is to assuage an anxiety through the fact of their availability. (Who would like to drive through a desert without a spare tire?) They are, in fact, very much like insurance policies in that they underwrite the possibility of acting by minimizing the risk associated with the act. But once installed, once used to replace a worn-out or broken part, a spare part no longer relieves one of anxiety. It ceases to be a spare. Spare parts thus might be said to exist in the gap between the actual and the potential, deriving their value from the combination of their potential usefulness and their actual nonuse. (I want to suggest that this is a manifestation of the gap between essence and existence, or more properly, existence and essence. But this is to anticipate.)

Perhaps our most important moments of truth are composed of our willful lack of recognition of the futility of bridging gaps between the actual and the potential. Kafka seems to stage such a moment. It results from the failure of a seemingly superfluous part of the apparatus, not a gear or lever, but the felt gag that is forced into the mouth of the condemned by the officer. When the old gag is placed in the condemned man's mouth, "in an irresistible access of nausea [he] shut his eyes and vomited."

> "It's all the fault of that Commandant!" cried the officer, senselessly shaking the brass rods in front, "the machine is befouled like a pigsty." With trembling hands he indicated to the explorer what had happened. "Have I not tried for hours at a time to get the Commandant to understand that the prisoner must fast for a whole day before the execution. But our new mild doctrine thinks otherwise. The Commandant's ladies stuff the man with sugar candy before he's led off. He has lived on stinking fish his whole life long and now he has to eat sugar candy! But it could still be possible, I shouldn't have anything to say against it, but why won't they give me a new felt gag, which I have been begging for the last three months. How should a man not feel sick when he takes a felt gag into his mouth which more than a hundred men have already slobbered and gnawed in their dying moments?"[7]

The claim of the officer concerning the treatment of the condemned man is totally at odds with an earlier depiction provided by the officer. In the earlier account concerning the condemned man's arrest and sentencing, he makes it clear that he has no concern about the condemned man's fasting for a day

before the execution of sentence. Moreover, the condemned man is constantly in the custody of the officer from the time of his arrest, and hence not
accessible to the ladies.[8] So what is happening in this rant?

One reading of this passage would give to the new commandant's ladies
the role of feminine resistance to and subversion of male political order. At
the psychoanalytical level they could be seen as the (male) hysterical elements of the officer's fragmented self that rise up in resistance to his phallo-
centric death drive.[9] I believe that the disordered temporality as represented
by the coexistence of incommensurate time frames can also be understood as
an example of one of Kafka's special techniques for highlighting the spatial
paradox associated with thinking about the gap between the actual and the
potential. He is writing this story not as a fable but as a description of the
fullness of time itself. Walter Benjamin, one of Kafka's greatest readers, suggests, "What Kafka could see least of all was the *gestus*. . . . Like El Greco,
Kafka tears open the sky behind every gesture; but as with El Greco—who
was the patron saint of the Expressionists—the gesture remains the decisive
thing, the center of the event."[10] Benjamin sees Kafka's work as an attempt
to make the spirit of the world concrete by bringing what has been forgotten
to the surface. But rather than understand this exercise psychoanalytically,
Benjamin argues that it must be understood as "never something purely individual. Everything forgotten mingles with what has been forgotten of the
prehistoric world, forms countless, uncertain, changing compounds, yielding a constant flow of new strange products. Oblivion is the container from
which the inexhaustible intermediate world in Kafka's stories presses toward the light."[11] This capacity to make the gesture serve as a substitute for
narrative explanation gives Kafka's work its importance. While the experiences that Kafka describes are highly individualized, he paradoxically limns
these experiences in such a way that they can never be received by individuals *qua* individuals. As Benjamin notes, "Kafka lives in a *complementary*
world."[12] By this phrase, Benjamin seems to mean that in establishing
through gesture what is usually noted through narrative, Kafka establishes
a world of meaning that is not beholden to tradition, and enables us to see
how tradition itself might appear to us as a sickness.

Kafka's overrich phrase concerning the condemned man's "irresistible access of nausea" uncannily rests upon an arcane meaning of the
word "access" as a synonym for "outburst." But it also suggests that the
nausea is something he was able to retrieve from a place. It already existed in the oblivion: the contents of the condemned man's stomach move,
thanks to the gag, from the dark recesses of his gut to the light that is soon
to be a high noon. In contemporary computer jargon, the word "access" has
transmuted into a verb meaning to retrieve something from a file, to bring it
on screen or "on line." It is to call forth that which already exists. The
officer's insistence that minor disorders (such as vomit on the machine) are
of no matter is consistent with the idea that it is the gesture, in this case the
nausea, that matters, and not the consequence, the vomit. This gestural un-

derstanding of meaning is consistent, I think, with an Emersonian view of compensation.[13]

Thus it is not what is breaking down that is of interest as much as it is the moment when breakdown is imminent. I want to know what the characterization of that moment might mean for the idea of compensation. In Kafka's story there is a weariness conveyed by the officer under his hysterical enthusiasm. His gestures, his muttering, his spoken asides, his concern to keep things moving, his fretting over the apparatus's condition, his willingness finally to submit himself to the apparatus, his ultimate hope for a return to an old order would not immediately signal the sort of calm confidence I first associate with the idea of compensation as Emerson presents it. And yet it still seems to me to suggest the gestural shape that a desire to elevate compensation to a transcendental value might take. In a time and place such as our late modern "united states," when minor moments of farce reveal important elements of the texture of existence, and when the overlooked or unobserved returns to haunt the human capacity to act, Kafka's detailed observation of a complementary world is not an imaginary escape from the pain we suffer, but a alternative perspective concerning the meaning of present reality from which we might better see the tradition of our judgments. It shows us the connections between the representation of an act and the act itself, and how the former incompletely completes the latter, never fully or finally, only as a piece of a puzzle that seems to generate new pieces every time we come close to solving it.

EMERSON

Emerson begins his essay on compensation by noting the ubiquity of the subject, a ubiquity that is for him a major source of its fascination. His fascination with compensation has to do with more than its appearance in all dimensions of human life. His fascination is a consequence, not only of compensation's ubiquity but of its special essence. Emerson suggests "that in it might be shown men a ray of divinity, the present action of the soul of this world, clean from all vestige of tradition, and so the heart of man might be bathed by an inundation of eternal love, conversing with that which he knows was always and always must be, because it really is now."[14] Compensation is here, is now. Emerson suggests that if we learn something about compensation—perhaps only the smallest arc of "the path of the law of compensation"—we might know that we are better than we know we are. We are better than we know, Emerson asserts, because we adhere to the law of compensation. But what is that law?

Emerson contrasts compensation to the popular understanding of justice. He relates how one preacher argues, from the doctrine of the Last Judgment, that the wicked are successful in this life but just compensation might be (should be) rendered to those who are good in the next one. Emerson objects: "The legitimate inference the disciple would draw was—'we are to have *such* a good time as the sinners have now'; or, to push it to the extreme import—'You sin now, we shall sin by and by; we would sin now, if we could; not being successful we expect our revenge to-morrow.'"[15] This notion "defers to the base estimate of the market of what constitutes manly success, instead of confronting and convicting the world from the truth; announcing the presence of the soul; the omnipotence of the will; and so establishing the standard of good and ill, of success and failure."[16] Compensation is misapprehended as a causal mechanism of justice, and justice as a consequence of the human balancing of good and bad.

Emerson understands compensation otherwise. It is intrinsic to nature itself, everything that is other than that which is human—an element of the dualism that pervades nature, whether in its general laws, in its specific mechanisms, or even in the nature and condition of human beings as a part of nature. He writes, "An inevitable dualism bisects nature, so that each thing is a half, and suggests another thing to make it whole; as, spirit, matter; man, woman; odd, even; subjective, objective; in, out; upper, under; motion, rest; yea, nay. . . . Whilst the world is thus dual, so are every one of its parts. The entire system of things gets represented in every particle."[17] Emerson describes this dualism in reference to human affairs in a series of prescient observations concerning the fortunes attendant on political fame and personal genius. But these descriptions are only illustrations of what he would suggest is a fundamental fact of life in the universe. "All things are moral," he suggests. "That soul, which within us is a sentiment, outside of us is a law. . . . What we call retribution is the universal necessity by which the whole appears wherever a part appears."[18]

Yet Emerson is at care to note that the wholeness of things is constantly challenged by the inevitably partial responses of human beings to existence. For him, this partiality, this incompleteness, is an aspect of the dualism of body and soul:

> Every act rewards itself, or in other words, integrates itself, in a twofold manner; first in the thing, or in real nature; and secondly in the circumstance, or in apparent nature. Men call the circumstance retribution. The causal retribution is in the thing, and is seen by the soul. The retribution in the circumstance is seen by the understanding; it is inseparable from the thing, but is often spread over a long time, and so does not become distinct until after many years. The specific stripes may follow late for an offense, but they follow because they accompany it. Crime and punishment grow out of one stem. Punishment is a fruit that unsuspected ripens within the flower of the pleasure which concealed it. Cause and effect, means and end, seed and fruit, cannot be severed; for the effect already blooms in the cause, the end preexists in the means, the fruit in the seed.[19]

For Emerson is it human to resist the wholeness of the soul that underwrites the varying experience of our bodies. We seek to act partially because we cannot do otherwise. We are bodily beings. That is our nature. In our moral strivings in particular, we seek the pleasure of the senses and not the requirements of character. Nonetheless, we will be thwarted in our delusions by the inevitability of a retributive action. "There is a crack in everything God has made," he notes.[20] That sentence accounts for both the resistance of the body to the soul and the inevitable connection of the two. The connection of the two is what makes compensation such a difficult idea. When placed in the context of human being, the doctrine of compensation is remarkable for its toughness, a toughness that comes from the harsh indifference of this insight when applied to specific circumstance, to the always partial responses we are capable of mustering to the wholeness of the soul. As Emerson suggests, in nature nothing is given, and all things are sold.[21] But the idea that there is a crack in everything God has made also suggests that while it is inevitable that we will resist the imposition of wholeness with our bodies, it is also useless to do so, because our bodies cannot be completely separated from our souls. The crack is not a gap, but a fissure, a space of both opening and connection. It is what enables us to see the whole in every part, an encoding of everything in each thing. It is also what prevents us from evading the reaction that attends every action.

The harshness of our knowledge of compensation might lead us to a stoicism or a passive nihilism. Should we simply become indifferent to action as a consequence of what Emerson himself calls "the indifferency of circumstance"?[22] He insists we should not. As ubiquitous as compensation is in the nature of things, he suggests,

> There is a deeper fact of the soul than compensation, to wit, its own nature. The soul is not a compensation, but a life. The soul *is*. Under all this running sea of circumstance, whose waters ebb and flow with perfect balance, lies the aboriginal abyss of real Being. Essence, or God, is not a relation or a part, but the whole. Being is the vast affirmative, excluding negation, self-balanced, and swallowing up all relations, parts and times within itself.[23]

Emerson wants us to remember that life is a progress, not a station. We thus have ways of measuring our uncertain movement toward better and away from worse. The absolute measure of ourselves is the whole, but such a whole is not available to us. Thus underlying Emerson's discussion of compensation, and in fact enabling that discussion, is the question of the relation of compensation to the real Being of the soul. And as he puts it, "In the nature of the soul is the compensation for the inequalities of condition."[24]

Emerson understands the soul as constantly quitting its whole system of things, worldly relations hanging loosely to the circumstances of its existence, the soul "becoming as it were a transparent fluid membrane through which the living form is seen, and not, as in most men, an indurated heterogeneous fabric of many dates and of no settled character, in which the man is imprisoned. Then there can be enlargement, and the man of to-day scarcely recognizes the man of yesterday."[25] Thus the consistency of the soul paradoxically consists of the mutation of character through time. For this reason he suggests that whatever sadness attends the human condition consists of the lack of faith that follows from the exclusive realization of the partial character of indiviual experience, and not from the greater knowledge of the unity of things in the soul. Our failure to "believe in the riches of the soul, in its proper eternity and omnipotence," leaves us in a horribly uncertain estate. "We cannot stay amid the ruins. Neither will we rely on the new; and so we walk ever with averted eyes, like those monsters who look backwards."[26]

Emerson presents us with ourselves as "organs of the soul."[27] The soul is a great sublimity, or God.[28] But Emerson's limitless vision is limited by his piety, precisely by his inability to get beyond God. He nonetheless leaves us with an Emersonian quest. Is it possible to think of advancement, to observe growth and development, without thinking of a god, even nostalgically? If we need a god to explain the spiritual laws of compensation, do we not also need a law of compensation to aid us as we free ourselves from belief in a god? To return to the idea of this essay, can God be considered just another spare part?

The soul need not be God when it can be light.[29] Imagine that Emerson without a god is Kafka. We then might begin an inquiry into the terms through which we could imagine a politics that could attend compensation in this disenchanted era, whatever name we might want to attach to it. The beginning of such a politics might be found in the actions through which we compensate for the lack of a god. We might repair to an appreciation of our existence for what it lacks, and in understanding better our lack, be able to note how full (perhaps overfull) it is. Emphasizing its connection to the emergence of modern democracy, and evoking (sometimes more, sometimes less) Kateb's evocations of democratic individuality, I would provisionally suggest that the death of God is the historical event that gives rise to the possibility of political theory as compensation. This does not mean that political theory comes into play as the activity that ensouls us, but rather that it becomes the activity that allows us to imagine our destinies as connected to one another free of the encumbrances of a metaphysics that demands of us that we understand ourselves as having a common soul. In short, it might enable us to imagine a kind of community otherwise, one compatible with free citizenship.

LIMBO

What happens after the condemned man is freed from the apparatus of the penal colony? He stays in the immediate vicinity of the apparatus, and, against the wishes of the explorer, witnesses the apparatus's breakdown and the subsequent death of the officer, after the officer submits himself to the apparatus. The explorer then seeks the help of the soldier and the condemned man to remove the officer from the harrow:

> But the other two could not make up their minds to come; the condemned man actually turned away; the explorer had to go over to them and force them into position at the officer's head. And here, almost against his will, he had to look at the face of the corpse. It was as it had been in life; no sign was visible of the promised redemption; what the others had found in the machine the officer had not found; the lips were firmly pressed together, the eyes were open, with the same expression as in life, the look was calm and convinced, through the forehead went the point of the great iron spike.[30]

"What the others had found in the machine the officer had not found." The spirit that animated the machine is gone.

The condemned man and the soldier follow the explorer to a teahouse, where the explorer seeks out the grave of the old commandant (hidden under a table). The inscription on the gravestone reads:

> Here rests the old Commandant. His adherents, who must be nameless, have dug this grave and set up this stone. There is a prophecy that after a certain number of years the Commandant will rise again and lead his adherents from this house to recover the colony. Have faith and wait![31]

The people at the teahouse smile at the explorer after he reads this inscription, "as if they too had read the inscription, had found it ridiculous and were expecting him to agree with them."[32] The explorer leaves. He is followed by the condemned man and the soldier.

> Probably they wanted to force him at the last minute to take them with him. While he was bargaining below with a ferryman to row him to the steamer, the two of them came headlong down the steps, in silence, for they did not dare to shout. . . . They could have jumped into the boat, but the explorer lifted a heavy knotted rope from the floor boards, threatened them with it and so kept them from attempting to leap.[33]

A probable reading of this final passage from the story suggests that the soldier and the condemned man seek to leave the colony, to regain the voices silenced by their experience. The explorer seeks to prevent their leap (of faith?) by waving a knotted rope (a phallus) at them, casting them back into their heart of darkness, to the pagan ignorance that makes the people at the teahouse smile at the prophecy of a resurrection and return of the commandant.

"Probably," writes Kafka, but Kafka is not a probable writer. He is interested in the gesture, not the motive. The soldier and the condemned man may as easily have sought to prevent the explorer's departure. How does one prevent someone from "attempting to leap"? One would only know that an attempt had failed if an attempt had been made. In this last sentence we see the logical paradox of spare parts. To know that an attempt to leap is prevented is only to know that no attempt to leap was made, and to assume the rest.

Let us assume otherwise. The condemned man and the soldier could have known that the explorer would resist the good of the immediate, life in limbo. Maybe they wanted to explain to him what that life is like. It is a life of gestures, pauses, moments of transition, life exactly like our life except for one difference, and that difference is something we will never know. It is life as oblivious, life in oblivion; to repeat Benjamin, "Oblivion is the container from which the inexhaustible intermediate world in Kafka's stories presses toward the light." It is a place where the explorer would lose his voice because he would lose himself, where nothing is purely individual, even as each individual shines in an irreparable light.

Giorgio Agamben presents this interpretation in a passage that has as its raison d'etre an observation about an artist's representation of people in limbo:

> Like the freed convict in Kafka's *Penal Colony*, who has survived the destruction of the machine that was to have executed him, these beings have left the world of guilt and justice behind them: The light that rains down on them is that irreparable light of the dawn following the *novissima dies* of judgment. But the life that begins on earth after the last day is simply human life.[34]

Agamben uses the phrase "irreparable light," and in so doing combines Kafka and Emerson. For Emerson the soul is light; for Kafka we are still in this world, even though our world is as uncertain as the gap between essence and existence shows it to be. The idea of the irreparable, for Agamben, is: "That things are thus and thus—that is still in the world. But that this is irreparable, that this *thus* is without remedy, that we can contemplate it as such—this is the only passage outside the world."[35] "Thus," for Agamben, means (at least) not otherwise. Being otherwise depends upon recognizing that the "thus" is not attached to God (Agamben understands that God must be recognized as the world, understood profanely). A "thus" without remedy rejects the profane understanding of the world (the world as God) and gives us a Nietzschean affirmation, a yes in the fullest sense of existence, the world *as thus*. For Agamben, this idea validates the eternal return of the same.[36] He moves even further:

> Seeing something simply in its being thus—irreparable, but for that reason necessary; thus, but not for that reason contingent—is love.
>
> At the point you perceive the irreparability of the world, at that point is transcendence.[37]

The ecstasy of the world made divine through the disconnection of thusness from God constitutes an obscure Emersonianism. Essence and existence are related through the irreparable, which is expressed by Kafka as the strange temporality that attends a world that is emptying itself of meaning, and by

Emerson as the crack in everything God has made. Transcendence is simply human life, in whatever eternity we can make of it.

For Agamben, the negative community that can emerge through the idea of the irreparable is one that will recognize itself in political struggle between the state and the nonstate. He writes:

> The novelty of the coming politics is that it will no longer be a struggle for the conquest or control of the State, but a struggle between the State and the non-State (humanity), an insurmountable disjunction between whatever singularity and the State organization.[38]

Expressed in terms of American political experience, we might say that this is a struggle between whatever contemporary form self-reliance can take in a world of massification and the force of massification itself. More precisely outlined in response to Kateb's Emersonian concerns, "[i]ndividualism must battle massification, more and more."[39] The battle occurs not between individuals and groups, exclusively or even predominantly, but in the massification of the individuality given to us through the happenstance of "whatever singularity," a struggle against the fascism in us all, the art of learning to live counter to all forms of fascism, but especially the fascism inside each one of us in our duly constituted individuality. We might call the struggle the struggle to attain the state of democratic individuality.

In this way political theory as compensation becomes clearer to me when it is understood as the preparatory study of human existence. We should always be ready to be human, for those times when our humanity fails us (as it so regularly does). Political theory operates as a kind of spare part, a spare humanity. Its practice is the activity, moral, inclusive, philosophical, and general, but also ethical, distancing, practical, and specific, of turning away from the centralizing forces of our age, most especially the moral forces of guilt and justice, which by dint of their orientation to final judgments are too often the elements of our human failure not to have them evoke our suspicion. Political theory moves *thusly* when it contributes toward a perception of the partiality of the human project, and opens the closed circle by realizing the incompleteness especially of its own project. When done well, it tutors us in the idea of a moment of truth in our concerted actions, fleeting but eternally recurring. And finally, for now, it places that eternality dangerously out of reach, by making it always irreparable, always incompletely thus. Among other things, it is a compensation for the fact that we will die, someday.

NOTES

1. See Jane Bennett, "Kafka's Genealogical Idealism," *Journal of Politics* 56, no. 3 (August 1994): 650–670.
2. Franz Kafka, "In the Penal Colony," in *The Penal Colony: Stories and Short Pieces*, trans. Willa Muir and Edwin Muir (New York: Schocken, 1961), p. 192.

3. *Ibid.*, p. 223.

4. *Ibid.*, p. 205.

5. *Ibid.*

6. *Ibid.*, p. 209.

7. *Ibid.*, p. 207.

8. *Ibid.*, pp. 198–199.

9. I think there is ample textual evidence to support a reading of "In the Penal Colony" as a feminist tale. For instance, the ladies' handkerchiefs could be interpreted to play a role as a form of cross-dressing, and might even be understood as the officer's attempt to fashion breasts for himself. The officer, early in the story, "looked uncommonly limp, breathed with his mouth wide open and had tucked two ladies' handkerchiefs under the collar of his uniform." *Ibid.*, p. 192. Indeed, the major theme of this story is the breakdown of a *penal* colony. But there is also reason to resist the psychoanalytical approach to understanding Kafka, as I discuss elsewhere in this chapter.

10. Walter Benjamin, "Franz Kafka: On the Tenth Anniversary of His Death," in Benjamin, *Illuminations*, ed. Hannah Arendt, trans. Harry Zohn (New York: Schocken, 1969), p. 121.

11. *Ibid.*, p. 131.

12. Walter Benjamin, "Some Reflections on Kafka," in Benjamin, *Illuminations*, p. 143.

13. Though not, I think, consistent with the Sartrean idea of radical choice, even though the idea of nausea works so powerfully for Sartre as a metaphor in ways that I think closely parallel this passage.

14. Ralph Waldo Emerson, "Compensation," reprinted in Emerson, *Essays and Lectures* (New York: Library of America, 1983), p. 285.

15. *Ibid.*, p. 286.

16. *Ibid.*

17. *Ibid.*, p. 287.

18. *Ibid.*, pp. 289–290.

19. *Ibid.*, p. 290.

20. *Ibid.*, p. 292.

21. *Ibid.*

22. *Ibid.*, p. 299.

23. *Ibid.*

24. *Ibid.*, p. 301.

25. *Ibid.*, pp. 301–302.

26. *Ibid.*, p. 302.

27. See Ralph Waldo Emerson, "Spiritual Laws," reprinted in Emerson, *Essays and Lectures*, p. 321. Emerson suggests that this essay is a continuation of "Compensation."

28. For a discussion of religiosity in Emerson that influenced my imagination of Emerson without God, see George Kateb, *Emerson and Self-Reliance* (Thousand Oaks, Calif.: Sage Publications, 1994), ch. 3.

29. *Ibid.*, p. 72.

30. Kafka, "In the Penal Colony," pp. 224–225.

31. *Ibid.*, p. 226.

32. *Ibid.*

33. *Ibid.*, pp. 226–227.

34. Giorgio Agamben, *The Coming Community*, trans. Michael Hardt (Minneapolis: University of Minnesota Press, 1993), pp. 6–7. The artist whose work is being described is Robert Walser.

35. *Ibid.*, p. 102.

36. *Ibid.*, p. 103.

37. *Ibid.*, p. 106.

38. *Ibid.*, p. 85. Emphasis omitted.

39. Kateb, *Emerson and Self-Reliance*, p. 195.

PART TWO

Democratic Individuality and the Politics of Identity

Politics and Transparency

TRACY B. STRONG

> [T]he spread of equality over the earth dries up
> the old springs of poetry. We must try to show
> how other springs are revealed.
>
> —Tocqueville, *Democracy in America*

THUS TOCQUEVILLE. His discussion of poetry in a democratic society goes on to suggest that it is only in a democratic society that "one can form a picture . . . in which a nation counts as a single citizen." Then, he continues, "all mankind can be seen together in broad daylight."

What does it mean to see the world as a democratic poet would see it? A poet makes the world in words: the gift of the poet is made possible because words are (just barely) more accessible than is the world. So poetry enables those who read it. A poet of democracy makes a world available, according to Tocqueville, in which all are seen in one picture. Part of the distress in Tocqueville's musings comes from the fear that no world will be available to the new democrats, whom he sees as sweeping all history from in front of them. Tocqueville's concern, however, is the subject that this poetry must make available for it to be truly democratic poetry. The subject of the poetry of democracy, Tocqueville intimates, is neither the ideal nor even nature; it is certainly not community and is not even properly the self. What would democratic poetry give its reader?

> In democratic societies where all are insignificant and very much alike, each man, as he looks at himself, sees all his fellows at the same time.[1]

I think that Tocqueville means here exactly what he says. It is not that I see a great community in the vista of democratic poetry but that I see, as I see myself, every other person as myself. This is not identity, but equality and possibility. This egalitarian vision, originally that of Hobbes,[2] holds that from the point of view of democratic politics anything that can happen to anyone can happen to me. No identity is foreclosed on the basis of race, color, creed, ethnicity, gender—*anything*.

This is not the same position as that adopted by most liberals. John Rawls suggests that just political institutions will best be chosen from behind a "veil of ignorance," that is, by systematically bracketing all those qualities that make me different from an other. Tocqueville is pointing at something different in America. He is not suggesting that for a just society to exist I must choose institutions without reference to my identity, but that in a just democratic society I really have no identity that is my own, nor one that is of my "group." In this case, in a democratic society there is nothing I need to veil in order to choose justly.

The most extraordinary, not to say outrageous, moment in George Kateb's 1992 book, *The Inner Ocean*, comes in his final discussion of Whitman:

> All the personalities that I encounter, I already am: that is to say, I could become or could have been something like what others are. . . . I am potentially all personalities and we equally are infinite potentialities.[3]

Whatever Kateb's position is, it is not Rawlsian liberalism. And, I might say, Kateb's position is certainly more exciting than such liberalisms. Kateb raises a different question about the democratic agent: what if the self for democratic politics were not "thin," in Rawls's words, but transparent, no thing? Such a self would have no historical substance— that is, it would not be defined by that which it was not. Such a self could not be Hegelian— that is, having no substantial identity, even a partial one, it could not be recognized by an other.

What kind of self is not defined by recognition from others, from that which it is not? There is nothing that the democratic self is not: thus it is not simply a literary conceit that leads Kateb to find a paradigm of democratic individuality in the song of Whitman. Such a self would be, I might say, the stuff of poetry, of art, a self that, as Emerson says of beauty, "comes unsought and comes because it is unsought."[4]

In 1836, Tocqueville thought that there was as yet no American poet, but he was sure that there would be. Within twenty years there clearly was: the first edition of *Leaves of Grass* was published in 1855. That Kateb finds this vision of the democratic individual available in the poetry of Walt Whitman is a confirmation of Tocqueville's anticipation. For Kateb, Whitman, at his best, incurs the full risk of democratic individuality: it is the risk that one runs when all need for a substantial self has been cast aside.

What is that risk? What is the attraction of running it? I wish to spend some time here exploring this space.

The passage quoted above from Kateb's essay on Whitman indicates that there is nothing any human being has become or done that I could not have become or done (neither Kateb nor Whitman exclude questions of gender). This is not a claim that I can be "anything I want," but (not so) merely a claim that anything anyone has been has something to do with me. Any substantial fixed conclusion as to "who I am" must therefore do violence to others. Such a condition seems to me to be what is meant by "transparency." The self that can be all selves does not have an other, for it is transparent to them.

In Emerson, this is notorious: "Standing on the bare ground . . . all mean egotism vanishes. I am become a transparent eyeball; I am nothing."[5] I presume that a transparent eyeball sees without being seen, that is, claims no position of privilege over its perception. Note also that Emerson is concerned to differentiate his claims for individuality from those of a "mean egotism." "I am nothing" is a claim about the being of the democratic individual. It is a claim of transparency of the self to the self, such that no quality may claim privilege or permanence.

Let me assert here that what Tocqueville pointed at in his discussion of the poetry of the democratic polity finds its realization in the poetry of Whitman and the writing of Emerson. In these great American writers of the last century, George Kateb has uncovered a source of thinking—of conversing with himself. Like them, he writes for Americans, the nation of the possibility of democratic individuality. What is there to say about and to the question of the transparency of the democratic agent and the politics that are and can be attached to it?

To approach what I think to be right in Kateb's thought, I want to bring his Emerson back into the world of Emerson's friends. On occasions Kateb parts company with his sources, typically claiming that at these moments they are, still, "too religious."[6] A thinker is "too religious," I think he means, when he or she does not honestly try to make the world more available to us. And, by not doing so, such thinkers run the risk of assuming that all evil is forgivable.[7] They recoil, as it were, from the irreality and fragmentary quality of the democratic world and do not quite have the courage to take it as it is.

Kateb does not quite tell us what a world without religiosity would be except to indicate that religion can simply be "severed" from the rest of Emerson and Whitman. In that operation, transparency is presumably a nonreligious quality. Yet Kateb is not the first to have argued this. The claim that Emerson was too religious was also, I think, quietly that of Emerson's good friend, Nathaniel Hawthorne. Hawthorne calls Emerson a "priest," and suggests, not to his credit, that Emerson might "solve [him] the riddle of the universe."[8] Kateb never to my knowledge deals with Hawthorne. By bringing Emerson into contact with Hawthorne, I hope to show something about each, and to be able to return to the poetry of individuality in a democracy.

Hawthorne and Emerson are of the same generation. Born within a year of each other, Emerson in Boston, Hawthorne in Salem, they spent their formative years in New England. Neither stood out as a student in college. Emerson moved first to the ministry; Hawthorne was always a writer.

They knew each other well enough by 1842 to take a long walking trip together to visit the Shaker community in Harvard, Massachusetts; they both were involved with the initial phases of the utopian community set up at Brook Farm by Bronson Alcott and other transcendentalists. In 1840, Emerson had declined to join Brook Farm, not wanting, he said, "to remove from my present prison to a prison a little larger." In 1841, Hawthorne had resigned from his first position (as weigher and gauger) at the Boston Custom House to join Brook Farm. He left after eight months, proclaiming that "I can best attain the higher ends of my life by retaining the ordinary relation to society." Around this time, Emerson published the First Series of essays, which included "Self-Reliance." Upon leaving Brook Farm, Hawthorne rented the Emerson ancestral home (the Old Manse) and wrote many of his first tales and sketches in the very office in which, he noted, Emerson had written "Nature." Hawthorne noted that he, Hawthorne, was the first lay occupant to profane the parsonage.[9]

If it is usual to "explain" Hawthorne in terms of his reaction to his "Puritan background," it is important to remember that Hawthorne thinks of himself as a secular being. In any case, such an explanation must to some degree be mistaken (for one thing, that background was distant enough for Hawthorne to have been raised as a Unitarian). More important, he explicitly distinguishes himself from Emerson on these grounds. Hawthorne sees Emerson as the last of the "mighty Puritan divines," and he claims to "seek nothing from him as a philosopher."[10] Emerson, contrariwise, notes in his *Journals* in September 1842 that "Nathaniel Hawthorne's reputation as a writer is a very pleasing fact, because his writing is not good for anything, and this is a tribute to the man."[11]

This difference—perhaps that of philosophy and literature—points to the most obvious difference between the two men: Hawthorne's writings are filled with other characters; Emerson's notably are not. In the rare cases in his *Essays* that Emerson mentions another individual who shares the same time and space as he (as with the death of his son, Waldo) it is to subsume that person into himself. (Emerson notes as a *danger* to the individual of those whom we "cannot choose but love."[12]) Thus part of the difference I am circling around here has to do with that between those who formulate individuality in a world filled with others and those who formulate it in thought with themselves. When Hawthorne dedicated *Our Old Home* to Franklin Pierce, he apologized for not having dealt with "matters of policy and government," having written instead essays belonging "entirely to aesthetic literature,"[13] thereby drawing attention to the fact that his essays were political, even if not about politics.

Despite, or because of, the perception of mutual differences, Emerson and Hawthorne were and remained friends. However, they ask two different questions. Wonderfully, their questions have the same words: they are both the question that starts Emerson's essay "Experience." The questions are the question of American political identity: how does the democratic self catch itself? "Where do we find ourselves?" asks Emerson. Now, both of them give the same general, common answer to this. We find ourselves in America.[14] But there are numerous ways of getting to that answer. Hawthorne, one might say, would read this sentence as "Where do *we* find *ourselves*?" What is in question for him is the "we." Emerson would instead read it as "*Where* do we *find* ourselves?" with a concern for the kind of space in which finding becomes a natural act. What does it mean to start this question with the question of the "we"?

Let me look first at Hawthorne's most sustained questioning of the problems of the "we." This comes in two places, the first in the discussion of the rule-governed regulatory world of "The Custom House," and the second in his portrayal of the elective community of *The Blithedale Romance.*

Hawthorne notes that it was a highly "strange vicissitude" indeed that took him from the Custom House to the Old Manse.[15] From the Old Manse he looks back at his time at Brook Farm and in the Custom House. The stay at the Custom House (a job secured by a presidential appointment) was, says Hawthorne, an attempt "to nourish [himself] with food for which [he] had hitherto had little appetite."[16] It was a time of his life from which he firmly expected providence to deliver him; dominated by a senior "patriarchal" figure, bound with endless rules, it would have ended by destroying him:

> A Customs Officer, of long continuance, can hardly be a very praiseworthy or respectable personage, for many reasons; one of them, the tenure by which he holds his situation, and another the very nature of his business, which—though, I trust, an honest one—is of such a sort that he does not share in the united effort of mankind.[17]

"His own proper strength departs from him," Hawthorne goes on to say. "The Custom House" is the preface to *The Scarlet Letter*, and Hawthorne indicates that it was while working at the Custom House that he discovered the manuscript that (he avers) formed the basis of the novel. One might, then, think of the Custom House as leading to the need to understand the guilt-ridden world of *The Scarlet Letter*. In opposition to these cousin worlds of Puritans and officials might stand the world of a freely chosen community of like-minded individuals. Such would be the world of Brook Farm, which, however, was a world he chose to leave to live at the Old Manse. The Old Manse is thus worth exploring as that space from which Hawthorne can write about the various choices made and refused in the world around him.

I am struck by the way in which his description of the history of the Old Manse resembles the house in Salem that was the focus for *The House of the Seven Gables* (it, too, is said to be haunted, filled with portraits, and so on). Indeed, the world of *The House of the Seven Gables* mediates the tension between the other two. For Hawthorne, the tension between the freely chosen community and the regulated world derives from the inescapability of hereditary conditions (what Emerson in "Self-Reliance" calls the

"corpse of memory"[18]). *The House of the Seven Gables* is about the inexora-
bility of what one has been and how the American attempt to escape the
hold of the past merely returns one to what one is. "In ages of democracy,"
writes Tocqueville, "men are always on the move from place to place. . . .
Democracy engenders a sort of instinctive dislike for what is old."[19]

It is important here to see, however, that Hawthorne does not wish to
escape from heredity—any more than, say, Nietzsche did. Every act that one
undertakes to escape one's heredity merely ties one to it the more. The problem for Hawthorne is to be with one's world, not without one.

For example, at one point in *The Blithedale Romance*, the question arises
of who will do what labor. Coverdale has assumed that housework will be
done by the women, whereas heavy work in the fields will remain the province of the men. Hawthorne has Zenobia "laughingly" suggest that these
conditions may change, that women may go to the field and "leave our
weaker brethren to take our places in the kitchen." Indeed, when the men
then offer to work in the kitchen, the women (perhaps wisely) "utterly decline."[20]

Gender, for Hawthorne, certainly is a major question; but even in its inherited form (as in division of labor) Hawthorne presents it neither as something inexorable nor as that which simply must be excised. The past (here,
gendered division of labor) is a *problem*, which can perhaps be dealt with.
What is clear in *The Blithedale Romance*, it seems to me, is that community
must be the by-product of life with others, and never its intention.

This can be developed with a second example, which suggests that Hawthorne does have a vision of how to achieve the joining of inner self and
democratic society, but his vision is neither of elective community nor of the
regulated heart. Take the character of Clifford Pyncheon at that moment
and in that place toward the end of *The House of the Seven Gables*, when he
flees Salem in an attempt to escape the blood curse, both past and possibly
renewed.[21] He has boarded a train and purchased a ticket, Hawthorne tells
us, for no direction in particular, just to ride for pleasure, as far as his money
will take him. Called to accounts by a "gimlet-eyed" old gentleman as to this
strange mode of pleasure, Clifford claims that his pleasure is superior to the
old staid ideas of fireside and home.

"In the name of common sense," asks the old gentleman, "what can be
better for a man than his own parlor and chimney corner?" Clifford replies
that these things have not the merit that many good people attribute to them:
"My impression is that our wonderfully increased and still increasing facilities of locomotion are destined to bring us around again to the nomadic
state." He goes on to argue that this time the nomadic state will have been
perfected:

> These railroads—could but the whistle be made musical and the rumble and jar
> gotten rid of—are positively the greatest blessing that the ages have wrought for
> us. They give us wings; they annihilate the toil and dust of pilgrimage; they

spiritualize travel. Transition being so facile, what can man's inducement be to stay in one spot? Why therefore should he build a more cumbersome habitation than that which can readily be carried off with him? Why should he make himself a prisoner for life in brick and stone and worm-eaten timber, when in one sense he may easily dwell nowhere—in a better sense, wherever the fit and beautiful shall offer him home?[22]

Well, why not? What is wrong with this vision of motor homes and airplanes? Why, to take over Gertrude Stein's question, should there be a "there" there? What is wrong with being a winged angel? Clifford Pyncheon wants to "annihilate pilgrimage," to escape the possibility of walking with others, simply by an act of will, as if the past were not part of him. He discovers that it is to no avail. As the railroad leads away, the telegraph pursues him, reminding him of, without ever giving him, his past. What good will it do to find himself in some strange town only to discover that everyone is talking about the blood of a dead person that may be on his hands?[23]

Pyncheon now insists that he is "transparent"—that is, that he has no fixed self. But the old gentleman, no matter how hard he tries, "can't see through [him]." Transparency, for Hawthorne, appears as a dream we give ourselves, the wish not to be defined by others but to be transparent to their view. America is fraught with those who could not stand how they were seen and sought someplace else not to be someone, who abandoned the definition of the gray plains of Kansas for the magical technicolor—the irreality—of somewhere over the rainbow.

Hawthorne's overall point is, I think, this: no one can become a person by trying to be one. (Nor can one escape being by trying not to be one.) "We" and "I" cannot be the result of a project. This is what is wrong with Blithedale. It is a romance about place and friendship, a place destroyed by the intentional pursuit of self and community. Writing of Hollingsworth, the chief offender, Hawthorne has Coverdale say:

> [Those who] incorporate themselves into an over-ruling purpose finally are converted to little else save that one principle. Such men had no heart, no sympathy, no reason, no conscience. They keep no friend, unless he make themselves the mirror of their purpose . . . and [they] will smite and slay you the more readily if you take the first step with them and cannot take the second.[24]

What is there instead? Hawthorne refers to the "free gifts of Providence," to the centrality of receiving the unplanned. It is, rather, in the affirmation of accidents that, for Hawthorne, individuality is to be found—and not in elective community, nor in the Puritan covenant (so criticized in "The Custom House"), nor in the revolutionary foundations. In the "The Old Manse" preface to the *Mosses*, in explicit contrast to his chosen pursuits at Brook Farm, Hawthorne notes that he relishes "best the free gifts of Providence."

And later in the same piece, he suggests without rancor that it is Providence that took him from the Old Manse to the Custom House.[25]

A being whose person is the free gift of Providence is a being who is what has happened to it, as well, therefore, as what can happen to it. In this it has some relation to Kateb and Whitman's vision. But does it have substance, place, definition? What does Hawthorne make of the free-floating spirit, the beautiful soul, the transparent self? Is this not an alternative to the self that is a remembrance of Providence? Such a figure does appear in *The Blithedale Romance*: it is Priscilla. Priscilla "loves everybody"; her heart dances within her; she has "nothing dismal to remember"; for her, "the past never comes back again."[26]

Hawthorne presents Priscilla both as the free spirit and as "the Veiled Lady." She appears as the former when Coverdale finally realizes he is in love with her. As the latter, she appears three times. As such she is apparently insubstantial (well, thinly substantial), gratefully free, and unembarrassed, self-reliant. We are told that "[s]he beholds the Absolute." But we also find out that in this appearance she is no transparent eyeball, but a mesmerized girl, who has been "disembodied" by Westervelt's hypnosis, and who is susceptible to seeking safety in Hollingsworth's command.[27]

I do not know if Hawthorne had Emerson in mind when he gave us Priscilla in *The Blithedale Romance* or Clifford Pyncheon in *The House of the Seven Gables*, but there is a lot of disembodying and a lot of transparency in Emerson. In "Nature," Emerson suggests that when "stimulated to a more earnest vision," Reason moves beyond the "animal eye," so that "outlines and surfaces become transparent, and ... causes and spirits are seen through them."[28]

Suppose we ask what may be the claim that the political realm may have on our lives. Politics is, as all have known since Plato, the realm of appearance, of surface and outline. Emerson's text seeks—it can be read as seeking—to make us transparent to the claims of politics. Transparency of the self is necessary to democratic politics, in this view, if we are not to be caught in outline, made into a cartoon. Democratic politics are thus the politics that allow the most motility to the self.

Kateb addresses these questions in an essay on Emerson's essay "Experience," which he reads as Emerson's most important commentary on the political.[29] Kateb has more brilliantly than anyone else used political theory to restrict the claims of politics and community, especially communities of interest, elected communities and, I believe, communities of accident. He has done this, I believe, because he is well aware of the appeals of the political community, and equally aware that these appeals are the stuff of the Cave, what Emerson calls in the poem epigraph to "Experience" the "lords of life." Kateb responds, I think, to this passage from "New England Reformers":

> The world is awakening to the idea of union, and these experiments show what
> it is thinking of. It is and will be magic. . . . But this union must be inward, and

not one of covenants, and is to be reached by a reverse of the methods they [The New England Reformers] use. *The union is only perfect, when all uniters are isolated.* It is the union of friends who live in different streets or towns.[30]

Or, I might add, coasts and countries. In "Experience," Emerson refers to this as "consanguinity." Nothing could be less spatially situated than this. The Emerson/Kateb vision of union is not and cannot be spatial, for space is what causes our vision to rest on surfaces and outlines. I find much that is attractive in this presenting of Emerson, but there are prices to pay, and perhaps not only personal ones. To be in the same space as someone is to be near them, to have a share with them, to have the ordinary in common with them. What is it to be near to someone, to share with them? Heidegger remarks in "The Thing" that "the frantic abolition of all distances brings no nearness; for nearness does not consist in the shortness of distance."[31] Do Emerson and Kateb share this vision?

In "Self-Reliance," Emerson, like Hawthorne, attacks traveling, calling it a "fool's paradise." The reasons are, however, different. Hawthorne thought travel often to be an attempt at escaping the space of one's home.[32] For Emerson, the danger of traveling is that it leads us to bring things back, to imitate, to quote others.[33] The reason this is bad, presumably, is that no imitator can be a genius, and genius is the tonic of the essay: "To believe in your own thought, to believe that what is true for you in your private heart is true for all—that is genius."[34]

In *The American Scholar*, Emerson calls genius "the sound estate of everyman."[35] Genius is the basis for democratic community as Emerson (and Kateb) envisage it.

Hegel, whom Emerson surely had in mind here, caught this well. In a passage that echoes in "Self-Reliance" and "New England Reformers," he wrote in *The Phenomenology of Spirit*:

It is the moral genius which knows the inner voice of what it immediately knows to be a divine voice; and since, in knowing this, it has an equally immediate knowledge of existence, it is the divine creative power which in its Notion possesses the spontaneity of life. Equally it is its own self divine worship, for its action is the contemplation of its own divinity. This solitary divine worship is at the same time essentially the divine worship of a community. . . .[36]

This passage is from the section on "The Beautiful Soul" and calls to mind Tocqueville's discussion of poetry in a democratic society. Hegel goes on to suggest that in this state one is assured of always being right without regard to what one is right about. The "beautiful soul" cannot externalize itself and endure existence.

Such a soul thus has no need to exist in space, that is, to exist in a world where one is necessarily caught by the sight of others. (Rousseau knew this and made it the basis of both the awful realm of inequality and the society of the social contract). But Hegel's critique of the limitations of the beautiful soul does not completely capture the Emersonian notion of genius.

Emerson's notion—so central to Kateb—is both subject and not subject to Hegel's critique.[37] Clearly, genius, as Emerson understands it, is impossible unless I know that I am not alone in the world. How, then, does Emerson's genius know that? One answer is that s/he lets him- or herself be known. But how might this happen? The Emersonian answer is in the notion of "provocation." In the "Divinity School Address," Emerson writes:

> Truly it is not instruction but provocation that I can receive from another soul. What he announces I must find true in me, or wholly reject.[38]

Kateb reads the first sentence as referring to books and suggests they will do "no more than inspire and provoke." In my reading, he has kept the passage at arm's length: souls are not (quite) books, and this calling forth is a test. Here, for Kateb, I might say, community threatens: when I find myself in you and you in me, reciprocity cannot be far behind. In Hegel, the spirit will move on to embodiment. And this Kateb must resist.

It is essential to Kateb that no self-reliant person so provoked—so revealed—be caught unthinkingly twice in the same self. This is why he turns to "Experience" in the second part of his essay: it is the cure for the danger of permanence, of self-imitation that will destroy the genius of democracy and the democratic geniuses. In "Experience," Emerson says:

> Our love of the real draws us to permanence, but health of the body consists in circulation, and sanity of mind in variety or facility of association. We need change of objects. Dedication to one thought is quickly odious.[39]

This, for Emerson (and Kateb), is the demand of honesty, and, explicitly, not that of morality.[40] This is Emerson at his most radical. Life is a miracle, has no memory—"I am ready to die out of nature and be born again into this new yet unapproachable America I have found in the West." Contrary to the judgment of the late Judith Shklar, Kateb is right that "Experience" is in fact the most political of Emerson's essays: it provides a way of being American that is constantly that of genius.

Can we, can one—who can—live like this? To what dangers does it open America? Emerson continues: "It is very unhappy, but too late to be helped, the discovery we have made that we exist" (presumably as Americans). Emerson calls this discovery "the Fall."[41] The reason it is unhappy is that such a self will combine the worst of all worlds. The fallen American self will be without moral restraint ("[c]ivilized in externals but a savage at heart," says Melville in *Israel Potter*), but self-certain of a given identity. There is, I believe, (even) in Emerson a recognition of the lack of restraint built into the democratic genius. "Where do we find ourselves?"—a dangerous answer is given after the Fall and given in action. I suspect that the reason that Kateb insists that this American identity is properly understood as located in thought alone is that he is aware of these dangers.

It is against this danger—in recognition of the Fall—that I think Hawthorne wrote. I do not think that this makes Hawthorne "religious." At least, I do not think that the Katebian accusation of "religious" carries the day. As Marx knew, the task for modernity remains not to get rid of religion but to make it unnecessary. Hawthorne, I think, affirms the everyday, the ordinary, not in its natural form, but as accident. The affirmation of accident that I find in his work is less exalted than the "Onward and onward" call in Emerson. Look again at Hawthorne. At the end of "The Custom House," he reflects on his dismissal from his post. He had thought that with the victory of Zachary Taylor he might nevertheless retain his position.

> But who can see an inch into futurity, beyond his nose? My own head was the first that fell!
>
> The moment when a man's head drops off is seldom, or never, I am inclined to think, precisely the most agreeable of his life. Nevertheless, like the greater part of our misfortunes, even so serious a contingency brings its remedy and solution with it, if the sufferer will but make the best, rather than the worst, of the accident which has befallen him.

Hawthorne goes on to suggest that his case resembled that of a man who having entertained the idea of committing suicide should have then the good fortune to be murdered. But then he concludes that these accidents have moved him on. Salem and the Custom House have ceased "to be a reality" of his life. But he has not ceased to belong, even though this new life was not a choice. "I am a citizen," he continues, "of somewhere else now."[42] It is this acceptance of the accident of spatial limitation and embodiment—and thus of citizenship—that differentiates Hawthorne from Emerson.

The world of Hawthorne is, I think, one in which characters struggle with the dream of transparency. Think of "The Birthmark." Here, Hawthorne depicts a man of science married to a woman whom he finds perfect in every way, except for the stain of a red, hand-shaped birthmark on her cheek. The mark is many things, among them, certainly, the mark of shame and passion, for it blends in when the woman, Georgiana blushes. "The Crimson Hand," intones Hawthorne, "expressed the ineludible gripe, in which mortality clutches the highest and purest of earthly mould."[43] Alymer, the husband, tries to erase the mark—he would have her transparent to the sign of her mortality and her humanity. Does the genius of democracy die? And what of it? What is a space without death?

Can poetry give us such space? Kateb lauds Whitman as possibly the "greatest philosopher of democracy" and supports his judgment with a discussion almost entirely centered on Whitman's poetry. Let me suggest with no argument here that it is no accident that the first great Western elaboration of citizenship comes in the funeral oration that Pericles gives for the first to die in the Peloponnesian War. Death makes citizenship possible and defines the human as the political. Death is like an accident: the only human relation we can have with it is to choose it freely.

What vision of citizenship (as opposed to that of individuality) do we get from Whitman and Kateb's discussion of him? Kateb certainly wants to claim that Whitman's poetry is of a piece with those democratic institutions that create democratic space.[44] But he is equally strong in rejecting any possibility that institutional mechanisms can legitimately require participation by individuals. Rights can never be instrumental to anything.[45]

"Where do we find ourselves?" The answer must be in America. The society to which this is addressed has a mixed record of success in these matters. For many, for long periods, the transparency of the democratic self has transmogrified into the kneejerk valetudinarianism of "I can be anything I want to be." The union of isolates has become the relentless avoidance of strangers. The vision of genius has become a rationalization of the lot of those who share nothing but the world of the upper middle class. The tendency to be what Melville called the "John Paul Jones of nations" has often been present in our lifetimes. There is eloquence in Kateb's discussion of the dangers of the docility that seems to characterize many modern states. Tocqueville had commented towards the end of *Democracy in America* that in democratic societies, some may even come to like their (kinder, gentler) chains. Is the problem docility or banality, even, sometimes, something close to the banality of evil? To what transformations does the motility of the democratic individual open the world?[46]

I do not know—I cannot here pursue the question—whether the democratic individualist soul is insufficient to resist its transformation. The nature of this soul, as Plato first saw, is change, and for Plato, the direction of that change was tyranny. Becoming has the character of being in a democracy.

Another parting word is Hawthorne's. The "solitary man," whose life has exemplified the darker side of democratic individuality, does finally come home, both spatially and substantively. He returns to the place that is his. And he worries first that others will be tempted to pursue the course from which he is now returning:

> But I would save him. "He shall be taught," said I, "by my life and by my death that the world is a sad one for he who shrinks from its sober duties. My experience shall warn him to adopt some great and serious aim, such as manhood will cling to, that he may not feel himself, too late, a cumberer of this overladen earth, but a man among men. I will beseech him not to follow an eccentric path, nor, by stepping aside from the highway of human affairs, to relinquish his claim upon human sympathy. And often, as a text of deep and varied meaning, I will remind him that he is an American."[47]

Does a genius have a sober duty? Can a free-floating spirit become a person among others? The quiet, reluctant, but clear answer in Hawthorne— "blue-eyed Nathaniel," D. H. Lawrence called him—is that that which will bring them to earth is a historical substance, a substantive opacity gained only in the life with others, a life not sought, not constructed, not inherited. The historical life we have is—no matter how much we want to resist it—the only life we have. The question one must face, in Emerson, in Whitman, and in Kateb, is whether democratic individuality has an American substance, or simply is what is best about America. If the later only, it may not resist what becomes of America.[48]

Are we, as Whitman wrote to Emerson, "blooded with our own blood"? Whitman wrote:

> Long, too long America,
> Traveling roads all even and peaceful you learn'd from
>   joys and prosperity only,
> But now, ah now, to learn from crises of anguish, advancing,
>   grappling with direst fate and recoiling not,
> and not to conceive and show to the world what your children
>   en-masse really are,
> (For whom except myself has yet conceived what your children
>   en-masse really are?)[49]

Such is the possibility. Two generations later, Frost saw the dangers:

> MIST
> I don't believe the sleepers in this house
> Know where they are.
> SMOKE
> They've been here long enough
> To push the woods back from around the house
> And part them in the middle with a path.
> MIST
> And still I doubt if they know where they are.
> And I begin to fear that they never will.
> All they maintain the path for is the comfort
> Of visiting with the equally bewildered.
> Nearer in plight their neighbors are than distance.[50]

I take this verse to have Emerson as part of its audience. And I take it to be in friendly critique of Emerson and thus probably of Kateb. But even in Frost's occasional lover's quarrel with his country it does take the transparency of mist and smoke to see things through. And I am grateful to George Kateb for it.

NOTES

Alexis de Tocqueville, *Democracy in America* (reprint, Doubleday Anchor, 1969), p. 484. My thanks to Sonia Alonso Saenz de Oger for recalling this passage and discussing the relation of Whitman and Tocqueville with me.

1. *Ibid.*
2. See my "How to Write Scripture: Hobbes, Words and Authority," *Critical*

Inquiry 20, no. 4 (Autumn 1993): 128–178. See also George Kateb, "The Irrationality of Politics," *Political Theory* 17, no. 3 (August 1989): 355–391.

3. George Kateb, *The Inner Ocean* (Cornell University Press, 1992), p. 247.

4. Ralph Waldo Emerson, "Nature," reprinted in Emerson, *Essays and Lectures* (Library of America, 1983), p. 18.

5. *Ibid.*, p. 10.

6. Kateb, *Inner Ocean*, pp. 35, 266.

7. *Ibid.*, p. 220.

8. Nathaniel Hawthorne, Preface to *Mosses from the Old Manse*, reprinted in Hawthorne, *Tales and Sketches* (Library of America, 1982), pp. 1124, 1146.

9. See *ibid.*, pp. 1123, 1124–1125.

10. *Ibid.*, pp. 1135, 1146.

11. *Selections from Ralph Waldo Emerson*, ed. Stephen E. Whicher (Houghton Mifflin, 1960), p. 213.

12. Emerson, *Essays and Lectures*, p. 31. Thus Frost in "The Death of the Hired Man" remarks, "Home is where, when you go there, they have to let you in," recognizing that there is something limiting to that compulsion.

13. I owe this reference to Wilson C. McWilliams, *The Idea of Fraternity in American Politics* (University of California Press, 1973), p. 302.

14. See Stanley Cavell, *In Quest of the Ordinary* (University of Chicago Press, 1988), p. 28.

15. Hawthorne, *Tales and Sketches*, p. 1148.

16. Nathaniel Hawthorne, *The Scarlet Letter*, reprinted in Hawthorne, *Novels* (Library of America, 1983), p. 140.

17. *Ibid.*, p. 151.

18. Emerson, *Essays and Lectures*, p. 265. Nietzsche borrows this and other images in *Thus Spoke Zarathustra*, especially the Preface and the chapter "On Redemption."

19. Tocqueville, *Democracy in America*, pp. 485, 484.

20. Nathaniel Hawthorne, *The Blithedale Romance*, reprinted in Hawthorne, *Novels* (Library of America, 1983), pp. 645–647. The passage continues: "So away she ran, and fell down on the green grass, as it was often her luck to do, but got up again without any harm."

21. The next several paragraphs draw upon my *The Idea of Political Theory* (University of Notre Dame Press, 1990), pp. 150ff.

22. *The House of the Seven Gables*, reprinted in Hawthorne, *Novels*, p. 575.

23. *Ibid.*, pp. 574–580.

24. Hawthorne, *Blithedale Romance*, p. 693.

25. Hawthorne, *Tales and Sketches*, pp. 1131, 1148.

26. Hawthorne, *Blithedale Romance*, pp. 697–698.

27. *Ibid.*, pp. 807–808.

28. Emerson, *Essays and Lectures*, p. 33. See the very interesting essay by Lee Rust Brown, "The Emerson Museum," *Representations* 40 (Fall 1992): 57–80.

29. George Kateb, *Emerson and Self-Reliance* (Sage, 1995).

30. Emerson, *Essays and Lectures*, p. 599 (my italics).

31. Martin Heidegger, *Poetry, Language, Thought* (reprint, Harper and Row, 1973), p. 165.

32. In addition to *The House of the Seven Gables*, "The Celestial Railroad,"

and other well-known texts, see "Fragments from the Journal of a Solitary Man," reprinted in Hawthorne, *Tales and Sketches*, pp. 487–500.

33. Emerson, *Essays and Lectures*, pp. 277ff.

34. *Ibid.*, p. 259.

35. *Ibid.*, p. 57.

36. G.W.F. Hegel, *The Phenomenology of Spirit*. trans. A. V. Miller (Oxford University Press, 1979), p. 397.

37. I might note here that Kateb need not be so worried about Emerson's religiosity—he is thinking of religion in the same way Hegel does, as an exteriorization of moral self-certainty. But if this is the direction Emerson goes in, it is not one in which Kateb wishes to follow.

38. Emerson, *Essays and Lectures*, p. 79.

39. *Ibid.*, p. 476.

40. *Ibid.*, p. 483.

41. Kateb does not cite this passage here, but he does cite it in his essay "Democratic Individuality and the Claims of Politics," in Kateb, *Inner Ocean*, p. 83, in conjunction with a discussion of the limitation of the claims of citizenship.

42. Nathaniel Hawthorne, "The Custom House," reprinted in Hawthorne, *Tales and Sketches*, pp. 135ff.

43. Nathaniel Hawthorne, "The Birthmark," reprinted in Hawthorne, *Tales and Sketches*, p. 766.

44. Kateb, *Inner Ocean*, pp. 84–85.

45. *Ibid.*, p. 226.

46. The title of Benjamin Barber's new book, *An Aristocracy of Everyone* (Ballatine, 1992), is a sign of the need he perceives to resist this danger.

47. Hawthorne, *Tales and Sketches*, p. 499.

48. Kateb might answer me by referring to rights and his idea of a "rights-based individualism." I see this as a response, but I do not see what in democratic individuality *requires* the notion of rights. But that is a longer argument.

49. Walt Whitman, "Long, too long America," in *Leaves of Grass* (reprint, Norton, 1965), pp. 311–312.

50. Robert Frost, "In the Clearing," in *In the Clearing* (Holt, Rinehart, Winston, 1962), p. 16.

Evil and the Imagination of Wholeness

WILLIAM E. CONNOLLY

> K was informed by telephone that next Sunday a short
> inquiry into his case would take place. His attention was
> drawn to the fact that these inquiries would now follow
> each other regularly, perhaps not every week, but at more
> frequent intervals as time went on. It was in the general
> interest, on the one hand, that the case should be quickly
> concluded, but on the other hand the interrogations, must
> be thorough in every respect, although; because of the
> strain involved, they must never last too long. For this
> reason the expedient of these rapidly succeeding but short
> interrogations had been chosen. Sunday had been selected
> as the day of inquiry so that K might not be disturbed in his
> professional work. . . . He was given the number of the
> house where he had to go. It was a house in an outlying
> suburban street where he had never been before.
>
> —Kafka, *The Trial*

THE FIRST INTERROGATION

Why would an omniscient, omnipotent, salvational god allow evil in the
world? No one has ever answered that question without remainders, doubts,
and uncertainties clinging to the answer. Even Augustine, who draws "the
will" into philosophical discourse first and foremost to protect his god from
responsibility for evil, found the labyrinth opened by this question too invo-
luted to navigate. Some of us find the question itself to be perverse, asking in
retort, What inordinate demand or hope lies behind such a question? Does
a demand for wholeness by the questioners support the introduction of a
salvational, omnipotent god? Does the demand to support cultural self-
confidence in this construction then foster the temptation to punish those
whose beliefs and identities jeopardize the self-confidence of this faith? Does
the form and urgency of the question foster the very phenomenon—evil—

the questioners seek to understand? Epicurus identified cultural pressures in this direction, even before the advent of Christianity.[1] And so did Nietzsche, many centuries after its advent. Epicurus speaks through Nietzsche when the latter says "that to quiet the heart it is absolutely not necessary to have solved the ultimate and outermost theoretical questions. Thus to those tormented by 'fear of the gods' it sufficed him [Epicurus] to say: 'if the gods exist they do not concern themselves with us.'" Nietzsche suggests that to seek further consolation, to demand a definitive answer to the problem of evil by offering a final answer to the outermost theoretical questions is very likely to foster evil. It is wiser to stop before becoming too definitive, fixed, and dogmatic in these matters, even though it is impossible to live without posing basic questions and harzarding contestable answers to them:

> Thus he who wishes to offer consolation—to the unfortunate, ill-doers, hypochondriacs, the dying—should call to mind two pacifying formulae of Epicurus, which are capable of being applied to very many questions. Reduced to their simplest form they would perhaps become: firstly, if that is how things are they do not concern us; secondly things may be thus but they may also be otherwise.[2]

George Kateb, by temperament and theoretical proclivity, is far closer to Epicurus than to Augustine. But, unlike Epicurus, he has witnessed the great political evils of the twentieth century—the Holocaust of Hitler, the exorbitant sacrifices of human life by Stalin, Mao, and Pol Pot—and he is alert to the incredible violence accompanying both the conquest of the Americas and the American enslavement of Africans. K, as he will be named during these interrogations, is therefore impelled to enter the labyrinth opened up by the question of evil, particularly by evil in politics.

I find K's account of political evil insightful, partly because of the cautious way in which the presumptions governing the account are advanced and partly because of the substantive themes supported by those presumptions. I also find it, somehow, to be surprisingly unpolitical, unpolitical to some degree in its comprehension of political evil but even more so in its mode of response to evil. The task is to retain K's insights while modifying the framework in which they are set. Since the power of these insights forms one of the attractions of the framework, full success in this task is unlikely.

Evil, K says, is "the deliberate infliction (or sponsorship or knowing allowance) for *almost* any reason whatever, of suffering of great intensity . . ."[3] *Political* evil is the infliction by governments or movements of intense suffering. It is most extreme when it inflicts suffering on "a large scale." Political evil is not the same as oppression or despotism, though the latter two can slide into the former. What, though, contributes to political evil on a large scale?

The answer does not reside principally in the contrariness of the human will, or in an innate tendency to cruelty in individuals. The move from individual cruelty to collective violence, while it occurs, does not sufficiently explain the latter. K finds the key source of political evil to reside in the abstract character of political calculation and action, in the ability of leaders to distance themselves from violences they command, in the difficulty those commanded to violence have in publicizing the concrete experience of suffering they experience or encounter while carrying out orders, and in powerful tendencies among leaders and subjects to invest this or that collective identity (a nation, a state, a collective movement) with sanctity through dualistic ideologies. "Political commitments transform human beings, making them capable of acting more terribly (in methodical, detached, even self-sacrificing ways) than wickedness ever could."[4] And most political theorists "in the canon" exacerbate these tendencies: in their quest to fashion or retain a legitimate collective identity, they invest the idea of collectivity with far too much sanctity, legitimacy, freedom, unity, and morality. Leaders of states and political theorists "are constantly taking *an invented group reality* for *a natural reality* and allowing it to impose itself, to dictate a logic or pattern that must complete itself."[5]

The strengths of K's analysis are apparent. Group identities do tend toward closure, dogmatism, and dualism. Political action is typically abstract in conception and execution. This tendency is intensified today when the consumer/citizen/viewer of a CNN battle report targets the enemy through the eye of the sovereign, as a sleek plane on the TV screen locks an abstract target onto *its* radar screen and as the hit is verified through a flash of light on both screens. In this scenario the commander, the pilot, the reporter, and the citizen all assume the same angle of vision: each views "the target" through the abstract eye of the sovereign on an attack mission. Generalization of this line of vision mobilizes collective celebration of abstract violence while screening out the complexities that engendered the war and the suffering of target populations. The abstract character of politics and war is conducive to the evil of unnecessary violence, then. But, still, the very pertinence of K's appreciation of political abstraction may point to a defect in his analysis.

In his passion to emphasize the artificial, inflated, ideological, dangerous character of group identity, K is tempted to contrast it to the ordinary, contractual, self-correcting perception of the concrete individual. K sometimes writes as if individual identity were concrete and natural and group identity abstract and invented. He knows better, but still this tendency comes into play whenever K is motivated to distinguish between the abstract character of the state and the concrete world of "the individual." But such a contrast contains its own tendencies to foster evil and to conceal it from those implicated in it. First, the story of a contract between discrete individuals is as abstract and ideological as any story of natural group identity; second, the formation and maintenance of the modern individual requires as many supporting institutional conditions as does the formation of an organic collectivity; and third, contemporary individuals' participation in the world of consumption, entertainment, news, politics, and war renders much of their everyday experience as abstract as that of political leaders and "the nation" as a collectivity. The experience of the individual who eats a tender pork chop is detached from the pig butchered at the meat factory. And the individual who eats a nice red apple with no worms or marks on it is screened from perception of the pesticides that give cancer to apple pickers and pollute the environment.

Citizens' independent perception of distant events, as K knows, are framed by the same media that mediate the perceptions of leaders. And the mechanisms by which leaders acquire distance from actions close to hand are also the mechanisms by which ordinary individuals do so. K resists "dualism," on the ground that it provokes the categorical divisions between us and them through which evil occurs. But he repeatedly risks installing a dualism of his own in this essay on political evil, the dualism of a natural distinction between the concrete individual and the invented group. K comes close; he even draws upon this dualism to locate the worst evils in the abstractions of state and collective politics. But he never quite completes the maneuver. Reluctantly and against the grain of "On Political Evil," K eventually acknowledges the necessity of group identity to life:

> I cannot imagine human life without some measure of group identity, but I also cannot imagine a comparatively decent life (at least internationally) unless group identity is mitigated considerably by the doctrine of individual human rights.[6]

I suppose something that is necessary hovers between the natural and the invented. It may be invented, but since some sort of invention of this type is indispensable to human life, it also possesses strains of the natural. But the very way K acknowledges the necessity of group identity forecloses him from engaging politics affirmatively as one of the potential media to identify and resist the politics of evil. K (almost) acknowledges the participation of the modern individual in abstract perception, passion, judgment, and action through the individual's multiple and layered implications in modern institutional life. But he withdraws to a conception of the ordinary, concrete individual when it comes to thinking about how to resist evil. He appreciates superbly the role individual rights play in resisting evil, but he evinces too little appreciation of how the politics of rights can also be a vehicle of arbitrary violence against constituencies explicitly or implicitly defined as falling below the standard of the normal individual. Thus "homosexuality"—conceived as an illness, a moral defect, or both—was defined at least until the 1970s in this culture as falling below the threshold of an individual right; the (still precarious) shift in its standing has resulted from a robust political movement to reconstitute established cultural norms of sexuality. Similarly, the "right to die" was a nonstarter in this predominantly Christian culture until a variety of constituencies moved it onto the register of political debates over rights. In each of these cases, and numerous others as well, what counts as falling within the legitimate province of the regular individual shifts through active *political* mobilization by collective constituencies previously marked by the culture as falling below the threshold of the normal individual. These collective modes of politics both reveal the densely acculturated character of "the individual" and show how a pattern of individual rights can contain undetected or demoralized violences within it.

The demand that the ordinary individual serve as the basis of rights sometimes draws K's attention away from the cultural constitution of the individual; it also deflects his attention from how destructive exclusions can be structured into the very social organization of individual rights. It is not that K is entirely unaware of these issues; it is more, perhaps, that he finds too many dangers attached to efforts to pursue them. K's drive to the solidity of the individual—to the one whose perception is his or her own, whose joys and pains are palpable, whose skin cannot be worn by another, and who ultimately cannot assign another to die for it—enables him to illuminate shadows in the politics of evil. But a desire to dissolve the source of evil into the abstract solution of collective politics may lead K to devalue the way in which the ordinary individual and the practice of rights can themselves participate in abstract evil.

THE SECOND INTERROGATION

K does not discuss *why* he cannot imagine life without "some measure of group identity." Would the answer carry K to an outlying suburb where he has never been before? Is it too dangerous to disrupt the individual as the ground of being and the brake against political evil? What if the individual does not provide the basis of rights, but rather, a particular type of collective identity provides the ambiguous conditions of possibility for the individual and rights? Does the solid ground K (sometimes) seeks now turn into a swamp?

Enter René Girard. Girard insists that the desire of the individual is implicated "from the start" in the social life that constitutes it, that powerful tendencies toward collective violence flow from the terms of this implication, and that any viable response to the problem of evil must engage this volatile, incorrigible set of relations between the cultural consolidation of individual desire and the social production of evil. Girard pursues these connections by addressing the formation of a pattern of desire in the individual. "In the traditional view," Girard says, "the object comes first, followed by human desires that converge independently on this object. Last of all comes violence, a fortuitous consequence of this convergence."[7] Such a set of assumptions resonate with the individualist model of self and rights K is sometimes tempted by. But desire, Girard insists, does not flow from the individual to an object existing outside the individual; the very organization of desire involves a triangular relation between a fractured subject, a model/ rival who appears to possess wholeness, and an object the model already desires. Girard explores the social structure of desire (as opposed to, say, the *need* for food) through a series of interpretations of biblical and classical narratives, such as the Book of Job, *Oedipus Rex*, and *The Bacchae*, and through critical readings of, well, *rivals* for interpretive hegemony in this domain, such as Freud, Nietzsche, and Lévi-Strauss.[8]

The key to desire resides in the twofold relation the fractured subject assumes to the model(s). First:

> In all the varieties of desire examined by us, we have encountered not only a subject and an object but a third presence as well, the rival. It is the rival who should be accorded the dominant role. We must take care, however, to identify him correctly; not to say, with Freud, that he is the father; or, in the case of the tragedies, that he is the brother. . . . Rivalry does not arise because of the fortuitous convergence of two desires on a single object; rather, *the subject desires the object because the rival desires it*. In desiring an object the rival alerts the subject to the desirability of the object.[9]

But what makes another being serve as a model? Here, we arrive at the crux of the Girardian theory:

> When modern theorists envisage man as a being who knows what he wants, or who at least possesses an 'unconscious' that knows for him, they may simply have failed to perceive the domain in which human uncertainty is most extreme. Once his basic needs are satisfied (indeed, sometimes before), man is subject to intense desires, though he may not know precisely for what. The reason is that he desires *being*, something he himself lacks and which some other person seems to possess. . . . It is not through words, therefore, but by the example of his own desire that the model conveys to the subject the supreme desirability of the object.[10]

The model appears to the subject to possess being, to possess a wholeness and self-sufficiency that might stem the subject's own uncertainty and incompleteness, if only the subject could possess it, too. Thus the desire of the fractured subject is essentially mimetic, directed toward an object bound up with the apparent wholeness of the model. It is only from the perspective of the subject, however, that the model appears to possess the completeness the subject lacks. In fact, nobody *possesses* wholeness or "being"; every individual is constituted through the models he or she engages.[11] These paradoxical conditions of individual desire—setting cultural conditions of possibility for the flow of desire and impossibility for the consolidation of a complete or whole individual—accentuate the probability of collective violence. Here, K and Girard converge again, momentarily. K's endorsement of the saying of Jesus on the Cross, "Forgive them, Father, for they know not what they do," is susceptible to a Girardian reading. Models and subjects do not understand

the implications of the relations in which they are implicated; they are repeatedly caught by surprise, therefore, by the eruptions of violence that
punctuate the politics of desire.

Out of this vortex of reciprocal uncertainty, unavoidable misrecognition,
and mimetic desire, rivalry escalates. Violence intensifies and spreads. Some
parties to these rivalries eventually seek alliances that define a weak or vulnerable member as the source of collective violence: that member's elimination or expulsion promises to restore the community to a fictive wholeness
it never actually possessed. Hence the Girardian readings of *Oedipus Rex*
and Job, texts taken to show how the surrogate is retroactively elevated to
a sacred status to support the future stability of the community. The production of surrogate victims temporarily stabilizes a violence that would otherwise escalate interminably; the surrogate victim becomes a sacred being the
community worships, partly out of dim, deniable indebtedness to the victim
for the role he or she plays in concealing violences installed in the unstable
structure of desire. A secret alliance among violence, wholeness, and the
sacred is born; a brake on the future escalation of violence is precariously
installed through the sacralization of scapegoats.

For Girard, evil occurs offstage, so to speak, in the production of scapegoats to sustain the cultural imagination of wholeness. Girard reminds us,
indirectly, that members of a surrogate constituency defined as the source of
evil are made to forfeit any rights given to ordinary individuals (if they live
in a culture of rights). An examination of how such surrogates are culturally
projected, treated as responsible for suffering, and punished might prove
particularly pertinent, then, to reflection on arbitrary violences uncon-
sciously installed in a culture of rights.

Girard generalizes too radically and dogmatically from mythic forms of
life to human culture in general, and from some forms of social life to others.
He ignores, to present a timely example, the crucial role that abstraction
plays in the contemporary production of political evil; and he deflates, as K
does, too, the role that politics might play in exposing and combating a
cultural dialectic of exclusion and violence.[12] His theory is too crude, dogmatic, and general. But, still—partly for these very reasons—it poses a valuable counterpoint to absract conceptions of individual rights that remain
hegemonic and undercriticized in this culture. Let us return momentarily to
the Girardian reading, then, to discern the line of connection between the
individual quest for wholeness and the cultural production of evil.

Girard's theory of mimetic identification, bearing affinities to Hegel's
presentation of lordship and bondage, also bears an unacknowledged debt
to the Lacanian theory of the imaginary. In the Lacanian "mirror stage," the
infant, experiencing "discordance with its own reality" through the lack of
control over its inner perturbations and motor activities, eventually appears
to itself in a mirror to be more full and whole than it *feels* itself to be. The
mirror effect, which can be achieved in a variety of ways, eventually draws
the discordant self toward an agenda: to become whole. The imagination of

wholeness, in relation to the actual experience of "primordial discord," is embellished and extended through identification with caretaking adults who appear complete to the infant.[13] They become objects of identification and, later, rivals the infant may seek to displace in the interests of becoming whole.

One adult male effect of this early experience, as represented in the Lacanian model, is illustrated in the film *Where Angels Fear to Tread*, based on E. M. Forster's novel of the same name. At a pivotal moment in the story, when the son of English aristocrats attends an Italian opera in pursuit of the Italian man who is about to seduce his sister-in-law from her place in English society, a large soprano appears on stage. Her appearance transforms everything. Young men in the audience become mesmerized, as this larger-than-life woman trills in a high, lilting voice. So does the Englishman, even though his female ally (also from England) finds it remarkably easy to resist this moment of identification. The soprano at once crystallizes and shields from articulation a dim memory haunting many aristocratic men in the audience. The high, lilting voice of this large woman recalls the mother or nurse, appearing so large to the infant, whose reassuring sounds once filled the nursery. The soprano summons the inarticulate memory of apparent wholeness in the other, a wholeness the small, discordant child once attributed to large, female adults who attended it. The response of the men to this larger-than-life soprano reveals how the imagination of wholeness still circulates through the grammar of adult male life—if not in this particular way for some, then perhaps in other ways. For these others desire, too, and these desires, too, may be motivated by the experience of a lack engendered by the appearance of wholeness in the other.

Such an imaginary, taking a variety of forms depending upon the specific relations children establish to adults and, later, those adults establish to other adults and groups to other groups, may never disappear entirely from social life. It may provide at once a condition of possibility for the constitution of desire and identity and a powder keg from which social division and violence can erupt. The modern individual's imagination of wholeness is a source of both good and evil.

Girard forms an entire social theory at the level of the imaginary, when he should expose the partial role the imaginary may play in the formation of desire, the pursuit of freedom through identity, and the generation of violence in social relations and should strive to identify counterforces inside desire and identity capable of struggling against these pressures. In reducing desire and identity to the imaginary, Girard forgoes consideration of political ways and means to fend off evil in political life. For if the imaginary were the only thing and if it also assumed only one form, then only the conversion of everyone from one kind of imagination to another single type could resolve violence. Girard effectively compromises the division between the concrete individual and the invented collectivity, but his reduction of social life to the imaginary in his early work prefigures the introduction in his later work of Christology as the unique solution to the problem of collective violence.[14] Only a faith formed from the perspective of the victim, Girard thinks, can both expose the dialectic of violence in the social structure of desire and respond sufficiently to it. K and Girard converge for a fleeting moment here, too, as K flirts with the theme of forgiveness of evil in the Gospels. But K recognizes this response to be insufficient to the scope and scale of political evil. And neither Girard nor K appreciates enough the indispensable role of political movements to the identification and relief of evil.

THE THIRD INTERROGATION

Is there a fugitive imagination of wholeness, circulating through desire, installed in the formation of collective identities in late modern societies? If so, it also finds expression in the lives of concrete individuals in these same cultures. For the constitution of each individual is bound up with the collective identities through which the individual is recognized and with those fugitive energies that exceed the individual's cultural identifications. The imagination of wholeness can attach itself anywhere, and a pattern of imagination at one level can resonate with the imagination of wholeness at others. The imagination of wholeness readily attaches itself to political ideals of the individual as well as to the collective experience of a nation. In "the canon" of political theory, the imagination of wholeness is discernible in Augustine's plea for unity of the individual will (to be approximated only if and as the divided will becomes obedient to the will of god) and in his notion of a dim memory of a time of human wholeness before the first sin, in Rousseau's imagination of a general will that is "constant, unalterable and pure," in Hegel's aspiration to a realized State (as K notes), in contemporary ideals of a rational consensus, in maternal versions of feminism, in modern ideals of nationalism, and in some models of the intact, whole individual in contemporary liberal discourse.

The cultural imagination of wholeness readily attaches itself to collective politics whenever the state is established as the central agency of collective action and freedom. The attachment may take the form of memory of a putative unity lost, the projection of fictive unity into the actual variety of contemporary life, or the demand to attain national unity against the forces that press against it. But it can also attach itself to the image of the individual in those same regimes, where some attend to the dangers of collective identity but forget the forgetfulness built into the image of the whole individual. The imagination of wholeness is even discernible in pluralist political politics, where a particular pattern of diversity functions to screen out arbitrary exclusions and violences upon which that pattern is grounded. Take, for example, the nineteenth-century "America" that Tocqueville registers and affirms.

Tocqueville, famously, celebrates local democracy, an independent judiciary, separation of church and state, and an independent and plural press, but he also recalls longingly the (putative) unity of the past provided by aristocracy. And he insists explicitly that the diversity of democracy itself must be contained within a common "civilization," burned deeply into the religious convictions, social mores, principles of reason, and cultural imagination adopted by the people. In the Tocquevillian imagination, the mores of the nation are burned into the imagination and rationality of each individual:

> What keeps a great number of citizens under the same government is much less a reasoned desire to remain united than the instinctive and, in a sense, involuntary accord which springs from like feelings and similar opinions . . . ; only when certain men consider a great many questions from the same point of view and have the same opinions on a great many subjects and when the same events give rise to like thoughts and impressions is there a society. . . . Although there are many sects among the Anglo-Americans, they all look at religion from the same point of view.[15]

"Involuntary accord," "like feelings," "similar opinions," "same point of view," "like thoughts and impressions," and (elsewhere on the same page) "a single nation"—all these point to the efficacy of a national culture within the individual. Tocqueville's imagination of the possibility of action in concert through the state is controlled by the idea of a common moral life imprinted in each individual: the individual is a microcosm of the nation, and the nation a macrocosm of the individual. While modest variations are possible and even admirable, everyone must be basically the same in the moral source they draw upon and the mores they embody. Tocqueville's imagination is thus confined to an arboreal image of pluralism, in which several limbs branch out modestly from a common trunk. He evinces little appreciation of a more rhizomatic pluralism with multifarious nodes of connection among diverse identities appealing to multiple moral sources: a pluralism in which the lines of connection and division proliferate so that no single line becomes overcoded, so that no single constituency is set up to become the necessary object of terror around which the pursuit of wholeness is organized. The higher unity upon which Tocquevillian "civilization" rests involves profession of the same basic god, an agricultural way of life in which the members are possessed by the territory that possesses them, and numerous universal imperatives installed in the common "mores." These onto-ethical requirements of civilization itself eventually accumulate to render it impossible to allow "wandering nomads," "pagans," and "Indians" to modify this ethos by participating in it. The land of America has to be territorialized to exclude those nomads whose way of being is incompatible with territorial civilization. Tocqueville, explicitly, reluctantly, and regretfully concludes that since the monological unity of civilization provides morality with its necessary conditions of existence, it cannot be immoral to exclude from America those whose nomadic way of life insults the wholeness of civilization. His monotheist, monomoral, monoterritorial imagination, closing down numerous possibilities otherwise available for respectful engagement and connection between "nomads" and "settlers," numbs Tocqueville, the America he registers, and numerous admirers today to the fires of violence ignited by it.[16] The evil of the Euro-American holocaust against millions of Amerindians is grounded in the insistence on homology between the structure of the regular individual and the mores of the nation.

Less virulent effects of this imagination are discernible in Tocqueville's treatment of women, Irish-Americans, slaves, atheists, and Frenchmen who run off into the wilderness with Amerindian women. The atheist in the nineteenth-century world of Tocqueville's America, for instance, functions as an internal corollary to the external affront of the "nomadic Indian." Atheists are defined as restless, selfish, materialistic, amoral individuals, who must be excluded from effective eligibility for moral leadership or political office because of their tendency to amorality and unreliability. Tocqueville valorizes the indispensable role of politics in fending off evil, but the conception of identity with which he begins impels him to produce evil even while trying to avoid it.

THE FOURTH INTERROGATION

If the imagination of wholeness flows freely into a variety of containers, if this imaginary wholeness cannot and should not be stilled entirely, and if it all too readily spawns arbitrary violence, how could it be modulated and chastened? We might address this question first by relocating the key source of one aspect of the problem of evil in politics, and then by responding politically to the problem so posed. The hope is to maintain contact with K, Girard, and Tocqueville while moving the response to political evil more actively onto a political register.

Evil resides as immanent possibility in the social currents that carry individual desire, collective identity, and moral goodness along. The capacity for evil—as fundamental and undeserved suffering—is lodged in the paradoxical structure of identity\difference relations themselves. It is lodged in a paradox of difference, which, on this reading, reaches deeply into the grammar of social relations. Nietzsche grasps this ambiguity in Zarathustra's presentation of "On the Three Evils."[17] And Nietzsche's characterization of *ressentiment*—which often expresses itself as resentment against constituencies whose way of being disturbs the imagination of wholeness individuals, groups, and nations regularly project into being—parallels loosely Girardian and Lacanian presentations of the imagination of wholeness. But the strategies Nietzsche commends for subduing *ressentiment* differ significantly from Girard's and Lacan's.

Things get off on the wrong foot if you first distill individuals from social life, and then either connect them to a collective identity that promises to fulfill them or warn them against a collectivity that stifles their freedom. Each individual simultaneously (1) crystallizes a particular (perhaps unique) combination of identities made available by the socially established fund of possibilities, (2) contains differences that mark that individual as departing from social norms in particular ways, and (3) embodies fugitive currents of energy and possibility (i.e., di/erence) exceeding the cultural fund of identities and differences through which that individual is organized. The value of the language of identity and difference is that it already mediates among the terms of the individual, the collective constituency, and the nation. Thus, if you "are," say, Amerindian, female, gay, Catholic, and an American citizen today, each of these collective identities participates in your constitution as an individual. In this case, as in many others, it is probable that some of the identifications through which you are organized and recognized will require political work to enable the set to coexist in the same self without intense suffering. The essential participation of individuals in culturally established layers of collective identity is rendered both more intensive and more contingent in the contemporary age, when cultural communication circulates much faster and further and the organization of identities is more detailed and meticulous. In such contexts, the politics of cultural interruption provides an indispensable means to combat the closures and violences of identity.

Identity requires difference to exist: it requires differences to provide it with contrasts that enable it to exist. But whenever the imagination of wholeness captures an identity, some of those enabling differences are also perceived to jeopardize the possibility of self-security and wholeness at which it aims. This is the paradoxical element circulating through relations of identity\difference. This paradoxical element can become productive as long as the imagination of wholeness does not overwhelm one or more parties, as long as, to note one example, "men" do not first constitute "women" as sources of nurturance from which to develop their unique capacities for agency, and then define them as spectators and/or objects through which to confirm their individuality. Wherever the imagination of wholeness acquires hegemony, the perception of difference becomes a threat to identity. Perhaps you (an individual, group, class, or nation) convert a range of differences into otherness to fix blame for the sense of uncertainty or incompletness you feel. Or your very mode of being may pose a threat to the insistent demand for wholeness by the other. Or, alternatively, the appearance of wholeness in some with whom you are identified may drive you to replace them to gain the prize they seem to possess. All identities in which the theme of a primordial "lack" or "alienation" is central are susceptible to one or more of these political operations. The pursuit of wholeness is a fundamental source of evil in politics.

Thus identity\difference relations enable the consolidation of particular constituencies, but the pursuit of fictive unity also propels drives to violence against the other. How do you participate in the positive effects of cultural identity without resorting to the production of otherness to render identity whole? How do you enjoy the manifold efficacies and pleasures of contingent, constructed identities without becoming the target of aggression from identities whose pursuit of wholeness requires them to treat you as other? I do not have a sufficient answer to these questions, though I find them to be the right questions. At any rate, the reponses that seem to make the most sense cannot promise to eradicate the danger. For the danger keeps recurring within identity\difference relations. The responses, rather, are set in a tragic sensibility in which the essential ambiguity of being fosters both the dangers and the ethical incentive to struggle against them.

Nietzsche and Foucault provide promising leads to pursue, though it is not my intention to claim that the insights I draw from each correspond exactly to his intentions. Nietzsche pursues strategies by the self applied to the self to subdue resentment against the absence of wholeness in being. The ethical objective is to become more alert to the historically contingent character of the identities in which you participate and to develop a character able to affirm what it has become without the wholeness of being. The self as a modest work of art is not governed by a fixed model of being; the crafting involved is always experimental to a considerable degree, and the type of self to be crafted varies with the distinctive natural and cultural materialization already there before you begin to do your work. The goal is to work modestly upon a self that already is—working upon selective contingencies that have become engrained, crafting them into a distinctive form; working on yourself to deepen your experience of the element of contingency in it and to increase the extent to which you affirm *this* condition of life; working on the self, therefore, to overcome the demand to be an intrinsic self or to conform to some fictive model of the universal individual. The self as a "work of art" is a modest, distinctive artifact crafted from a self that has already acquired considerable definition through the vissicitudes of fate: it becomes an ethically successful artifact to the extent it is able to love life without demanding wholeness of being. There is no guarantee that every self will succeed in such experimentation, even if it undertakes it. And—it almost goes without saying—in a highly stratified society, many selves will not find themselves in cultural positions that support a lot of this work. This fact, though, does not diminish the importance of such work upon the ethical character of those who do find themselves in such a position. It increases it.

The goal of self as a work of art is neither to discover a true self existing underneath those numerous layers of sedimented contingency nor to create the self entirely by the self. The ideal of self as a work of art, in fact, is defined in resistance to those two familiar moral models. This does not mean, however, that the self as a work of art is unconnected to ethics. Its most compelling ethical objective is to overcome the source of evil installed in the the imagination of wholeness already circulating within most selves. Such an ideal makes contact with K's ideal of individuality, though it contests the language of the individual that K sometimes adopts when disparaging invented collectives. For many of the materials the self works upon in itself are cultural and collective.

Foucault, the second figure, appreciates the significance of arts of the self while also seeking to politicize more actively identity\difference relations. He does so to interrupt those collective identities too thoroughly consumed by the demand to make themselves whole. The key to Foucault is the attempt to challenge by political means violence, fundamentalism, and the drive to wholeness in identity wherever they rear their ugly heads.

Nietzsche, then, emphasizes the significance of distinctive practices of self-fashioning by a being already formed to a considerable degree; Foucault, the importance of distinctive political mobilizations to redress racial, religious, gender, sexual, national, or ethnic identifications resting upon the pursuit of wholeness through the negation of difference. Each domain of action—strategies of the self and political interruption of drives to wholeness—is closely bound up with the other. Let us focus on the second, presupposing a political culture in which the electoral apparatus of democratic accountability is already installed.

If you define democracy simply as a mode of rule or governance, where elected representatives legislate, execute, and enforce general policies, and where the primary debate is whether officials should represent the electorate (the idealist view) or be insulated from it in order to govern rationally (the realist view), then the democratic state all too readily becomes a conduit for evil. In fact, in neo-Rousseauian and neo-Hegelian traditions of democratic discourse—where citizens seek a general will or citizen voters seek a unified nation-state—democratic governance easily degenerates into the organization of unity through the demoralization of otherness. These forms readily become vehicles for consolidation of violence against the internal other (those within the state who deviate from the nation or general will), the interior other (that in the self which differs from its socially consituted identity), and the external other (those outside the state who threaten the self-confidence of its identity). But if you imagine democracy not only as a particular organization of governance but also as a distinctive culture or ethos in which constituencies have a significant hand in modeling and moving the identities that constitute them, then cultivation of a democratic ethos becomes very pertinent to struggles against the violence of wholeness. When a democratic ethos is operative, productive tension is maintained between governance of a populace through electoral processes and the periodic interruption by social movements of those standards and constituencies whose privilege depends upon the conversion of difference into otherness. Of course, a democracy constituted in such an ambivalent way itself generates some exclusions and limits. It limits the reach, for instance, of religious, gender, sexual, and national identities whose mode of being depends upon maintaining the claim of wholeness by the conversion of difference into otherness.

The greatest danger in such a democratic ethos is that its very success might spur into being reactive, fundamentalist movements that insist that what they are is intrinsic, exclusive, and good. Its corollary virtue is that the positive ethos it foments can support a more multifarious pluralism than currently found in any formal democracy, a pluralism in which multiple possibilities of connection are enabled because more of the parties involved appreciate contingent and relational dimensions in their own being, a democracy in which cultural limits are imposed on contestation between contending identities because more constituencies recognize their own ambiguous implication in the differences they engage. Such an ethos provides ethical support to critical movements that interrupt the exclusionary drives of naturalized identities. And critical politicization of recurrent drives to wholeness in identity forms a linchpin of the battle against evil in democratic politics. For democratic politics, on this conception, both generates reactive drives to wholeness among numerous identities and contains within itself the best available antidotes to those tendencies. It is the ways in which it turns against some of its own ugliest tendencies that makes the ethos of democracy so valuable.

Cultural appreciation of the constitutive ambiguity of identity can provide a spur to the cultivation of mutual respect among constituencies locked into ambiguous relations of interdependence and strife. For a constituency identity is formed by the organization of fleeting possibilities within it into a settled form, by definition of that which varies from its form into modes of difference, and by reception and resistance to definitions projected upon it by oppositional constituencies.

In identity\difference relations, empathy, flowing from the experience of difference and signs of diference circulating through your identity, provides a significant source of the democratic ethos. The irony, which Nietzsche, Foucault, and Emmanuel Levinas (in different ways) understand so well, is that moralities that insist upon grounding themselves in a universal matrix of reason, the fixed commands of a single god, the intrinsic identity of the solid individual, or the higher unity of the harmonious community risk securing themselves by converting difference into otherness *and* difference into emptiness; they thereby dry up some of the sources from which agonistic empathy for difference might be cultivated.[18] Empathy emerges from appreciation of the ambiguous, relational character of identity itself, when this ambiguity is affirmed for its revelation of the abundance of life over identity rather than regretted for a lack of being it signifies. One form such a relation assumes, in the (refigured) language of Nietzsche, is a "pathos of distance," an attachment to that which differs from you through a certain distantiation from it.

This attachment across the space of distance insinuates forbearance into strife and generosity into interdependence; it does so because neither party is hell-bent on achieving wholeness by erasing entirely the distance between them. When such an ethos of democracy is operative, freedom is fostered by building multiple possibilities of coalition, conflict, and indifference among diverse identities, and by forming cushions of respect around contending identities so that colliding parties bounce apart with less injury inflicted on either by the force of impact. But, of course, such an ethos of democracy is never sufficiently developed. It is always in need of repair or revivification along some dimension or other.

It is possible to read Nietzsche—the arch-adversary of democracy as a Rousseauian mode of rule and the carrier of nostalgia for an aristocratic ethos—as an involuntary contributor to the ethos of democracy needed in the late modern age. Nietzsche's central adversary in late nineteenth-century Europe was the culture of Christianity, wherever that culture achieved sufficient hegemony to overwhelm contending spiritualities. But he still felt a certain pathos for this adversary, not because it might become what he already was, but because he needed it to crystallize what he was and because it embodied a contending way to respond to persistent mysteries of existence. Consider Nietzsche's formulation of the "spiritualization of enmity" with respect to this arch-adversary:

> The Church has at all times desired the destruction of its enemies: we, we immoralists and anti-Christians, see that it is to our advantage that the Church exists. . . . In politics, too enmity has become much more spiritual—much more prudent, much more thoughtful, much more *forbearing*. . . . We adopt the same attitude toward the "enemy within"; there too we have spiritualized enmity, there too we have grasped its *value*. One is *fruitful* only at the cost of being rich in contradictions; one remains *young* only on condition the soul does not relax, does not long for peace.[19]

It is to "our" advantage that the church exists—its existence helps us to cultivate nontheistic *reverence* for the ambiguity of being through contrast and selective indebtedness to several forms of theistic devotion. Christianity provides a spur—an advantage—to us, even while we fight against drives by a large subset of (Tocquevillian/American) Christians to constitute us as amoral, negational atheists, held to forsake reverence and ethical forbearance in general because we do not bow before the idol they project into being. Adding "Judeo" in front of "Christian" does not help all that much. For, here, too, the suggestion is that a common (now extended) "Judeo-Christian heritage" is necessary to American, democratic, civilized morality. What does help is the affirmation by theists of multiple sorts of agonistic respect for constituencies who draw ethical inspiration from nontheistic (and nonsecular) sources.

Nietzsche contended that only a noble few are prepared to spiritualize enmity in such a pluralized, generous way. He might exaggerate an important truth here. It *is* unlikely that such an orientation will ever form the ecumenical ethos of a pluralistic democracy. We may never live in a world in which a definitive majority of "Christians," "pagans," and "secularists," for instance, fold the spiritualization of enmity into their reciprocal relations. But, equally, such a spirituality already has *some* presence in modern democracies. Moreover, *such a cultural disposition will not find an active expression anywhere today unless it establishes an active presence in democracy.* Finally, unless such a reciprocal spirituality does acquire a significant presence in operational democracy, democracy itself will be more stingy, dogmatic, and exclusionary than it has to be. The old aristocratic world, even Nietzsche would agree, cannot be reinstated today (if it ever existed), and the Nietzschean compensatory ideal of nobility for a few above and beyond the reach of state politics is no longer sustainable either.[20] Today, the spiritualization of enmity either assumes a larger presence in a democratic culture or it finds no significant foothold anywhere.

The historic, self-aggrandizing American/Christian constitution of "the atheist" as amoral, selfish, restless, materialistic, and unreliable must be reconfigured before those culturally marked by that identity can become full-fledged participants in public life. For Tocqueville's dictum that the overt atheist in nineteenth-century America could not be elected to public office still holds today. Even though the Tocquevillian/Christian/American demonization of "the atheist" has now lost some of its historical fervency, there are signs of the latter's returning. What is most important about this example, though, is that it provides a model of how those attempts to avoid evil bound up with a quest for wholeness end up creating collective models of otherness potentially eligible for collective violence or suppression. And the Nietzschean/Foucauldian responses, taken together, reveal what must be done to roll back such potentialities.

What contribution can constituencies marked as atheist make to such a process? Well, a political movement designed to convert the identity of "atheism" into that of nontheistic reverence for the ambiguity of being might have salutary effects. It would challenge the definition of the other upon which some versions of theism depend, and it would introduce into the terms of ethical discourse an alternative orientation, reducible to neither the form of theism nor the form of secularism with which we are most familiar. It would, that is, *enact politically* a new cultural identity out of an old negated difference. To the degree it succeeded in crossing the threshold from an other subsisting below the level of cultural respect to a legitimate alternative existing on the register of public discourse, it would jostle and disrupt old patterns of secular reason and theistic faith by juxtaposing them to an ethical perspective that fits into neither mold. Individualist theories of rights and communitarian theories of national identity both obscure the ambiguous *politics of enactment* by which a new entity is propelled into being out of injury, energy, and difference and through which arbitrary exclusions and violences in previous constellations of identity and rights are revealed retrospectively.[21]

Once the critical threshold of enactment/recognition is crossed by political means it would become possible to render critical engagements among theists, nontheists, secularists, and atheists more "prudent," "thoughtful," "forbearing" and "fruitful." Interdependencies among contending spiritualities would become more multiple, more dissonant, and more spiritualized.

You would now exercise reciprocal forbearance toward adversaries who help to crystallize your identity, even while deflating claims they may advance to self-sufficiency. And you would invite them to do the same. You would do so partly from appreciation of how the reciprocal production of agonistic respect opens up cultural spaces through which new possibilities can be propelled into being, partly from respect for the way the periodic introduction of new identities enhances the broader experience of contingency and relational interdependence among existing identities, partly out of gratitude to the difference of the other in helping you to be what you are, partly through experience of the traces of the other in your identity that are regulated to maintain what you are, and partly out of prudence in a world in which you seldom know which allies you may need in the future.

The spiritualization of enmity forms a cardinal virtue in a vibrant democratic ethos. It expresses and appreciates the common understanding that no single orientation to the fundaments of being can establish its own certainty or universality. To the degree such a spiritualization is absent, formal democracy gives off the odor of stagnation or the offensive smell of dogmatism. For the spiritualization of enmity exposes and fends off violences grounded in the pursuit of wholeness, wherever those pursuits acquire hegemony. It encourages a pathos of distance among interdependent and dissonant constituencies, each of which may detect traces of itself in the others, including traces in itself of the drive to wholeness it discerns in the others.

•

Once you fold the imagination of wholeness into K's presentation of the individual as well as the nation, critical politicization of identity\difference relations at many sites becomes a crucial vehicle through which to subdue the violence of identity. The primary task of these interrogations, then, has been to show how the drive to wholeness enters into the identity of individuals in ways that resonate with its entry into collective politics. If K already knows this, so much the better. If he periodically forgets it through an eagerness to ground rights in the common sense of the individual and a corollary desire to minimize the positive possibilities of politics, then this essay may point to gaps in his engagement with evil.

My identification with K remains significant amidst these possible differences in the distribution of emphasis. Both of us, for instance, think that it is when the politics of nationality harnesses religion to itself that the risk of political evil becomes extreme. Both of us draw critical sustenance from forerunners such as Epicurus and Nietzsche, and each of us breaks with these forerunners' respective conceptions of democracy. Both of us, as nontheists, also insist upon reopening the labyrinth of evil, even though it is thought by many to be the reserve of theology; we do so because the language of evil remains the most pertinent discourse through which to engage political sources of profound suffering. Finally, both of us strain to hear the fugitive excess of being over identity: K's attention to the "inner *ocean*" points to this dimension. It is just that the ocean resides *between* and *around* as well as *within*.

It is ethically imperative to show how the quest for wholeness can enter into the desire of the individual, the political practice of rights, constituency movements, the politics of nationalities, and the reason of state. It is also imperative to interrupt by political means pressures toward dogmatism in each of these domains. Nonetheless, it still remains pertinent to explore how the very ambiguity of individual rights enables them to function as crucial barriers to evil. In this domain, K may return to his accustomed role as interrogator of the presumptions of others. For electoral democracy minus a robust culture of rights equals a repressive regime.

NOTES

1. "But the intellect, by making a rational cacluation of the end and the limit which govern the flesh, and by dispelling the fears about eternity, brings about the complete life, so that we no longer need the infinite time. But neither does it shun pleasure, nor even when circumstances bring about our departure from life does it suppose, as it perishes, that it has in any way fallen short of the best life." Epicurus, in *The Hellenistic Philosophers*, vol. 1, ed. and trans. A. A. Long and D. N. Sedley (Cambridge: Cambridge University Press, 1987), p. 150.

2. Friedrich Nietzsche, *Human, All Too Human: A Book for Free Spirits*, trans. R. J. Hollingdale (New York: Cambridge University Press, 1986), p. 305.

3. George Kateb, *The Inner Ocean: Individualism and Democratic Culture* (Ithaca, N.Y.: Cornell University Press, 1992), p. 200.

4. Kateb, *Inner Ocean*, p. 205.

5. *Ibid.*, p. 210 (my italics).

6. *Ibid.*, p. 209.

7. René Girard, *Violence and the Sacred*, trans. Patrick Gregory (Baltimore: Johns Hopkins University Press, 1972), p. 144.

8. Girard never characterizes his own relation to interpretive rivals in these terms, but he is particularly severe with them and very eager to distinguish his thinking from theirs. Does this structure have some applicability to the essays in this volume, many of which are written by students or younger colleagues of George Kateb? Let me leave the point here: if you, George, recognize traces of rivalry in several essays in this volume, you might be moved to consider a theory that accounts for this relation, taking into account the effects such relations have on your conception of the individual. Ahhh, the pleasures of discourse.

9. Girard, *Violence and the Sacred*, p. 145.

10. *Ibid.*, pp. 145–146. My thinking on this topic is aided by Michael Shapiro, whose essay, "That Obscure Object of Desire," in *The Political Subject of Violence*, ed. David Campbell and Michael Dillon (New York: Manchester University Press, 1993), pp. 114–136, brings out both how the Buñuel film *The Obscure Object of Desire* fits this structure of desire and how it can be drawn upon to illuminate the constitution of the Iraqi other by America during the Gulf War.

11. Do not assume that I know what wholeness is, though it is impossible to attain. It seems to me that no one knows what it is and that it often functions as an end state in the imagination. We may know how it appears in the other, but not what it is as an experience. It is thus always experienced as a lack. Augustine comes close to saying this in his discussion of how we "remember" a state before the Fall that was full and innocent.

12. Through the vissicitudes of authorial production and press publication, this essay was written before a book that explores the question of desire more closely. In my "The Desire to Punish," in William E. Connolly, *The Ethos of Pluralization* (Minneapolis: University of Minnesota Press, 1995), I discuss the Girardian theory of desire extensively and critically.

13. Jacques Lacan, *Écrits*, trans. Alan Sheridan (New York: W. W. Norton, 1977), ch. 1, "The Mirror Stage." Lacan says: "What I have called the mirror stage is interesting in that it manifests the affective dynamism by the subject who originally identifies himself with the visual gestalt of his own body: in relation to the still very profound lack of coordination of his own motility, it represents an ideal unity, a salutary imago; it is invested with all the original distress resulting from the child's intra-organic and relational discordance." This "will crystallize in the subject's internal conflictual tension, which determines the awakening of his desire for the object of the other's desire . . . the primordial coming together is precipitated into aggressive competitiveness from which devlops the triad of the others, the ego, and the object." *Ibid.*, p. 18. Lacan qualifies the effects of the imaginary by indicating how it changes when drawn into the realm of the symbolic. Luce Irigaray, in *This Sex Which Is Not One*, trans. Catherine Porter (Ithaca, N.Y.: Cornell University Press, 1985), offers a compelling critique of the masculine version of "the real" and "the symbolic" in Lacan and also reveals how alternative enactments can modify the effects of the imaginary on life. I have responded to the Zizekian appropriation of Lacan in the Epilogue to the second edition of my *Political Theory and Modernity* (Ithaca, N.Y.: Cornell University Press, 1993).

14. See, for example, René Girard, *The Scapegoat*, trans. Yvonne Freccero (Baltimore: Johns Hopkins University Press, 1986).

15. Alexis de Tocqueville, *Democracy in America* (2 vols.), trans. George Lawrence (New York: Doubleday and Co., 1966), p. 373.

16. I discuss the relation between Tocqueville's "civi-territorial complex" and the violent displacement of Amerindians from "American" territory in greater detail in my "Tocqueville, Religiosity and Pluralization," in Connolly, *Ethos of Pluralization*.

17. Friedrich Nietzsche, *Thus Spoke Zarathustra*, trans. Walter Kaufmann (New York: Penguin Books, 1966), pp. 186–191. The best discussion of *ressentiment* in that volume is in "On The Tarantulas," pp. 99–102.

18. I have tried to show how this operates and how Nietzsche and Foucault represent viable responses to this impoverished ethos in my *The Augustinian Imperative: A Reflection on the Politics of Morality* (Beverly Hills, Calif.: Sage Publications, 1993). The version of this perspective developed by Emmanuel Levinas is well represented in Levinas, *Totality and Infinity,* trans. Alphonso Lingis (Pittsburgh: Dusquesne University Press, 1969). The issues involved in a Levinisian ethic are presented compellingly in Simon Critchley, *The Ethics of Deconstruction: Derrida and Levinas* (Oxford: Basil Blackwell, 1992).

19. Friedrich Nietzsche, *Twilight of the Idols*, trans. R. J. Hollingdale (Middlesex: Penguin Books, 1969), p. 44. I deleted the sentence "A new creation in par-

ticular, the new *Reich* for instance, has more need of enemies than friends: only in opposition does it become necessary . . . ," partly because the terms "friends" and "enemies" are misleading here, and partly because even when they are clarified within the broader meaning of the "spiritualization of enmity," the very form the nation-state assumes in the late modern age makes the cultivation of this form of enmity particularly dangerous. My Nietzsche is not a proto-Schmittian. Indeed, Schmitt's "decisionism" grows out of the insistence that the absence of wholeness is a lack that must be remedied by the decisionism of the state.

20. Nietzsche himself argues somewhere in *The Gay Science,* trans. Walter Kaufman (New York: Vintage Books, 1974), that modern individuals are no longer "stones in an edifice." We are much more like "actors" who expect to have a voice in the cultural parts we are called upon to play. This change in self-conception forms a crucial part of the democratic ethos. But if the old Nietzschean world of aristocratic politics is not reinstatable, the secondary Nietzschean ideal of nobility above politics is not likely to be operationalized either. I argue in chapter 5 of my *Identity\Difference: Democratic Negotiations of Political Paradox* (Ithaca, N.Y.: Cornell University Press, 1991) that the space for this Nietzschean world above the "poisonous flies" of politics has been squeezed out by the intensification of organizational life in late modern culture. Thus I work with Nietzsche on behalf of the self as a work of art and the spiritualization of enmity and against him in defining democracy as the most favorable soil for cultivation of these possibilities. I know someone will announce (as if it were a surprise) that these uses of Nietzsche do not correspond to the Real Nietzsche.

21. This presentation makes the politics of enactment sound slightly less paradoxical than it must be—for a new enactment, in bringing something new into being out of difference (rather than removing the ideological cover from an entity/identity that was there all along), does expose violence concealed in a previous pattern of practice. But it does not expose the new exactly as it was before its enactment. Previously, "it" was, perhaps, a difference constituted by the hegemonic identity. It was "atheism," say, defined as lacking reverence because it did not revere a deity. The new enactment exposes the old violence, but it does so while moving the identity of that which had been injured. This temporal ambiguity, I want to say, is built into many social movements, inluding the civil rights movement, the feminist movement, and the gay rights movement. The language of individual rights misses this crucial ambiguity.

Multiculturalism between Individuality and Community: Chasm or Bridge?

BENJAMIN R. BARBER

THE HEALTHY TENSION between democracy and individuality to which most modern political philosophers subscribe is understandably hard to comprehend within a single politics because however creative the interaction between liberty and equality in theory, in practice the politics of individuality and the politics of community have starkly contrary entailments. The happy phrase "democratic individualism" conceals armies of libertarians and communitarians who necessarily find themselves implacable antagonists on almost every significant policy issue: police powers, welfare, conscription, public health, and income redistribution. Individuals may be embedded in communities and communities may be composed of and justified by individuals, but the entailments of serving individuals and those of serving communities are frequently incompatible. Indeed, democratic individualism disguises fundamental differences over the function and legitimacy of the democratic state: is it forever a potential encroacher on the rights of individuals? Or is it the vehicle by which individuals secure their common interests? Is it defined by the preservation of private rights or the pursuit of public goods? Both? Yes, of course, both, but does this mean Ronald Reagan or Lyndon Johnson, Newt Gingrich or Jesse Jackson, supply-side or welfare economics? Anyone who thinks the sharp dichotomies thrown up by such choices can be easily blunted need only look at such contributions to the liberal-communitarian debate as Amitai Etzioni's *The Spirit of Community* or Stephen Holmes's book-length broadside against communitarianism called *The Anatomy of Liberalism*.[1] Or better yet, read *The Inner Ocean: Individualism and Democratic Culture*, George Kateb's cogently spirited collection of essays in which the idea of democratic individualism plays a prominent role.

Kateb is himself well aware of the instability of the tension and, having given lip service to the interdependence of individualism and democracy, has little trouble in articulating an eloquent argument on behalf of the individual, stripped of all communitarian entailments. "Government is always under suspicion," he concludes, scarcely before his argument is begun.[2] He favors a delicate balance, but there is little doubt that forced to choose, he would prefer the politics of Emerson to those of Jefferson, would prefer Thoreau to Paine, and if he had to cross the waters (he'd probably prefer not to), would prefer Nietzsche to Rousseau.

Yet his commitment to the linkage between democracy and individuality is sincere, as (for example) his deep devotion to racial equality makes evident. As slavery was a source of outrage to Thoreau, so racial injustice remains a source of outrage to Kateb. Slavery was a private economic system, ultimately defeated by the army of a state, and then constitutionally outlawed by that state. Here, democracy served individual rights through the state—though, some would say, it was the judiciary and not the democratic legislature that played the critical role. Is there, then, a missing piece that can help forge a more than hypothetical relationship between democracy and individualism? Between the adversarial state and the citizen individuals who in a democracy are its proprietors? I wish to suggest here that civil society and its ideology—the constitutional faith once identified with pluralism and now often associated with multiculturalism—may provide a civic culture within which individuality and democracy may coexist just a little less uncomfortably. My strategy will be to explore multiculturalism in a global perspective and hope that the comparative framework reinforces the arguments I have offered elsewhere about strong democracy, civil society, citizenship, and civic education.[3] France, where I recently spent a year occupying a "Chair of American Civilization" (the French deem it an oxymoron), is a particularly vivid exemplar of the challenge of a civic multiculturalism from a parallel but historically distinctive perspective.

America and France, "sister republics," share a need to reconcile multicultural and plural societies with an integral civic ideology of democracy. Issues that as recently as the 1980s seemed peculiarly American are now plaguing France as well. At the beginning of 1993, an American newspaper headline declared, "France Jails Woman for Daughter's Circumcision."[4] According to the article, Muslim women living in France are no longer to be allowed to "mutilate" their infant children's genitals. Having banned the chador from state schools, France can hardly honor the multicultural practice of clitorectomy.

Multiculturalism has also become an issue elsewhere. Turks with long-standing residence as guest workers in Germany have been burned out of their homes as "foreigners," at the same time their own country was persecuting the Kurdish minority at home. Muslims and Hindus in Britain have replicated the sectarian violence tearing India to shreds. Afghanistan has been unofficially (and unceremoniously) partitioned into three ethnic sections populated by warring tribes of Uzbeks (with a few Tajiks thrown in), Panthans, and Persian Afghans; China is threatened at the village level by a renewal of ancient clan rivalries; and under the euphemism "ethnic cleansing," the zealous tribes of the former Yugoslavia—until finally separated in 1996—engaged in mutual genocide in accord with an anarchic pecking order, which, while making every ethnic group the enemy of every other ethnic group, consistently put Muslims at the bottom of everyone's heap. Even Switzerland, Europe's traditional standing tribute to sustained multicultural nationalism, is at risk, its Francophone and Germanic populations angrily divided over the new relationship to the rest of Europe. In the autumn of 1992, a substantial majority of German-speakers aligned against any deepening of the relationship with the new Europe outvoted and thereby outraged the French-speakers, nearly 80 percent of whom had voted to strengthen the European connection. While the dismantling of the Helvetic Confederation (founded in 1848 in its modern form) is not at hand, Switzerland's troubles do not bode well for either Swiss multiculturalism or a united Europe. The *New York Times* welcomed Warren Christopher, President Clinton's Secretary of State, into office with an editorial noting that no incoming foreign minister "since World War II has inherited so varied and chaotic an agenda: turmoil in Bosnia, Iraq, Somalia, Haiti, Russia and a score of former Soviet Republics."[5]

These harrowing developments in a Europe in which history had supposedly drawn to a close (Fukayama) and that as recently as the early 1990s was supposedly undergoing an uneventful process of "democratization" in the east and forging a single European political and economic entity in the west have brought a once predominantly American debate into global relief. However acclaimed as a cultural appurtenance it has been in America, multiculturalism has become a haunting specter for Europe and the world beyond. Hence, although political correctness, a preoccupation with race and gender, and controversies about the "canon," along with the generic focus on multiculturalism that gives rise to them, may still generate more rhetoric in the United States than elsewhere, the pertinence of the debates to other continents is finally becoming apparent, and the lessons that America's experience can offer are being recognized. By the same token, the toxicity of cultural rifts in Europe may give pause to Americans who think cultural difference is exclusively an occasion for celebration and who tend to disregard the warnings of those, such as Arthur Schlesinger, Jr., who worry about the fragility of American unity.[6] The startling fact is that less than 10 percent of the modern world's states are truly homogeneous, and in only half does a single ethnic group comprise even 75 percent of the population.[7] Multiculturalism is the rule, homogeneity the exception. Widespread as multiculturalism is, can it reconcile individualism and the communities by which individuals identify themselves? Is America a model of such reconciliation?

Possibly. In fact, even the world's more traditionally homogeneous integral nations have good reason to pay the lessons of American multiculturalism some heed. The increasing economic and communicational interdependence of the world means that such nations, however unified internally, must nonetheless operate in an increasingly multicultural global environment. Ironically, a world that is coming together culturally and commercially is a world whose discrete subnational ethnic, religious, and racial parts are also far more in evidence. Forced into incessant contact, postmodern nations cannot sequester their idiosyncrasies. Post-Maastricht Europe, while it falls well short of earlier ambitions, has become integrated enough to force a continentwide multicultural awareness, whose consequences have by no means been happy, let alone unifying. The more "Europe" heaves into view, the more reluctant and self-aware its reluctant national constituents become. What Gunter Grass said of Germany—"Unified, the Germans were more disunited than ever"—applies in spades to Europe: integrated, it is more disintegral than ever.[8]

The American debate over national identity, multiculturalism, and the canon, which only a few years ago seemed esoteric in that exceptionalist way that American political debates can be, is suddenly attracting international attention.[9] How pertinent is it really? Can the Europeans and would-be multicultural democracies beyond Europe learn from America's national experience with pluralism?

AMERICA'S CONSTITUTIONAL FAITH

Perhaps the first question is whether the history of America's multicultural identity really has much in common with the revived tribalisms so prevalent elsewhere. The exceptionalist thesis has always exempted America from the world's currents, and some might argue that the American experiment in multiculturalism, like the American experiment *tout court*, is not a fit model of anything for anybody else at all. George Kateb has certainly treated America as a special case, and it is hard to know whether his take on individualism is intended for an audience beyond these shores or whether America remains for him, as it has been for so many other exceptionalists, a last best hope for liberty. Despite his enormous analytic skill, Kateb has remained an American parochial, reveling in America's virtues and worrying its vices like so many rare bones.

Yet underlying America's multicultural paradox is a Tocquevillean dilemma, poignantly rehearsed by Kateb, that is universal. Tocqueville noted that free liberal societies were likely to nourish a diversity that could undermine the social cohesion on which they depended for their stability. The nineteenth-century alliance of nationalism and liberalism had, after all, brought together two contradictory principles inclined to work in contrary directions—a nationalism that fostered uniformity, and a liberty that encouraged diversity. To the extent that societies were defined by an integral nationalism, they became hostile to liberty. Yet at the same time, free societies, more than most others, needed the unity and cohesion that their liberty tended to deny them (or, when unity arose out of religion or nationalism, that liberty undermined).

America faced this dilemma early on, seeking a surrogate for religion in new civic beliefs—what Justice Hugo Black later called constitutional faith (*Verfassungspatriotismus*, in the term used by Habermas.) Because—as with so many so-called "peoples" elsewhere today—Americans then were divided by private religious faith, by race and gender, and by class and ethnic origins, they could have no faith in common other than a faith in the commons: a fidelity to the Constitution as a set of broad principles uniting them under common democratic and legal processes. Whereas in places such as the former Yugoslavia, private faith has become a public identity subject to civic repression, the American constitutional faith is faith in a civil society that, precisely by separating public from private, permits private differences and private freedoms to flourish without jeopardizing the political commons.

Now, to be sure, the actual story of America has often failed to live up to and has frequently even contradicted its constitutional aspirations. As Judith N. Shklar wrote in her remarkable last book, *American Citizenship*, "[F]rom the first, the most radical claims for freedom and political equality were played out in counterpoint to chattel slavery, the most extreme form of servitude."[10] And George Kateb tends with some justification to regard resisters and dissenters, such as Thoreau as better friends to equality than the mainstream "democratic" civic culture that tolerated slavery for so long. Yet even where constitutional faith has been bad faith, it has offered a promise of unity in an otherwise vast and diversified republic of continental extent. The quarrels over multiculturalism today are not really new: when Arthur Schlesinger, Jr., worries that the celebration of difference may occlude a fragile unity, he only rehearses nineteenth-century anxieties about America's capacity to absorb wave after wave of non-WASP immigrants.[11]

Is it possible, then, that the American constitutional faith that has helped to bridge individual rights and community identity proffers a solution to Europe's recidivist tribalisms? Is there an equivalent of constitutional faith for India or Nigeria or the former Yugoslavia or Somalia that would pull the tribes off one another and nurture a framework for political unity? In America, constitutional faith has lost its novel artificial look. It has become conventional. Like an old shoe, it fits comfortably, and its wearers need not examine too carefully how it was cobbled or whether its origins are legitimate. But beyond American shores, constitutional faith has to be manufactured afresh each time a fractious nation-state tries to dissuade its fragments from flying apart. In the absence of a history of commitment to common civil practices, such an aridly secular faith is unlikely to draw much fealty. For what is its substance to be? Who is the "We" in Europe's or India's or Russia's "We the people"? Are the common principles exclusively commercial and technological, as Eurocrats in Strasburg and Bruxelles often intimate? Or is there a potential civic element as well? For example, democracy?

THE RETRIBALIZATION OF THE WORLD

America has fifty states and perhaps a dozen or two powerful ethnic, racial, and religious subcultures. The membership roll of the United Nations, on the other hand, is approaching two hundred, and only a handful of its subscriber nations are culturally homogenous (less than twenty). When we count the civil wars being tracked by the U.S. Department of State, an even more complex reality is revealed.[12] In this tumultuous world, the real players are not nations but tribes of one kind or another, perhaps even clans—this is a world in which the United Nations could quickly grow to as many as a thousand ethnically based "nations." It is not too difficult to imagine a constitutional faith that would be apposite to the French or Germans. But for Basques and Normans and Alsatians and Bavarians and East Prussians? And what of Kurds, Puerto Ricans, Ossetians, East Timoreans, Quebecois, Abkhasians, Catalonians, Tamils, Slovaks, Inkatha Zulus, Palestinians, Kurile Islander Japanese—peoples without countries inhabiting nations they cannot call their own, tribes wanting to seal themselves off not just from other tribes but from modernity and all its commercial and technological integrating forces? How will peoples who define themselves by the slaughter of tribal neighbors residing next door be persuaded to subscribe to some flimsy artificial markets? Is the American model really of any relevance at all?

There is considerable irony in the revival of nationalism in the postnationalist world—for nationalism was initially a force for unification in Europe, bringing together rival clans and tribes under the figment of a larger territorial nation bound together by language and culture if not blood and kinship. But having won its victories of integration, nationalism changed its strategy, becoming a divisive force in the territories it once helped tie together. Back in the 1920s, in his *Revolt of the Masses*, Ortega y Gasset observed how during periods of consolidation, nationalism tends to be a unifier with a "positive value," while in less coherent periods it becomes fractious and negative, a kind of identity "mania."

In America, identity politics have served to define one-half of a hyphenated personality: an "Italian-American" or a "African-American." The distinctive prefix is how immigrants get assimilated into the common suffix. The only "American-Americans" are native American Indians, so to be an American *is* otherwise to have a distinctive pre-American identity. To be hyphenated *is* to be an American! But elsewhere, ethnic particularity has been a basis for isolation, separation, and hostility. And as traditional multicultural nation-states are destabilized, subnationalist movements have a nightmarish tendency to crop up like cancerous cells within cancerous cells, each anarchic fragment threatening to destroy the larger segments of which it is a nominal part. America had to endure a civil war in which one great region attempted to secede from the whole. Once secession gets under way, it is hard to stop—which is why Americans worry that identity politics may be carried too far, even in America's assimilationist culture.

The experience elsewhere is not encouraging. Russia's secession from the Soviet Union was scarcely completed when Northern Ossetia became an internal problem for Russia. Since then, the Ingush minority (less than 10 percent of Northern Ossetia's population of 650,000) has risen against the Ossetians, with Russian troops trying at once to keep the two factions from each other's throats and to preserve the unity of Russia from the secessionist inclinations of both. Yeltsin's deputy administrator in Vladikavkaz has said, "The task is to make a man forget his memories"[13]—a task about as promising as pursuing universal peace by hoping that men will forget their will to aggression.

OLD IDEOLOGIES AND A NEW CONSTITUTIONAL FAITH

In truth, old memories linger on, poisoning every attempt at establishing new forms of artificial unity. There were once colonial and neocolonial alternatives to constitutional faith—effective, if costly, antidotes to ethnic factionalism—but their time is past. Ethnic nationalism was frequently kept in check and the politics of difference offset by imperialism in both its capitalist-colonialist and its neocolonialist communist variants. Ironically, these two versions of civic faith have themselves been rival ideologies for the last hundred years, not least of all during the cold war. Yet both communism and capitalism hoped to unify the peoples over whom they sought dominion through the imposition of radical economic secularism, whether in the form of transnational capital markets or in the form of transnational proletarian rule. The cry "Workers of the world, unite," like the call for free trade and open markets, is always a threat to ethnic identity. Imperialist economic strategies (whether statist or market), however odious they might have been, did keep rival ethnic factions in check. The great nineteenth-century empires, rooted in economic rather than ethnic suzerainty, held together quite astonishing coalitions of peoples who were naturally at odds. The Ottoman, the Austro-Hungarian, and the Russian empires were among the most inclusive associations of peoples the world has known, at least since the time of the Roman Empire. Whatever their depredations with respect to liberty, rights, and self-determination, they did inhibit the centrifugal instincts of the multiple tribes and factions they held together through a combination of coercion and economic interest, and they inoculated the nineteenth century, endowing it with a relative immunity to large-scale war (if not to revolution) that has been the envy of our own, all too bloody century.

Communism played a similar role in holding together the old Russian empire after its dissolution, keeping the lid on secessionist and fractious sentiments among the nationalities by the ruthless imposition of a secular ideology of collectivism. In the Soviet Union, communism worked against domestic insurrection for over seventy years, and even in Eastern Europe and the Baltics, where it came as an entirely alien intrusion imposed by force, it kept rival peoples from one another's throats for at least forty years.

The rapid disintegration of whatever unity had been achieved in the Baltics, Eastern Europe, the former Yugoslavia, and the former Soviet Union reveals both how important to continuing transnational unity the victory of communist imperialism was and how Pyrrhic it turned out to be in the long run. What, then, is left that can bind together multiethnic and multireligious societies? Neither liberals concerned with individual rights and the rule of law nor communitarians interested in local democracy are happy with the choices. Both seem loathe to support the classical nineteenth-century liberal principle of self-determining nations, for fear of underwriting global balkanization. President Wilson's own Secretary of State, Robert L. Lansing, failed to share his chief's enthusiasm, asking whether self-determination would not "breed discontent, disorder and rebellion? The phrase is simply loaded with dynamite. It will raise hopes which can never be realized. It will, I fear, cost thousands of lives. What a calamity that the phrase was ever uttered! What misery it will cause!"[14] No wonder that even Amitai Etzioni, an ardent American supporter of communitarianism, worries about the "evils of self-determination,"[15] while Joseph S. Nye editorializes in the *Washington Post* about "The Self-Determination Trap."[16]

The capitalist market remains an alternative of sorts: I have written about it elsewhere under the rubric of "McWorld"—encompassing "economic and ecological forces that demand integration and uniformity and that mesmerize the world with fast music, fast computers, and fast food—with MTV, Macintosh and McDonald's—pressing nations into [a] commercially homogenous global network: one McWorld tied together by technology, ecology, communications, and commerce."[17] McWorld certainly remains tribalism's most formidable rival, and in the long run it may even manage to attenuate the force of the world current recidivist tribalisms. But in the short run, it does little to soften ethnic passions. We have seen Croat irregulars standing over the bodies of innocent civilians they have just slain, smoking American cigarettes, wearing Adidas and blue jeans, and otherwise sporting all of the insignia of the global markets as they pursue policies of sectarian genocide and ethnic cleansing. As certain strains of American and Caribbean rap music have become anti-Semitic and homophobic, certain varieties of German rock have become a virulent propaganda instrument of skinhead bigotry. Pop music as a global harmonizer is a fading 1960s dream. "We are the world," sing the do-good musical naifs from Memphis and Hollywood, but they clearly are not the world: Sony, Time-Warner, Microsoft, Pepsico, and Disney are the world.

Yet it is only in the esoteric domain of rational choice theory that economic calculation seems to outweigh ethnic passion, so even if McWorld ultimately succeeds in integrating the world commercially, there is little guarantee that it will render it more democratic or rights-regarding. Hence, we come back to the question with which we started: can some version of constitutional faith on the American model bring relief to multicultural societies under duress from tribalism and thus prone to anarchy? Can it even be counted on to bridge radical individual rights and insistent communitarian values in America, where, "democratic individualism" notwithstanding, they seem to be increasingly at odds?

DEMOCRATIC CONSTITUTIONAL FAITH
AS TRIBALISM ANTIDOTE

There may be a form of constitutional faith that responds to the new tribal-ism, but it will not be a faith simply borrowed lock, stock, and barrel from America, Switzerland, or some other successful multicultural society. Civic faith depends in part precisely on its adaptability to the circumstances and conditions of particular peoples at particular historical moments. There are different kinds of difference, alternative versions of multiculturalism—even in America, where, for example, the difficulties of the African American heirs to slavery are very different from those of black immigrants from the Caribbean (who are very successful in their assimilation into America).

Attempting to paper over the fissures in the former Yugoslavia by import-ing an American civic ideology is no more likely to succeed than attempting to prop up its democracy by importing American political party institutions. Technology transfer sometimes works; institution transfer almost never does. Democratic institutions succeed because they are molded to the land-scape in which they are grounded and planted in the soil of a well-established civil society. This has been the lesson of all political theory from Montesquieu and Rousseau to Madison and Tocqueville, both of whom demanded a new science of politics for a new society.

Nonetheless, several of the formal principles involved in establishing a successful civil society are relevant. A constitutional faith pertinent to na-tions comprising rival ethnic fragments requires a civic ideology in which difference itself is recognized and honored. This is the secret of Switzerland's remarkable multicultural, multiconfessional success: Italian, though the lan-guage of only a tiny minority of Swiss, remains a national language; Raeto-Romansch, though spoken by only a few tens of thousands in the single canton of Graubuenden, is an official language of that canton.[18]

Second, the honoring of difference must be accompanied by some territo-rial or geographical expression of it, ideally through federal or confederal institutions. Partition destroys a civil society; federation preserves it, while acknowledging the relative autonomy of the parts. The failed Owen/Vance solution for Bosnia tried to find its way between partition and federalism, in a situation that manifests the worst case situation: hostile ethnic groups intermingled in populations that are not geographically discrete and nearly impossible to disentangle other than by relocation (a euphemism for expul-sion). The Owen/Vance plan multiplied the number and reduced the size of confederal units to a point where every small ethnic neighborhood had some autonomy, but, of course, this finally cannot work unless a society is carved into units the size of a town street or three or four adjacent houses or apartments. Such solutions that try only to keep rival groupings apart are not so much dealing with bigotry and hatred as yielding to them. Bloody as the American Civil War was, it was fought in the name of union, not dissolution. Most modern civil wars are fought by both sides in the name of partition, the point of contention being only who gets how much of what.

Furthermore, in the American case, separation has always been a short-term tactic belonging to a long-term strategy of integration. The parts are honored to strengthen their tie to the whole and to demonstrate that the ideology of the whole represents not the hegemony of one group but a (potentially) genuine inclusiveness. Unless working together is seen as crucial to the survival of the parts, the parts will inevitably come to view themselves as a diaspora of some other (perhaps invisible) blood nation, whose reconstruction will come to be seen as the only avenue to preservation. Unhappily, the antagonism of one group may actually ignite a defensive separatist identity in some other group that had previously seen itself as assimilated. Thus, Bosnian and Croatian Muslims, secularized and assimilated into Yugoslav life, became self-consciously Islamic and separatist only in the face of continuing aggression by their erstwhile countrymen and neighbors. Likewise, a Greek Orthodox minority that was not respected inside Croatia became a force not only for an independent Macedonia but a likely inducement for Greek (and then Turkish) intervention into Croatian affairs.

Federalism is probably too aggressive and centralist a solution for countries as fractured as Croatia or Afghanistan. Confederalism may be more promising. The *Federalist Papers* have been required reading for foreign nationals seeking an American solution to their multicultural difficulties for some time now, but I would offer the *Articles of Confederation* as a far more relevant document. Article III of the *Articles* would seem to provide a relatively modest framework for holding rival nations, such as Czechland and Slovakia or Serbia and Croatia, together. It provides for the autonomy of the member states and honors their independence, but it also declares:

> The said states hereby severally enter into a firm league of friendship with each other, for their common defense, the security of their liberties, and their mutual and general welfare, binding themselves to assist each other against all force offered to, or attacks made upon them, or any of them, on account of religion, sovereignty, trade, or any other pretense whatever.

Article IV provides that "the free inhabitants of each" state "shall be entitled to all the privileges and immunities of free citizens in the several states, and the people of each state shall have free ingress and regress to and from any other state, and shall enjoy therein all the privileges of trade and commerce." Similar provisions held together the Helvetic Confederation from 1291 down to 1800, when Napoleon tried in vain to impose a unitary constitution on the recalcitrant cantons. The splintered factions of many a ruptured nation could do worse than reconceive themselves in terms of a "firm league of friendship."

The problem remains what to do with minorities *within* each confederal region. Initially, in the most volatile regions, where, as in Bosnia, deeply hostile groups are inextricably mingled (the Vance/Owen map trying to separate them was a nightmarish, ultimately futile exercise in micro-gerrymandering), some form of external intervention will probably be required: a security shield that protects them from civil fratricide while they labor to establish a civil society. The shield need not necessarily be the United Nations, which has had a mixed record in its peacekeeping efforts. A coalition of forces, such as NATO or the Common Market, or a powerful neighbor (Russia in Serbia or the United States in Haiti, for example) can also offer outside authority. It certainly seems unlikely that any map, however tortured, can bring peace to Armenia or the former Yugoslavia or the Sudan in the absence of armed enforcement—no lasting peace without war, or its threat. Even America failed to secure its multiculturalism in a setting of tolerance until it had fought a bloody civil conflagration.

Yet the presence of foreign peacekeepers, even when effective in the short term (and it often is not), cannot do more than buy time and a provisional setting for long-term internal solutions. The American Civil War set the stage for a Reconstruction that failed to pay off on the promise of justice. How much did Lincoln's battle for the American soul achieve? The proof ultimately is in the internal, noncoercive settlement.

Some still think there is hope in economics, but as the discussion of what I have called McWorld suggested, economic markets, while they may attenuate the sharpness of internecine divisions, do little to soften hatred or reduce the sorts of deep-seated bigotry that lead to tribal war or ethnic cleansing/genocide. Russia has become an exemplar of both wild capitalism and criminal fratricide. Germany's economic miracle and its leadership in the Common Market did not translate into immunity against domestic violence or against the rage aimed at foreigners. The integrating forces of McWorld operate best where there is relative tranquility and social order. They are no substitute for internal reconciliation.

Here, there may be no alternative to a civil religion of reciprocal rights and mutual respect. Such a civic faith cannot be contrived from scratch but must emerge out of civil institutions, such as public schools, civil associations, charitable organizations, common customs, and a shared civic consciousness—the very institutions that constitute a robust civil society and that either have never taken root or have failed in so many of Eastern Europe's disintegrating states. Such institutions create the basis for multiple identities: cross-cutting cleavages that allow people to think of neighbors separated from them by ethnic or religious background as sharing other objectives and ends—the common values arising out of, for example, union or parent-teacher association or political party membership. Difference needs to be offset against common membership ("As African Americans, we deserve equal respect and equal treatment before the law"), rather than being used as an argument for separation ("As Croatians, we deserve a country of our own"). In America, difference has served to legitimize inclusion; in Europe it has too often served to rationalize exclusion. Our civic faith in "We the people" as a formula for inclusion has much to do with whatever success Americans have had in forging democracy.

For most important of all in establishing a viable constitutional faith, is democracy itself. Democratic institutions put flesh on the bones of civic identity and give to individualism something more than the sterility of abstract personhood. They turn mutual respect into a set of necessary political practices. More than anything else, it has been the absence of democratic institutions in Russia, the former Yugoslavia, Afghanistan, Somalia, Liberia, Czechoslovakia, and all the other disintegrating multicultural nations that has aided and abetted tendencies to ethnic fragmentation and national dissolution. By the same token, it has been America's and Canada's and Belgium's and Switzerland's democratic practices that have held together peoples and civic cultures that on their own would have been little less vulnerable to the siren call of ethnicity than the Yugoslavs or the Afghans.

As strategy, this suggests a need to reprioritize: put democracy first as the foundation of civil society, and resistance to fragmentation may follow. Ethnicity is unlikely to create a form of democracy that can contain and limit it; democracy can create a form of ethnicity that is self-limiting. When rights are taken seriously and perceived as defining individuals and groups, it is easier to attach them to minority ethnic groups under pressure and to persuade majority ethnic groups that expressing their own identity as exclusion violates their civil faith. Putting democracy first means treating it as a way of life, not just as a set of institutions. When democratic political practice is rooted in membership in the community and empowers community members in a larger civic polity, ethnic and religious traits grow less crucial in forging a public identity. The American separation of church and state not only protected the state from religion, it protected religion from the state and from other rival belief systems, and thus strengthened it. When liberal democracy separates the public and the private, it actually enlarges the space for the exercise of private religion and ethnicity, while insulating them from their potential public consequences—intolerance, for example.

Ethnicity is a healthy expression of identity, which, however, like a healthy cell, is susceptible to pathologies that turn the growth mechanism against itself. Like many anxious pathologists of community, George Kateb sometimes seems to mistake the pathology for the normal cell. It is true that a cell gone bad results in a cancer that destroys not only the body around it (the larger nation) but the cell itself (the ethnic entity), but the cure for cancer is not a preemptive strike against cells simply because, like all normal cells, they are cancer prone. Rather, the object is to immunize them. Democracy, as it turns out, appears to be part of the cure. It is ethnicity's immunological key: the source of its normalcy and its capacity to control its own growth to make it compatible with the growth of other cells, and hence the basis for its ability to participate in the building of a stable body politic.

Perhaps the time has come for those states around the world falling into warring pieces to stop worrying about keeping the parts together and to start worrying about how to make the parts democratic—to recognize that the true source of America's measured and all too partial but still significant success as a multicultural society is its democratic civic faith. Likewise, one might say to George Kateb, the goal of a modern Emersonian should not be to protect individuals from communities but to assure that communities and the individuals who comprise them are genuinely democratic and thus less in need of protection from one another.

NOTES

1. Amitai Etzioni, *The Spirit of Community* (New York: Crown Publishers, 1993); and Stephen Holmes, *The Anatomy of Liberalism* (Cambridge: Harvard University Press, 1993).

2. See George Kateb, *The Inner Ocean: Individualism and Democratic Culture*, (Ithaca, N.Y.: Cornell University Press, 1992), p. 1.

3. See Benjamin R. Barber, *Strong Democracy: Participatory Politics for a New Age* (Berkeley: University of California Press, 1984); and Barber, *An Aristocracy of Everyone: The Politics of Education and the Future of America* (New York: Ballantine Books, 1992).

4. "France Jails Woman for Daughter's Circumcision," *New York Times*, January 11, 1993, p. A8.

5. "Reinventing Foreign Policy," *New York Times Week in Review*, January 24, 1993, sec. 4, p. 10.

6. Arthur Schlesinger, Jr., *The Disuniting of America* (New York: Norton, 1993).

7. Joseph Nye, "The Self-Determination Trap," *Washington Post National Weekly Edition*, December 21–27, 1992, p. 28.

8. Gunter Grass, quoted in Marla Stone, "Nationalism and Identity in (Former) East Germany," *Tikkun* 7, no. 6 (November/December, 1992): 41–46.

9. The Spring 1992 issue of *Le Débat* carried several essays (including one by François Furet) on the American experience with multiculturalism, political correctness, and gender studies.

10. Judith N. Shklar, *American Citizenship: The Quest for Inclusion*, (Cambridge: Harvard University Press, 1992), p. 1.

11. See Barber, *Strong Democracy* and *Aristocracy of Everyone*.

12. In the early 1990s, a front-page story on ethnic wars listed forty-eight trouble spots. David Binder with Barbara Crossette, "As Ethnic Wars Multiply, U.S. Strives for a Policy," *New York Times*, February 7, 1993, pp. 1, 14. The Carter Center in Atlanta, Georgia, has an even more comprehensive and startling list.

13. Quoted in *Newsweek*, December 7, 1992, p. 34.

14. Cited in David Binder, "Ethnic Wars Multiply," *New York Times*,

February 7, 1993, p. 1. Of course, Lansing was no friend of Wilson's vision, and actually worked to undermine aspects of his policies.

15. Amitai Etzioni, "The Evils of Self-Determination," *Foreign Policy*, no. 89 (Winter 1992–93): 21–35.

16. Nye, "Self-Determination Trap."

17. Benjamin R. Barber, *Jihad versus McWorld*, New York Times Books, 1995.

18. For a discussion see Benjamin R. Barber, "Participation and Swiss Democracy," *Government and Opposition* 23, no. 1 (1988): 31–50.

Walden Three:
Postmodern Ecology and Its Precursors

LESLIE PAUL THIELE

THIS IS AN ESSAY about conceptual revolutions. It concerns modern and postmodern developments in the seemingly perennial struggle between the individual and the environment. With a scope so grandiose, this essay predictably indulges in generalization, and perhaps caricature. In apology, I can only say that my chief concern—a conceptual analysis of the postmodern ecological revolution—gains a needed historical background from the cursory tales told of its predecessors. My presentation of the postmodern ecological revolution is informed by Martin Heidegger's own conceptual upheaval.

Let me present the argument succinctly. America has experienced five conceptual revolutions that have significantly affected social and political thinking—the bourgeois revolution, the socialist revolution, the romantic revolution, the behavioral revolution, and the postmodern ecological revolution. The dynamic force of these revolutions consists of a confrontation between the individual and the perceived demands and dangers of the natural and cultural environments. I call these events revolutions not because they were all conceived in secrecy and initiated in blood, or because they all effected historic institutional change. I call them revolutions because each undermined or overturned prevalent conceptions of the individual's relation to the environment and because the stakes for each were freedom.

I shall discuss these revolutions in what amounts to a rough chronological order, submitting each to three questions: (1) Which theorist (native or non-native) best serves as the revolution's conceptual parent? (2) What is the revolution's central conflict and tentative resolution? (3) Whom might we designate as its internal critic, that is, which adversary best illustrates the revolution's dangers and shortcomings because he or she shares certain of its most crucial assumptions? While the stories of these conceptual revolutions are told in an American context, one might generalize to consider them features of Western social and political thought at large.

THE BOURGEOIS REVOLUTION

America's bourgeois revolution played itself out concretely in the struggle for independence and constitutional stability. Its representative theorist is

John Locke, who held an unrivaled position of influence in the minds of the Founders. Locke had declared that "in the beginning, all the World was America."[1] The Founders did, indeed, conceive of America as a land of inexhaustible riches and a pristine world of its own. But the advent of property and trade, or more specifically, the advent of its taxation without representation, changed all that. Property, the Founders agreed with Locke, was safe neither in conditions of anarchy nor under tyranny. Tyranny, after all, was simply a kind of anarchy. It was a state of war—not of all against all, but of one against all.

Locke understood the bourgeois revolution's central conflict to be between the individual and a natural environment of relatively unrestrained animal instincts. The chief purpose of the revolution was to ensure the individual's escape from this state of nature and the insecurity to property that it fostered. In the American colonies, this anarchic state was established by a (foreign) monarch whose relation to his subjects was not mediated by law and right but by arbitrary rule. With the revolution of independence, a savage land, or rather, a land savaged by a lawless king, became a just and productive society bonded equitably by means of a social contract. A *novus ordo seclorum*, a new order of the world, was achieved through the revolutionary struggle for freedom from monarchical oppression. It was a victory of the socialized group over the tyranny of (the king's) unrestrained drives.

Locke assumed the individual to be a tabula rasa, a blank slate, upon which the social environment inscribed its dictates. The revolutionary social contract constituted a reinscription of the American *tabula*, at once wiping out the lessons learned in the anarchic-tyrannic state of nature while instituting the habits of cooperative production. The freedom struggled for and won was chiefly the negative liberty safeguarding the sanctity of property, which, for Locke, included the property of one's body. The American bourgeois revolution established the individual's sovereignty, mediated by law, over its private domain.

As an internal critic of the bourgeois revolution, Jean-Jacques Rousseau shared with Locke the goal of a social contract that politicized a former state of nature and curtailed despotic power. For Rousseau, however, the bourgeois contract was a tragic resolution. The reason is that Rousseau conceives "natural man"—that is, the human being in the state of nature—in much better terms than does Locke. Instincts are for the most part benign and nonacquisitive. Consequently, the state of nature remains largely hostility-free. Rousseau's charge (leveled chiefly at Hobbes but also applicable to Locke) is that the theorists of the bourgeois revolution project back onto natural man the degenerate traits that develop only in society. For all that, Rousseau does not believe that we might regain our noble savagery. Unadulterated liberty has been forever lost. Rousseau therefore concludes that our socialization and politicization must be more extensive than was assumed by the bourgeois theorists.

"The course of human misery is the contradiction between man and citizen. Give him wholly to the state or to himself," Rousseau grandly writes.

"If you divide his heart you tear him apart."[2] Once contaminated by the amour propre of social life, the individual can never again be given wholly to him- or herself. Accordingly, Rousseau seeks to transform the individual egoism of the bourgeoisie into a collective egoism. Ideally, *amour de patrie* would replace amour propre. The individual is to be given wholly to the state in order to rediscover liberty (now in positive form) under its aegis. The prospects for success in this endeavor, however, are not good. The bourgeois revolution won its victory primarily at the expense of the state of nature. But it also won at the expense of the state, and, Rousseau laments, at the expense of nature itself. The sense of organic collective life—the impulse behind political theory from Plato and Aristotle through the medievalists—was effectively extinguished by the bourgeois revolt against monarchy. Rousseau concludes that the liberal social contract, by championing the negative liberty of the productive individual, not only subdued the savage but destroyed the savage's natural nobility as well.

In sum, the bourgeois revolution marks the struggle of the individual with a lawless environment of brute instinct. The socialization of anarchic drives, for Locke, yields productive, acquisitive individuals, who define their freedom as sovereign control over a private domain. Once aggregated, these individuals, whose separate domains of sovereignty can be sustained only by law, constitute an independent republic. Internal critics of the revolution, like Rousseau, worry that an aggregation of sovereign individuals will not a community make. Only a transfer of sovereignty from the individual to the state can ensure community while at the same time giving birth to liberty in its positive form.

THE SOCIALIST REVOLUTION

As with the bourgeois revolution, the story of the socialist revolution has been told too many times to require more than a sketch. The revolution's chief theorist is Marx. Its object is to turn the bourgeois revolution on its head, allowing society to subdue the egoistic individual and reestablish a natural, organic community. What is natural to humankind is not its property-producing labor, as Locke has it, but its essence as a *Gattungswesen*, a species-being. The struggle between the possessive, bourgeois individual and the proletariat (or its vanguard, the species-being *in ovum*) constitutes the socialist revolution's central conflict. Once revolutionary struggle destroys classes, an unalienated communal life may be reestablished. History then reaches its culmination, and stops. Positive liberty is achieved in the self-realization of humankind. Individuals are repatriated to their true nature, which at this historical juncture corresponds to a technologically productive and materially abundant life in a classless society. Humankind becomes master of itself and its history.

The socialist revolution was experienced in America mostly vicariously and in a much attenuated form. Its bloodier European (and later Asian) variants served as a warning or confirmation of what social needs required addressing, but what social battles should not be fought. In the New World, the mitigation of class conflict was achieved by the relatively successful governmental intervention into the dynamics of a capitalist economy and, perhaps more important, by a uniformly strong culture of liberal individualism. The revolution's attenuated form corresponds chiefly to the early stirrings of trade unionism and the subsequent era of the New Deal. The proletariat would not emerge from these periods so much victorious as co-opted. The bourgeois individual, in turn, was coaxed into the management of a welfare state.

"I believe in individualism," the populist Franklin Roosevelt remarked, "up to the point where the individualist starts to operate at the expense of society." These words, from Roosevelt's acceptance speech at the 1936 Democratic National Convention, indicate the extent to which the pragmatic, liberal American mind strayed toward a socialist worldview. American society gained the semblance of a corporate existence. Though not exactly conceived as organic, neither was it reduced to an aggregate of atomized egos. Society deserved protection from its more rapacious elements. But the head of government, it was assumed, could safeguard the body politic from the greatest indignities perpetrated by its self-seeking limbs, the all-too-rugged individuals. A more radical remedy was shunned.

As an internal critic of the socialist revolution, we might choose the social anarchist Mikhail Bakunin. If Rousseau makes us uneasy with the celebration of Locke's victorious rule in America, then Bakunin serves an analogous purpose with regard to Marx's successes elsewhere. Bakunin claims that the dissolution of community fostered by the bourgeoisie is very insufficiently and very dangerously remedied by the revolutionary state. Like Marx, Bakunin conceived the socialist revolution as a means to escape economic and political domination and achieve a radical freedom. Like Marx, Bakunin hoped the socialist revolution would secure the victory of renaturalized humanity over those betrayals of its species-being perpetrated by bourgeois society. But unlike Marx, Bakunin was suspicious of the dictatorship of any organized group, however temporary its proposed tenure.

Any vanguard acceding to power, Bakunin warns, "will no longer represent the people, but only themselves and their claims to rulership over the people." Bakunin concludes, "Those who doubt this know very little about human nature."[3] Bakunin was chary of the pastoral professions of governing elites. Their revolutionary ideals, he held, masked a lust for power that would never exit history's stage. Karl Marx, taking this criticism rather personally, counseled Bakunin to "send all his nightmares about authority to the devil."[4] Apparently a nerve had been struck.

In sum, the socialist revolution marks the struggle between the inherently social individual and an environment of economic exigencies that foster egoism. Precipitated by artificial scarcity and labor-based alienation, the revolution aims to secure freedom through social sovereignty and material abundance. No longer isolated and oppressed, liberated individuals rediscover and recreate their humanity through the production of a public domain and public goods. Internal critics, such as Bakunin, suggest that any newly anointed priesthood presiding over society will quickly assume all the powers and prerogatives of the old. Both social sovereignty and individual liberty will then be sacrificed upon the altar of expediency by the revolutionary vanguard.

THE ROMANTIC REVOLUTION

The romantic revolution erupted in defiance of the institutions of the bourgeois revolution and the insinuations of the socialist revolution. Unlike its predecessors, the romantic revolution is characterized more by philosophic musing, poetic recollection, and individual lifestyle than collective practice. But its enduring effect on the American psyche is evident.

The revolution's characteristically American architects are Ralph Waldo Emerson, Henry David Thoreau, and Walt Whitman. These thinkers and poets contemplate, practice, and sing paeans to the life of the renaturalized spirit. Their goal is, primarily, to escape the conventions and constraints of bourgeois society, and, secondarily, to eschew the seductions of communal life. The American romantics demurely applaud the ideals of the socialist revolution but reject its program. Aspects of species-being are celebrated, to be sure, but the essential solitude of thought and spirit militates against its actualization. The American romantics affirm the organic whole of humankind. But this affirmation occurs chiefly in poetry and thought. It bespeaks less a desire for the individual's inclusion in the whole than the individual's expansion to a whole. Whitman opens his *Leaves of Grass* with celebratory ambivalence: "One's-self I sing, a simple separate person, / Yet utter the Democratic, the word En-Masse." His *Song of Myself* begins with a similar panegyric—not to the individual *in* community but to the individual *as* community. Whitman writes, "I celebrate myself, and sing myself, / And what I assume you shall assume, / For every atom belonging to me as good belongs to you."[5] Thoreau and Emerson declare a similar allegiance.

Like Marx, Thoreau sees the division of labor as the chief evil. When that division is built upon slavery and war, it necessitates, for Thoreau, a "peaceable revolution." The division of labor robs the individual of the most precious experiences, foremost being harmony with life's natural processes. It makes one less than a whole person. Unlike Marx, however, Thoreau maintains that indenturing oneself to the community is no better than selling oneself to the capitalist. In both cases, the individual is robbed of the breath and breadth of life. Unlike Marx, Thoreau does not believe that technological progress will facilitate escape from alienation or win freedom. More than likely, technology will only further distance individuals from the earth and encourage their servitude. The realm of necessity will simply be expanded to incorporate a dependence on mechanical contraptions and the social customs they engender. Thus Thoreau waxes philosophic on the freedom of time and spirit gained by walking to the next town rather than taking the train, for the latter project entails submitting to wage labor in order to earn the fare.

With these thoughts in mind, Thoreau set out with an axe in hand for Walden Pond. There, he would attempt to "live deliberately" and "deep," and "suck out all the marrow of life."[6] At Walden, Thoreau sought to prove both Locke and Rousseau wrong at once: individuals could retain their civilization and yet regain their savage nobility and radical liberty. The key to squaring this circle, it seems, was being an American. Thoreau writes, "The Atlantic is a Lethean stream, in our passage over which we have had an opportunity to forget the Old World and its institutions."[7] Thoreau's image of the New World and its opportunities has become an indelible part of the American dream. In this dream, the sovereign individual becomes the analogue of the sovereign state: interfering with and harming no one, yet benefiting all by distant example. Perhaps this dream is the only one Thoreau could have dreamt. It was consistent with a character that dictated an educated solitude. Ralph Waldo Emerson, Thoreau's one-time close friend, would see fit to remark: "If I knew only Thoreau, I should think cooperation of good men impossible."

Emerson, like Whitman and Thoreau, celebrates the community via the individual. Ultimately, the individual is part of an organic whole, as conceived in heaven if not on earth. "It is one soul which animates all men," Emerson declares in *The American Scholar*. Elsewhere, we discover the ethical component of this faith. "Only the good profits," Emerson writes, "which we can taste with all doors open, and which serves all men."[8] However, Emerson himself declined to participate in the organized attempt to live with all doors open. He would politely refuse when asked to join the experiment in communal living at Brook Farm. While Emerson held the motives of this experiment to be "noble and generous," he did not "put much trust in any arrangements or combinations, only in the spirit which dictates them." Emerson venerated the aspiration of an unselfish communal life, but he could not abide its inconveniences. More important, he could not tolerate its threat to an autonomous mind and spirit.

Emerson's work, like his life, is a celebration of the "infinitude of the private man." We are truly free only when we think, Emerson declares. And one decidedly cannot think en masse. Emerson insists that "no society can ever be as large as one man," that the "perfect State" consists of the "republican at home," and that a political "union is only perfect when all the uniters are isolated." With emendation of Thoreau in mind, we suspect, Emerson adds that this isolation must not be "mechanical." It must be "spiritual," a sort of "elevation." Emerson's chief concern is cultivating individual freedom within the realm of social necessity. His goal is the elevation and expansion of the beautiful soul in the midst of a useful but spiritually and intellectually threatening social existence.

The American romantics are wary of the ideals of the socialist revolt and reject its practicalities. But their chief struggle is waged elsewhere. They rally themselves against the insidious effects of bourgeois life. The bourgeoisie perpetrate through convention what the socialist threatens to impose through revolution: the dissolution of the individual into the social. The society that Emerson castigates in his *Self-Reliance* as a "conspiracy" against the individual was not to be found at Brook Farm. It was evident in the complacent, conventionalized life of hometown Concord. This is the life, as Thoreau lamented, that is "frittered away by detail." The chief threat to the great and infinite individual issues not from fledgling socialist visions of universal accord, but from hegemonic, philistine yearnings for commodities, comforts, and everyday habits. The texts of heroism that Emerson lauded as "sallies of freedom" were fast disappearing from the world around him, and for the most venal of reasons. Social conformity and the pursuit of wealth had gone a long way to exterminating what was great in the individual. "Not till we have lost the world do we begin to find ourselves," Thoreau insists. The discovery of the infinite self is only to be made upon the grave of materially acquisitive and spiritually complacent bourgeois lives, lives of "quiet desperation."

The romantic individual's task is not to escape the anarchy or tyranny of base instincts so that productive social life becomes possible, as Locke envisioned. Nor is the romantic to escape individual egoism so that species-life becomes possible, as Marx proposed. Rather, the romantic individual seeks to escape both the collective egoism and conventionalized productivity of social life. The goal is a radical, yet moral, individual freedom. The assumptions that ground this vision are relatively straightforward: individual sovereignty; "higher laws," as Thoreau writes, that ground the individual's potential for an elevated, spiritual life; and a natural world that constitutes an exemplary cosmos rather than a nihilistic chaos.

Friedrich Nietzsche may serve as an internal critic of the romantic revolution. Nietzsche was a great admirer and fond reader of Emerson, and might well have found his inspiration for the Overman in Emerson's description of the Over-Soul. Nietzsche shares Emerson's suspicion of social mores, celebrates with Emerson the heroism of the self-reliant individual, and applauds Emerson's disdain for herd life. However, Nietzsche does not share Emerson's faith, or the faith of Thoreau and Whitman, in the goodness of natural man, in the essential beneficence of nature, or in the existence of higher laws that might ground and validate our autonomous and infinite individuality.

George Kateb, in a wonderfully terse Nietzschean critique, suggests that "God is not dead enough" for the American romantics. That is to say, Emerson, Thoreau, and Whitman remain "religious in that they cling to a belief or hope in the more-than-human, in the not-ourselves. They think they detect in the world some force or spirit that though it may be beyond the human mind nevertheless also corresponds to it. The source of their wonder at existence—a wonder they express in describing or imagining their moments of contemplative ecstasy—is still, to a significant degree, wonder at the lurking divinity of nature."[9] Divinities lurking in nature are the opiates of romantic individualists. Nietzsche called them the shadows of God.

Nietzsche wants to banish these specters and spurn their intoxications. He prompts us to look askance at Emerson's announcement in *Spiritual Laws* that "there is a soul at the center of nature," and he chides our naïveté would we side with Thoreau's belief that "the laws of the universe are not indifferent, but are forever on the side of the most sensitive." In his correspondence, Nietzsche wrote of Emerson as a "brother-soul," and spoke of him as the man "richest in ideas in the nineteeth-century." But he was sharply critical of Emerson's quasi-religious zeal. Nature, for Nietzsche, had no soul or purpose, beneficent or otherwise. To succumb to such romantic delusions is to lose that probity of intellect that befits the truly heroic individual, the "higher type" who chooses to remain ungrounded and self-supporting and does not shrink from nihilism. Emerson, Nietzsche concludes, was simply "too much infatuated with life."[10]

In sum, the romantic revolution marks the struggle between the poetic individual and a socially conventionalized environment. Freedom becomes identified with the individual's intellectual independence and spiritual autonomy. This independence and autonomy is grounded upon faith in a natural cosmos. Nietzsche contests this faith, suggesting that the romantic revolution is built upon metaphysical self-delusion. Despite successfully shedding the cloak of social convention, the romantics fall back upon a divinely ordered nature to clothe their heroic individuals.

THE BEHAVIORAL REVOLUTION

If the romantic revolution reintroduced God into the world through the divinity of nature, then the behavioral revolution might be seen as a final exorcism. While the romantic revolution found its representative text in *Walden*, the behavioral revolution is epitomized in *Walden Two*.[11] B. F. Skinner published this utopian novel in 1948, 101 years after Thoreau had finished his stint at the New England pond. Skinner's book portrays an isolated community, Walden Two, which secures economic self-sufficiency and social harmony through behavioral engineering and innovative technology. Its contented inhabitants manipulate and reconstruct their natural and social environments, achieving both the "conquest of nature" and the "conquest of man."

Far from being poetically divinized at Walden Two, nature is subdued and mastered at the hands of *homo faber*. The "tyranny" of weather is conquered through mechanical engineering. Almost everything is simply made accessible indoors. In turn, the tyranny of social nature is conquered through behavioral techniques that substitute benign drives, conventions, and habits for their noxious counterparts. Thus Walden Two, as its chief engineer quips, is really a "Walden for Two." It is an idyllic existence that, unlike Thoreau's model, does not merely escape the problems of collective life but actually resolves them.

God is certainly dead enough at Walden Two. Its founder announces in Feuerbachian fashion that "religious faith becomes irrelevant when the fears which nourish it are allayed and the hopes fulfilled—here on earth." Priests have effectively been replaced by psychologists. For the same reason that Walden Two does without priests and gods, it is also a "world without heroes." A society that functions for the good of all cannot tolerate "individual figures" that disrupt its equilibrium. More important, it must do without myths about the freedom that great individuals are supposed to incarnate.

At Walden Two, there is no such thing as free, uncontrolled, and therefore heroic human behavior. Every act is a product of "operant conditioning." This is not to say that freedom stops at the gates of Walden Two. The world outside this technological utopia, its denizens assert, is no more free, and no more disengaged from manipulative control. It is simply a matter of who is doing the controlling: enlightened psychologists and skillful social engineers or deluded priests, ill-informed parents, hucksters, and demagogues. Walden Two is considered the "freest place on earth" because its behavioral technicians modify behavior through positive reinforcement rather than physical coercion. In this way one may simultaneously "*increase the feeling of freedom*" while ensuring social conformity. At Walden Two, humanity's essential unfreedom is finally put to good use. Quiet desperation gives way to contented problem-solving.

The central conflict of the behavioral revolution, and its tentative resolution, are most straightforwardly described by Skinner in his subsequent work, *Beyond Freedom and Dignity*. The book begins with a familiar litany of environmental woes: the population explosion, the nuclear threat, world famine, pollution. After explaining the theory behind operant conditioning, Skinner concludes *Beyond Freedom and Dignity* with a plea to abandon belief in freedom and autonomy, a belief, he insists, that is chiefly responsible for inhibiting the timely resolution of our worsening problems. What is being abolished by the science of behaviorism, Skinner writes, is the romantic individual, the individual "defended by the literatures of freedom and dignity." That abolition, we are told, is long overdue:

> Autonomous man is a device used to explain what we cannot explain in any other way. He has been constructed from our ignorance, and as our understanding increases, the very stuff of which he is composed vanishes. Science does not dehumanize man, it de-homunculizes him, and it must do so if it is to prevent the abolition of the human species. . . . Man himself may be controlled by his environment, but it is an environment which is almost wholly of his own making. The physical environment of most people is largely man-made. . . . the social environment is obviously man-made. . . . An experimental analysis shifts the determination of behavior from autonomous man to the environment—an

environment responsible both for the evolution of the species and for the reper-
toire acquired by each member. . . . We have not yet seen what man can make
of man."[12]

Like Locke, Skinner believes the individual is a tabula rasa when born.
But Skinner asserts that behavioral scientists might become sovereign authors, perfecting those techniques needed to wipe slates clean and etch them
anew.

The object of the behavioral revolution is the conquest of social pathologies and natural constraints through technical knowledge and skill. The age-
old conflict between the (autonomous) individual and the environment becomes a working relation between the behavioral scientist and the natural
and social environments he or she controls. Properly conditioned, Skinner
maintains, individuals will think and act how they must think and act in
order to survive and prosper collectively—and they will do so feeling freer
than ever.

Michel Foucault serves as an internal critic of the behavioral revolution.
Foucault may seem an unlikely candidate for this task. He has consistently
pitted himself against the psychologists, technicians and social engineers
whose successes are said to describe modernity. He rallies us against the
panoptic society and pastoral state that Skinner enthusiastically endorses.
Yet Foucault vociferously decries the behavioral revolution only because he
accepts so many of its premises.

Foucault, like Skinner, believes that the individual is a malleable, social
construction. Both theorists identify in detail techniques developed for the
purpose of shaping souls. Foucault, like Skinner, claims that these disciplinary techniques are ubiquitous. The webs of power/knowledge that constrain and condition us are inescapable. We are all necessarily caught in a
game of mutual manipulation. Such exercises of power/knowledge are not
bad in themselves, both Skinner and Foucault acknowledge. Power/knowl-
edge is simply the medium in which humans exist. It forms and sustains
them. It is the crucible of humankind.

We may resist disciplinary techniques, Foucault, like Skinner, acknowledges, but not because there are realms of pure freedom in which to gambol.
Rather, resistance is simply the pitting of one form of power/knowledge
against another, the short-circuiting of one technique by another in a brave
new world. Thus freedom, both Skinner and Foucault conclude, is not something we ever really secure. Freedom is something we feel in the struggle to
take hold of the reins of power/knowledge, or, better said, in the effort to
exchange certain reins for others.

Foucault encourages us, the participant victims of power/knowledge, to
engage in a "hyper- and pessimistic activism."[13] Skinner, on the other hand,
advocates a hyper- and optimistic activism on the part of social engineers.
Skinner's object is to extend the domain and deepen the reach of the matrices
of power/knowledge. Foucault's object is to proliferate the guerilla struggle

against these matrices. The behavioral revolution was an effort centrally to manage scientific knowledge and technical power over the human subject. Foucault seeks to disperse this technical power anarchically by way of the genealogical undermining of all claims to scientific knowledge. The threat of behaviorism, Hannah Arendt once said, is not that it is true, but that it could become so. More than any other theorist, Foucault has taken this message to heart.

Skinner applauds the denouement of the human odyssey as directed by a technical elite. Foucault asks us to subvert the power of this elite in order to become the technicians of our own lives. He speaks of this struggle against the apparatuses of power/knowledge in aesthetic terms. We are to create ourselves as works of art. The justification for this inventive resistance is clear: if we do not shape ourselves into works of art, someone or something else will inevitably do the shaping for us.

In sum, the behavioral revolution marks at once the environment's victory over the individual and science's victory over the environment. It is grounded upon the conceptual and practical deconstruction of freedom. Once the quest for technical control usurps the vain pursuit of liberty as society's organizing principle, behaviorists argue, a life of social harmony and material well-being may be achieved. Internal critics of the revolution, such as Foucault, acknowledge the social construction of the individual. However, Foucault suggests that we scramble the disciplinary matrices that constrain and condition us so that we might create ourselves as works of art. As the ephemeral product of this self-invention, in the individual's exercise of creative self-mastery, something called freedom may be experienced.

THE POSTMODERN ECOLOGICAL REVOLUTION

Foucault, one might suggest, is ill placed in this dialectical tale. He rightly deserves to be discussed as a theorist of the postmodern revolution. I have cast him as a critic of behaviorism, however, to make a point. His effort, like the efforts of many others understood to be postmodern, is largely reactive.[14] He promotes a politics chiefly defined by the resistance of beleaguered individuals caught in the apparatuses of normalization. Offered no hope of escape from these apparatuses, yet encouraged not to submit, postmodern individuals resign themselves to a deconstructive monkey wrenching with the system.

This reactive postmodernism may be contrasted with an active postmodernism that embraces the irony of the deconstructive mind, yet moves beyond its purely defensive positions. While benefiting from the tactical insights of genealogical theorizing, active postmodernism also moves beyond the reactive postmodern conception of freedom as an individualistic form of artistic self-mastery or linguistic guerilla warfare.

Active postmodernism evidences itself today in many forms. I shall focus on one of its primary manifestations, the contemporary environmental movement. It has been said that radical environmentalism constitutes "the first fully postmodern *Weltanschauung*, thoroughly surpassing the modernist paradigm of the last three centuries."[15] This is misleading. Contemporary environmentalism, like most, if not all, active postmodern phenomena, surpasses modernism only by building upon it. Indeed, modernism is not so much uprooted by the environmental movement as selectively cultivated. Like all revolutions, despite their more radical intentions, the postmodern ecological revolution never fully escapes its parentage. In turn, what is remarkable about the contemporary environmental movement, including its "radical" wing, is that it celebrates many Weltanschauungen, but no one Weltanschauung. The postmodern ecological revolution has always been pluralistic and will likely remain uncongealed.[16] Still, common features of an otherwise fragmented movement may be discerned, and the kinship between environmentalism and postmodernism is demonstrable.

Modernism is often identified with the drive for sovereignty, universality, (instrumental) rationality, homogeneity, simplicity, clarity, and limitless progress. A correspondingly synoptic statement about environmentalism might be made by listing the "three laws of ecology" that are said to orient it: (1) interconnectedness and interdependence (of humans and other species) is ubiquitous; (2) the security and stability (of human and nonhuman ecosystems) derives from diversity and complexity; and (3) a finitude of resources and distinct limits to human growth exist.[17] The contemporary environmental movement posits humankind as an intrinsic part of an ecological web of life. Human freedom is understood not as a technological mastery over this web, but as a self-conscious integration into it. Ecological concerns for interdependence, complexity, and the limits to growth align well with postmodern celebrations of contingency, ambiguity and antiteleology. These concerns pit themselves sharply against the panoply of modernist drives mentioned above.

Stephen White states that postmodernism is best identified by four features, the first three of which are an "incredulity toward metanarratives" (to employ Lyotard's well-worn phrase), a "new awareness of the dangers of societal rationalization," and a susceptibility to "new information technologies." These three features speak primarily to postmodernism's reactive struggle against the totalizing character of modernist rationalism and progressivist teleology. The fourth feature identified by White largely constitutes the active side of postmodernism, namely, the appearance of "new social movements," such as the feminist, peace, and ecological movements.[18]

New social movements are conglomerations of grass-roots organizations involved in normative critiques and practical transformations of established beliefs, values, and patterns of behavior. These movements engage in social, cultural, and political struggles against modern modes of subjectification.

They contest the means by which identities are established and maintained. Particular targets are modernism's anthropocentric humanism, patriarchal chauvinism, rationalistic essentialism, economic imperialism, and technological totalism.

New social movements are fluid amalgams whose size, constitution, and course are largely determined by the social, cultural, and political terrain they navigate. As social composites with diverse and fluctuating memberships, their strategies and goals are neither static nor internally uncontested. Directing these characteristics back to the question of postmodernity, Stephen White writes: "What stands out about new social movements is an irreducible pluralism and a suspicion of totalistic revolutionary programs. For such groups, the growth of incredulity toward traditional metanarratives is particularly unlikely to be seen as a source of fear and trembling, but instead as source of some cognitive space within which new orientations may have a better chance to flourish. This is especially clear in the case of the women's movement and radical ecologists. . . . The qualities of new social movements make them the most plausible immediate addresses to those theorists who celebrate the emergence of 'local' resistance (Foucault), a 'border conflict' (Habermas), 'local determinism' (Lyotard), and particularistic 'lines of flight' (Deleuze) from the societal or revolutionary rationalization of life."[19]

New social movements are not wholly new.[20] Nor are they uniformly successful at selectively cultivating the desirable features of modernism. Questionable modernist tendencies certainly persist within the environmental movement, most noticeably among those environmentalists who advocate the creation of an international Leviathan to ensure global ecological stability. In turn, premodern orientations are also in evidence, particularly among those "deep ecologists" who believe, to borrow a phrase from Joni Mitchell, that we might somehow "get ourselves back to the garden." The environmental movement is replete with modernist eddies and nostalgic cross-currents. Yet such modernist aspirations and nostalgic leanings are, it seems to me, peripheral to the surge of the environmental movement as a whole.

Born out of and in reaction to modernism's penchant for univocality, homogeneity, simplicity, and clarity, and schooled in the intricate interdependencies of complex ecosystems, contemporary environmentalists have been largely inoculated against both nostalgic and progressivist yearnings for transparent order. Despite their reliance on metaphors such as "Spaceship Earth," the majority of environmentalists do not seek to rechannel power, knowledge, and technology from the statist pursuit of wealth and weaponry to global ecological administration. The Green vision is much more eclectic and decentralized. As Wendell Berry writes, "The only true and effective 'operator's manual for spaceship Earth' is not a book that any human will ever write; it is hundreds of thousands of local cultures."[21]

While tensions exist between the promotion of local self-management and global oversight within most environmental organizations, these tensions tend to be fecund ones and are recognized as such.

New social movements have described themselves as "fractal" organizations, meaning that homologous activities are conducted throughout the levels and organs of the movement in an effort to marry the roles of educator and educated, mobilizer and mobilized. As Alberto Melucci put it: "The medium, the movement itself as a new medium, is the message. As prophets without enchantment, contemporary movements practice in the present the change they are struggling for."[22] The transformation of identities that social movements advocate finds its staging ground within the movement itself. Movement activism, for this reason, entails more than the instrumental pursuit of group interests. It also involves the self-conscious questioning, reassessing, and reformulating of private and public interests and identities.[23]

New social movements are characterized by their rejection of the political fictions of organicity that would foist upon them a too-disciplined regimentation and counteridentity. They generally refrain from claiming the status of unified and universal agents of historic change. They do not pose as the functional equivalent of the proletariat whose revolution did not come. For the most part, they eschew blueprints. Instead, they engage in creatively demonstrating that *what is* is not necessarily so, and that, in the long term, it is not sustainable. As Melucci observes, "[T]hrough what they do, or rather through how they do it, movements announce to society that something 'else' is possible."[24]

As a whole, then, the environmental movement remains suspicious of totalizing programs of action and homogenizing demands for solidarity. It rejects a static, uniform identity for itself and forgoes utopian enchantments. One might label it an "eco-ironic" revolution in an effort to capture the nature of its self-conscious and chary activism.

This brings me to my reason for outlining the conceptual features and dynamics of the bourgeois, socialist, romantic, and behavioral revolutions. In contrast to these previous upheavals, the postmodern ecological revolution dismisses Promethean mythologizing that posits the human odyssey in terms of a basic opposition between the individual and the environment. Integration, not autonomy and mastery, is the goal. The postmodern environmentalist seeks neither the sovereignty of the possessive individual over a private domain (as was the object of the bourgeois revolution) nor the absolute control of the communal individual over the realm of necessity and history (as was the object of the socialist revolution) nor the victory of the autonomous, spiritualized individual over the conventions of a social world (as was the object of the romantic revolution) nor the technical power of the scientific individual over a natural and social environment (as was the object of the behavioral revolution). Each of these four revolutions was actuated by a self-assertion, namely, the self-assertion of the human being as individual or species, as body or spirit. The prize to be won by this self-assertion was always a form of freedom. But it was a freedom wed to possession and mastery. New social movements, and the environmental movement in particular, oppose this marriage. Human freedom, environmentalists suggest, is to be found through a self-conscious living within limits and an active interdependence. There is something decidedly postrevolutionary, then, about the ecological revolution.

Throughout the Western world, the essence of human being has been consistently identified as the capacity for freedom. This freedom has been understood in many ways and has undergone many transformations. Yet from its inception, the Western consciousness of freedom has remained tied to what might be called possessive mastery. We witness this relationship from that early freedom discovered through the domination of master over slave (and man over woman) in ancient Greece. It persists in the freedom sought through the domination of the higher self over the lower self by Plato, by Aristotle, and increasingly by the Stoics and Augustinians. It has been reasserted in various forms in the modern age. Possessive mastery is the type of freedom won in the self-assertive struggles of the four modernist revolutions. And it endures within certain forms of postmodern (Nietzschean and Foucaultian) revolt, wherein self-mastery is recast as a form of artistic self-invention.

The pursuit of a freedom that entails mastery over others, over nature and things, or over the self, has found its way into the scriptures of all Western ideologies. It sits at the center of the cultural and political drives that constitute modernism, and it continues to fuel postmodern reactions. This pursuit of a masterful and possessive freedom has a rather damning legacy regarding humanity's relation to the natural environment. In the Western world, freedom has been identified since Adam with dominion over the earth. Contemporary understandings of freedom still bear out this legacy. Positive liberty, as developed out of Platonic, Stoic, Christian, Rousseauian, Hegelian, and Marxian notions of the higher self, celebrates dominion over the earth as the prerogative of human rationality and its political or otherworldly telos. Negative liberty, as developed out of liberal traditions, has proved a useful prophylactic against tyranny (and this tyranny has often been carried out in the name of positive liberty). Nonetheless, negative liberty has fostered the domination of nature in no lesser degree. For the negative libertarian, the nonhuman world is incapable of bearing rights or dignities of its own. If nature is not accorded protection, respect, and care under the auspices of private property, it receives none. But private property, as Locke understood it, is an extension of the self, a product of its labor. Property may be disposed of as the individual sees fit. Indeed, its use and efficient using up is to be encouraged as a measure of the expanding realm of human freedom. Thus Locke would justify the violent expropriation of American Indian lands without recompense on the ground of their insufficient exploitation by the original inhabitants.[25]

Positive and negative conceptions of liberty are spurned by postmodernists as misleading and inadequate. The postmodern critique of rationality and teleology has exposed many of the strategies of positive liberty to be insidious. The postmodern exposition of the permeability of the self and the productivity of power has demonstrated the defensive project of negative liberty to be naive. Thus reactive postmodernists pursue freedom as the heroic, albeit tragic task of aesthetically creating the self in the face of ubiquitous webs of power. This artistic struggle is portrayed as a highly individualistic endeavor. Collective effort is often maligned because of its normalizing entanglements. Here, we witness Nietzsche's tenacious legacy. The pursuit of individual freedom remains key, but now freedom is chiefly found in the mastery of the postmodern artist whose work is him- or herself. Turned inward, postmodern aesthetes have little to say about the preservation of the natural world. And they harbor enervating suspicions about collective efforts to protect it.[26]

With the postmodern ecological revolution, the understanding of freedom shifts ground. Environmentalists understand freedom not as the possessive mastery of self, other, or nature, but as the dynamic integration of the individual into a social and natural ecology. Human freedom is not forged out of sovereign power. It is discovered through interconnectedness. Social and biological interdependence is not an obstacle to freedom, but its source.

Postmodern environmentalists observe that preferences and identities are not innate, but are elicited and produced. In a world of ubiquitous advertising, the production and seduction of preferences and identities may become overpowering. Safeguarding negative liberty proves an inadequate project in such a context. The unrestrained market can no longer serve as the bastion of individual liberty. For what is hidden about the market's hand is not only, or even primarily, *pace* Adam Smith, its efficient regulation of production to meet demand. What is hidden, and insidiously so, is the market's capacity to stimulate demand by shaping the appetites of consumers and perforce its capacity to shape our identities as consumers.

The hidden hand of the market decidedly lacks a green thumb. Environmentalists insist that we may no longer leave this hand wholly unrestrained. Regulation is necessary not only to protect the health of individuals from harmful products but also to protect the welfare of present and future generations, and the viability of other species from ecologically destructive patterns of consumption and production. At issue, however, is not only the standard (liberal) problem of politics: namely, who gets what, when, and how. It is not simply a matter of cutting up and redistributing the pie in different ways—though the problem of distributive justice will be with us always and takes on a heightened complexity with the intergenerational concerns of environmentalists. Rather, it is a matter of challenging the way in which our identities have been reduced to that of pie-producing and pie-consuming beings, whose overriding obsession is making the pie grow indefinitely.

New social movements contest the cultural and political categories sustained by late capitalism. They contest, as Habermas states, the "colonization of the life-world" that was ushered in with the modern growth of instrumental rationality and market-oriented life styles.[27] As Suzanne Berger observes, much of the protest in Europe since the late 1960s marked "an explosion of doubt about the quality and direction of life in advanced industrial societies, about the kind of human relationships that develop in mass consumer societies. . . . This was a protest not against the failure of the state and society to provide for economic growth and material prosperity, but against their all-too-considerable success in having done so, and against the price of this success."[28] Likewise, the strength of the environmental movement in America is a function of the perceived ecological costs of a "successful" market economy. As a result of its vast and vastly wasteful consumer culture, environmentalists point out, the United States poses a grave ecological threat. It is considered the most "overpopulated" nation in terms of the environmental degradation it visits upon the earth.[29]

More than anything else, a heightened ecological consciousness has undermined the global victory of capitalism. As one theorist put it, the ecological crisis has "blown the cover" of the liberal economic ideology of growth, undermining the widespread belief that we can have our pie and eat it too, simply by making the pie grow indefinitely.[30] The "detoxification" of a "growth-addicted society" brought about by the ecological crisis also fosters society's effective "repoliticization."[31] This repoliticization arises because the ideology of growth has hitherto obfuscated the demands of social justice. In the United States in particular, where "trickle-down" economics was born, disparities in wealth between the richest and poorest segments of society continue to increase at unprecedented rates despite stable economic growth. As Herman Daly explains, "We are addicted to growth because we are addicted to large inequalities in income and wealth. To paraphrase Marie Antoinette: Let them eat growth. Better yet, let the poor hope to eat growth in the future."[32] The ideology of growth masks a depoliticized economy. The ecological crisis is wearing away the mask.

The environmentalist's rejection of unrestrained market growth is not an embrace of a state-controlled economy. Centralized power is recognized as inherently dangerous. Moreover, postmodern environmentalists are unwilling to adopt the sovereign collective as an unqualified good, any more than the sovereign individual. If the surplus material acquisition, waste, and technological mastery that threaten the biosphere remain socially predominant, collectivizing their pursuit will hardly solve the problem. Moreover, the global nature of the most pressing ecological problems makes environmentalists suspicious of the restrictive tribal solidarities that statist and collectivist ideologies may foster. They remain wary of any understanding of freedom, whether personal or popular, individual or collective, that is cast as an unrestrained sovereignty.

Contemporary environmentalists do not articulate a singular understanding of freedom. I believe, however, that freedom understood as a form of possessive mastery is implicitly challenged by their activities. With the dual aim of giving voice to this reformulation of freedom and preventing its reification, I shall briefly examine Martin Heidegger's role as both a conceptual parent of the postmodern ecological revolution and its internal critic. Heidegger's locutions are unlikely ever to find their way onto environmentalists' banners (thankfully). Yet he supplies an account of the freedom that structures much of their work.[33]

HEIDEGGER AND ENVIRONMENTALISM

Heidegger is frequently identified as a progenitor of postmodernism. Stephen White draws out this relationship, observing that Heidegger, even better than Nietzsche, prepares the ground for postmodern thought by focusing explicitly on the nature and importance of language, by directing the force of his attack at "modernity's instrumental-technological orientation to the world," and by critically examining Nietzsche's understanding of the will to power, which, in another form, underlies modernity's technological orientation.[34] Heidegger's work is also frequently appropriated as a philosophical grounding for ecological concerns.[35] Often this appropriation is based on Heidegger's understanding of human being as "care," his emphasis on learning how to "dwell" upon the earth, his understanding of the importance of tending to a "homeland," his notion of humanity as the "shepherd of Being," his promotion of "guardianship" and "preservation," his confrontation with technology, and his critique of anthropocentric humanism. In turn, Heidegger insists that Human being is a Being-in-the-world, and that the rigid, modernist binary of the individual versus the worldly environment is fictitious and dangerous.

Michael Zimmerman suggests that such aspects of Heidegger's thought "help to support the claim that he is a major deep ecological theorist."[36] In the same vein, Charles Taylor writes that "Heidegger's understanding of language, its *telos,* and the human essence can be the basis of an ecological politics, founded on something deeper than an instrumental calculation of the conditions of our survival (though that itself ought to be enough to alarm us). It can be the basis of in one sense a 'deep' ecology."[37] However fertile the relationship between Heidegger and environmentalism, one should avoid straightforward translations of his philosophy into ecological thought. To the extent that ecological thinkers attempt to ground human existence (and ethics) in a biological or evolutionary essence, Heidegger proves a formidable critic.

Heidegger does prompt us "to experience truth as the preservation [*Wahrheit*] of Being; and to understand that, as presencing, Being belongs to this preservation." But he is also quick to point out that "as protection of

Being, preservation belongs to the herdsman, who has so little to do with bucolic idylls and Nature mysticism that he can be the herdsman of Being only if he continues to hold the place of nothingness."[38] Heidegger's ontological shepherd is often transfixed by anxiety, tottering above an existential abyss. This is quite out of keeping with romanticized notions of a life fully synchronized with natural rhythms. The preservation of Being is a preservation not of things, but of nothingness, of that no-thingness that is Being. Thus Heidegger designates human being not the shepherd of beings [*das Seiende*], but the shepherd of Being (*das Sein*). He maintains that "Guardianship of Being is not fixated upon something existent. . . . Guardianship is vigilance, watchfulness for the has-been and coming destiny of Being."[39] The same sorts of caveats are required regarding Heidegger's understanding of dwelling and care. In each case, it is illegitimate to leap from an ontological description to an ontic prescription, regardless of its ethical or ecological thrust.

For all that, Heidegger's philosophy offers support for the environmental movement and for ecological concerns at large. The key to moving from philosophical thought to worldly involvement rests with the relationship that our identities have to our behavior. The fact is that our actions stem from, and in turn help to mold and transform, our sense of self. As Heidegger maintained, we are, for the most part, what we do. The corollary is that what we do is largely an expression of who we (think we) are. Our relation to the world is grounded upon the identities we have established, or have had established for us. These identities develop, in part, out of a culturally mediated understanding of the nature of human being.

Like most Western philosophers, Heidegger identifies the uniqueness and dignity of human being by its capacity for freedom. Like his Western counterparts, Heidegger holds that freedom occupies the center of the philosophic (and political) enterprise. He writes that "the question of the essence of human freedom is the fundamental question of philosophy, with even the question of Being entwined in it."[40] But Heidegger rejects the understanding of freedom as a radical autonomy, the power to satisfy one's wants, or a sovereignty over the self, over others, or over a private realm of things. Rather, freedom emerges most fundamentally in our witnessing of Being as it comes to be manifest in beings. "Freedom," he writes, "is the condition of possibility of the disclosure of the Being of beings, of the understanding of Being."[41] The unique relation to Being that human being enjoys, Heidegger insists, is a product of our capacity for freedom.

As a way of summarizing the human disposition that facilitates this freedom, Heidegger employs the term *Gelassenheit*. *Gelassenheit* is generally translated as "releasement." It indicates the disposition of letting be, subjecting things neither to domination and control nor to an objectifying possession, but rather opening oneself to them that they may be appreciated and understood for themselves. Freedom is that preservation and shepherding of Being that allows us fully to dwell in the world of things, as befits human beings understood as beings who care. No longer restricted to the exhibition of beings as objects of possession, manipulation, or mastery, human being may reformulate its identity in terms of its capacity for a disclosive freedom.

Heidegger establishes a link between our ontological understandings and our ontic, worldly involvement. He insists that "Man is not the lord of beings. Man is the shepherd of Being," and thus challenges our historically sedimented sense of self.[42] "Mortals dwell in that they save the earth," Heidegger writes in an ontological description of the human condition. But he immediately extrapolates the ontic ramifications of this identity: "To save really means to set something free into its own presencing. To save the earth is more than to exploit it or even wear it out. Saving the earth does not master the earth and does not subjugate it, which is merely one step from spoliation."[43] To be free, for Heidegger, means to free that which is other, to disclose the world in thought, word, and deed in a way that preserves and safeguards difference. Such a disclosive freedom is incompatible with the objectification of others and things that the totalized attempt to acquire, control, or dominate entails.

Heidegger's understanding of a freedom distinct from the anthropocentric objectification of the world is not, however, grounded in the ontological homogenization of human and nonhuman life. Unlike certain deep ecologists, Heidegger is unwilling to equate humans, ontologically or ethically, with all other species. Rather, the capacity to experience freedom through participation in the disclosure of Being accords human being a unique status. Heidegger writes: "Compared with the duration of cosmic galaxies, human existence and its history is certainly quite fleeting, only a 'moment.' But this transiency is nevertheless the highest mode of Being when it becomes an existing out of and towards freedom."[44] While Heidegger supports a nonanthropocentric approach to the earth and world, he rejects its replacement with a biocentric approach. This does not depreciate his status as an ecological theorist. Arguably it makes his candidacy stronger. Celebrating the unique capacities of human being to disclose in a way that preserves best ensures humanity's benign stewardship of the earth.

The human capacity for disclosure, and for the experience of freedom as disclosure, is threatened by the unmitigated pursuit of freedom understood as a form of possessive mastery. Heidegger identifies the culmination of this pursuit with modern technology. In contrast to releasement, which lets things be disclosed in manifold ways according to their various natures, Heidegger defines technology as a way of revealing all things in a singular manner. Technology reveals everything as standing-reserve (*Bestand*), as that which awaits its most efficient use and using up by human minds and hands. This technological mode of revealing receives the name enframing (*Gestell*). Enframing, then, is the essence of modern technology, a totalizing ordering that challenges everything forth (to be revealed) as raw material for human craft and consumption.

If there is any claim to greatness to our being, Heidegger insists, it does not arise from the human capacity to dominate and possess the earth, enframing it as a quarry for our exploits. Human greatness and dignity emerge most fundamentally from our capacity and concern to preserve and bear witness to that which stands outside and beyond us. In stark contrast to the homogenizing totalizations of enframing, disclosive freedom evidences itself in multiple modes of worldly revealing.

To achieve mastery over the earth, one must presume to comprehend it. Yet according to Heidegger, nature is inexhaustibly mysterious. One of Heidegger's favorite Heraclitean fragments was "Nature loves to hide." However one reveals the natural world, something else remains hidden: relationships of interdependence are left undiscovered, evolutionary legacies unexplored, biological, aesthetic or physical properties untouched. The vast diversity of nature is matched by the manifold modes of disclosure to which humans are privileged on account of their capacity for freedom. Modern technology effectively robs nature of its ability to hide by robbing human beings of their capacity to disclose nature in multiple, preservative ways.

When enframed, everything equally and inclusively becomes appropriated as standing-reserve. Everything is made available for our calculation and assessment, becoming at once "overseeable, controllable, definable, connectable, and explicable."[45] Yet every such attempt to "penetrate" the earth with "calculating importunity," Heidegger insists, will turn to destruction: "This destruction may herald itself under the appearance of mastery and of progress in the form of the technical-scientific objectification of nature, but this mastery nevertheless remains an impotence of will. The earth appears openly cleared as itself only when it is perceived and preserved as that which is by nature undisclosable, that which shrinks from every disclosure and constantly keeps itself closed up."[46] Heidegger identifies the will to mastery as an actual impotence of will. Only when we preserve the earth by restraining our reach, do we gain the freedom to perceive the earth as earth, in all the splendor of its diversity.

Environmentalists struggle against the calculating importunity that turns everything on earth into standing-reserve. As one Sierra Club newsletter states, "The truth is, we've been managing our national forests as though they were outdoor warehouses of living trees, held in inventory until the lumber companies are ready to take delivery. And it's got to stop!" Eventually it will stop, environmentalists hold, if for no other reason than that there are physical limits to economic and industrial growth. In large part, the ecological revolution is the product of the increasing awareness of these limits.

Heidegger's philosophy buttresses this awareness. He presents us with a philosophy of limits. He describes our freedom as dependent upon rather than threatened by the worldly boundaries of human being. "It is misguided to think one understands freedom most purely in its essence if one isolates it as a free-floating arbitrariness," Heidegger writes. "Moreover, the task is precisely the reverse, to conceive freedom in its finitude and to see that, by proving boundedness, one has neither impaired freedom nor curtailed its essence."[47] Boundedness does not threaten disclosive freedom because disclosive freedom, unlike its historical namesakes, is not wed to possessive mastery.

Hannah Arendt, one of Heidegger's more illustrious students, suggests that the political realm can be put aright only by abandoning the Western world's misconstrued understanding of freedom as a form of sovereignty.[48] Likewise, Heidegger suggests that the boundless enframing of the earth that is at the heart of so much environmental degradation is likely to stop only once we transform our understanding of freedom. As a capacity to bear witness to what is rather than an opportunity or duty to master and possess it, human freedom can become the cornerstone of an ecological ethic.

CONCLUSION

I chose the name *Walden Three* to designate the postmodern ecological revolution because it highlights two important characteristics. First, the postmodern ecological revolution signifies a move beyond the Thoreauian retreat from social life at Walden Pond. Postmodern environmentalists are committed to a politically active, public caretaking of nature. Like Thoreau, they are unsatisfied with traditional political structures and patterns of social behavior. Unlike Thoreau, they involve themselves in a *social* movement whose object is to repoliticize rather than depoliticize worldly life. In turn, the postmodern ecological revolution signifies a move beyond the technological control and conquest of nature as it was fictively consummated at Walden Two and as it is concretely evidenced in contemporary life. The growth of human population and power has made the isolationist retreat to Walden One impossible. The tenacious relationship between mastery and spoliation has revealed the centralized, technical conquest sought at Walden Two to be dangerous and unsustainable.

Technological power allows us to wrest more and more of nature from its hiding place and stamp it with humanity's imprimatur. Environmentalists resist the seduction of this power to possess and master, extolling the beauty of that which remains other and the wisdom of letting it remain so. In a shrinking world, the ecological other requires collective caretaking and preservation. The task at hand, however, is not simply to institute better environmental laws and regulations, as important as these are. The struggle is to discover a new way of being-in-the-world and a new way of understanding the freedom that actuates this being.

NOTES

1. John Locke, *Two Treatises of Government,* ed. Peter Laslett (New York: Mentor, 1960), p. 343.

2. Jean-Jacques Rousseau, "On Public Happiness," *Oeuvres Complètes,* vol. 3 (Pleide, 1964), pp. 510, 881.

3. Michael Bakunin, *Bakunin on Anarchism*, ed. Sam Dolgoff (Montreal: Black Rose Books, 1980), p. 331.

4. Karl Marx, *Selected Writings,* ed. David McLellan (Oxford: Oxford University Press, 1977), p. 563.

5. Walt Whitman, *Leaves of Grass and Selected Prose* (New York: Holt, Rinehart and Winston, 1949).

6. Henry David Thoreau, *Walden and Civil Disobedience* (New York: W. W. Norton, 1966). Subsequent quotations of Thoreau are from this edition unless otherwise specified.

7. Henry David Thoreau, "Walking," in *Great Short Works of Henry David Thoreau* (New York: Harper and Row, 1982), p. 304. One institution best forgotten, for Thoreau, is imperialistic statecraft. Needless to say, this institution, at least since the Mexican War and the Monroe Doctrine, has become as American as gunboats and Coca Cola.

8. Ralph Waldo Emerson, *Selected Writings of Emerson*, ed. Donald McQuade (New York: Modern Library, 1981). Subsequent quotations of Emerson are from this edition.

9. George Kateb, *The Inner Ocean: Individualism and Democratic Culture* (Ithaca, N.Y.: Cornell University Press, 1992), p. 170.

10. Letter of May 26, 1876, in Friedrich Nietzsche, *Nietzsche Briefwechsel, Kritische Gesamtausgabe,* ed. Giorgio Colli and Mazzino Montinari (Berlin, N.Y.: Walter de Gruyter, 1988), div. II, vol. 5, p. 164.

11. B. F. Skinner, *Walden Two* (New York: Macmillan, 1948).

12. B. F. Skinner, *Beyond Freedom and Dignity* (New York: Vintage, 1971), pp. 191, 205–206.

13. Michel Foucault, "On the Genealogy of Ethics: An Overview of Work in Progress," in *Michel Foucault: Beyond Structuralism and Hermeneutics,* 2d ed., ed. Hubert Dreyfus and Paul Rabinow (Chicago: University of Chicago Press, 1983), pp. 231–232.

14. Foucault was better known for his political activism than most postmodernists (see Keith Gandal, "Michel Foucault: Intellectual Work and Politics," *Telos* 67(1986): 121–134). My characterization of him as a reactive postmodernist pertains to the limitations of his theoretical positions.

15. Robert Frodeman, "Radical Environmentalism and the Political Roots of Postmodernism: Differences That Make a Difference," *Environmental Ethics* 14 (Winter 1992): 318–319.

16. I have identified some of the conceptual cross-currents within the environmental movement in Leslie Paul Thiele, "Nature and Freedom," *Environmental Ethics* 17 (Summer 1995): 171–190.

17. Taken from 1976 Greenpeace Declaration of Interdependence, in *Radical Environmentalism: Philosophy and Tactics*, ed. Peter List (Belmont, Calif.: Wadsworth Publishing, 1993), pp. 134–136. The second law is contested within ecological circles, and its obverse has been argued. That is to say, the development of diverse, complex ecosystems may be dependent upon stability. In the aftermath of radical ecological change or destruction, one witnesses the ascendancy of relatively simple ecosystems, such as the growth of grasses and weeds after forest fires. A more diverse and complex ecosystem only develops in time, barring more disruption.

18. I offer a broader analysis of new social movements in Leslie Paul Thiele, "Making Democracy Safe for the World: Social Movements and Global Politics,"

Alternatives 18 (March 1993): 273–305. Though this essay focuses on the environmental movement, I do not mean to discount the importance of the feminist, peace, or other new social movements, or to subsume them under the environmental banner. However, peace and ecological security increasingly go hand in hand today, and there is much overlap in movement membership. Eco-feminism, on the other hand, makes up only a small portion of the current feminist culture. Nonetheless, many feminist issues are of prime ecological concern. The Green movement (and party) in the United States, for example, explicitly maintains feminism as one of its Ten Key Values, and arguably advocates core feminist concerns in the other nine. From a global perspective, in turn, the decrease of patriarchy and the gaining of greater economic, political, and reproductive rights for women are widely recognized as the key to combating the ecological devastation caused by overpopulation. For a concise summary of the literature and debate about the relationship of gender, ecology, and peace, see Virginia Held, "Gender as an Influence on Cultural Norms Relating to War and the Environment," in *Cultural Norms, War and the Environment*, ed. Arthur Westing (Oxford: Oxford University Press, 1988).

19. Stephen K. White, *Political Theory and Postmodernism* (Cambridge: Cambridge University Press, 1991), p. 11.

20. See Charles Tilly, "Social Movements, Old and New," in *Research in Social Movements, Conflicts and Change*, vol. 10, ed. Lewis Kriesberg and Bronislaw Misztal (Greenwich, Conn.: JAI Press, 1988).

21. Wendell Berry, *What Are People For?* (San Francisco: North Point Press, 1990), p. 166.

22. Alberto Melucci, "The Symbolic Challenge of Contemporary Movements," *Social Research* 52 (1985): 801.

23. Certainly professionalism and the instrumental pursuit of group interests are evident within the environmental movement. Indeed, many of the larger, national environmental organizations are highly professionalized, and some peddle themselves in ways that betray a willingness to do almost anything to increase their market share of contributions and memberships.

24. Melucci, "The Symbolic Challenge of Contemporary Movements," p. 812.

25. Locke, *Two Treatises of Government*, pp. 336–337. See also Wayne Glausser, "Three Approaches to Locke and the Slave Trade," *Journal of the History of Ideas* 51 (1990): 199–216. Roderick Nash observes that women, children, and slaves used to be viewed as property but came to have their own rights under the liberal paradigm. He argues that the animal rights movement, and the deep ecological movement in general, may be seen as a radical extension of the liberal tradition. See Roderick Frazier Nash, *The Rights of Nature: A History of Environmental Ethics* (Madison: University of Wisconsin Press, 1989).

26. Robert Frodeman writes: "Postmodernism criticizes the epistemological basis of modernism while assuming the individualistic outlook that was the political correlate of modernist metaphysics. It is the ecological consequences of this political allegiance to Cartesian subjectivity that places postmodernism at odds with radical environmentalism." Frodeman, "Radical Environmentalism," p. 315.

27. Jürgen Habermas, "New Social Movements," *Telos* 48 (1981): 37.

28. Suzanne Berger, "Politics and Antipolitics in Western Europe in the Seventies," *Daedalus* 108 (1979): 32.

29. See Paul Ehrlich and Ann Ehrlich, *Healing the Planet* (Reading, Mass.: Addison-Wesley, 1991), pp. 8–9.

30. To the extent that economic growth arises not from an increase in the consumption of raw materials and energy but from the growth of services that do not increasingly tax the environment, there is no reason to condemn it. In turn, when economic growth derives from increases in the value of goods it may be benign if, for example, more expensive biodegradables are substituted for less expensive materials that would create unmanageable waste streams. The lion's share of today's economic growth, however, remains environmentally destructive. It is unsustainable in the long term and far from cost free in the here and now.

31. Joel Jay Kassiola, *The Death of Industrial Civilization: The Limits to Economic Growth and the Repoliticization of Advanced Industrial Society* (Albany: SUNY Press, 1990).

32. Cited *ibid.*, p. 71. The largest, mainstream national environmental groups have been frequently criticized for being white, upper-middle-class organizations that until recently paid little heed to issues of environmental racism and social justice. For a discussion of these criticisms, and the tensions that persist between national organizations and local activists, see Robert Gottlieb, *Forcing the Spring: The Transformation of the American Environmental Movement* (Washington, D. C.: Island Press, 1993).

33. I have written about Heidegger's understanding of freedom in Leslie Paul Thiele, "Heidegger on Freedom: Political Not Metaphysical," *American Political Science Review* 88 (June 1994): 278–291, and at greater length in Thiele, *Timely Meditations: Martin Heidegger and Postmodern Politics* (Princeton: Princeton University Press, 1995).

34. White, *Political Theory and Postmodernism* , p. 31.

35. Heidegger's work is the theme of a greater number of articles appearing in *Environmental Ethics* than that of any other major theorist (save Marx) who is not primarily known for his or her environmental writings.

36. Michael Zimmerman, *Heidegger's Confrontation with Modernity: Technology, Politics, Art* (Bloomington: Indiana University Press, 1990), pp. 242–243.

37. Charles Taylor, "Heidegger, Language, and Ecology," in *Heidegger: A Critical Reader*, ed. Hubert Drefus and Harrison Hall (Cambridge: Blackwell, 1992), p. 266.

38. Martin Heidegger, *Early Greek Thinking,* trans. D. Krell and F. Capuzzi (New York: Harper and Row, 1975), p. 36.

39. Martin Heidegger, *Poetry, Language and Thought,* trans. A. Hofstadter (New York: Harper and Row, 1971), p. 184.

40. Martin Heidegger, *Gesamtausgabe,* vol. 31 (reprint, Frankfurt am Main: Vittorio Klostermann, 1982), p. 300 (my translation).

41. *Ibid.*, p. 303.

42. Martin Heidegger, *Basic Writings* (New York: Harper and Row, 1977), p. 221.

43. Martin Heidegger, *Poetry, Language and Thought,* trans. A. Hofstadter (New York: Harper and Row, 1971), p. 150.

44. Martin Heidegger, *The Metaphysical Foundations of Logic,* trans. M. Heim (Bloomington: Indiana University Press, 1984), p. 18; cf. Heidegger, *Being and Time,* trans. J. Macquarrie and E. Robinson (New York: Harper and Row, 1962), pp. 28, 35. Zimmerman quotes this passage as indication that Heidegger "overestimated our importance" compared to that of nature (Michael Zimmerman, "Toward a Heideggerian *Ethos* for Radical Environmentalism," *Environmental Ethics* 5 (1983):

121). Zimmerman overlooks Heidegger's statement, made a few paragraphs earlier, that this fundamental questioning is "far removed from any noisy self-importance concerning the life of one's own soul or that of others" (*The Metaphysical Foundations of Logic*, pp. 16–17). Heidegger insists that the ontological priority of human being in no way determines that the natural world, or the material world at large, exists (solely) *for* human beings. "That all functional relations are grounded ontologically in a for-the-sake-of," Heidegger writes, "in no way decides whether, ontically, all beings are as beings for the sake of the human Dasein." Heidegger, *Basic Problems of Phenomenology,* trans. A. Hofstadter (Bloomington: Indiana University Press, 1982), p. 295.

45. Martin Heidegger, "Heidegger's Letter to the Boss's Daughter," *Telos* 77 (Fall 1988): 126.

46. Heidegger, *Poetry, Language and Thought*, p. 47.

47. Heidegger, *Metaphysical Foundations of Logic*, p. 196.

48. Hannah Arendt, "What Is Freedom?" in Arendt, *Between Past and Future* (New York: Penguin, 1968).

PART THREE

Culture, Sensibility, and the Self

Wollstonecraft as a Critic of Burke

DAVID BROMWICH

MARY WOLLSTONECRAFT'S *Vindication of the Rights of Men* was the first published reply to Edmund Burke's *Reflections on the Revolution in France*. Later replies from the radical side challenged and in a measure qualified Burke's report of the events of 1789, brought out the selective emphasis that guided his record of French history, showed the inadequacy of his sources (a bias sometimes passing into caprice), and sought to unmask his private motive for publishing, so late in life, a work of aristocratic propaganda. It was agreed by the detractors as by the vindicators of Burke that the *Reflections* were addressed more to England than to France, as a sequence of coded warnings against the politics of the Revolution Society and other associations for reform; this, the pamphlet writers knew, would have been a primary reason for his choice of the word "reflections." On matters like these, Wollstonecraft is not a distinctive guide, and her sparing use of contemporary data may have made her reply appear at once preliminary and oddly aloof. Where Thomas Paine stands out against Burke as a rival narrator of the revolution and of the miseries of the people which Burke denied a place among the causes of the revolution, where James Mackintosh shows that the changes of 1789 may be consistent with the principles of 1688 and approval of the French Revolution continuous with the traditional Whig view of the "settlement" of 1689, where Joseph Priestley sees how Burke's historicism must be taken to qualify his sense that the British political system "is placed in a just correspondence and symmetry with the order of the world"—in this company, Wollstonecraft can seem to have missed her cue. If, in 1790, one wanted pragmatic help in winning the debate, she would not be one's first choice of an ally. And yet she seems to me a more original moral thinker, and a deeper reader of Burke, than any of the large and capable regiment of anti-Burke pamphleteers.

Two facts about the composition of the *Vindication of the Rights of Men* have a circumstantial interest. Wollstonecraft wrote it quickly. The *Reflections* appeared on the first day of November 1790, and by the last day of November, copies of the *Vindication* were on sale. An intimate detail gives a more personal coloring to the achievement and may say something, too, about how to read her argument. Wollstonecraft took on the task of writing against Burke at the suggestion of the radical publisher Joseph Johnson, whose *Analytical Review* she assisted as a reviewer of romances and books of moral philosophy. Some way into the writing, she found that she could not continue; as William Godwin relates the incident in his *Memoir of the Author of the "Rights of Woman"*:

> It was sent to the press, as is the general practice when the early publication of a piece is deemed a matter of importance, before the composition was finished. When Mary had arrived at about the middle of her work, she was seized with a temporary fit of torpor and indolence, and began to repent of her undertaking. In this state of mind, she called, one evening, as she was in the practice of doing, upon her publisher, for the purpose of relieving herself by an hour or two's conversation. Here, the habitual ingenuousness of her nature, led her to describe what had just past in her thoughts. Mr. Johnson immediately, in a kind and friendly way, intreated her not to put any constraint upon her inclination, and to give herself no uneasiness about the sheets already printed, which he would cheerfully throw aside, if it would contribute to her happiness. Mary had wanted stimulus. She had not expected to be encouraged, in what she well knew to be an unreasonable access of idleness. Her friend's so readily falling in with her ill-humour, and seeming to expect that she would lay aside her undertaking, piqued her pride.[1]

And so, says Godwin, she finished. But in this anecdote, I find the explanation of "torpor and indolence" unlikely. A young political writer undertakes to rebuke, in public, the greatest political writer of the age on the appearance of a work in which he seemed to turn against the cause of liberty for which he once fought heroically: how shall we describe the mood of such a person at such a time? Idleness may have been her word, but we are not bound to repeat it. Possibly she "began to repent of her undertaking" from a scruple about the sort of attack she had launched against a mind of Burke's stature. Anyway, the sentiment that Godwin paraphrases from the delicate persuasive tactic of Johnson—that she ought "not to put any constraint upon her inclination"—is in the context equivocal; one may suspect the constraint was prompted by decorum, by feelings of respect and awe, rather more than by idleness.

In its final form, her reply to Burke is free of the virulent strain of slander and insinuation common in the pamphlet wars of the 1790s. She writes ad hominem when she pleases, but exhibits, much of the time, a strong mixture of respect for the author of *Reflections on the Revolution in France*:

> From the many just sentiments interspersed through the letter before me [i.e., the *Reflections*], and from the whole tendency of it, I should believe you to be a good, though a vain man, if some circumstances of your conduct did not render the inflexibility of your integrity doubtful; and for this vanity a knowledge of human nature enables me to discover such extenuating circumstances, in the very texture of your mind, that I am ready to call it amiable, and separate the public from the private character.[2]

Compare Paine on Burke's "periods, with music in the ear, and nothing in the heart," and on Burke's character, "accustomed to kiss the aristocratical hand that hath purloined him from himself." Or Priestley, certain that had

Burke lived at the time of the first apostles, "[Y]ou would, according to your general maxim, have cherished your old heathen 'prejudices, because they were old' and have lived and died a humble worshipper of the Gods, and especially the *Goddesses,* of ancient Greece and Rome." Or a smaller talent, Brooke Boothby, avowing, before an all-out parody of Burke's lament for the "age of chivalry," that "Twenty years ago you would not have thought of this revolution as you do now. In the sage caution I think may be discerned something of the timidity of age."[3] These reactions typify the mischief and the confidence of the radical opposition. By contrast, the steadiness of Wollstonecraft's engagement with Burke gives her book its special authority as an act of moral imagination.

She understood, as Paine and the suffrage of radical opinion did not, that the basis of Burke's political argument lay in an argument about morality. And she knew that morals in Burke's view—and it was a view she accepted—were themselves constituted by taste and manners. The subtlety with which she illustrates this understanding and brings it to bear in practical criticism, makes Wollstonecraft's proper company not Paine and Priestley and Mackintosh, but Wordsworth and Hazlitt in the next generation. Unlike these later authors, however, her purpose in writing about Burke is not appreciative, not even antithetically appreciative. She wants to isolate a truth in his idea of the coherence of taste and morality in order to reverse the direction in which Burke believed his idea necessarily pointed. She will therefore argue, from similar intuitions about the authority of feelings and habits of thought, to a radically different conclusion than any entertained by Burke. Recall that in the *Reflections,* Burke says we must feel the evil of wicked acts sensibly, that is, with the feminine virtue of sensibility enlivening our judgment, and this most pressingly when we feel for the weak and the wronged—his great example being the queen of France during the October days of 1789. Wollstonecraft will answer that we must feel the evil of wicked acts strongly, sympathetically, with the weight of a judging conscience that is neither masculine nor feminine, and on behalf of the weak, who are bound neither to be nor to resemble women. To defeat Burke's soliciting of delicate feelings of pity for the aristocracy, Wollstonecraft had determined to break up his association of aristocracy with a specialized kind of feminine character. She has here a larger interest in exposing the social wrong of any specializing of a virtue to either sex; for this reason, as I hope to show, the *Vindication of the Rights of Men* holds the germ of the *Vindication of the Rights of Woman,* which she wrote less than two years later.

For a critic of Burke, to engage him on the subject of taste means to ponder the implications of his elegiac rhapsody on Marie Antoinette. Wollstonecraft mentions the passage only once, when she considers his provocative judgment that under the system of chivalry in Europe, "vice itself lost half its evil, by losing all its grossness." Quoting those words, she says with shock and dismay: "What a sentiment to come from a moral pen!" Because she never confronts the description more directly, yet her reading of it generates her revision of Burkean morality, one needs to recall the peculiar character of the passage: the way it expands an analysis of a single moral response to serve as the paradigm for the ordering of a whole morality, and the hints by which it characterizes the person whom such a response may be supposed to inhabit. In summarizing again the best-known pages of *Reflections,* I aim to describe them from Wollstonecraft's point of view. There is something arbitrary in such a procedure but nothing finally unjust if one believes as I do that she got Burke right.

On October 6, 1789, a crowd of hunger marchers from Paris, who had grown turbulent when they assembled at Versailles, pursued the queen to her chamber with the intent of subjecting her to indignities difficult to imagine. Two of her bodyguards were killed, but the mob was held off by the National Guard and later appeased by the intervention of Lafayette. However, Burke pauses at the moment of impending catastrophe to praise the conduct of the queen, and to narrate his own sympathetic response. She has "borne that day (one is interested that beings made for suffering should suffer well) . . . in a manner suited to her rank and race, and becoming the offspring of a sovereign distinguished for her piety and her courage."[4] An homage equal to what Burke feels for the queen can only come in the form of a personal memory:

> It is now sixteen or seventeen years since I saw the queen of France, then the dauphiness, at Versailles; and surely never lighted on this orb, which she hardly seemed to touch, a more delightful vision. I saw her just above the horizon, decorating and cheering the elevated sphere she just began to move in,—glittering like the morning-star, full of life, and splendor, and joy. Oh! What a revolution! and what an heart must I have, to contemplate without emotion that elevation and that fall! Little did I dream when she added titles of veneration to those of enthusiastic, distant, respectful love, that she should ever be obliged to carry the sharp antidote against disgrace concealed in that bosom; little did I dream that I should have lived to see such disasters fallen upon her in a nation of gallant men, in a nation of men of honour and of cavaliers. I thought ten thousand swords must have leaped from their scabbards to avenge even a look that threatened her with insult.—But the age of chivalry is gone.—That of sophisters, oeconomists, and calculators, has succeeded; and the glory of Europe is extinguished for ever. Never, never more, shall we behold that generous loyalty to rank and sex, that proud submission, that dignified obedience, that subordination of the heart, which kept alive, even in servitude itself, the spirit of an exalted freedom. The unbought grace of life, the cheap defence of nations, the nurse of manly sentiment and heroic enterprize is gone! It is gone, that sensibility of principle, that chastity of honour, which felt a stain like a wound, which inspired courage whilst it mitigated ferocity, which ennobled whatever it touched, and under which vice lost half its evil, by losing all its grossness.[5]

Burke traces this amelioration of vice by refinement—of wicked policy by an inherited decency of manners—to the "mixed system of opinion and sentiment" that "had its origin in the ancient chivalry." It was a system "which mitigated kings into companions, and raised private men to be fellows with kings." All this was accomplished by "the soft collar of social esteem," which cushions and gently coerces all ranks of society from high to low. As certain compunctions were prescribed for rulers, so certain deferences were inculcated upon their subjects; and so long as both observed the unquestioned practice of such manners, a revolutionary mob was as improbable a social result as an arbitrary ruler. This thought about the tacit yet compelling authority of manners pervades the *Reflections*: Burke has in mind the same symmetry of conduct between high and low within a society when he writes, "Kings will be tyrants from policy when subjects are rebels from principle." The agreement that cements a tranquil society is all the more real for being tacit. It betokens a standard so far beyond challenge that it need never be positively recorded.

So much for the materials of any living morality. How was the work of personal choice, or ratification, on which such a morality must depend, successfully performed in the gracious time Burke says is past? It was done by a habit of justifying actions that never exposed them to the glare of estimates from sheer utility. Rather, moral judgments were rendered complex, and were made more sure of themselves, by virtue of "the decent drapery of life." This drapery, as Burke explains, is a metaphor for "all the super-added ideas [concerning the worthiness of beauty, for example, just because it is beautiful, and the rightness of docility toward established power], furnished from the wardrobe of a moral imagination."[6] As he elaborates the conception, the super-added ideas are like the clothing of a woman, naturally respected by all but those who think such layers are *just* ideological coverings. Little as we know about modern revolutionaries, we know this kind of assault is within the reach of their character. So the victim in the Burkean scene of revolutionary catastrophe turns out to be a woman who should have been rescued. The spectator, whom Burke imagines as capable of actually saving her, is a man of a certain sort—a man who feels himself to exemplify "the spirit of a gentleman"; who thinks that "to make us love our country, our country ought to be lovely"; who, when he feels differently from others, or when he feels the same, can justify himself with confidence by saying, "It is *natural* I should." For such a man, the responses of moral action are directly related to the judgments enforced by the delicacy of taste. He will unquestioningly associate the proprieties of social life with the proprieties of art. When he feels doubtful, he will apply for direction to the masters of "the moral constitution of the heart," an ideal tribunal which consists, above all, of poets who know "the feelings of humanity." His mind filled by the teaching of the imaginative school of moral sentiments, such a man, contemplating the sufferings of the queen on October 6, will say with Burke, "Some tears might be drawn from me, if such a spectacle were exhibited on the stage." The theatrical test is conclusive.

I have described the susceptible male character Burke represents when he writes as a spectator of the Revolution informed by chivalric ideas, and I have done so as if one were obliged to approach the character schematically, or from an unfamiliar distance. But the truth is that the character was well known at the end of the eighteenth century—writers and readers had a name for him. He was the "man of feeling," the "man of sensibility." Imagine now the situation of Mary Wollstonecraft as she set out to describe this book on France by an admirer of the queen of France. It is important never to forget that Wollstonecraft hated the violence against Marie Antoinette. She saw it as a savage and regressive act—not an excusable excess and not a liberating stroke against piety—and four years later her *View of the French Revolution* makes a conclusive judgment of the October days. She calls the mob "vagabonds," and the raising of the mob by the Duke of Orleans

> one of the blackest of the machinations that have since the revolution disgraced the dignity of man, and sullied the annals of humanity. Disappointed in their main object, these wretches beheaded two of the guards, who fell into their hands; and hurried away towards the metropolis, with the *insignia* of their atrocity on the points of the barbarous instruments of vengeance—showing in every instance, by the difference of their conduct, that they were a set of monsters, distinct from the people.[7]

She will not allow the conduct of the mob to cool her advocacy of the people, any more than she will be seduced by zeal to palliate the crimes of a revolution.

But Wollstonecraft would have intensely disliked Burke's symbolic and rhetorical use of the interlude. Half of her life, she sometimes felt, had been wasted in reading novels intended to instruct and please, whose heroines shared the traits of the queen of France as Burke painted her. In these novels, too, a unique power of agency was assigned to the man capable of acting on the heroine's behalf. In order to feel properly for her, the hero was emotionally disposed to be something like a woman, yet his displays of valor were such as to obviate any moral action by the woman herself: "[T]en thousand swords must have leaped from their scabbards to avenge even a look that threatened her with insult." She notes dryly in the *View of the French Revolution* that "*swords had ceased to leap out of their scabbards* when beauty was not deified,"[8] but even without the later testimony, one can see well enough what the plot of the *Reflections* must have looked like to her. The worst feature of the book, as she read it, was the narrowing of scope that followed from the "gothic affability" of a narrator like Burke, and his consequent indifference to what she calls "the silent majesty of misery." Meanwhile, phrases like "decent drapery" worked as eulogistic concealments for a heroine who did nothing because it was her place to do nothing but supply gentle bait for the hero of sensibility—a heroine whose moral duty was to be, so that men might do, and whose practice of the special feminine virtue of modesty could disarm any accusation of artful dealings or moral obliquity. In the *Vindication of the Rights of Woman*, Wollstonecraft would quote Catherine Macaulay: "There is but one fault which a woman of honor may not commit with impunity"—namely, the fault that would give her a character of immodesty. This much, Wollstonecraft had already discerned from Burke's portrait of the queen; for his queen was no different in kind from the well-rewarded girl of humbler birth who formed the weak moral center of the standard novel or romance.

Once Wollstonecraft has established that Burkean chivalry is another name for the cult of sensibility, she has her target well in view. I do not underrate the power of irony that was necessary to reach that point. It took genius to get there, and an accompanying clarity of purpose comes out in incidental touches—for instance, in the way she alludes in passing to "cold, romantic characters" who are full of artificial feelings; where by a simple juxtaposition (cold, romantic), she catches Burke's sentimental theory in a contradiction it engenders from within. Once we concede that all moral feelings are learned to the point of being second nature and seeming in retrospect to have been untaught, what is to prevent the responses they prompt from becoming unfelt as well as unreflective? But the allusive arguments in Wollstonecraft are often more pointed than this. She traces in literal detail the consequences of Burke's aphorism about vice losing half its evil by losing all its grossness. Fully worked out as a prescriptive ethics, his sentence implies that virtue stained by grossness has a lower position in the moral scale than vice given luster by refinement. Wollstonecraft reduces the thesis to a pair of examples. "Stealing, whoring, and drunkenness" are on this theory more blamable than "over-reaching [in its old sense of fraud], adultery, and coquetry"[9]—though the former vices, gross as they are, need not "obliterate every moral sentiment," while the latter "reduce virtue to an empty name" and thus threaten the very principle of society. The examples are calculated to bring a maximum of discomfort to the reader who has understood and taken satisfaction in Burke's paradox. *Vice lost half its evil, by losing all its grossness*: he meant, with those words, to defend hypocrisy as a practice consistent with the socialized understanding of shame, and to maintain that the Jacobins, by tearing the veil from every moral practice, had created an ethic at once antihypocritical and perfectly shameless. Wollstonecraft here replies that it is a condition of the paradox that Burke should blame vices that are merely self-destructive or bluntly transgressive, while he spares vices that entail a hardened contempt for the moral being of others. The half-virtues of the hypocrisy that Burke wants to half-praise all have this in common, that they treat persons as means. This refined morality will sooner tolerate Valmont than Sir Toby Belch, and that is part of what Wollstonecraft has in mind when she remarks (addressing Burke in person): "[Y]our politics and morals, when simplified, would undermine religion and virtue to set up a spurious, sensual beauty, that has long debauched your imagination, under the specious form of actual feelings."[10] The key phrase seems to me to be "undermine religion." Burke, she judges, has an irreligious conception of virtue; for her, virtue will prove inseparable from religious faith. It is not an innate quality, to be calmly accepted, but must be acquired by struggle. If things were otherwise, with what possible purpose could we associate our experiences on earth?

Like Paine after her, Wollstonecraft agrees with many particulars of Burke's criticism of the National Assembly and of the Paris mob that was first the servant, then the master of the assembly. Like Paine, too, she blames their errors on the history of corrupt social relations in France. Not the wrong judgments of the revolutionaries but the depaved feelings that are the legacy of despotism have produced these effects. It would have been better if the abolition of titles had not been the work of those who "had no titles to sacrifice," and whose conduct might accordingly be construed as simple revenge. This repeats Burke's strictures against the lawyers of a low type who formed a great proportion of the National Assembly—"men not taught habitually to respect themselves; who had no previous fortune in character at stake; who could not be expected to bear with moderation, or to conduct with discretion, a power which they themselves, more than any others, must be surprized to find in their hands."[11] Wollstonecraft observes, in the same key: "Weak minds are always timid. And what can equal the weakness of mind produced by servile flattery, and the vapid pleasure that neither hope nor fear seasoned?"[12] But in a society where equal claims were granted to men and women, or to those with much property and those with little, strong minds would be formed by the clash of independent opinions so as mutually to fortify the contending parties. As it is, the only opportunity for rich and poor, for men and women, has been mutual corruption. There is much additional evidence in the *Rights of Men* that Wollstonecraft already supposed a society is good to the exact degree that it permits the development of the moral courage of individual minds: "To argue from experience, it should seem as if the human mind, averse to thought, could only be opened by necessity; for, when it can take opinions on trust, it gladly lets the spirit lie quiet in its gross tenement."[13] Her phrasing is scrupulous and has an uncommon resonance for those who have read Burke with care.

Necessity is a crucial idea everywhere in Burke, but an idea whose influence is often hidden. A thinker gifted with a potent imagination of disaster, who virtually defines prudence as the accommodation of diverse interests to obviate sudden change, Burke conceives of necessity as the moment of privation or blank at which a political order disintegrates because it has lost all faith in the givenness of its arrangments. Inertia, and the presence of an inert class in society, come into his idea of political health at some cost in paradox, just for the sake of avoiding the necessity that supplies a main motive for action in more volatile theorists. The thought of necessity is to Burke what the thought of death is to Hobbes. In the face of this aversion, Wollstonecraft argues that the sheer stimulus or excitement that comes from necessity may be requisite to the spiritual activity of an individual mind. She writes vividly against the conception of virtue as an innate capacity with which Burke has guarded his idea of an uninterrupted order:

> Every thing looks like a means, nothing like an end, or point of rest, when we can say, now let us sit down and enjoy the present moment; our faculties

and wishes are proportioned to the present scene; we may return without repining to our sister clod. And, if no conscious dignity whisper that we are capable of relishing more refined pleasures, the thirst of truth appears to be allayed; and thought, the faint type of an immaterial energy, no longer bounding it knows not where, is confined to the tenement that affords it sufficient variety.[14]

That the development of virtue has no visible termination and no point of rest seems to Wollstonecraft "one of the strongest arguments for the natural immortality of the soul."

Burke in the *Reflections* sometimes writes as if he believes that virtue is a habit, sometimes as if he believes that it is an instinct; the famous aphorism "[P]rejudice renders a man's virtue his habit" splits the difference. Wollstonecraft, I think, confirms his preponderant emphasis when she denies that virtue can be an instinct. But she parts company with him in identifying the kind of acquired power virtue is. It does not, she says, spring from and does not trace its authority to the conventional life of society, which could hardly advance two moments together without the work of habit. It is rather a habit acquired by the soul in its contest with adversity, or the soul struggling in the usual current of unforeseeable questionings. Burke said that the people of England "know we have made no discoveries in morality. We know that no discoveries are to be made." It may be true that all societies are partial successes—true enough to discourage any revolution that induces sudden and widespread suffering in any class in society. Maybe, in this sense, no discoveries have been made. But Wollstonecraft, because she believes in "genuine acquired virtue," sees what a sophistical gloss Burke's "we" incorporates. Is it true of each person subsumed by his "we" that he or she has made no discovery in morality, through the medium of thought and feeling in a world that allows both thought and feeling some inroads in action? To deny this freedom seems to Wollstonecraft an act of metaphysical supererogation as bad as anything Burke castigates in the Jacobins; for, to her, virtue has reality only as a personal discovery that is wholly guided neither by its beginning nor its end:

> If virtue be an instinct, I renounce all hope of immortality; and with it all the sublime reveries and dignified sentiments that have smoothed the rugged path of life: it is all a cheat, a lying vision; I have disquieted myself in vain; for in my eye all feelings are false and spurious, that do not rest on justice as their foundation, and are not concentred by universal love.
>
> I reverence the rights of men.—Sacred rights! for which I acquire a more profound respect, the more I look into my own mind; and, professing these heterodox opinions, I still preserve my bowels; my heart is human, beats quick with human sympathies—and I FEAR God!
>
> I bend with awful reverence when I enquire on what my fear is built.—I fear that sublime power, whose motive for creating me must have been wise and good; and I submit to the moral laws which my reason deduces from this view

of my dependence on him.—It is not his power that I fear—it is not to an arbitrary will, but to an unerring *reason* that I submit.[15]

Some precise inferences are to be made from the phrasing of this credo. By her assertion that "If virtue be an instinct, I renounce all hope of immortality," Wollstonecraft may seem to evade analysis by retreating to an intuition. But her intent is plain from the earlier passages of the *Rights of Men* concerning the tyranny of prescription in society and the deference to prejudice as "untaught feelings," of which she speaks with the bitterness one may justly feel against a social scheme that promotes satisfaction with things as they are. If the finite and given sources of contentment are all we exist for, she says, "Let us eat and drink, for tomorrow we die—and die for ever!" On this view, God created human life for no more inventive purpose than is evident in the creatureliness of animals, each with its designated and undeflectable function—so that, quite oddly, the idea of innate virtue returns us to the anti-imaginative and even the utilitarian measure of things that Burke himself acutely satirized: the measure by which "a queen is but a woman; a woman is but an animal; and an animal not of the highest order." To the reader of the *Rights of Men* who keeps the *Reflections* in view, it becomes gradually clear that Wollstonecraft does think of Burke as an irreligious mind.

This is at least so far warranted that one cannot conceive the words "I FEAR God" or anything remotely like them inhabiting the structure of the *Reflections* unless the words were quickly followed by allusions to Burke's coequal fear of the king and parliament and the ancient constitution. Society is his God; and Wollstonecraft sees this clearly: a page after the declaration I have just quoted, she transcribes a paragraph of Burke in which he writes of the happy result "when the people have emptied themselves of all the lust of selfish will." In that state, "in their nomination to office," says Burke, "they will not appoint to the exercise of authority as to a pitiful job, but as to an holy function." At the last turn of phrase, Wollstonecraft pounces:

> Sir, let me ask you, with manly plainness—are these *holy* nominations? Where is the booth of religion? Does she mix her awful mandates, or lift her persuasive voice, in those scenes of drunken riot and bestial gluttony? Does she preside over those nocturnal abominations which so evidently tend to deprave the manners of the lower class of people? ... Yet, after the effervescence of spirits, raised by opposition, and all the little and tyrannic arts of canvassing are over—quiet souls! They only intend to march rank and file to say YES—or NO.[16]

How did Burke arrive at a habit of thinking of politics as sacred?—a habit so deep it could surprise, one imagines, even him in his casual choice of a word, and a habit the more curious in view of its resemblance to a leading fault he will later impute to the Jacobins: that they have been led by political fanaticism to "compound with their nature," and so have cheated themselves of the knowledge that only human feelings are sacred and the deepest of those feelings are reserved for a person who suffers. Wollstonecraft thinks she knows how he fell into the error; I take her to be describing that process when she says he was misled by "the sophistry of asserting that nature leads us to reverence our civil institutions from the same principle that we venerate aged individuals." This she calls "a palpable fallacy 'that is so like truth, it will serve the turn as well.' "[17] In what does the sophistry consist? Burke has perhaps deceived himself before deceiving others, by the ascription of natural and metaphorical dignity to a fact in itself sufficiently artificial and banal. He has linked two disparate kinds of feeling by selecting out the mere common quality of age—as if that alone, which does bring associations of respect or habitual regard, necessarily brought also associations of dearness and heartfelt attachment. The truth is that a corporate body has no soul, and we do not feel, even for living institutions of which we ourselves are members, quite in the same way that we do for individuals.

It will now be clear how thoroughly Wollstonecraft assimilates Burke's thinking about morality to her separate aim as a political moralist. Her argument for genuine acquired virtue builds on his argument for a moral imagination, but it need not therefore support the whole pattern of prescriptive usages he saw as the inevitable consequence. Wollstonecraft shows that Burke's beliefs, followed in their whole length, are by nature no more reactionary than they are revolutionary—though, under a system where inveterate abuses have grown habitual, they will tend to the revolutionary side. Yet this substantial accomplishment still leaves something wanting from the author of a book called *A Vindication of the Rights of Men*. "The rights of men," as invoked by anyone in the 1790s, implied a conviction of the necessity of righting the balance between the happiness of a few and the unhappiness of many; but so vast a change is bound to look like a sacrifice to some, in their capacity as individual minds which Wollstonecraft holds sacred. She is aware that an answer is expected here, and her response is so intricate, yet so deliberately stated, in contrast with the rapid controversial style which dominates the pamphlet, that her emerging argument can easily pass unobserved. She writes:

> The justice of God may be vindicated by a belief in a future state; but, only by believing that evil is educing good for the individual, and not for an imaginary whole. The happiness of the whole must arise from the happiness of the constituent parts, or the essence of justice is sacrificed to a supposed grand arrangement. And that may be good for the whole of a creature's existence, that disturbs the comfort of a small portion. The evil which an individual suffers for the good of the community is partial, it must be allowed, if the account is settled by death.—But the partial evil which it suffers, during one stage of existence, to render another stage more perfect, is strictly just. The Father of all only can regulate the education of his children. To suppose that, during the whole or part of its existence, the happiness of any individual is sacrificed to promote the welfare of ten, or ten thousand, other beings—is impious. But to suppose that

the happiness, or animal enjoyment, of one portion of existence is sacrificed to improve and ennoble the being itself, and render it capable of more perfect happiness, is not to reflect on either the goodness or wisdom of God.[18]

It is important to see what place this apology leaves for political action, and what kind of action it eminently permits or prohibits. By the argument above, Wollstonecraft is committed unconditionally to renounce all political acts that require the sacrifice even of one individual for the welfare of ten thousand. To assume that such an act could be justified involves the belief that the account is settled by death, the belief that the only life after death is the life of society which we agree to make our religion, the same belief that Burke found unacceptable in the Jacobins and that Wollstonecraft finds unacceptable in Burke. Her strictures also evidently rule out a defense of any general proscription or persecution ending in killing, or in the punishment of unsuspecting persons found newly guilty under a new law. The argument does not rule out the compelled transfer of property, nor does it exclude certain forms of late, and perhaps of compelled, education for offenders whose crimes descend from the regular habits of an old regime. The last would have been a main implication to Wollstonecraft (who thought of herself primarily as an educator) of the phrase about one portion of existence being "sacrificed to improve and ennoble the being itself, and render it capable of more perfect happiness." The sacrifice is tolerable within an individual life, to advance individual happiness. Very likely, she agreed with Richard Price that the future improvement of humankind as promised in the words of the Lord's Prayer, "on earth as it is in heaven," was providentially intended to bring earthly life into conformity with the Christian imagining of heaven. But the change may feel devastating. "Virtue can flourish only amongst equals," she will say near the end of the book;[19] and this discovery may be initially shocking to some of those whom it finally benefits.

The last observation seems to presuppose the idea that the rich are unconscious sufferers on account of their own advantages. Wollstonecraft does see them in that light, and in doing so she borrows uncannily from Burke, even as, once again, she shifts the weight of his conclusion. It remains today a puzzle about the *Reflections* that a man of talent and energy such as Edmund Burke should have chosen to devote a panegyric to the inertia of the aristocracy. What had he in common with them? "Is it," asks Wollstonecraft, "among the list of possibilities that a man of rank and fortune *can* have received a good education? How can he discover that he is a man, when all his wants are instantly supplied, and invention is never sharpened by necessity?"[20] Education itself makes us conceive fresh wants, makes us also interested in distinction, and therefore, whether we please to think so or not, makes us interested in something besides the present state of things. At least, this holds true for individuals as we reflect on ourselves. Nothing but the limits of our imagination prevents us from applying the moral generally. Burke, as Wollstonecraft means to suggest, is himself a typical beneficiary of education. In fact, she thinks he wrote the book mainly with a thought of distinction for himself: "You have said many things merely for the sake of saying them well." And again, "You make as much noise to convince the world that you despise the revolution, as Rousseau did to persuade his contemporaries to let him live in obscurity."[21] Had Burke been a Frenchman, she surmises, he would have stood with the advocates of the revolution. It is an affectation in him to plead for those whose every want has been assured in advance.

In all this train of thought, Wollstonecraft is as close as usual to the texture of the *Reflections*. She is remembering a passage so equivocal that most of Burke's commentators for two centuries have overlooked it—a paragraph strangely touched by apologetic pity for the rich, and impossible to reconcile with Burke's announced purpose of acquitting the dignity of the aristocracy.

> They too are among the unhappy. They feel personal pain and domestic sorrow. In these they have no privilege, but are subject to pay their full contingent to the contributions levied on mortality. They want this sovereign balm under their gnawing cares and anxieties, which being less conversant about the limited wants of animal life, range without limit, and are diversified by infinite combinations in the wild and unbounded regions of imagination. Some charitable dole is wanting to these, our often very unhappy brethren, to fill the gloomy void that reigns in minds which have nothing on earth to hope or fear; something to relieve in the killing languor and over-laboured lassitude of those who have nothing to do; something to excite an appetite to existence in the palled satiety which attends on all pleasures which may be bought, where nature is not left to her own process, where even desire is anticipated, and therefore fruition defeated by meditated schemes and contrivances of delight; and no interval, no obstacle, is interposed between the wish and the accomplishment.[22]

I am uncertain what to make of this passage—how to fit it into any construal of the *Reflections* or even to explain by what means it got there. It has going somewhere underneath it the very cold and savage style of wit that five years later will dominate Burke's *Letter to a Noble Lord*; and, with that, a tone of continuous vexing irony that is pragmatically serviceable to no political side. But Wollstonecraft could with equal plausibility have read this passage as one more bizarre exercise of overwrought sensibility—a faculty, she says, by nature liable to perverse and self-regarding displays. What could top the aristocratic sensibility of an author who sees that the aristocrats themselves labor under a pathetic want of interest in life, and who concludes that they can be helped, if they can be helped at all, by a "charitable dole" of sentiments from someone both below and above their rank, a moralist uniquely charged with the memory of the sentiments of humankind?

A view of Wollstonecraft's engagement with Burke ought to end where it begins, with the passion that animated her revolt against sensibility. This was a lifelong argument for her, and I close by looking back at her source and forward to the results in the second *Vindication*. Further back than the

Reflections, her prompting came from the Burke of *A Philosophical Origin of Our Ideas of the Enquiry into the Sublime and Beautiful*. To recall the broad divisions of that book, the beautiful is feminine, and its typical qualities are to be fair, little, smooth, weak, unimpeding. The sublime is masculine, and its typical qualities are to be irregular or infinite in successiveness, grand, rough, strong, and so much an obstacle that we can only encounter it safely as an idea. The beautiful is a possession we can care for; the sublime, a threatening encumbrance that may possess us. Burke makes plain how far the sexual character of the distinction may reach when he says that the authority of a father is too mixed with an idea of strength to admit the sentiment of love we feel for a mother. (Not so, or much less so, in the case of a grandfather, where terror is mitigated by distance and a less severe regimen of compelled docility.) In short, "we submit to what we admire, but we love what submits to us; in the one case we are forced, in the other we are flattered into compliance."[23] Thus, not only is sublimity associated with admiration and unwilling submission, and beauty with love and voluntary submission, but, in Burke's identification of sublimity with pain and beauty with pleasure, he admits no possibility of combination between the beautiful and the sublime that does not entirely destroy the beautiful. The sublime, on the other hand, may on occasion be softened without altogether losing its character of power. It follows that the beautiful, the containable thing that solicits but does not demand compliance, may endear itself to us by its very irregularities or defects; and Part III, Section ix, of the *Sublime and Beautiful*, under the heading "Perfection not the cause of beauty," includes these sentences in Burke's empiricist-dandyish style, which Wollstonecraft must have known by heart:

> So far is perfection, considered as such, from being the cause of beauty; that this quality, where it is highest in the female sex, almost always carries with it an idea of weakness and imperfection. Women are very sensible of this; for which reason, they learn to lisp, to totter in their walk, to counterfeit weakness, and even sickness. In all this, they are guided by nature. Beauty in distress is much the most affecting beauty. . . . I know, it is in every body's mouth, that we ought to love perfection. This is to me a sufficient proof, that it is not the proper object of love.[24]

To present Wollstonecraft's reply to this thought has been part of my motive in discussing the *Vindication of the Rights of Men*. The reply is still going strong in the *Vindication of the Rights of Woman*.

She there observes that in a Burkean or sentimental morality, women are trapped by the requirement that they seek love by display of the same characteristics that defeat self-respect. "As a moralist, I ask what is meant by such heterogeneous associations, as fair defects, amiable weaknesses, etc.? If there be but one criterion of morals, but one archetype for man, women appear to be suspended by destiny, according to the vulgar tale of Mahomet's coffin."[25] It may be said in extenuation of the *Sublime and Beautiful* that four decades of sentimental novels had done more to corrupt morality than a single, early, though very widely read, theoretical romance by Edmund Burke. Wollstonecraft concedes as much; but the particular damage of Burke's morality of manners was, as she saw it, to give a sanction, in the higher walks of art and politics, to a way of thinking that might otherwise have fallen into disrepute as an obvious outgrowth of libertinism. She herself in the *Rights of Men* had called sensibility a libertine morality; in the *Rights of Woman* she associates it with "a kind of sentimental lust," which she thinks peculiarly French. But the polemical victories she scored in the *Rights of Men* were not fully recognized, and so she returns to the topic in earnest and at length. The *Rights of Woman* offers a notable positive program, and if one numbers among its achievements the reasoned case for coeducation, and the unforgettable challenge to the idea of heroic virtues, it makes no sense to trace those elements to Wollstonecraft's dispute with Burke. Yet in the later book, it is again her polemical motive that prods her invention, and the tactics she discovered two years earlier now emerge as more than tactics.

In writing explicitly for the advancement of women, Wollstonecraft saw that she had to do two things: first, to show that fair defects are not only the property of the fair, by tracing how in society the same traits are picked up by others whose accidents or disproportions of education closely resemble those of women; and second, to cast doubt on the thesis that the beautiful can allow no admixture of the sublime unless it would renounce its claim to beauty. The persons, besides women, who exhibit most conspicuously the presence of fair defects turn out to be soldiers—an adventurous comparison that no other pamphleteer would have dared and none could possibly have carried off:

> Soldiers [like women] acquire a little superficial knowledge, snatched from the muddy current of conversation, and, from continually mixing with society, they gain, what is termed a knowledge of the world. . . . Soldiers, as well as women, practise the minor virtues with punctilious politeness. . . . It may be further observed, that officers are also particularly attentive to their persons, fond of dancing, crowded rooms, adventures, and ridicule. Like the *fair* sex, the business of their lives is gallantry.—They were taught to please, and they live only to please.[26]

The case is clinched by the unprejudiced plainness of the analogy. By contrast, the argument that gentleness, suffering, and a passionate endurance may be elements of the sublime as well as the beautiful, seems impossible to advance against Burke, until one thinks of the example of Jesus Christ. Conscious that some of what appears most chivalric in the Burkean morality is also unchristian, Wollstonecraft simply marks the example with everything it may prove: "Gentleness of manners, forbearance and long-suffering, are such amiable Godlike qualities, that in sublime poetic strains the Deity has been invested with them; and, perhaps, no representation of His goodness so strongly fastens on the human affections as those that represent Him abundant in mercy and willing to pardon."[27] This sentence closes the confrontation. The divergence of premises between Burke and Wollstonecraft turns out to be greater after all than appeared from their unexpected affinity of motives in 1790. In answer to Burke's identification of prejudice with untaught feelings, Wollstonecraft remarks in the *Rights of Woman*: "A prejudice is a fond obstinate persuasion for which we can give no reason; for the moment a reason can be given for an opinion, it ceases to be a prejudice."[28] But there are obstinacies that outlast every reason even in the thoroughly educated. Burke's fear of disorder was a prejudice of this kind, and the religion of society was his rational-sounding answer to the fear. In the end, Wollstonecraft's faith in individual conscience is a prejudice of the same kind, and fear of God and of herself is the name she finds for a rational obstinacy equal to Burke's.

NOTES

1. William Godwin, *Memoir of the Author of the "Rights of Woman"* (London and New York: Penguin, 1987), p. 230.

2. *The Works of Mary Wollstonecraft* (7 vols.), ed. Janet Todd and Marilyn Butler (London: Pickering, 1989), vol. 5, pp. 7–8. I use this volume of the *Works* hereafter for the text of both *Vindications*.

3. Thomas Paine, *The Rights of Man* (London and New York: Penguin, 1984), pp. 46, 51; Joseph Priestley, *Letters to the Right Honourable Edmund Burke, Occasioned by his Reflections on the Revolution in France*, 3d ed. (London: Joseph Johnson, 1791), p. 61; Brooke Boothby, *A Letter to the Right Honourable Edmund Burke* (London: J. Debrett, 1791), p. 21.

4. Edmund Burke, *Reflections on the Revolution in France*, ed. Conor Cruise O'Brien (London and New York: Penguin, 1968), p. 169.

5. Burke, *Reflections*, pp. 169–170.

6. *Ibid.*, p. 171.

7. Mary Wollstonecraft, *An Historical and Moral View of the Origin and Progress of the French Revolution and the Effect It Has Produced in Europe*, in *Works*, vol. 6, p. 206.

8. *Ibid.*, p. 189.

9. Wollstonecraft, *Works*, vol. 5, p. 25.

10. *Ibid.*, p. 48.

11. Burke, *Reflections*, p. 130.

12. Wollstonecraft, *Works*, vol. 5, p. 47.

13. *Ibid.*, p. 19.

14. *Ibid.*, p. 16

15. *Ibid.*, pp. 33–34.

16. *Ibid.*, p. 36.

17. *Ibid.*, p. 49.

18. *Ibid.*, pp. 52–53.

19. *Ibid.*, p. 57.

20. *Ibid.*, p. 42.

21. *Ibid.*, pp. 29, 44.

22. Burke, *Reflections*, p. 201. "Even," in the penultimate clause, looks like a printer's error for "every."

23. Edmund Burke, *A Philosophical Enquiry into the Origin of our Ideas of the Sublime and Beautiful*, ed. J. T. Boulton (Notre Dame and London: University of Notre Dame Press, 1968), p. 113. A sensitive consideration of the *Rights of Men*, in the light of Burke's feminine definition of beauty, can be found in Harriet Devine Jump, *Mary Wollstonecraft: Writer* (London: Harvester, 1994), ch. 3.

24. Burke, *Philosophical Enquiry*, p. 110.

25. Wollstonecraft, *A Vindication of the Rights of Woman*, in *Works*, vol. 5, p. 103.

26. Wollstonecraft, *Works*, vol. 5, pp. 92–93.

27. *Ibid.*, pp. 101–102.

28. *Ibid.*, p. 182.

CHAPTER ELEVEN

As Time Goes By:
Justice, Gender, Drama, and George

HELENE KEYSSAR

GEORGE KATEB is the most private of men, but, when speaking of movies, he establishes a stunning intimacy with others. During the years when I saw George Kateb regularly and casually, it occurred to me more than once that George was put on earth primarily to enliven our lives with conversations about movies, or, more precisely, about ourselves as mediated by the movie of the moment. In *Robert Altman's America*, I speak briefly about the power of movies to provoke gossip, to allow us to speak our hearts with others while we are simultaneously speaking our minds about the stars and their characters, the world in which we live and the world projected on screen. When I think about film and such conversation, I think about George Kateb. "Transport me," he said, "but bring me back to gossip over the fence about *Waiting for Mr. Goodbar* or *The Crying Game*."

George's taste in movies has always been surprising in the moment, and yet, over time, I thought, predictable. Once, he told me—or perhaps sought my agreement—that there were no real movies before the 1950s. I half agreed and later wrote that the movies had come of age in the decade between the mid-1950s and mid-1960s. I meant by this that what had been unusual—color, wide-screen projection, stereophonic sound, location shooting that often required the use of a zoom lens, sound that acts as commentary on characters, plot, and period and can no longer be dismissed as background music—was, after the early 1960s, commonplace on the movie theater screen. And George and I both thought this was good. So when I began to think about writing something that had to do with things I think about and things George Kateb thinks about, I thought about such movies as *Rebel without a Cause* and *Paths of Glory*, *Dr. Strangelove* and *Bonnie and Clyde*, *Johnny Got His Gun* and *Easy Rider*, *Midnight Cowboy*, *The Wild Bunch*, *2001*, and *M*A*S*H**. (I reflected briefly on the important European movies that intellectuals were meant to see in the 1960s—*Jules and Jim* and *Persona* and *Blow-Up*—but I do not believe that was what George had in mind.)

It was thus somewhat disconcerting to find that, when asked indirectly some months ago to name his favorite movie, George's unhesitant answer was *Casablanca*. "But," I sputtered to myself, "George, *Casablanca* was made in 1942." "So it was," I could imagine him saying. "So it was."

Perhaps George had forgotten his claim about post-1940s movies, but I am more tempted to think that he found no significant discrepancy between his admiration and affection for *Casablanca* and his expressed preference for post-1940s movies. Still, why *Casablanca?* Why not *Citizen Kane* or *Rules of the Game?* I want to take these questions seriously enough that we can actually think about *Casablanca,* an activity few critics have attempted. To do this, I want to look first at another movie, George Cukor's *Adam's Rib,* made just at the end of the 1940s (but really, at least a 1950s if not 1960s film), and then at Aeschylus' *Oresteia.* I propose to approach *Adam's Rib* and the *Oresteia* (especially the *Eumenides*) as pre-texts, facades as well as entries to a few reflections on *Casablanca.*

•

Early in *Adam's Rib,* Amanda and Adam (Katherine Hepburn and Spencer Tracy) are sipping breakfast coffee in their elegant bedroom, when Amanda excitedly begins to read Adam an item from the morning paper. The story she reads to her husband has already been told to us in part by the camera in the opening sequence of the film: provoked by her husband's persistent infidelity, a working-class woman named Mrs. Doris Attinger (Judy Holliday, in her first major role) has discovered her husband with his mistress and shot at him (but not killed him).[1] During much of this opening sequence, the camera's point of view is proximate to and occasionally identical with that of Mrs. Attinger, but the camera retains a measure of directorial omniscience as well.

The newspaper story reveals that the woman we saw shooting at her husband has been arrested for attempted murder; her husband is recovering in a hospital from his wife's assault. Hepburn's face shows that she is immediately alert to the social implications of this incident, an event peculiar in its reversal of the conventional domestic triangle in which a husband defends his honor and his role as husband in the face of a wife's infidelity by killing or at least challenging the wife's lover. It will take another half-hour, however, for Amanda to articulate her initial perception that here is a case where sexual identity may alter the reading and judgment of an act . What Amanda grasps instantly is that both the public who read newspapers and the jurors who try the accused will judge the woman who assaults her husband for adultery in a fashion different from the way they would judge a man's attack on his wife and/or her lover for a similar act of infidelity. As if to orient us from the start to the importance of these differing perceptions, Adam proceeds to confirm Amanda's fear: trying to hold Adam's attention to the newspaper account, Amanda sputters, "This lady, this lady. . ." "What lady?" Adam interjects. "What *lady?*"

Cukor points in this exchange to the exact territory to explore if we are to appreciate the complex concerns of this film. The two opening sequences of *Adam's Rib* together establish complexities of gender, class, and point of view that make conversation—on and off screen—inevitable and necessary. All of us—George Cukor, Adam, Spencer Tracy, Amanda, George Kateb, and I know that if ever there has been an image of a lady in America it is that of Katherine Hepburn. On a leech-ridden river in Central Africa (*The African Queen*) or with a leopard and a beau in jail in Connecticut (*Bringing Up Baby*), Hepburn can only be a lady, no matter how hard she tries to be other, as actress or character. (This is not to make an essentialist claim about Hepburn or the qualities of a lady. In 1993, the concept of a lady still bears a thin tie to its origins in the aristocracies of the West, as is clear when we speak of "ladylike" behavior, and even the most fervent believers in biological origins of gender would not likely deny that a lady is a construct of culture.)

But Hepburn/Amanda is not the lady to whom Amanda and Adam refer in the scene just described, a scene that is, in fact, the second opening of *Adam's Rib*. The lady in question in Adam and Amanda's bedroom is Doris Attinger, whom we have already seen as a lonely, awkward, garishly dressed woman chewing a candy bar on a street corner. We have also seen this person nervously pursue a man onto the subway and finally through the street to a dingy apartment, where we watched her discover her husband embracing a woman named Beryl Kane, whom Mrs. Attinger and we correctly take to be Mr. Attinger's mistress. Then we watched Mrs. Attinger shoot at her husband, an act she accomplished with embarrassing clumsiness, ignorance, and ineptitude.

I can think of two reasons why Cukor screens the story of Doris Attinger's pursuit of her husband for the movie audience before we hear the same story from the newspaper mediated by Amanda. Ostensibly, we see what "actually happened," and thus from the beginning, our point of view is distinct from that of Adam and Amanda, and, one could argue, we are better informed than either of them. It is not the case, however, that my seeing of this scene ensures an objective or fair judgment of the accused, Mrs. Attinger. Presumably, the structure of a court in a democracy is rooted in an understanding that truth is a matter of interpretation, justice a matter of choice. The jurors will be presented with two distinct views of what Doris Attinger did and why she did it. Her motives will also affect the jurors' understanding of what Doris Attinger did. Our view of what we saw is mediated by the movie camera and by each of our contexts for viewing; we are privileged, but we are also made responsible for judging by our viewing.

Everything we see of Doris Attinger before she is arrested for attempted murder of her husband might be seen as defining what a lady is not, the better to recognize what a lady is when we cut to Amanda in her satin dressing gown, picking up the breakfast tray and newspaper outside the bedroom door, shutting the door with her foot, and moving back to a huge bed, all the while chattering wittily. This is the elegance and grace of a lady. This woman would be too competent to miss her target if she shot "at" her husband. This, too, is the woman who herself is a lawyer and can defend another woman's life.

If the double opening of *Adam's Rib* seems for a moment unnecessarily confusing or unusual, we might recall that the double-couple, double-plot structure has its origins at the latest in Roman comedy. And if we are led to ask, as I am, why the role of Doris Attinger is defined as that of an "unlady-like" working-class housewife, we might consider that Roman comedy and most of its descendants deployed the same conventions and structure, in order, in part, to set gender issues in a frame that allows us to judge consistencies and inconsistencies across contexts. Why complicate the already tricky gender equality issue with this injection of class differences? Possibly because gender oppression is more vividly or publicly represented in a working-class context. Or because class relations function as a metaphor for gender relations and thus double the issues of difference. Or, as several post-1960s feminists have argued, because understanding class politics is essential and prior to gender conflicts. The rest of *Adam's Rib* can be read as a response to these questions and possibilities, but it is not until we finally get the case of Doris Attinger into court that we are fully present at what is at stake.

At the trial, Doris Attinger no longer appears cheaply overdressed; in place of the broad-brimmed, overly dramatic hat she was wearing in pursuit of her husband, in court Doris wears a delicate hat, a romantic bouquet of small flowers. Her new hat is definitely a "lady's" hat. It is, in fact, the hat bought by Adam as a present for Amanda. With this crucial costume prop, Doris Attinger pretends to be a civilized, reasonable woman. (Any actor or actress can tell you the magic that can be done with just one key costume piece: suddenly you are the character.[2]) She is well instructed by her defense lawyer, who, of course, is none other than Amanda. Class can be bought and taught; Doris can become a lady, just as Eliza does in *Pygmalion*. But, at least in 1949, gender was less purchasable; it was attached not only to genes but to values, behaviors that could not be so readily exchanged.

Or could they? Let us assume for a moment that the difference between being a man and being a woman is a different kind of difference. Different than, say, as I have been suggesting, the difference between a woman who is a lady and one who is not. That, I think, is the possibility this film wants to raise. *Adam's Rib* is, after all, made soon after World War II, during a time when American men advertised their desire to put their women back in their own homes and take them out of the workplace. Now Amanda has obviously resisted these social pleas, but sometimes, and certainly this time, Adam at least believes she goes too far. In court, Amanda is not a lady. A lady knows the rules of the elite and plays by them. A lady is "civilized."[3] That is what Adam means when he appears incredulous when Amanda calls Mrs. Attinger a lady. But in court, Amanda violates both the decorum of the court and the rules of her marriage. She acts unconventionally—what Adam calls disrespectfully. With the gift of her own hat, careful makeup, and additional costuming, combined with the efforts of several pretrial rehearsals, Amanda transforms Doris from a pathetic shrew to a ladylike victim of her husband's infidelities. To the degree that image is role here, both Doris's class role and her gender one are altered for her court appearance.

It is not only Doris, however, who is transformed for the jurors and judge. The court itself becomes, from Adam's point of view, a "circus" in Amanda's hands. The women witnesses Amanda brings to court bear no evidence of Doris Attinger's assault on her husband. They serve, instead, as testimony to the equal and sometimes superior abilities of women as compared to men. A chemist with innumerable academic degrees represents women's intelligence; a corporate manager who oversees the work of hundreds of others suggests women's organizational skills. Last but far from least, a "lifter" appears in Doris Attinger's defense. This notably large woman gymnast is called to the stand to demonstrate women's physical strength; she does not talk about her prowess but demonstrates her power by somersaulting in front of the judge's bench and then hoisting Adam in the air.

To make certain that we and the jury undertand that justice is a matter of point of view, Amanda asks us through the device of these unconventional witnesses to try to see things differently. To ensure that the jurors, and the parallel film audience, realize the potential to see differently, Amanda next asks the jurors to use their imaginations. She then asks them and us to see two women, Doris and her rival, Beryl Kane, as men, and to see Mr. Attinger as a woman.

Had we any doubts where we stand or sit at this point in the film, by this cinematic transformation, Cukor confirms the audience's role as an extension of the jury by screening an image that each of us might conjure when asked by Amanda to see Doris and Beryl as men and Mr. Attinger as a woman. Before our eyes, the camera transforms the object of its gaze: Doris becomes a smooth-cheeked young man; Beryl gains a mustache and thick, slicked hair suggestive of a caricature of the young male seducer of melodrama; Mr. Attinger appears with the gaunt features, tight curls, and cheap dress of a grim, pathetic woman. If we use our imaginations, Amanda implies, we can not only see a woman as a man but we can be led to admit that we would judge the actions of the accused differently were she a man.[4]

I understand the explicit, self-conscious transformation of the on-screen image called forth by Amanda to be intended to accomplish two distinct but related goals. First, it is intended to make clear that we do see a person differently when we see him or her as another sex. Doris Attinger does look different when she is presented on screen as a man; the jury's eventual verdict of innocent must be read by us as evidence that for the jurors, the image of Doris as a man was possible and persuasive. Secondly, seeing Mrs. Attinger as a man makes clear that what we should wish for on the screen and off is not for women to become men. If men are the problem, then becoming one is not an answer. Third, this segment reveals the film's ability to transform persons into something, someone, other than they were initially. That this particular film's explicit transformations suggest a kind of technical amateurism and silliness is a problem that we might call a limit in this film and this instance. The editing here is not equal to the idea Amanda has in mind; it is not, indeed, equal to our imaginations. Notably, however, this production of Amanda's in court might be thought of as the equal of Adam's home movie, each of which is as unprofessional as the other. I think, nonetheless, that we do get and accept the concept of gender change as a concept of difference from Amanda's stunt. This in turn, I risk claiming, presents us with the possibility of transforming and transcending our own selves off-screen in daily life. If a film can transform a woman into a man, than it is also capable of transforming a woman or a man into a sex object, certainly, but it is capable, too, of transforming a woman or man into almost anything else—or into someone who is not just a more honest, realistic image of women as we know they exist off-screen but a person more complex than the screen or our society usually imagines.

Amanda wins her case; she persuades the jury that were Mrs. Attinger a man, as they imagined for a moment she/he was, they would have seen "his" shooting of his wife's partner in adultery as justifiable revenge. Adam's response, a reasonable summary of events and their relation to law, rests on what he believes to be the crime committed and his concomitant belief that the criminal or noncriminal nature of an act has nothing to do with gender. Adam's refusal to consider gender as an issue in the case may well be meant to treat men and women equally, although Amanda hears his words as that of the enemy. So, it seems, do the jurors, who reject Adam's argument and find Doris Attinger to be innocent. This verdict is not obvious. At most we can infer that Mrs. Attinger is found not guilty because Amanda manages to transform the trial from that of one woman to that of all men and women who do not treat women in the same way they treat men.

In the meantime, Cukor and his colleagues also enlarge the picture of what is on trial. We are gradually shown that it is not simply a matter of the evidence in the case or even of sorting out our gender and class biases. What we are witnessing in court is two very different processes of persuasion, two different ways not just of judging but of thinking about the world. Adam's mode is traditional, careful, rational, logical, abstract—most of the time. Amanda's approach is markedly not illogical or stupid, sentimental or inept; it is dramatic, theatrical. She stages performances and brings forward evocative, tangible images; Adam argues careful, legally based points. In one memorable segment of the trial sequence, Amanda presents three women gymnasts who are walking, tumbling examples of competence. While these samples may be irrelevant to the logical argument about Mrs. Attinger's guilt, Amanda makes her point that women are, but should not be, seen as unequal to men.

The court finds Doris Attinger innocent of all crimes against her husband and his mistress, but the trial of men and women in *Adam's Rib* is not over when the court has reached its verdict. Depressed and newly cynical, Adam seeks a divorce from Amanda, although he continues to fight the case—the case of Doris Attinger, the case of justice as he sees it, but also what he now sees as the case of Amanda and Adam. Following the trial, Adam has made moves to move out of the apartment, but he lingers, and in his lingering, discovers Amanda seeking solace in the company of the ever-leering neighbor, Kip, whose song, "Farewell, Amanda," has repeatedly punctuated the film. Out comes Adam's gun. Out comes Amanda's outrage: "You can't do that," she tells Adam. "It's against the law." In a word, Adam's retort is "Gottcha." He reveals that his gun is made of chocolate, and exits, triumphantly.

This is, of course, a Pyrrhic victory for Adam. He has humiliated Amanda in a classical recognition scene by making her perceive her own double standard: faced with Adam's gun as his response to what he might read as her infidelity, Amanda has called forth the authority of the law she has just undermined in court. By this trick, Adam wins back some of the pride and power he has lost in court. But his softly phallic stunt does not win back Amanda. Only when Adam weeps, or appears to weep, during a meeting with their accountant, does Amanda believe that perhaps all this battling has oppressed Adam, too. With the recognition that their suffering might be equal, Adam and Amanda now retreat to their country house, where they end up where we discovered them at the beginning—sitting on a bed, each with a hat on, talking, recovering each other, as they remove themselves from the public eye, our eye.[5]

"It shows that I've been right all along." Amanda declares, "Men. Women. The same." (Her claim reminds me of the very odd habit they have of calling each other Pinky/Pink*ie*. Pinkie for her, Pinky for him, she tells the court recorder.) "Except," she adds, "for a few little differences." "Viva la différence!" he declares, and when she requests a meaning, he translates, "Hooray for that little difference!" Adam, taking the last word as his, celebrates. Each closes a side of the bed curtain, a suggestion that this is the beginning of their play and the end of ours. We know, and she knows, however, that this is not anyone's last word on the topic that has been at hand throughout the movie.

Her last word would be more like those we hear in *Pat and Mike*, that other enchanting exploration of male-female partnership on film enacted by this same duo. There, as Molly Haskell reminds us, it is the Spencer Tracy character who proclaims, "What's good for you is good for me is good for you."[6] In *Adam's Rib*, Adam does not claim that everything that is good for him is good for Amanda. He wants a wife, he tells Amanda near the end of the film, not a competitor. And as if to test that this is what he has, his nearly last words are an announcement that he is going to run for a judgeship. When Amanda wonders aloud if the Democrats have as yet chosen a candidate, Adam augments his news with two words that are simultaneously question and command: "You wouldn't!" And, for the moment, she agrees she wouldn't. It is not she, however, who is celebrating difference in the end.

Not just Doris Attinger, but "all women are on trial in this case," Amanda claims.[7] The end of *Adam's Rib* confirms that this is as true of the film as it is of the court case within the film. Now we hear an echo, something familiar and troubling on the wind. The echo is of Aeschylus' *Oresteia*, of lines spoken and actions performed in the drama of twenty-five hundred years ago. *Adam's Rib* is not the first (or last) time in the history of Western culture that a fictional trial created by performers has been the site of the representation of conflict between men and women as man and woman in relation to justice. Yet the similarities between *Adam's Rib* and the *Eumenides*, the third part of Aeschylus' trilogy, are too striking to ignore. In both works, a trial structures the tension, and in both the role of women as much as the deeds of any individual are to be judged. While it is Orestes who is officially the defendant in the *Oresteia*, his mother, Clytemnestra, whom he killed, is also indirectly on trial for her slaying of her husband, Agamemnon, who is Orestes' father. The question before the jury in the *Oresteia* is whether Orestes deserves to be punished for killing his mother. This matricide, the chorus of Furies who have pursued Orestes claim, is a crime for which vengeance is rightly sought. Orestes' argument, made for him by Apollo, is that the killing of his father, Agamemnon, by his mother, required the killing of his mother. If these killings are seen as equal crimes, than clearly Orestes must be punished. Apollo, as defense attorney, argues, however, that killing Agamemnon was a worse crime than killing Clytemnestra because Agamemnon was a father, a man, a hero, "the source of life," and Clytemnestra, only a woman who mistakenly acted like a man, was "not the parent, just the nurse to the seed."[8]

Among the various transformations of culture enacted in the *Oresteia*, few are as blatant as the privileging of the authoritative discourse of the male citizen and the silencing of countervoices, associated throughout every situation with women. One of the key paradoxes of the trilogy, and a source of its resolute tension, is located in the contradiction between the dramatic efficacy of polyphony, of the multivoicedness of the personae, and the political efficacy of law, compromise, and consensus, of community as unity.[9]

By the end of the *Eumenides*, limits have been placed on the polyphony, the multivoicedness of the polis. The "lethal spell" cast by the voices of the female Furies and their "salt black wave of anger," all of which are response to the vindication of Orestes, are excluded from the land and hence from the discourse that shapes the city, much as Oedipus is finally banished from Thebes. Athena's last action in the drama is to call forth all of the women of the city to dress and praise the Furies; as if to ensure that no female escapes, Athena specifies that girls, mothers, and aged women sing the final chorus of the play. In so doing, the women of the city acknowledge and take on themselves the agreement to repress their most threatening voices and to relegate themselves to a fixed and constrained domain focused on reproduction and nurture.

This, however, is an uneasy agreement, notably confirmed in dance more than in words. Within the social and political world projected in the drama, the women of Athens have nothing to say, and their song dutifully mimics Athena's blessings and the language of the Furies. But the final theatrical gestures are neither so simple nor so definitive. The appearance of a new chorus at the end of the performance would have been disconcerting to the audience. And Athena's speech makes it difficult to ignore the ironic redundancy in the representation by male performers of this chorus of women of the city who are brought forward explicitly to confirm their submission to the new laws and practices of men. The medium of the male chorus that speaks as and for women is the message, but to call attention to this medium, as Aeschylus does, is also to call it into question. The talk in the *Oresteia* may resolve by debate the problem of justice, but, ironically, by confirming the establishment of democratic processes, processes that should, by definition, be polyphonic, the verbal representations of the drama assert and demand a unified understanding of the polis.

This is the strongest impression we are left with, but it is not the only meaning of the last moments of the *Eumenides*. In the end, as J. P. Vernant contends, "an equilibrium is established, but it is based on tensions. In the background, the conflict between opposing forces continues."[10]

It is remarkable that Cukor's film, *Adam's Rib*, could be as easily the object of Vernant's comment as is the *Eumenides*. The descendents of the jury of the *Eumenides*, a jury torn between a case made for the superiority of men over women and a case made for the equality of men and women, are still divided in the mid-twentieth century. The verdict is not yet in. What is at stake in *Adam's Rib* is justice and whether equal justice for all means not only justice for women as well as for men but the same justice for women as for men. What is also at stake in *Adam's Rib* is the role of the court in the demos or city, the relation of law to private lives. And, not very finally, what is at stake in *Adam's Rib* is the celebration of polyphony (called difference in *Adam's Rib*) versus monology. All these were at stake in the *Oresteia* as well. In political terms, I would argue, the big stake is democracy, a form of life, not just of government, a form of life that we must choose over the tyranny of patriarchy, or our liberty will be as much an illusion as Adam's tears. And this, finally, George, brings me to *Casablanca*.

Both *Adam's Rib* and the *Oresteia* remind us that women and theater have languages other than the verbal. As women, the men in the chorus can, as Aeschylus writes, "carry on the dancing on and on." Mediated by men playing women, the Dionysian elements of the theater are reasserted in the *Eumenides* and reclaimed by Amanda in the courtroom of *Adam's Rib*. Women may be excluded from the polis and the theater, they may be frequently reduced to objects of a male gaze or situated in the margins of the worlds of film, but as long as drama requires Dionysian elements and as long as movies move, the idea of women must be present in dramatic representations, and the threat of polyphony remains. In *Adam's Rib*, Adam knows he must respect the different voice his wife brings to their society, but he is uneasy precisely with her "carrying on."

Casablanca tells another story. *Casablanca* is the favorite American movie, not just of George Kateb but of uncountable millions of Americans, of several generations. Curiously, however, it is a movie about which almost any American can say something but about which few critics have had anything interesting to say.[11] We remember this film in moments and in cycles, one scene picking up on the events and patterns of relationship in another: Rick and Ilsa met and loved and parted at a Paris train station in the past; in Casablanca, they meet again, fall in love again, and this time part at an airport. A young Bulgarian couple are impeded in their quest for an exit visa from Casablanca by the police captain Renault; when the young woman decides to go to bed with Renault in exchange for the visa, the apparently apolitical, insensitive cafe owner, Rick, intervenes and facilitates the acquisition of funds to purchase the visa. Rick makes much the same gesture for Ilsa and her husband, Victor Laszlo, but in, this instance, the loser is Rick himself.

After a first viewing (and who has seen *Casablanca* only once?) we remember these events less as narrative than as a string of dramatic poems. As the style of much American poetry is epigrammatic, so is the style of *Casablanca*. There is Sam, the African American piano player, playing "As Time Goes By," first for Ilsa, and then for Rick. There is Ilsa's entrance, and Rick's sighting of Ilsa as he rushes angrily to stop Sam from playing "their" song. And, always but sparingly, there are the soft-focus close-ups of Ilsa, the straightforward distance shots of Victor Laszlo, and the shadowy shots of Rick. Knowing that Bergman and Bogart are what we came for, the camera teases us, resists finding them, finds Rick's back, Ilsa in a corner of his room.

The script of *Casablanca* is all one-liners, oral epigrams to match the visuals. "Kiss me as if it were the last time," Ilsa commands Rick. And Rick toasts Ilsa, "Here's looking at you, kid." "Go back to Bulgaria," Rick tells the young couple when they ask what else to do other than have Annina, the young woman, go to bed with Captain Renault. "We'll always have Paris," Rick reminds Ilsa. (Or is it Ilsa who says this to Rick?) And then there is the last line of *Casablanca*: "You know, Louis, this could be the beginning of a beautiful friendship," Rick tells Renault as the two men disappear into the dark.

If you are shocked, shocked by this reductive response to *Casablanca*, please bear with me. That we might remember *Casablanca* in the way I have suggested is not to discredit the film or its viewers. We do not simply remember the film and each of its moments—we cherish *Casablanca*, and some of that sentiment has to do with its availability.[12] We use our memory of lines and images to connect to other viewers, to attest to a common memory.

Released in 1942, but set in 1939–1940, unlike most American films, *Casablanca* is a blatant piece of political propaganda. "Join the army," it tells us. "It's time to take sides." And if *Casablanca*'s director, Michael

Curtiz, is not an auteur and does not match Germany's Leni Riefenstal, it matters not because we had Bogart and Bergman. Americans in 1942, isolationists many of them, needed a shot of patriotism, and the legend has it that more than a few young men went right from the movie theater to the nearest draft recruitment station.

But why do we still watch, and love, *Casablanca*? Why, twenty-three years after the war, would the entire audience of the Brattle theater in Cambridge stand and join the on-screen customers at Rick's Cafe Americain to sing the "Marseillaise"? Perhaps because *Casablanca* transports us to a time and place where ordinary people could be heroes. Perhaps because in each of us there is a desire to take our place at the barricades. To imagine doing that, we must be led by the movie to put reason aside; we must, momentarily, be enchanted.

Beyond this, *Casablanca*, ironically, may be our most American film. Rick's cafe is an open boat, as much a ship of international fools and wisefolk as any imagined by American writers. Rick and Sam call forth Huck and Jim; Captain Renault replays Melville's and Fitzgerald's confidence man. *Casablanca* represents two of our most attractive movie genres—the Western and the war film. And Bogart's particular, politicized way of "inhabiting the social role" of the American cowboy hero is central to the movie's power as an American film.[13] The Western hero, as Stanley Cavell describes the type (drawing from Baudelaire), is also seen in Western culture as the dandy. He is a loner, except for the occasions when he bonds with other men. He is attractive in a particularly erotic way, but he hides his own emotions, especially his attractions, and this serves only to increase his appeal. Most crucially, the dandy has an inner fire, an ineluctable and unalterable commitment and set of convictions, which we know only indirectly, from the cold glance he gives to his foes or the tension in his body in the face of love or kindness. Cavell argues that the dandy still holds power over our imaginations, and that "[O]ur most brilliant representatives of the type are the Western hero and Bogart."[14] If this is so, then Rick in *Casablanca* is the model of the type and its most potent instantiation.

The American Western hero is notable for his own privacy, and this in turn, again borrowing from Cavell, makes him, necessarily, a defender of privacy. I would add that our heroes, including Rick, use their courage to encourage and protect civilization—they defend the vulnerable soldiers who appeal to them for aid, much as Rick helps Laszlo get his exit visa, but if they have a companion, he is usually a maverick, at the fringe of society, not its center. Women love the American dandy, as occasionally he loves them, but his need to live outside the law allows him only passionate moments, not sustained domestic relations. Think of Shane. Like Shane and other Western heroes, Rick deserves to be condemned by feminists for his willingness to do the thinking for himself and his woman and for inspiring women such as Ilsa to ask him to think for both of them. The American hero kisses as if it were the last time—and the first. He resides outside history as well as outside the law, and he resides in his memories of Paris or does not take much notice of time going by. For Rick, time is cyclic and history belongs to someone else.

In *Casablanca* we find this hero and the mythology of his world as richly represented as I can imagine its ever being. *Casablanca* is our Athens, and Rick's Cafe Americain surely looks like a home for democratic individuals, a site where a man can keep his secrets and help others keep theirs.

Yet something is wrong in *Casablanca*, the movie, and it is not just the depiction of women, as brave, beautiful creatures who yield thinking for themselves to the men they love. Ilsa is a painful reminder of how far we have not gone since the Greek women of the *Eumenides* agreed to yield their wills and desire to the will of men in order to keep the peace. Think of Amanda next to Ilsa, and then remember Clytemnestra. Crudely, *Casablanca* is nostalgic sexist filmmaking, and we not only indulge it but love it. Worse, however, is that the authority of the dandy and the submission of the woman in *Casablanca* powerfully confirm the identity of the democratic individual[15] as a man whose single voice will suffice. This should sound like a contradiction. I think it is a contradiction. We hear many voices projected within the frame of *Casablanca*, but in the end, Ilsa is silent, as is Laszlo, and Rick speaks for them—and us.

After the Athenians saw the *Oresteia*, and, indeed, while they watched its performance, they talked, argued with one another, continued to dispute the equality of men and women and the space that justice was to fill. In my experience, something like what I imagine to be comparable conversations occur among those who have seen *Adam's Rib*. We condemn or applaud Adam's chocolate gun and fake tears, Amanda's transformations of others and herself. Now think about what we do after viewing *Casablanca*. Perhaps we long for the causes we aren't fighting for, and, more likely, we grieve for the loves we found and lost, the laws we never broke, the friendship we never saved. I weep. Every time. But now, thinking about *Casablanca*, I wish for conversation. That, after all, is what democracy is about. Isn't it, George?[16]

NOTES

1. Mr. Attinger behaves like a terrified rabbit when confronted by his armed wife. The key wound Doris Attinger inflicts is to her husband's macho pride; he loses more face than blood.

2. Stanley Cavell, *Pursuits of Happiness* (Cambridge, Mass., 1981), pp. 228–229. Cavell recalls a vague memory of hats as a symbol of liberty in his bountiful reading of *Adam's Rib*.

3. Cavell, *Pursuits of Happiness*, p. 197. Cavell calls attention to Adam's claim that the rest of the world will think of him and Amanda as "uncivilized" because they have taken a private battle into the public courtroom and because they (not Amanda only, just more she than he) have challenged conventional gender role behavior. I

presented these thoughts about civilization and *Adam's Rib* in a lecture several years before I read Cavell's essay on *Adam's Rib*, but this is not to deny the richness and wonder of illumination Cavell brings to this movie, especially its deployment of the home movie, which I deliberately ignore because Cavell says all that needs to be said about it.

4. *Ibid.*, pp. 217–218. Cavell finds these cinematic transformations to be unsuccessful and discomforting. I am unclear as to whether he thinks of them as the failure of director Cukor or of Amanda trying to be a director. At any rate, I empathize with his unease—the images thrust us outside the movie, as Cavell notes—but contend that this is at least a remarkable attempt to press the edges of film's possibilities.

5. *Ibid.*, p. 195.

6. Molly Haskell, *From Reverence to Rape* (New York, 1973), p. 227. Like Haskell, I think of *Pat and Mike* and *Adam's Rib* as films that can be profitably read together. I also want to acknowledge Haskell's originality in her discussion of *Adam's Rib*, a film she sees as distinct from other 1940s movies in its portrayal of a marriage in which each member respects the other.

7. Cavell, *Pursuits of Happiness*, p. 224. Cavell also cites this line from *Adam's Rib*, but while I take the line to resonate strongly with all that happened in other courts, historical and theatrical, where women have been on trial, he takes the oppositional position of Beryl Kane, Attinger's mistress, as successfully countering Amanda's claims of sisterhood. I see Cavell's point, but, as with almost every other aspect of gender in this film, the weight of Beryl Kane's case against the feminist position is a matter of interpretation, not fact.

8. Aeschylus, *The Oresteia* (New York: Penguin Classics, 1977), pp. 260–261.

9. M. M. Bakhtin, *The Dialogic Imagination* (Austin, Tex., 1981), esp. p. 428. I use the term "polyphony" to mean multivoicedness—that quality of texts that resists authority and monologue and insists on the interaction of two or more "languages" and points of view. Polyphony is closely related to two key ideas in Bakhtin's work—dialogism and heteroglossia. "Dialogism" refers to the constant interaction between meanings that is characteristic of the novel from Bakhtin's perspective. Heteroglossia is the basic understanding of language as context-driven; according to Bakhtin and his followers, the meaning of any given word will depend on the particular time and place in which the word is uttered, and will change under different conditions. This, of course, means that we are always negotiating meaning, always struggling to understand and be understood, as both *Adam's Rib* and the *Oresteia* dramatize.

10. Jean-Pierre Vernant, "Greek Tragedy," in *The Structuralist Controversy*, ed. Richard Macksey and Eugenio Donato (Baltimore, 1970), p. 290.

11. Harvey R. Greenberg, *The Movies on Your Mind* (New York, 1975), pp. 79–105. Greenberg's chapter begins with an observation similar to my own about the popularity of *Casablanca* in the context of a critical abyss. Greenberg also notes some of the same qualities I remark on in Rick, qualities Cavell helpfully terms those of the dandy. But Greenberg's claims about the sexuality of various characters, especially his claims about Rick's Oedipal patterns, are unconvincing.

12. Georges Sadoul, *Dictionary of Films* (Berkeley, 1965), pp. 54–55. Even Sadoul, who does not mention *Adam's Rib*, describes *Casablanca* as "enchanting." Other critics, such as Pauline Kael, insist that it is what Kael in other contexts calls trash, but they all, including Kael and the auteur critic Andrew Sarris, admit that *Casablanca* entertains them and even brings tears to their eyes. See also Greenberg, *Movies on Your Mind*, p. 79.

13. Stanley Cavell, *The World Viewed* (New York, 1971), p. 56.

14. *Ibid.*, pp. 55–56.

15. Here and elsewhere in this paper, where I mention the "democratic individual," I have in mind specifically the figure that George Kateb describes in *The Inner Ocean* (Ithaca, 1992), especially as described in the chapter entitled "Whitman and the Culture of Democracy." For more reflections on gender, film, the social self, and Kateb's democratic individual see my "Becoming Women, Women Becoming: Film and the Social Construction of Gender," in *Social Selves*, ed. Christine Sypnovitch and David Bakhurst (New York, 1995).

16. This rhetorical question is posed with a Proustian memory of things past.

William James's Rugged Individualism

KIM TOWNSEND

IN HER SOPHOMORE year at Radcliffe College, Gertrude Stein began her English 22 theme for April 25, 1895, with the question, "Is life worth living?" Her answer was a resounding yes, "Yes, a thousand times yes." It was yes because she had just heard William James ask the same question in a lecture to the Harvard Young Men's Christian Association, and he had answered in the affirmative. It was yes, she said, because "the world still holds such spirits as Prof. James." James was "truly a man among men," a man (as she put it in the kind of sentence that would earn her lasting fame but a C in English 22) "who has lived sympathetically not alone all thought but all life." He embodied all that was "strongest and worthiest in the scientific spirit"; he was a metaphysician who did not worship logic or rely on mere reason; but most important of all, he was a true man:

> He stands firmly, nobly for the dignity of man. His faith is not that of a cringing coward before an all-powerful master, but of a strong man willing to fight, to suffer and endure. . . . He is a strong sane noble personality reacting truly on all experience that life has given him. He is a man take him for all in all.[1]

Given his example, the example of a man who embraced "all experience" and still persevered, life was indeed worth living.

When his lecture appeared as a booklet the next year, his friend Sarah Whitman—an artist (she did his portrait), as well as a woman who figured prominently in the social life of Cambridge and in the founding of Radcliffe—gave thanks to James for inspiring her generation to persevere in an age when God, if not dead, was in need of help. She recommended his talk to friends as one "wherein he constructs courage anew for those who must stand upon the little foothold of the naked human Will, and 'yearn upward' according to the conditions of that Will's higher necessities. An eager and noble cry from a brave and tender heart."[2] A reviewer in the *Harvard Advocate* credited James with possessing the pugnacious spirit that would make life worth living, and he said he hoped his talk would represent Harvard in the eyes of the world, that it would arouse "a man's fighting spirit, and his contempt for the half-hearted questioner. A few more such words from the University would give the world a new view of our Harvard spirit."[3] Attending to James's text ourselves, we may easily see what kind of individual he presented as proof of life's worth.[4]

James opened his lecture by asking his audience to "search the lonely depths for an hour" with him, to attend to "the profounder bass-note of life," and then, having set the tone with a long quotation from Thomson's *The City of Dreadful Night*, he talked about those who had said no in answer to his question—about suicides. There was little he could say that might have helped the majority of those suicides (numbering about three thousand a year, he noted), but like every young man seated there before him, he knew "that metaphysical *tedium vitae* peculiar to the reflective life," the "scepticism and unreality that too much grubbing in the abstract roots of things will breed," the "suicidal view of life" that came of "the over-studious career" and "too much questioning." ("I take it that no man is educated who has never dallied with the thought of suicide," he wrote off-handedly the following year.[5]) To be intellectually responsible—"nay, more, the simplest manliness and honor"—required that they consider suicides: "Their life is the life we share."

Appropriately enough, what he offered this audience as a remedy was religious faith, "nothing more recondite than religious faith," although, of course, no monistic or natural faith or religion, no faith or religion limited or corrupted by any theology, any "stall-fed officials of an established church," any formulation or definition of any kind. He was speaking of such faith as he would again, at great length, a few years later in his Gifford Lectures on *The Varieties of Religious Experience*, as the belief (or "over-belief," as he would then call it) in the existence of an unseen world, a source of higher energies, a higher order that lends significance to our mundane efforts. This religion "in the supernaturalist sense" had nothing to say against suicide, and that fact alone made it a deterrent: it's a comfort to know "you *may* step out of life whenever you please"; in the meantime, "you can always stand it for twenty-four hours longer, if only to see what to-morrow's newspaper will contain, or what the next postman will bring."

But religion and James's somber performance gave promise of more than the satisfaction of curiosity. Rather than devaluing life, the hardships and suffering that the suicide faced gave it "a keener zest." "The history of our own race is one long commentary on the cheerfulness that comes with fighting ills." Against "*our* petty powers of darkness" the potential suicide could be expected "to wait and see *his* part of the battle out," to do so not in supine, cowering resignation, but "on the contrary, a resignation based on manliness and pride." To make the struggle and the risk seem the more worthwhile, James could not point directly to Christ's example (the Higher Criticism had seen to that), so he reached back to his days as a medical student and came up with an analogous figure:

> Consider a poor dog whom they are vivisecting in a laboratory. He lies strapped on a board and shrieking at his executioners, and to his own dark consciousness is literally in a sort of hell. He cannot see a single redeeming ray in the whole business; and yet all these diabolical-seeming events are often controlled by

human intentions with which, if his poor benighted mind could only be made to catch a glimpse of them, all that is heroic in him would religiously acquiesce. (*Writings*, p. 499)

Oscar Wilde (on trial that year) might have had us remember the death of little Nell and laugh, but James's tone, like that of the other Victorians who preceded him—his favorite, Carlyle, Ruskin, late Wordsworth (all of whom he quotes), Arnold—remained quite stony throughout the lecture.

In closing, he made the point that if we believe in God's unseen world and believe that there is purpose to our struggles, then it and He are the more likely to exist and our efforts are the more likely to have meaning. As he put it in the very last words of his Gifford Lectures, "Who knows whether the faithfulness of individuals here below to their own poor over-beliefs may not actually help God in turn to be more effectively faithful to his own greater tasks?"[6] For now, if life is not "a real fight," if what we do does not contribute to the universe's success, then it is indeed "no better than a game of private theatricals from which one may withdraw at will." But "it *feels* like a real fight," so one must proceed as if it were. "Believe that life *is* worth living," he concluded, "and your belief will help create the fact."

To the obvious meaning of Stein's assessment of James as a "strong man willing to fight," we may add that he was a man who made himself by *willing* himself to fight. He was a man who, believing he could prevail, did, and thereby proved himself a man. By choice and with effort he was a masculine man, easily recognizable in such public performances as "Is Life Worth Living?" or "What Makes a Life Significant?" or "The Energies of Men." I would like to account for this particular man, to do so in a sampling of James's writing and in a reading of relevant passages in his life, which, as he often argued, could not be considered radically separate. I want to do so in a way that will suggest how much James was a man of his times as well as the individual genius of more common repute.

"Accentuation, foreground, and background are created solely by the interested looker-on," James wrote in "The Importance of Individuals." He was himself, he went on to confess, "a hero-worshipper."[7] My interest is not in debunking him, but I think we can learn more about him, more specifically, about the masculine presence that has been so influential, if we do not worship him. There is something heroic about him, but there is also something sad. He was an extraordinary individual, but he was also a figure who became increasingly familiar after the Civil War—the man forever struggling to be manly.

•

James' contemporaries agreed on the terms that applied to him, even if they did not always share Stein's enthusiasm. The quality that his student (and later professor of philosophy at Columbia), D. S. Miller thought most distinctive about James's presence at Harvard was "fellow-manliness," and he added: "[T]he sporting men in college always felt a certain affinity to themselves on one side in the freshness and manhood that distinguished him in mind, appearance, and diction."[8] Everyone recognized James walking, shoulders back, between the college and his home on Irving Street, or James bicycling in the early evening, or James in his Norfolk jacket and slightly rakish cravats, or James befriending students, bringing them home for lunch in order to continue a conversation (though capable, at times, of ushering them out as unceremoniously), or James following a train of thought, informally it seemed, in front of his students and willing to ask one of them, "What *was* I talking about?" if he lost his way, or to dismiss the class altogether.[9] The future musician and composer Daniel Gregory Mason thought James's colleague in the philosophy department, Josiah Royce, had a "deeper and more poetic" manner, but when James "moved restlessly about the platform chatting with us rather than lecturing us," Mason, too, found James's " frank manliness and friendliness . . . irresistible."[10] Set apart at Harvard by nationality, religion, and social and sexual preferences— disliked but swallowed, as he put it in his memoirs[11]—Santayana was less likely to fall under James's spell, but he recognized it for what it was. He appreciated it when "James was characteristically masculine and empirical in his wrath at the 'scandalous vagueness' of Spencer's ideas"; he "admired his masculine directness, his impressionistic perceptions, and his picturesque words"; he knew that "the normal practical masculine American . . . had a friend in William James."[12]

Though it may seem churlish to insist on the presence of these terms in assessments of James, they appear repeatedly in his own judgments of his environment, his judgments about college life, and—for him it followed— his judgments about the national health as well. In defining "The Social Value of the College-Bred" for the Association of American Alumnae meeting at Radcliffe in 1907, for example, he said that the best claim higher education could make for itself was that it enabled us "to *know a good man when we see him.*" Such a man set the proper tone. (" 'Tone,' to be sure, is a terribly vague word to use," he said, "but there is no other, and this whole meditation is over questions of tone.") For democracy to survive, it had to "catch the higher, healthier tone." The figure he invoked was that of the "judicious pilot," steering "the college-bred amid the driftings of democracy." The figure he set up in opposition was one Richard Elliot and his "feminine counterpart," possibly infecting the culture around Boston—"for priggishness is just like painter's colic or any other trade-disease." Good colleges would immunize their students against such effeminate infection, their "general tone being too hearty for the microbe's life."[13]

He thought Harvard did just that. At the Commencement dinner in 1903, in defining the independent and often lonely thinkers who set "the preeminent spiritual tone" of "the true Harvard," James did not associate them with sportsmen or battlers or seafarers, but he did invite his audience to indulge in a little laughter at the expense of the less hardy members of the student body. One of them had interrupted one of his lectures exclaiming, " 'But, doctor, doctor! to be serious for a moment,' " in "a high-pitched voice," and as James reported, "the whole room burst out laughing."[14] In the 1890s, in the debate over the so-called Three-Year Course, James honored the more independent thinkers among the students, but he also observed that the intellectual life they enjoyed seemed "unreal and fastidious" to most students. In characterizing the average student's needs, he became rhetorically feral:

> These excellent fellows need contact of some sort with the fighting side of life, with the world in which men and women earn their bread and butter and live and die; there must be the scent of blood, so to speak, upon what you offer them, or else their interest does not wake up; the blood that is shed in our Electives, fails to satisfy them for long. (*Writings*, p. 13)

More than three years, and the potentially mandarin nature of the institution will become apparent and "these excellent fellows" will become contemptuous. Or it might be that they will go on thinking, and their resistance to the disease of "priggishness" will get dangerously low.[15] The ideal, Adamic man whom he tried to rescue from the infamous "Ph.D. octopus" was a distinctly masculine man. Whereas "individuality and bare manhood" had once been the surest sign of "the very soul" of the country, he pointed out, they now had to be stamped and licensed in order to be acceptable. True value had been transferred "from essential manhood to an outward badge." All this brought him to the kind of conclusion that had so stirred Gertrude Stein: "Let us pray that our ancient national genius may long preserve vitality enough to guard us from a future so unmanly and so unbeautiful!"[16]

In his own intellectual exchanges, he preserved that vitality, with Frederic Myers, for one, whose devotion to psychic research made him grow "ever handsomer and stronger-looking," with that "athletic . . . ratiocinator" Bertrand Russell, or, most intensely, with Royce, to whom he wrote while composing the Gifford Lectures: "I lead a parasitic life upon you, for my highest flight of ambitious ideality is to become your conqueror, and go down into history as such, you and I rolled in one another's arms and silent (or rather loquacious still) in one last death-grapple of an embrace."[17] James himself found such combative or agonistic terms relevant to his appreciation of a man's work, but he would never allow for the erotic implications of his adulation of the manly. In *The Principles of Psychology* he made it clear that though he imagined most men might "possess the germinal possibility" of being sexually attracted to other men, the "fondness of the ancients and of modern Orientals for forms of unnatural vice" was not instinctual but rather an example of an instinct's being inhibited by habit. The sexual instinct, natural though it might be, was subject to inhibitions, to various temperamental conditions and impulses. It had to contend with shyness, for example, or with "the *anti-sexual instinct*, the instinct of personal isolation, the actual repulsiveness to us of the idea of intimate contact with most of the persons we meet, especially those of our own sex." James was repulsed by the idea of the practices "of the ancients and of modern Orientals" (it "affects us with horror," he says); therefore it is unthinkable that they acted on instinct. It could not be that they were *all* aberrant: "We can hardly suppose that the ancients had by gift of Nature a propensity of which we are devoid, and were all victims of what is now a pathological aberration limited to individuals." But he has to admit that "these details are a little unpleasant to discuss"; two years later, he omitted them from the *Psychology: Briefer Course* altogether.[18]

"*My* deeper levels seem very hard to find," he wrote toward the end of his life.[19] He was too late for Freud, who would, he knew, "throw light on human nature"—too late but temperamentally unreceptive as well. At the conclusion of his lectures on the *Varieties of Religious Experience* (1902), he announced that the "*subconscious self* is nowadays a well-accredited psychological entity," and—again with emphasis—that "*the unconscious person is continuous with a wider self through which saving experiences come*,"[20] but he was envisaging new understandings of why life was worth living. He was not interested in more complex readings of the family romance. After his famous meeting with Freud at Clark University in 1909, he said that he could make nothing of Freud's dream theories and that Freud himself impressed him as only "a man obsessed with fixed ideas."[21]

But James's openness to new ideas was as legendary as his manliness. Walter Lippmann's testimonial can be taken as summary of the many that exist. Fresh out of college, in his first signed article, he said that James was

> perhaps the most tolerant man of [his] generation. . . . He listened for truth from anybody, and from anywhere, and in any form. He listened for it from Emma Goldman, the pope, or a sophomore; preached from the pulpit, a throne, or a soap-box; in the language of science, in slang, in fine rhetoric, or in the talk of a ward boss.[22]

Some thought he embraced too much. John Jay Chapman said that "James saw too much good in everything, and felt towards everything a too indiscriminating approval."[23] Santayana reduced his religious beliefs to almost nothing; James, he said, "merely believed in the right of believing that you might be right if you believed."[24]

We must not fail to appreciate the play, the bravado, the energy (James would have us say) of James's writing. On the other hand, though he was forever depicting or dramatizing his points, imagining himself in situations in order to discover their significance, ready to reimagine them if necessary, he was at the same time testing his arguments and himself against what are clearly masculinist standards. There were beliefs and manners (the two so

often conjoined by James) for which he had little or no tolerance—"the hin-
doo and the buddhist" because they are "simply afraid, afraid of more experience, afraid of life," for example, or "quietistic religion" generally, any
religion "sure of salvation *any how*," for its "slight flavor of fatty degeneration," "thin and elegant logical solutions" as opposed to "thicker and more
radical empiricism," or just plain priggishness.[25] Closer to home—and with
the same figures of speech—he challenged his brother, Henry, "You skinny
bachelors know nothing of the thickness of life,"[26] and told him that when
their sister, Alice, referred to Henry as the "angel" (a habit that William
tired of), he searched his imagination for "something very 'oriental' "[27]—or
sexually perverse, as we know from *The Principles of Psychology*.

Presenting himself to his would-be wife, Alice, he described the lengths to
which he was willing to go to prove himself. Characteristic of his "particular
mental or moral attitude" was

> an element of active tension, of holding my own, as it were, and trusting out-
> ward things to perform their part so as to make it a full harmony, but without
> any *guaranty* that they will. Make it a guaranty—and the attitude immediately
> becomes to my consciousness stagnant and stingless. Take away the guaranty,
> and I feel (provided I am *uberhaupt* in vigorous condition) a sort of deep enthu-
> siastic bliss, of bitter willingness to do and suffer anything, which translates
> itself physically by a kind of stinging pain inside my breast-bone. (*Letters*, vol.
> 1, pp. 199–200)

From a little distance the image of this man testing his manhood to the point
of inducing chest pains seems sad or even slightly amusing, but no. "Don't
smile at this," James warned. "[I]t is to me an essential element of the whole
thing! . . . the deepest principle of all active and theoretic determination
which I possess."[28] Thirteen years later, in the chapter on "Will" in his *Psychology*, James presented his most stirring portrait of his hero, engaged in
what is surely a *real* fight or game, confronting challenges head on, welcoming them not least because their pressure is registered, once again, in the
chest. It is a peroration that deserves long quotation:

> If the "searching of our heart and reins" be the purpose of this human drama,
> then what is sought seems to be what effort we can make. He who can make
> none is but a shadow; he who can make much is a hero. . . . When a dreadful
> object is presented, or when life as a whole turns up its dark abysses to our view,
> then the worthless ones among us lose their hold on the situation altogether,
> and either escape from its difficulties by averting their attention, or if they can-
> not do that, collapse into yielding masses of plaintiveness and fear. The effort
> required for facing and consenting to such objects is beyond their power to
> make. But the heroic mind does differently. To it, too, the objects are sinister
> and dreadful, unwelcome, incompatible with wished-for things. But it can face
> them if necessary, without for that losing its hold upon the rest of life. The
> world thus finds in the heroic man its worthy match and mate; and the effort

which he is able to put forth to hold himself erect and keep his heart unshaken is the direct measure of his worth and function in the game of life. He can *stand* this Universe.[29]

In the same vein, though at first we might think we detect a slight air of casualness, if we bear these descriptions of "character" in mind, we know James is serious when he observes in 1907, in "The Energies of Men," that "[w]ars, of course, and shipwrecks, are the great revealers of what men and women are able to do and bear."[30] "To be imprisoned or shipwrecked or forced into the army would permanently show the good life to many an over-educated pessimist," he wrote in "On a Certain Blindness in Human Beings."[31]

Not having fought in the Civil War, the closest James came to facing a life-threatening test was his experience of the San Francisco earthquake the year he was teaching at Stanford. His response was one of "pure delight and welcome," he wrote in "On Some Mental Effects of the Earthquake." He had cried out (or almost did): "'*Go* it,' I almost cried aloud, 'and go it *stronger*.'" He took the earthquake personally; it seemed directed at him—"animus and intent were never more present in any human action." There were epistomological implications to which we must return—the earthquake seemed to want to make the meaning of its name manifest. There was also an impressive "readiness," an ability to regroup, that "like soldier-ing . . . lies always latent in human nature." The result was a striking "universal equanimity." "The commonest men," he discovered, "simply because they *are* men, will go on, singly and collectively, showing this admirable fortitude of temper."[32]

For days that seemed a lot like every other day—or as respite from the struggles that he welcomed—James recommended less dramatic therapies, the therapy of "The Gospel of Relaxation," for example. When James speaks in that lecture of "the many of our fellow-countrymen" who had collapsed and been sent abroad to rest their nerves," he refers to George Beard's and S. Weir Mitchell's diagnoses of the pressures of "modern civilization," but we cannot help thinking of his own trips to Divonne or Bad Teplitz or Bad Nauheim whenever his own nervous system threatened to break down. He explained that such men's problems were not overwork but rather feelings of "breathlessness and tension," a desire for results, or—in another tautology—"that lack of inner harmony and ease" of which he was speaking. It is as if he were in dialogue with himself, trying to explain, to say how to maintain and when necessary ease the tension that he told Alice characterized his being.

What James offers as a "cure" is a version of the only one of his theories that still makes its way into textbooks in psychology, the theory that action does not follow feeling but rather can influence or control feeling—the so-called Lange-James theory. The theory has it that if we could will ourselves to stay put in the face of danger, we would not experience fear; if we would "more or less deliberately" smile at people we don't like, "make sympathetic inquiries . . . and force ourselves to say genial things," we might arrive at "closer communion"; if we would sit up and look around and act cheer-fully—well, "[i]f such conduct does not make you soon feel cheerful, noth-ing else on that occasion can." To cite one more application, one that seems to reverse everything James says about the healthy-minded and sick souls in *The Varieties of Religious Experience*, melancholy feelings would disappear if we would but cease to worry, be less conscientious, think less about our-selves. "Stated technically," and with emphasis (as is so often the case with James), "*strong feeling about one's self tends to arrest the free association of ones's objective ideas and motor processes*." Exercise will prevent such feel-ings: "the tennis and tramping and skating habits and the bicycle-craze which are so rapidly extending among our dear sisters and daughters" will do more for neurasthenic women than Mitchell's rest cure ever did. Exercise would also enable Americans to emulate the English, the strength of whose empire lay in the strength of the character of each individual Englishman, he said, which in turn was nourished by nothing so much as "the national worship, in which all classes meet, of athletic out-door life and sport."

The pace and confidence experienced by the "muscularly well-trained human being" was to James "an element of spiritual hygiene of supreme significance." Cultivating "muscular vigor" would make it possible to fulfill not Christian but those stoical ideals he so impressively represented to Ger-trude Stein and Sarah Whitman and the men of Harvard.

•

The Ph.D. business, the whole "industry of building up an author's meaning out of separate texts leads nowhere," James once wrote to a candidate who was working on his "poor self"—unless, he said, "you have first grasped his centre of vision, by an act of imagination."[33] It is the kind of metaphor to which James would be inclined. But anyone trying to "grasp" James should also recall his sister's figure for him: "He is just like a blob of mercury, you can't put a mental finger on him."[34] One should bear in mind, too, that James was forever resisting final comprehension on principle. His great de-scription of "The Stream of Thought" in *The Principles of Psychology* teaches us that naming, arresting the articulation of our thoughts with nouns, with substantives, limits the lives of others in our imaginings, and limits our own creative possibilities.

Still, I think we can say more than James himself says about his habits, about the "tension" that characterized him, and about the way he con-structed an ideal of heroic masculinity for himself and for the men and women of his time. Another metaphorical rendering of him (it is Santa-yana's) may be of help:

> But he was really far from free, held back by old instincts, subject to old delu-sions, restless, spasmodic, self-interrupted: as if some impetuous bird kept

flying aloft, but always stopped in mid-air, pulled back with a jerk by an invisible wire tethering him to a peg in the ground.[35]

Not even something so reductive as an ideal, then, but something temperamental or instinctual, not the center of his vision perhaps, but something about it that must be acknowledged far more than is usual in assessments of James's individuality. And if one thing that was limiting about him, about the open-endedness of his being and his "philosophy," was a desire to establish and protect himself as an impressively masculine figure, we can appreciate his impulse the more by examining the ways in which he imagined its opposite, the feminine. He also tried himself against his friends and, what was obviously more challenging for him (and for any student of the James family), against his brother, but on this occasion I have chosen to stress the figuring of women that necessarily had to take place in order for him to establish himself as a man.

Santayana's image of the "peg in the ground" has more resonance if we recall James's extraordinary father, Henry James, Sr., and specifically his contention that it was not in "Man's nature" to soar unless he entered the state of holy matrimony. Henry James, Sr., insisted that there really *was* an angel in the house. He thought no man could live without her and be saved, and so, if he were to live up to the ideal that she represented, he would have to be more than a man. William devoted as much energy as he did to the construction of manliness in large part because he was so committed to his father's views of women and marriage.

Squirming under the pressure of his dutiful editing of his father's *The Literary Remains*, William was right in pointing out in his introduction, "With all the richness of style, the ideas are singularly unvaried and few. Probably few authors have so devoted their entire lives to the monotonous elaboration of one single bundle of truths."[36] The truth about woman was that she was man's only hope for salvation. She was created to show him the way out of his beastly state; in her, man could see the promise of his life, his otherwise "unseen spiritual manhood." The only way man, "by nature . . . in himself unsocial," could enter that state was to marry, "to leave father and mother, and cleave unto the wife alone, that is, to a new manhood symbolized by woman." She was (and here one begins to notice the "richness of style") the "patient bondsman of the latter's necessities, the meek unresisting drudge of his lusts both physical and moral, so wooing him, and at last winning him, out of his grovelling egotism into the richest social and aesthetic dimension." Through her he might become "divinely human, or characteristically *social*."[37] Fourier and Swedenborg escort him as he envisages woman patiently submitting to her husband so that gradually she may build up "the family, the tribe, the city, the nation, and every larger form of humanity, until now at last her helpless nursling has become developed into THE PEOPLE."[38]

Joining in discussion with Horace Greeley and Stephen Pearl Andrews about *Love, Marriage, and Divorce, and The Sovereignty of the Individual,* Henry James, Sr., said that he himself had discovered a divinity in his wife that was "the very opposite of everything I find in myself . . . a divinity infinitely remote from my own petty self, and yet a divinity in my very na- ture, so that I can't help becoming aroused to the meaning at last of living worship, worship consecrated by death to self."[39] By his account of Genesis (chapter 13, "Adam and Eve," of *Spiritual Creation,* in *The Literary Re- mains*), man is "the rudest, crudest, spiritually least modified—that is most *universal*—form of human nature, representing the base, earthly, material, centrifugal, *identifying* force in creation which is known as *selfhood . . .* that essentially evil, diabolic, or simply waste force in humanity." Woman, Eve, by delightfully rendered and blinding comparison, was the

> celestial counterpart of this vulgar deciduous Adam . . . his regenerate, *Divine*-natural, or individualizing soul, the dew of God's ceaseless, soft, caressing pres- ence in human nature, full of indulgent clemency and tenderness towards the dull, somnolent, inapprehensive, unconscious clod with whom she is associ- ated, and whom yet she is to educate and inspire by exquisitely ineffable divine arts into the lordship of the universe, or marriage sympathy and union with the universal heart of man. (*Literary Remains*, pp. 347–348)

"Anyone with half an eye can see" that Adam's fall was no death; it was "anything but disastrous"; rather, it was his rise "out of sheer unrelieved brutality" into "self-consciousness," his recognition of "*his soul,* or *spiritual nature*; for that is what Eve signifies in reference to Adam."[40] It is a recogni- tion, too, of his separation from God, a separation he can repair in marriage.

But not marriage as we know it. Marriage had been, for the father him- self, his "truest divine revelation." Without his wife he would have gone to hell, he said, not because of anything she had done but simply by her "un- consciously being the pure, good, modest woman she is." For marriage to succeed, it must serve not the family but society—and so while defending himself against Greeley's charge that he was advocating free love, he went on to argue the equally radical case that marriage had to be "relieved by greater freedom of divorce."[41] Otherwise a man will consider his wife his property, and though she was meant for submission, that very instinct would lead her to rebel, and he, in turn, to "some vile and dastardly re- venge." When it took the form of murder, he wrote in "The Logic of Mar- riage and Murder," the enraged husband was not so much to blame as "the social constitution under which we live, inasmuch as that constitution makes the true sanction of marriage to be force, not freedom."[42]

The gospel of free love "turns my stomach," he said. The divinity of his wife had aroused in him "the meaning at last of living worship, worship consecrated by death to self." The reason he was so "aroused" was quite simple: his wife no longer aroused him. Rather than lead a double life, he denied himself, saying proudly, "I will abide in my chains." And when his wife died, he was astonishingly true to his word: his worship was in fact consecrated by his death. Four months after Mary Walsh James died (of bronchial asthma), he wrote to their favored son, Henry: "She really did arouse my heart, early in our married life, from its selfish torpor, and so enabled me to become a man. . . . The sum of it all is, that I would sooner rejoin her in her modesty, and find my eternal lot in association with her, than have the gift of a noisy delirious world." He longed to die. "He had no visible malady," Henry reported to William, after their father's death five months later. "The 'softening of the brain' was simply a gradual refusal of food, because he *wished* to die. There was no dementia except a sort of exaltation of belief that he had entered into 'the spiritual life.'"[43]

"All my intellectual life I derive from you," William wrote to his father in one of those unparalleled letters the Jameses wrote one another as one or another approached death. Father and son often expressed themselves differently, but, William said, "I'm sure there's a harmony somewhere, and that our strivings will combine."[44] It would require many pages to read that acknowledgment properly, but in the present context his debt is relatively clear. I say his debt, but it was more likely to have been his handicap, for growing up as a sexual man and potential husband with such a father invoking such standards had to have required heroic effort—effort that required redoubling given a mother who favored his brother, the so-called angel, and bridled at what she perceived as his own (William's) hypochondria.

William James grew up contemplating the sexual male with more disdain and fear than did the stereotypical Victorian male. When he looked, what he saw was what he called "the carnivore within."[45] We have heard him on the *"anti-sexual instinct"*; his only other consideration of sexuality in *The Principles of Psychology* occurs in a paragraph on animal behavior in his discussion of "The Functions of the Brain," a consideration that leads him to conclude: "No one need be told how dependent all human social elevation is upon the prevalence of chastity. Hardly any factor measures more than this the difference between civilization and barbarism."[46]

As a young reviewer, he met the argument of Horace Bushnell, in *Woman's Suffrage: the Reform against Nature*, that if women become men's rivals, men will not hesitate "to push them to the wall wherever we find them," with the counterargument that however much men's and women's interests might conflict, no man would allow his sexuality to reveal itself to a woman. Her very power, her transcendent example, guarantees the suppression of his sexuality. Bushnell's argument, James wrote, "leaves altogether out of sight the mere animal potency of sex. An individual man, however his interests may clash with those of an individual woman, will always shrink from appearing personally like a brute in her presence."

He was reviewing Bushnell's book along with Mill's *The Subjection of Women*, which came out in the same year (1869); his father was also reviewing the two, and almost simultaneously. Of course there are many similarities: the father regrets the absence of sex in Mill's analysis because he, too, wants to celebrate woman's ability to dull "the edge of these rapacious delights, of these insane cupidities"; the son wishes that Mill had paid more attention to divorce; and the son puts in his own terms the father's belief (expressed at greater length and more emphatically in his "Woman and the 'Woman's' Movement") that woman is "naturally" inferior to man, "his inferior in passion, his inferior in intellect, and his inferior in physical strength" (facts no more deniable than gravitation nor less respectable than electricity, he says), and therefore have no business in the public sphere. William does not like the *way* Bushnell argues against women's participation in government, but he agrees with the phrases he picks out that describe their "nature":

> She is not "created" to mingle in any kind of strife, or "to batter the severities of fortune. . . . All government belongs to men. . . . Where agreement is impossible, one of the two must clearly decide, and it must be the man. The woman's law . . . requires it of her . . . to submit herself to his fortunes. . . . If he has no sway-force in him . . . to hold the reins, he is no longer what Nature means when she makes a man." Women are "naturally subject," "subordinate," meant to yield to evil and violence, not to combat them with answering evil and violence. So far so good.[47]

In her inequality and her submission lay her power to heal, the Jameses would argue. As for the man, "[h]owever he might shrink from expressing it in naked words," James wrote, "the wife his heart more or less subtly craves is at bottom a dependent being." Thirty years later, William would not be so absolute, but the habit of mind is still recognizable. He is writing to his friend Frances Morse from Bad Nauheim: "[I]n most women," he said, there was "a wife that craves to suffer and submit and be bullied."[48]

With such thoughts in mind, how might a man set about finding a wife? In James's case, as we know, his father did it for him. His own gestures in that direction were few and ineffectual: reports of a chance meeting or of time spent watching a woman through a telescope from his boardinghouse window, or sending flowers to another woman in a window and then beating a hasty retreat, all in letters from abroad, where he was studying and taking the waters; a half-hearted courtship of the woman who would later marry Oliver Wendell Holmes, Jr.; and, relatedly, attentions to his invalid sister, Alice, which her biographer, Jean Strouse, describes as a combination of commiseration for her illness and "self-centered seductiveness."[49] And there seems to have been another form of "self-centered seductiveness"—namely, masturbation.

Anyone interested in James will have pondered that passage in *The Varieties of Religious Experience* in which he offers himself up as an example of "the Sick Soul." His is the chapter's last example, his the "worst kind of melancholy," the one that "takes the form of panic fear." In recalling in

1902 an experience he had had at least thirty years before, and in doing so by means of a letter supposedly sent to him by a Frenchman, which he translates "freely," he may remind us of his brother at play with multiple points of view, but whereas Henry's fictions suggest the inevitable and undeniable elusiveness of "truth," the absence of any one truth, and the validity of contending truths as they are individually perceived (William's "pragmatic" idea of truth, we might say), William's performance in this instance hints at a truth that he would go to almost any lengths not to have to face.

But the case, James says, has "the merit of extreme simplicity," and he sums it up in

> the image of an epileptic patient whom I had seen in the asylum, a black-haired youth with greenish skin, entirely idiotic, who used to sit all day on one of the benches, or rather shelves against the wall, with his knees drawn up against his chin, and the coarse gray undershirt, which was his only garment, drawn over them inclosing his entire figure. He sat there like a sort of sculptured Egyptian cat or Peruvian mummy, moving nothing but his black eyes and looking absolutely non-human. This image and my fear entered into a species of combination with each other. *That shape am I*, I felt, potentially. Nothing that I possess can defend me against that fate, if the hour for it should strike for me as it struck for him. There was such a horror of him, and such a perception of my own merely momentary discrepancy from him, that it was as if something hitherto solid within my breast gave way entirely, and I became a mass of quivering fear. (pp. 149–150)

James's "correspondent" goes on to say that he was very careful not to give his mother any hint of what he was going through and that what he was going through must have had "a religious bearing." When James asked him (himself) to explain, he said that he had avoided insanity by quoting "scripture-texts," at which point, in a footnote, James cites his father's *Society the Redeemed Form of Man* as "another case of fear equally sudden." In another footnote, James refers his reader to Bunyan, who, like the Frenchman, registered his fears in his breast: "I felt also such clogging and heat at my stomach, by reason of this my terror, that I was, especially at some times, as if my breast-bone would have split asunder."[50]

James had started his letter by saying that at the time, he was in a state of "philosophic pessimism and general depression of spirits about my prospects," reminding us that his all but lifelong struggle with anxiety and the various physical ailments that both prompted and were caused by it—his battle with his form of neurasthenia—was obviously not just a reflection of difficulties he had meeting his culture's and his family's expectations of him. It mirrored his struggle with intellectual doubt and with the frustration and self-denigration that came of his not being able to settle on a career as well. And to reduce it to any one cause would be absurd, would be like reversing the logic of those who, having observed that lunatics often masturbated, terrified people with the argument that anyone who masturbated was insane. But in this one, deeply shrouded allusion, James revealed his fears about masturbation.

Cushing Strout speculates that James had read William Acton's *The Functions and Disorders of the Reproductive Organs* and been struck by Acton's warning that the habit of introspection could lead not to just "the suicidal view of life," as James had said in "Is Life Worth Living?," but to masturbation and then to madness.[51] Sander Gilman allows us to be more precise. He recalls an entry in the diary that James kept during the crisis years of the late 1860s and early 1870s in which he admits that he has tried "to associate his feelings of Moral degradation with failure"—that is, that he has been demoralized by his labyrinthine thinking and by not having settled on a career—"[b]ut in all this I was cultivating the moral . . . only as a means and more or less humbugging myself." Gilman then points to a text that is, indeed, French and that contains a full-length portrait of Aba (his only sounds being "ba ba ba"), a masturbator, in a coarse undershirt, his hair black, his eyes wild, and "his knees drawn against his chin." It is James's image of his profound depression, of his most melancholic, neurasthenic state. It is James in his most abject state as a man, having embraced what is most unmanly about himself. He would not utter a word about it to his mother, he would suffer the chest pains in silence, and he could not help recalling his father's "vastation" and thus intensifying his sense of shame and unworthiness and panic.[52]

James told his "Philosophy 2" class that those who put off marrying were mired in unwholesome leisure, that it was healthier to marry early,[53] but he himself was thirty-four when his father came home from an evening at The Radical Club on Chestnut Street in Boston and announced to the family that he had met the woman his eldest son would marry. The club's membership included the more advanced Transcendental and Unitarian thinkers of the day (Henry James, Sr., had lectured to them several times); the presence of Alice Howe Gibbens attested to her independence of mind and spirit. Twenty-seven at the time, and a teacher at Miss Sanger's school, she had begun to prove herself ten years before, when, her rakish father having died (probably by his own hand) and her mother having totally collapsed, she assumed responsibility for the welfare of her one remaining parent and her two younger sisters. Alice was clearly qualified to be James's wife. She embodied the ideal Henry James, Sr., had defined in his lecture on "Marriage" to the Radical Club: she would be able "to quicken in [her husband's] heart a flame of chaste, interior, spiritual tenderness, such as no other sexual tie would ever have evoked."[54] Nothing was to stand in the way. William was told by his father, "If you marry her I'll support you," and at the next club meeting he was introduced to his future wife by his friend Thomas Davidson.[55]

Their courtship lasted two years, or rather, having herself decided that she, too, had met her mate upon a first meeting, Alice persevered for two years while William came to terms with the idea of marriage. "Mother had never encountered anything remotely resembling his incandescent, tormented, mercurial excitability," their son later wrote.[56] In his first letter—crammed onto both sides of four postcards and a calling card—James presented Alice with his version of the proposition that a man was meant for spiritual regeneration and that it was a wife's calling to assist him on his way. He was going against the normal way of the world "*officially* recognized by society" in wanting to marry her; he did not meet "the standard of wholesomeness." There was but one justification for going ahead: "Crimes against its law, such as the marriage of unhealthy persons can only be forgiven by an appeal to some metaphysical world 'behind the veil' whose life such events may be supposed to feed." To subscribe to what he would call in *The Varieties of Religious Experience* "The Religion of Healthy-Mindedness," to "abandon my private spiritual advancement," would be, he said, "worse than a *crime* against nature . . . a *sin* against the holy ghost—metaphorically speaking." He was not going to do that, so the question he wanted to put to her at the very outset was, Was she willing to assist him?

> Now if the case come up with reference to matrimony, and I feel that it is a case of this kind, well and good for me! But if the other person through heedlessness, superficiality, or insensibility slide into the natural crime, without the imperative spiritual need wh [*sic*] alone can make it be forgiven what thank [*sic*] has she? She falls a prey to the Tragical, this time without atonement. Thus she must not take me unless she find it spiritually laid upon her as a tragic duty, to do so.[57]

Gradually James came to believe that Alice would complete him in the way his father had described: "I will feed on death and the negation of me in one place shall be the affirmation of me in a better. For this your undivided work I eternally thank you, and you ought to feel happy for it," he wrote seven months later. Around the anniversary of their meeting, he wrote: "To have you recognize me, to have your truth acquiesce in my better self, form henceforward the only possible goal of my better life. You *will* do it—you will value me, care for me." Five months after that, he wrote: "I approach more and more the conclusion that the mission of your sex is not to originate but to judge—to distinguish the better from the worse when they have it offered them—to do this really. . . . It shows how deeply a man needs the corroboration of the woman whom he respects, how something is missing until he gets it."

A few months later, in an Emersonian outburst, James went too far, claiming that given his loyalty to "the wider Not-me (the willingness to serve the Universe)," he would "not scruple to sacrifice" Alice, but soon after (and soon after a separation and a period in which he assumed their courtship was at an end), he regretted his "unspeakable impotence and culpability," and pleaded: "Forget, forget the sickening words. The loathing with which I now repudiate them, shows me how I am already changed."

Few of Alice's letters have survived. At one point she must have spoken of James's "doctrine" in something like protest. James' response was: "[D]o not speak of my '*doctrines*'—they are only provisional perceptions of the facts of life." He then assured Alice that she knew more about marriage than he ever would. They were married in July of 1878, and from what we can tell, though they may not have lived by the letter of Henry James, Sr.'s, "doctrines," Alice tried to do for William what his mother had done for his father. Alice's life was, as she defined it for her husband, "a quiet life of helping you." She wanted to feel her responsibility "a thousand times more keenly from *hour to hour*," and worried lest she would fail. But William assured her in words of which his father would have approved: "You have lifted me up out of lonely hell. . . . You have redeemed my life from destruction."[58]

James once described himself to his wife as "that poor diseased boy whom you raised from the dust."[59] In such a scenario, his incessant strugglings, his efforts to establish himself as a manly figure in it, make the more sense. No man is going to want support forever; against the elevating female principle in his life, he is bound to assert himself as masculine—bound, we might say, by the very way he formulated his and her existence to begin with.

•

Of the philosopher, James once wrote: "Whatever principles he may reason from, and whatever logic he may follow, he is at bottom an advocate pleading to a brief handed over to his intellect by his peculiarities of his nature and the influences in his history that have moulded his imagination."[60] "Temperament" was what he often called it. "The history of philosophy is to a great extent that of a certain clash of human temperaments," he claimed in *Pragmatism*:

> Undignified as such a treatment may seem to some of my colleagues, I shall have to take account of this clash and explain a good many of the divergences of philosophers by it. Of whatever temperament a professional philosopher is, he tries, when philosophizing, to sink the fact of his temperament. Temperament is no conventionally recognized reason, so he urges impersonal reasons only for his conclusions. Yet his temperament really gives him a stronger bias than any of his more strictly objective premises.[61]

Because this was the case, you could never expect "absolute illumination from human philosophizing. At most you can get arguments either to reinforce or protect certain emotional impulses."[62] On the other hand, as we know, he was dismissive of those who *did* philosophy, those who might reach conclusions but whose temperaments were not engaged in the logic-chopping or reasoning that they did to get there. His temperament—the "peculiarities of his nature and the influences in his history"—forced him to profess "human" as against what we might call professional philosophy, and to do so constantly. James could say, in a famous exchange with Santayana, "What a curse philosophy would be if we couldn't forget all about it!"[63] but one is hard put to think of a time when he ever did.

James's insistence on the seminal influence of "temperament" reminds us how much he owes to Emerson. Going back to "Experience" (if to nothing else), we find Emerson writing, "Temperament puts all divinity to rout," "Temperament is the veto or limitation-power in the constitution," and:

> Dream delivers us to dream, and there is no end to illusion. Life is a train of moods like a string of beads, and as we pass through them they prove to be many-colored lenses which paint the world their own hue, and each shows only what lies in its focus. . . . It depends on the mood of the man whether he shall see the sunset or the fine poem. There are always sunsets, and there is always genius; but only a few hours so serene that we can relish nature or criticism. The more or less depends on structure or temperament. Temperament is the iron wire on which the beads are strung.

In the same essay, we find Emerson praising the "man of native force" and decrying nicety of thought ("Intellectual tasting of life will not supersede muscular activity," he says), in ways that are wholly familiar to us by now. His sentences on our unhappy discovery that we exist surely inform James's thinking on "The Stream of Thought": "That discovery is called the Fall of Man. Ever afterwards we suspect our instruments. We have learned that we do not see directly, but mediately, and that we have no means of computing the amount of their errors." And his definition of the "spiritual," which would seem to follow, as "*that which is its own evidence*" may account in large measure for James's excitement when the earthquake struck San Francisco. It was what had been imagined for him by his friend. It was his earthquake, "an individualized being, B.'s earthquake, namely," manifesting "the full meaning of its name." It was an instance, maybe *the* instance in James's life, when mediation ceased and the Word became the thing.[64]

But in comparing him with Emerson, we should recall the homely remark James quotes in "The Importance of Individuals": "There is very little difference between one man and another; but what little there is, *is very important*."[65] The difference between James and Emerson is significant and unmistakable. It is one of style, style conceived of as it is by James on Emerson himself in his "Address at the Centenary of Ralph Waldo Emerson, May 25, 1903": "The style is the man, it has been said: the man Emerson's mission culminated in his style, and if we must define him in one word, we have to call him Artist."[66] James was a different kind of artist altogether.

"I had fancied that the value of life lay in its inscrutable possibilities," Emerson writes,

> in the fact that I never know, in addressing myself to a new individual, what may befall me. I carry the keys of my castle in my hand, ready to throw them at the feet of my lord, whenever and in what disguise soever he shall appear. I know he is in the neighborhood, hidden among vagabonds. Shall I preclude my

future by taking a high seat and kindly adapting my conversation to the shape of heads? When I come to that, the doctors shall buy me for a cent.[67]

Compare this with James on his own open-ended philosophy:

The pragmatism or pluralism which I defend has to fall back on a certain ultimate hardihood, a certain willingness to live without assurances or guarantees. To minds thus willing to live on the possibilities that are not certainties, quietistic religion, sure of salvation *any how*, has a slight flavor of fatty degeneration about it which has caused it to be looked askance on, even in the church . . . philosophy must favor the emotion that allies itself best with the whole body and drift of all the truths in sight. I conceive this to be the more strenuous type of emotion.[68]

It is not just a matter of James's squeamishness as he imagines hardness giving way to repellent softness (we have already noted that), but the almost total absence of play in the voice and in the few figures he allows himself. Whereas Emerson moves among the individuals to whom he wants to be open, finding them at the extremes of the social scale, while at the same time destabilizing his own position (my castle, my lord, now king, now cipher), and then dramatizes the pettiness of any elevated position with images of mere tops of heads and coins, James moves cautiously, his flexibility amounting to repeated qualification (a certain, a certain, a slight), as he establishes the hardy figure who can be responsive to "all the truths in sight" because he has finally managed to plant his feet so firmly. Richard Poirier's nice distinction between the way Emerson enacts "the struggles by which he tries to keep his own language from becoming 'faked'" and James's more theoretical skepticism about language can be extended to apply to their respective styles. James may acknowledge that "'language works against our perception of the truth,'" Poirier says, quoting from "The Stream of Thought," but "there are very few stylistic indications in his writing that he suffers for it, or that he feels it as a threat to his own stylistic self-assurance, to his way of carrying himself in the world."[69]

James honored and furthered many of Emerson's ideas, but the way he did so reminds us more of one of his most famous students: Theodore Roosevelt. He was as much a "strenuous" as a "self-reliant" man. "Military feelings," "pugnacity," he said in his most famous utterance, "The Moral Equivalent of War," are bred into us. And he would not have it otherwise: "Militarism is the great preserver of our ideals of hardihood, and human life with no use for hardihood would be contemptible."[70] "Man is essentially an adventurous and warlike animal, and one might as well preach against the intercourse of the sexes as against national aggrandizement by piracy," he wrote in 1901.[71]

When he preached against imperialism, he followed the advice of his student and friend John Jay Chapman: enter into your opponent's point of view, and *"then move the point."* "We must make new energies and hardihoods continue the manliness to which the military mind so faithfully clings," he argued. "Martial virtues must be the enduring cement; intrepidity, contempt of softness, surrender of private interest, obedience to command, must still remain the rock upon which states are built."[72] The new enemy was "*Nature*," the environment; young men, especially "our gilded youth," would "get the childishness knocked out of them" in what we might call a turn of the century version of the New Deal's Civilian Conservation Corps or, less exactly, the Peace Corps. When Roosevelt launched his resounding attack on the antiimperialists in the name of "The Strenuous Life" in 1899, James took great exception, but what infuriated him was not just Roosevelt's unbridled celebration of that life but the charge that those who opposed his, Roosevelt's, policies were any less capable of living it.[73] James's proposal in "The Moral Equivalent of War" was to keep "military characters in stock . . . keeping them, if not for use, then as ends in themselves and as pure pieces of perfection,—so that Roosevelt's weaklings and mollycoddles may not end by making everything else disappear from the face of nature."[74]

•

A few weeks after Gertrude Stein wrote that her professor was "a man take him for all in all," she was scheduled to take his exam—but "she just could not." Their exchange is part of the Stein legend:

> It was a very lovely spring day, Gertrude Stein had been going to the opera every night and going also to the opera in the afternoon and had been otherwise engrossed and it was the period of the final examinations, and there was the examination in William James's course. She sat down with the examination paper before her and she just could not. "Dear Professor James," she wrote at the top of her paper. "I am so sorry but really I do not feel a bit like an examination paper in philosophy today," and left.
>
> The next day she had a postal card from William James saying, Dear Miss Stein, I understand perfectly how you feel. I often feel like that myself. And underneath it he gave her work the highest mark in his course.[75]

The story serves to compliment them both, he for his insight and sense of proportion, she for being, manifestly, a genius. But one wonders, Would he have let a male student quit that way? Isn't his gesture of a piece with his self-representation as a manly figure, the more manly for dealing gently with a young woman?

Once again, he would fashion woman in such a way as to bring himself into clear definition. His relationship to Stein—his chivalric manner, the adoration he inspired—was of a piece with his larger understanding of the womanly and—by contrast—his own achieved manhood. She would be pure in order to help him transcend or suppress his brutish instincts, at ease in order to relieve his tension, strong in order to see him through his neurasthenic spells. When Gertrude Stein heard him argue for life's worth and went back and described him as "a man take him for all in all," she intended to pay him the highest of compliments. But comparing her words with those from *Hamlet*, we can see she was responding not so much to an ideal complex human being as to a male and to his style. She was responding to a particular temperament, the result of an especially anguished history, to a presence, there at the lectern, at a specific and exceptionally influential time in our cultural history.

NOTES

1. Gertrude Stein, quoted in Rosalind S. Miller, *Gertrude Stein: Form and Intelligibility* (New York: Exposition, 1949), pp. 146–147.

2. *Letters of Sarah Wyman Whitman* (Cambridge, Mass.: Riverside, 1907), p. 117.

3. *Harvard Advocate*, 62 (November, 1896): 64.

4. William James, *Writings* vol. 1, *1878–1899*, and vol. 2, *1902–1910* (New York: Library of America, 1992 and 1987, respectively), vol. 1, pp. 480–503. Unless otherwise noted, citations of James's writing are to and unreferenced quotations are from this two-volume edition.

5. *The Letters of William James* (2 vols.), ed. Henry James (Boston: Atlantic Monthly Press, 1920), vol. 2, p. 39.

6. James, *Writings*, vol. 2, p. 463.

7. *Ibid.*, vol 1, p. 648.

8. Quoted in James, *Letters*, vol. 2, pp. 11 and 14.

9. George Santayana, *Character and Opinion in the United States: With Reminiscences of William James and Josiah Royce and Academic Life in America* (New York: Charles Scribner's Sons, 1920), p. 96.

10. Daniel G. Mason, "Harvard in the Nineties," *New England Quarterly* 9 (1936): 66–67.

11. George Santayana, *Persons and Places* (New York: Charles Scribner's Sons, 1963), vol. 2, p. 159.

12. *Ibid.*, vol. 1, p. 242, and vol. 2, p. 166; Santayana, *The Genteel Tradition* (Cambridge: Harvard University Press, 1967), p. 55.

13. James, *Writings*, vol. 2, pp. 1242–1247.

14. *Ibid.*, pp. 1126–1129.

15. William James, "The Proposed Shortening of the College Course," *Harvard Monthly* 11 (January 1891): 127–137.

16. James, *Writings*, vol. 2, pp. 1111–1118.

17. "Ever handsomer": *ibid.*, p. 1260. "Athletic ratiocinator": *ibid.*, p. 963. "I lead": James, *Letters*, Vol. 2, p. 136.

18. William James, *The Principles of Psychology* (reprint, Cambridge: Harvard University Press, 1983), pp. 1053–1055.

19. James, *Letters*, vol. 2, p. 255.

20. James, *Writings*, vol. 2, pp. 457, 460.

21. James, *Letters*, vol. 2, pp. 327–328.

22. Walter Lippmann, "An Open Mind: William James," *Everybody's Magazine* 23 (December 1910): 801.

23. John Jay Chapman, *Memories and Milestones* (New York: Moffat, Yard, 1915), p. 24.

24. Santayana, *Character and Opinion*, p. 77.

25. James, *Writings*, vol. 2, pp. 615, 941, and 772–773.

26. *The Correspondence of William James: William and Henry* (3 vols.), ed. Ignas K. Skrupskelis and Elizabeth M. Berkeley (Charlottesville: University of Virginia Press, 1992–1994), vol. 1, p. 193.

27. *Ibid.*, p. 303.

28. James, *Letters*, vol. 1, pp. 199–200.

29. James, *Principles of Psychology*, p. 1181.

30. James, *Writings*, vol. 2, p. 1228.

31. *Ibid.*, p. 857.

32. *Ibid.*, pp. 1215–1222. There were newspaper reporters of looters, some so eager to get rings that they chopped off fingers, and of the drunkenness of troops sent in to restore order, but James either didn't read them or he ignored them. See *The Correspondence of William James*, vol. 3, p. 313n.

33. James, *Letters*, vol. 2, p. 355.

34. *The Diary of Alice James* (New York: Penguin, 1964), p. 57.

35. Santayana, *Persons and Places*, vol. 2, p. 166.

36. William James, Introduction to *The Literary Remains*, by Henry James, Sr. (Boston: James R. Osgood, 1885), p. 9.

37. William James, "Woman in Revelation and History," by permission of the Houghton Library, Harvard University.

38. H. James, Sr., *Literary Remains*, p. 262.

39. H. James, Sr., *Love, Marriage, and Divorce, and the Sovereignty of the Individual* (reprint, Weston, Mass.: M & S Press, 1975), pp. 92–93.

40. H. James, Sr., *Literary Remains*, pp. 346–359.

41. H. James, Sr., *Love, Marriage, and Divorce*, p. 95.

42. H. James, Sr., "The Logic of Marriage and Murder," *Atlantic* 25 (1870): 744.

43. Ralph Barton Perry, *The Thought and Character of William James* (2 vols.) (Boston: Little, Brown, 1935), vol. 1, pp. 112–113.

44. James, *Letters*, vol. 1, p. 219.

45. Quoted in John Owen King III, *The Iron of Melancholy* (Middletown: Wesleyan University Press, 1983), p. 182.

46. James, *Principles of Psychology*, pp. 34–35.

47. James's review appeared in *North American Review* 109 (1869): 556–565; his father's is " 'The Woman Thou Savest With Me,' " *Atlantic* 25 (1870): 66–72.

48. James, *Letters*, vol. 2, p. 135.

49. Jean Strouse, *Alice James* (Boston: Houghton Mifflin, 1980), p. 123.

50. James, *Writings*, vol. 2, pp. 149–151.

51. Cushing Strout, "William James and the Twice-Born Sick Soul," *Daedalus* 97 (1968): 1066–1067.

52. Sander Gilman, *Diseases and Representation* (Ithaca, N.Y.: Cornell University Press, 1988), pp. 74–78. James impressed a version of the same image on his son's mind when the latter went off to boarding school, warning him, "If any boys try to make you *do* anything dirty . . . either to your own person, or to their persons

. . . you must both preach and smite them. For that leads to an awful habit, and a terrible disease when one is older." See Alfred Habbegger, *The Father: A Life of Henry James, Sr.* (New York: Farrar, Straus and Giroux, 1994), p. 415 n.

53. Gerald E. Myers, *William James: His Life and Thought* (New Haven: Yale University Press, 1986), p. 490 n. 31.

54. *Sketches and Reminiscences of The Radical Club*, ed. Mrs. John T. Sargent (Boston: J. R. Osgood, 1880), p. 210.

55. Typescript of Henry James III on his mother, Alice Howe Gibbens, by permission of the Houghton Library, Harvard University, p. 34.

56. *Ibid.*, p. 35.

57. Unpublished letter, quoted by permission of the Houghton Library, Harvard University.

58. Quoted in Myers, *William James*, p. 37. All other citations from James's correspondence with his wife are by permission of the Houghton Library, Harvard University.

59. Henry James III on his mother, p. 45.

60. Perry, *The Thought and Character of William James*, vol. 2, p. 379.

61. James, *Writings*, vol. 2, pp. 488–489.

62. Perry, *The Thought and Character of William James*, vol. 1, p. 403.

63. Santayana, *Character and Opinion in the United States*, p. 92.

64. "Dream delivers": Ralph Waldo Emerson, "Experience," reprinted in *Selections from Ralph Waldo Emerson*, ed. Stephen E. Whicher (Boston: Houghton Mifflin, 1957), p. 257. Other Emerson quotes: *ibid.*, pp. 254–274.

65. James, *Writings*, vol. 1, p. 648.

66. *Ibid.*, vol. 2, p. 1120.

67. Emerson, "Experience," pp. 258–259.

68. James, *Writings*, Vol. 1, p. 941.

69. Richard Poirier, *Poetry and Pragmatism* (Cambridge: Harvard University Press, 1992), p. 27.

70. James, *Writings*, vol. 2, p. 1285.

71. Perry, *The Thought and Character of William James*, vol. 2, p. 199.

72. James, *Writings*, vol. 2, p. 1290.

73. Perry, *The Thought and Character of William James*, vol. 2, p. 311.

74. James, *Writings*, vol. 2, p. 1285.

75. *Gertrude Stein: Writings and Lectures 1909–1945*, ed. Patricia Meyerowitz (Baltimore: Penguin, 1967), p. 15.

CHAPTER THIRTEEN

American Political Culture, Prophetic Narration, and Toni Morrison's *Beloved*

George Shulman

HUMAN BEINGS tell stories; we may call them narratives. They are crucial to human life, and fruitful to study, because they mediate past and present, social condition and interior experience, inherited circumstance and agency, collective and personal identity. Collective artifacts internalized as part of identity, stories also foster the reflection that infuses them with new meanings. For a political theorist, then, narratives make visible the cultural dimensions in politics.

In American political culture, the prophetic story of captivity, deliverance, and foundation, thus of decline from founding origins, hence of redemption, has been especially important; in this essay I investigate how differently situated Americans have retold this story to authorize claims about rights, inequality, membership, history, and their meaning. I trace this narrative, first, in Anglo-American men defending liberal nationalism; next, in the oppositional politics of those they have excluded; then in current culture; and lastly in Toni Morrison's novel *Beloved*.

While other stories are important in American political culture, focusing on the resources, limits, and dangers of the prophetic narrative clarifies two issues. One is hegemony: how are we to assess the power of governing narratives in political life, and the limits and possibilities in retelling them? The other is redemption, an idea at the core of the prophetic story and American political culture: how are we to assess the dream of fixing the crimes and suffering that flaw our nation and past, to "make good" an originary but unfulfilled promise of freedom?

My retellings analyze hegemony, at first in terms of an Americanized Marx: I use Sacvan Bercovitch in particular to explore the role of prophetic narration in efforts to sustain, or challenge, liberalism. But then, as if using a democratized Nietzsche, I explore the hegemony not of liberalism but of redemptive rhetorics, in elite and oppositional politics, and in current political culture. By relating past and present versions of prophetic narration, I create a context for reading *Beloved* as a literary work of political thought: by narrating as tragedy the quest for deliverance, it retells a compulsively repeated story to confront the redemptive dream at its core.

The Narrative of the Good Son

Claims about liberal hegemony, master narratives, or national identity are risky: they can efface the agency and flatten the contest they profess to value. But such claims are needed to understand domination, the meaning of lived experience, and the fashioning of agency. My scaffolding for *Beloved*, then, begins with Sacvan Bercovitch's *American Jeremiad* because it links liberalism, prophetic narration, and ideals of nationhood to theorize hegemony in American politics.[1]

For Bercovitch, conflict and aspiration have been governed here by a liberalism itself sustained, contra Louis Hartz, by the hegemony of a prophetic and Puritan narrative form, and thus by a particular idea of nationhood. In the story he tells, "Anglo-American," propertied men formed a liberal and national identity by differentiation from Old World despotism, but also from native peoples, slaves, women, and propertyless men. Believing that a Puritan and constitutional legacy, partly by such exclusions, yielded personal and political self-government, self-declared heirs claimed to form a special nation, called by God to free humanity, but therefore vulnerable to decline and corruption.[2]

Through a prophetic view of deliverance in history, that is, they sacralized origins, wedding liberal principles to national identity, and endowing both with redemptive significance in a providentially authored history. But liberal hegemony has been sustained, Bercovitch argues, because differently situated groups continued to argue about inequality, identity, and difficulty through the genre of the "jeremiad," a "prescribed ritual form" that elicits and yet "contains" self-reflection and dissent.[3]

In its biblical form, the jeremiad roots both freedom and nationhood in origins. By positing a legacy that delivered founders from captivity, prophets narrated nationhood in a way that linked identity to originary commitments, their betrayal to enslavement, and their pious recovery to renewed freedom. Performatively, by blaming captivity, conflict, and suffering on deviation from founding norms, a jeremiad secures their authority: it elicits guilt about their betrayal, hence gives meaning to suffering, and thereby solicits recommitment.

As redemption means both deliverance and repossession, so a jeremiad recovers the commitments that deliver a chosen people from the impulses, activities, and groups deemed to cause captivity. As redemption also means making good what is flawed, so this story redeems a nation flawed by crime and suffering, but also redeems the very legacy it posits as a saving authority, neither admirable but irretrievable nor extant but problematic.

By a "traditional" jeremiad, then, elites recurrently use present problems to bind unequal Americans to a narrowly defined Puritan and liberal legacy, whose violation is construed to cause their difficulties. But, Bercovitch shows, this legacy also includes a "revolutionary mythos" of a people hostile to tradition, capable of the unprecedented. Thus, elites and those they dominate have used jeremiads to abstract from "actual" origins a promise whose realization justifies *change*, framed in progressive but still redemptive terms. What are the insights, and then the problems, in this view of jeremiads as a ritual of criticism?[4]

Most simply, Bercovitch shows the communitarian face of liberal politics: Anglo-Americans have authorized rights and formed nationhood by narrating a project of personally enacting and collectively fulfilling a redemptive purpose. Self and nation are profoundly joined because the sacred meaning of "America" authorizes the rights of self-making men, who bear and signal the fate of a national project. A class ideal has been interiorized and generalized, and "Americans" made, as people enter and use a narrative that elicits anxious effort to redeem their promise.[5]

Second, he shows how jeremiads mediated the inclusionary promise of this ideal community, and the exclusion of nonliberal otherness it requires. For jeremiads define membership by distinguishing the true heirs who honor an emancipatory legacy from those who threaten it, and thus can justify racial violence, imperial expansion, or assimilation supervised by good sons.

Third, Bercovitch shows how such jeremiads have been cast as false prophecy by major movements of opposition, which have argued about modernization and inequality by revising a story of redemptive purpose and betrayal. Speaking of literary artists, he depicts most American reformers: "The dream that inspired them to defy the false Americanism of their time compelled them to speak their defiance as keepers of the dream"(p. 180).

Fourth, he shows how jeremiads displace politics by culture: grievances are voiced not in strongly contrasted "moral and social" alternatives to a dominant order, but in competing calls for "cultural revitalization" of its authentic but jeopardized values(p. 179). Confirming the religiosity of a special nationhood, and moralizing conflicts that signify the fate of a more perfect union, critics occlude the political sense that any community is divided by conflicts of identity and interest.

These insights about "American" civic identity frame his notorious claim that jeremiadic criticism *necessarily* "contains" dissent. His goal is to identify not the range of dissent, but its legitimating center of gravity: to be legitimate, critics "must" invoke liberal rights or capitalist norms; racial or patriarchal ideology can be rejected, but "must" be deemed a *violation* of core values, such as self-determination and voluntarist community, which "must" appear both native and unproblematic. The "must" is contingent, yet intractable. It signals a cultural hegemony rooted in social power and narrative form; it marks the internal and strategic pressures driving critics to redeem the society they condemn, by naming their ideals "truly American."[6]

Still, there are profound problems. Simply put, Bercovitch renders American culture too monolithic. But rather than recover the complexity within the liberal tradition that he flattens, or voice the other narratives that make its hegemony more contested than he allows, I pursue three problems within his story of jeremiadic form and liberal hegemony. First is motivation: why do succeeding generations find a jeremiadic story meaningful and empowering? Second is variation: *does* it "work" to secure liberal hegemony, despite the differing social positions and intentions that shape oppositional efforts to *use* it? Third is redemptive American rhetorics: do they in fact exceed liberal limits, but impose other ones? Through these questions, I would explain the power, but also reconceive the foreclosure, that Bercovitch attributes to prophetic narration.

MOTIVATION: THE ANXIETY OF THE ISAACS

Why and how do declining classes and groups of "new men" repeatedly infuse tropes of decline and deliverance with specific meanings? Why do their narrations mobilize white men (and women) across class lines? Such queries expose the missing motivational core in Bercovitch's story, but have been addressed by scholars inspired by American literature. They depict an America founded not only on contract and rights, in markets and legislatures, but also on Indian graves, slave labor, rape, and incest.[7]

In these readings, Anglo-Americans formulate liberal rights, manly independence, and chosen nationhood by marking racial and gendered difference; in turn, the excluded enter and haunt the imagination of the enfranchised, who name difficulty and depict corruption in racial and gendered terms. A "rebirth of freedom," then, depends on overcoming the threats to personal autonomy and national unity that elite jeremiads lodge in the self, and in racial others and women, the city, and the state.

On the one hand, a liberal culture intensifies male anxiety about dependence because it celebrates the idealized independence Lawrence called "masterlessness," and because the market "makes men the playthings of alien powers," as Marx put it. In tropes of corruption as decline, propertied men recurrently voice an anxiety they blame not on their ideal, or on familial and market practices deemed to secure that ideal, but on impulses, groups, and activities that subvert both. Casting themselves as good sons rescuing a paternal legacy from corruption and other sons from dependence, self-declared Isaacs direct resentment of powerlessness in a way that empowers them as fathers, while binding widespread aspirations for autonomy to a liberal order.

On the other hand, their jeremiadic stories regenerate the sovereignty of self in a way that voices the dream of belonging inherent in liberalism. Liberal society generates communal aspirations that elite jeremiads lodge in the nation; as a "union" of rights-bearing individuals, the nation is what Marx called an "allegorical community," created by abstracting from the group power and conflict that represent earthly taint. This abstraction is enormously powerful, though, because it represents the gendered division between the "home" and the corrupt world. Adapting biblical jeremiads, which make the paternal household a metaphor for nationhood, elites recurrently depict antifamilial subversion of what otherwise would be a harmonious home, to justify the purification that restores it.[8]

Elite jeremiads, as in Reagan-era discourse, continue to be rhetorically powerful, and thus instrumentally effective, because they voice alienation and loss of purpose, while promising to recover a shared identity of self-determination. As a political theory, however, this poetry of rebirth is self-defeating for those it mobilizes. It enables them to lament acquisitive life, but demonizes alternatives; enables criticism of servitude, but premises freedom for some on subjugation of others; celebrates democracy, but also the industrializing capitalism that entombs it; voices longing for community, but empowers the state.

Such arguments have been articulated by an oppositional tradition that distinguishes true and false prophecy. Those cast as Sarahs, Hagars, and Ishmaels have reconceived autonomy and community by retelling a story of legacy and decline. Can oppositional *use* of a jeremiad contest the liberal hegemony Bercovitch attributes to its form?

VARIATION AND USE: OPPOSITIONAL RETELLINGS

Bercovitch rightly emphasizes the extent to which groups cast outside a middle-class fold have retold jeremiadic stories. Yet liberal hegemony has been more contingent and contested than he allows because jeremiadic form does not, in itself, foreclose criticism of liberal origins and norms. Briefly showing this, however, shifts attention to the redemptive rhetorics shared by contrasting jeremiads.

Middle-class female reformers, labor republicans, and abolitionists, agrarian populists, Debsian workers, Progressive reformers, and civil rights activists often used jeremiadic narration to diagnose their captivity and redeem the nation from the sins that caused it. In each case, critics and actors became true heirs of the American promise, even as they redefined the meaning of rights and redemptive community. They reenacted the emancipatory promise of liberalism by invoking individual rights against antiliberal despotism, but also claimed their community embodied a special virtue because of its location, suffering, and capacity for service and sacrifice. In the idioms of sisterhood, cooperative commonwealth, moral household, or beloved community, excluded and aggrieved groups have been reborn as protagonists in stories of redeeming the promise of a corrupted America.[9]

Their jeremiadic stories of corruption and rebirth linked rights and the ethos of care liberalism assigned to the home, to expose subjugation in a liberal legacy and to foster more inclusive and substantive conceptions of equality and freedom. Outgroups thereby displayed the legitimacy and empowerment derived from redemptive rhetoric: by invoking but revising widely shared ideals, critics revised familial, racial, and market practices, to fix what went wrong in the past and make good the "American" promise of delivering (all) people from captivity.[10]

Jeremiads, then, need not "contain" dissent in narrowly liberal terms. By folding conflict into narratives that redeem America's promise, though, outgroups mirror elites: claiming innocent virtue, antagonists piously invoke a legacy others betray; by redemptive service, each would actualize the dream of a nation both free and harmonious. In turn, contrasts of Eugene Debs and Emma Goldman, Jane Addams and Randolph Bourne, or Martin Luther King, Jr., and Malcolm X suggest the pressures that rhetorics of American redemption impose on historically excluded groups.

First, when legitimacy depends on defending a founding legacy against corruption, outcasts are pressed to redeem rather than question the very ideas and traditions that have required or sanctioned their exclusion. Second, when legitimacy requires speaking to and for *everyone* in a community, critics are pressed to deny rather than voice the depth of conflicting interests. Third, when legitimacy derives from the moral authority of a redemptive role, protagonists are pressed to disown in themselves the carnality, interestedness, and power that signify corruption in the social body they would purify.

REDEMPTIVE RHETORICS AND IDENTITY POLITICS

The marginality of certain critical voices suggests that jeremiadic criticism formed a gravitational field in which no legitimate discourse questioned whether crimes and suffering *could* be redeemed, let alone at what cost. But are group identities, arguments, and conflict still governed by this field? To engage this question, or identity politics in political culture now, I use claims about guilt and innocence to relate recent uses of nationalist jeremiads, and recent captivity stories that reject American origins.

Historically, our political rhetoric has echoed the two ways that biblical prophets explained but also used suffering. In one, worldly difficulty signals the guilt of those who must will their suffering as penance, to become worthy of pardon, and redemption. Thus did Lincoln insist on the guilt of his chosen people, atoned by willing the suffering of war, itself redeemed as "we the living" consecrate the dead by bearing their purpose. Thus did social movements name national failure, to elicit the guilt and justify the conflict that would redeem America's promise. So, too, many Americans internalize social position as a guilt they must redeem through sacrifice.

Yet American jeremiads emphasized more a second approach: worldly difficulty signals the innocence of those who will and use suffering to achieve vindication as redeemers of a guilty world. Thus do elite jeremiads lodge guilt in alien powers that hold innocent men captive; outgroups have disowned the (always reluctant) vengeance elites endorse, but wounded innocence appears in stories of captivity to the power of guilty others, or of a posterity that betrays the sacrifices of forebears.[11]

In turn, political argument since Nixon has refigured guilt and innocence by revising captivity narratives. A working class undergoing economic decline and cultural change has responded to nationalist jeremiads depicting innocent white victims of a demonic love triangle, an invasive state serving only blacks and middle-class women. Meanwhile, politicized women and minorities have come to narrate not jeremiads redeeming American origins but captivity stories that posit other origins, to relocate belonging in the subnational or supranational identities of innocently suffering and thus redemptive protagonists. Stories of countercommunity, though, echo jeremiadic rhetoric of pure origins, guilty deviation, and purifying renewal.[12]

Despite differences about authoritative origins, then, groups form and fight by drawing legitimacy from a narrative of innocent captivity. As a result, they "must" compete for and wed themselves to the status of oppressed victim, hence innocent, virtuous, and a redemptive protagonist. In these terms, good sons "save America" through nationalist jeremiads regulating literal and discursive access to a paternal estate endangered by guilty others, while those cast out are policed by appeals to authentic belonging in counterredemptive communities. In turn, critics have fashioned left-Puritan jeremiads in which consumer culture, narcissism, and victim politics subvert the producer ethos, civic culture, and self-restraint that secure democratic politics.[13]

At issue, however, is not the extent of conflict in a culture of complaint, for democratic politics should involve contrasting efforts to link private grievances and public causes. At issue, rather, is the form given to resentment and grievance. That form does not reflect the decline of a guilt culture, for its moral categories still produce legitimacy, or "fragmentation" of national culture, by whose governing terms identity still is articulated. Political culture thus displays not incredulity toward a master narrative of captivity and redemption but the narrative's continuing role in shaping resentment, legitimacy, and identity.

The contradictions in the Clinton administration and the Republican "contract" demonstrate Bercovitch's point, for many Americans still live within a closed circle of compulsive repetition. They speak within a discursive horizon of corruption and renewal to the degree they orient action and legitimacy only by a story of innocent American origins. They reiterate a moral logic of blame and vindication to the degree they use guilt and innocence to mark power and legitimacy. And they sustain rhetoric of betrayal and purification to the degree their suffering binds them to stories of redeeming it. But such symmetries appear in narrations that oppose the symbolism of "America," by redeeming the innocent otherness of a community suffering captivity within it. It is no accident, then, that Morrison retells a captivity story to diagnose the origins and history, the suffering and moralizing logic that bind masters and (ex-)slaves to repetition.

BELOVED: REDEMPTION AS A PROBLEM

Beloved was written more than one hundred years after the last slave narratives, in the fading shadow of both the civil rights and black power movements, during another "post"-Reconstruction resurgence of white racism, and amidst Africentric revivalism. In this novel, Morrison rethinks all the inherited stories of servitude and emancipation, the moral categories they entail, and the idea of redemption at their core. In my reading, *Beloved* retells a captivity narrative to theorize about servitude and freedom, but by linking various kinds of imprisonment to the pursuit of redemption. In this narrative, the deliverance sought by men and whites has enslaved others, but ex-slaves also risk imprisonment in the effort to redeem their past and themselves.

I focus on the meaning of the plot centered around Sethe, a woman who escapes from the plantation Sweet Home, the white father's household, and settles in a community of escaped blacks in the north. In this new community without whites, she sets up for herself and her children a home without husbands and fathers. Yet the past and the white world invade that world when her former owner appears. In what she considers a supreme act of love, she tries to kill her four children, but can send only one "through the veil . . . where she will be safe." That child is named Beloved at her burial, because Sethe cannot afford a full gravestone inscription. This is a flashback nineteen years later, as Sethe is isolated from the community, and haunted by a "spiteful" ghost who becomes flesh.

In Sethe's guilty effort to redeem her deed by sacrificing herself to gain the ghost's forgiveness, and in Beloved's effort to both punish Sethe and guarantee her love, we see the haunting legacy of a formally emancipated ex-slave and an understandable but destructive symbiosis between mother and child. Sethe's neighbors, guilty because their envious ill will against her was fulfilled nineteen years before, resolve that the ghost and past should not possess her or the present. As they face her house to exorcise the ghost, a white man appears, and a hallucinatory Sethe relives the terror that once led to murder. But she directs her rage at the man rather than destroy what she loves. As Sethe tries (but fails) to strike him, Beloved disappears.

Feeling loss and lost, Sethe laments, "She was my best thing," but only now can she begin to learn, as her lover, Paul D., insists, "You your best thing, Sethe, you are." The narrator, having retold a devastating captivity narrative and resurrected its ghosts, does not tell us Sethe's future, but appears to call for an end to the compulsive repeating of the past:

> It was not a story to pass on. . . . They forget her like a bad dream . . . quickly and deliberately. . . . Remembering seemed unwise. . . . It was not a story to pass on. . . . So they forgot her. Like an unpleasant dream during a troubling sleep. . . . This is not a story to pass on. . . . By and by all trace is gone. . . . The

rest is weather. Not the breath of the disremembered and unaccounted for, but wind in the eaves, or spring ice thawing too quickly. Just weather. Certainly no clamor for a kiss . . . (pp. 274–275)

"Pass on" means to transmit but also to "pass on that," in the sese of letting it go by: the story is not to be passed by, and yet not repeated as such; it must be confronted but not to be repeated in the way it is retold. As if confirming this core ambiguity, these passages are followed by the novel's last word, "Beloved."

The novel's protagonists are almost all African American men and women: the story obviously concerns the horrors and anonymous dead of the middle passage, the experience of slavery, and their legacy. Represented primarily in and by a mother/daughter bond, this legacy also suggests how motherhood under patriarchy has been enslaving. By depicting how the power of blacks and women to name, (re)produce, and nurture has been appropriated, *Beloved* shows the legacy ex-slaves take inside, and emplots how a struggle to become free is shaped by its haunting power. The novel thereby renders both the ambiguity of memory, for re-membering slavery and the dis(re)membered seems essential, yet imprisoning, and the ambiguity of narration, necessary to selfhood and to community, yet dangerous in its promise of closure.[14]

In turn, commentary focuses on race and gender, familial dynamics and psychology, memory and narrative, but severed from American political culture. Yet Morrison's protagonists do not exemplify difference alone, voicing only what Anglo-American culture silences; their haunting past, continuing servitude, and quest for personal rebirth and community also participate in and reveal core dreams of the culture they stand within and against. Her retelling of a captivity narrative, if situated in a dual context of difference and commonality, of entwined "nations," appears as a profound meditation on freedom and redemption, and thus as a transfiguring exercise in political education.

To contextualize the novel in this way, begin with the deed that Morrison says inspired it: Margaret Garner, who killed her infant to prevent its return to slavery, became a key symbol for slavery apologists, Frederick Douglass, and white abolitionists. Douglass used Garner to symbolize the horror of slavery, arguing that "every mother who . . . plunges a knife into the bosom of her infant to save it from the hell of our Christian slavery should be . . . honored as a benefactress." By narration, the deed is given a meaning both particular and general; at issue is how a story makes visible the ambiguities in constituency and condition, experience and responsibility, carried by the word "our."[15]

Following Douglass in part, the novel reiterates the slave narrative that inverts Anglo-American versions of jeremiadic prophecy: New World and Christian origins do not deliver from despotism, but impose hell on earth, an Egyptian servitude. By narrating the meaning of legacy and freedom from the position not of fathers and sons but of slaves as mothers and daughters, *Beloved* thus inverts the origins of culture and history, shifting from white to black and from paternity to maternity. But Morrison does not counter only the masters' discourses; slave narratives, she says, "drop a veil" over "proceedings too terrible to relate," as if survival required forgetting. But "the struggle to forget which was important to survive was fruitless, and I wanted to make it fruitless." She would "rip that veil and expose a truth about the interior life of a people who didn't write it."[16]

By a veil, slave narratives sever physical and formal emancipation from the psychic and cultural legacy of servitude. Since that veil sunders the internal and external and thus the past and present, Morrison tells a ghost story for the same reasons that Melville or Poe, she has argued, used the genre of romance to show the return of what is repressed in liberal narratives of self-making and political emancipation: "We live in a land where the past is always erased and America is the innocent future in which immigrants can . . . start over. . . . The culture doesn't encourage . . . coming to terms with the truth" about the past, which is made "absent or romanticized." Thus she rips a veil that has joined whites and blacks, whose emancipatory stories entail what she calls a "national amnesia" about a past and "interior life" that "no one wants to remember."[17]

This jeremiadic denunciation of forgetting frames her novel, but as it goes behind the veil, memory also appears as a problem because the past is uprooting, slavery, and death. The novel recovers not a betrayed legacy of freedom but a history that connects slavery and modernity, terror and rationalized labor, racial domination and liberal democracy. "Americans," to be sure for different reasons, "veil" a past that has divided but also shaped and entwined them. In *Beloved*, the haunting power of this past appears as the uncanny, the repressed returning within a family—in Anglo- and Afro-American discourse a key trope for community, for depicting the vicissitudes of history and interior, and thus for making a parable about politics.

Since for Morrison "modern life begins with slavery," those vicissitudes are particular to Sethe and slavery, yet prefigure what she calls a "modern" effort to forge self, freedom, and meaning from a crucible of uprooting, violence, and suffering. Since Sethe struggles to justify a suffering that arises partly from her own bloody choices, and since Beloved represents the claims and voraciousness of a wounding past, the story confronts in its particulars an interracial problematic binding suffering, moral justification, and redemption to freedom.[18]

That redemption is central to Morrison's concerns appears most obviously in the problem of naming crucial to and in the novel. Sethe evokes Seth, the third son of Adam and Eve, whose name means "anointed by God." In turn, Paul, a name associated with rebirth, is given to every male slave at Sweet Home by their deluded "liberal" owner, Garner. And Paul had rewritten Hosea's words, the book's epigraph: "I will call them my people, which were not my people; and her beloved, which was not beloved."

Here is announced the promise of redemption and who is to be redeemed; many readers of the novel thus contrast "Old Testament" law (of whites and fathers) and a "New Testament" promise of redemption, borne by those seeking deliverance. As Mae Henderson argues, Morrison "enacts . . . an opposition between Law and Spirit, redeeming her characters from the curse of the law as figured in the masters' discourse." Sethe "achieves redemption" through the "creation of a cohesive psychoanalytic and historical narrative" that links healing to beloved community. She is "delivered" from the cursed law and "made whole" through a story that "makes good" her suffering by endowing it with a special (redemptive) power.[19]

In my reading, in contrast, *Beloved* makes the epigraph's promise less secure, more troubling; it undercuts Christianized dichotomies to question the bond tying suffering to redemption. An effort to *become* free must begin with servitude as a legacy, but depends on confronting the dream of making good what went wrong in the past, which binds us to the past. In contrast to Bercovitch, though, Morrison subverts a compulsively repeated story of captivity and redemption by *retelling* it as tragedy.

Showing how this story has divided and yet entwined masters and (ex-) slaves, *Beloved* depicts the story's costs, explains its powerful appeal, elicits possibilities it forecloses, and thus reconceives its promise of freedom. By this repetition with a difference, a past not dead or even past is no longer denied, but neither is it redeemed; finally given its due, it can be put to a some kind of rest. This "working through" is achieved through three moments central to Sethe's story—southern slavery, northern haunting, and Beloved's disappearance.

The story originates in the plantation "Sweet Home" that white men created in pursuit of freedom through the right to own property and the idea of limited government. This first moment, which conditions all that follows, depicts the emancipatory masterlessness mythically and politically sought by those Anglo-American men D.H. Lawrence calls escaped slaves; fleeing mother and despotism, they define freedom as the absence of dependence. Their freedom thus requires the servitude of others, for if dependence is slavery, a free man must control those on whom he depends. But since fathers and sons depend on those they call Hagars and Ishmaels, they are haunted by specters, the estranged power their disclaimed dependence gives to their slaves.

To escape the dependence that signified captivity, southern and northern men invoked self-determination and property rights, but disagreed about slave labor; the North reenacted the emancipatory promise of liberalism to redeem the nation from the sin of slavery, to bring a rebirth of freedom to the father's house. Thus did Sethe flee north to join a community of escaped slaves. From their position, though, free labor meant wage labor and captivity within a despotic home writ large. Yet formal rights do enable the forming of a countercommunity, whose vicissitudes comprise the second moment in the novel's retelling of deliverance.

To the enslaved, servitude means that mother's milk and labor are "stolen"; they are forced to provide a nurturance and recognition they lack the power to demand and the right to receive. Masters, says Sethe, not only "work, kill, or maim you, but dirty you . . . so bad you couldn't like yourself anymore"(p. 251). For a people forbidden to desire, and unable to protect those they love, "loving small" seems crucial to survival, but the power to love and the right to be-loved is central to freedom. Insisting she has "enough milk for all," Sethe thus dreams of a community in which nurture as love and labor is not devalued and coerced, but chosen, reciprocal, and effective.

As freedom depends on bonds of love that promise to redeem a captive people, or nation, so escaped slaves invoke emancipatory rights to found a "beloved" community. But a ghost signifies their haunting by a past servitude they would "beat back" and forget; the story of Sethe's family thus relates the problem of remembering and redeeming the past and the problems in defining freedom as mutual nurture.

That relationship is first voiced by Sethe's grandmother, Baby Suggs. Freed by her son's labor, Baby Suggs has assumed the vocation of "unchurched preacher" by letting "her great heart beat" in the presence of her peers. "Yonder," she tells them, "they do not love your flesh. They despise it. . . . *You* got to love it," because "the only grace [you] could have was the grace [you] could imagine"(pp. 88–89). Baby Suggs felt defeated and chose to die, however, because whites "came into my yard" to destroy the love she defended, because "a community of other free negroes," envying her reunited family, stood back, and because Sethe's love meant murder(pp. 177–180).

Sethe faced love's powerlessness, but also exercised the frightful power it can justify. "Whites might dirty *her* . . . but not her best thing," those "parts of her that were precious and fine and beautiful"(p. 251); she gathered "every bit of life she had made," to "drag them through the veil . . . where they would be safe."(p. 163). Claiming her act was "right because it came from true love"(p. 251), and rejected by neighbors judging her "pride," Sethe and Denver, her daughter, retreat to a house haunted by a ghost both spiteful and "needing a lot of love"(p. 209). The arrival of Paul D, who seeks a present with Sethe, provokes the ghost's fleshly return, which exposes deeper ambiguities in love as a model for politics.

For Sethe *makes* herself captive to her past and ghostly other; she dreams of a seamless union of love and understanding to repair their wounds. To redeem her abandonment as a daughter, and her act of murder as a mother, Sethe resurrects her beloved other; in the name of love she sacrifices her mortal being. Becoming "like a chastised child while Beloved ate up her life . . . the older woman yielded it up without a murmur"(p. 250). While Sethe would "make up for a handsaw," Beloved is both "making her pay for it" and trying to satisfy a "longing" for love that is "bottomless"(p. 58). Bound to a past that each would fix by gaining wholeness and vindication from the other, they create a familial prison drained of life.[20]

In *Beloved*, life and freedom require the (mother) love that signifies food and recognition, but nurture is not all of life, and freedom requires more than its mutuality. In part, nurture must be a form of servitude for the mother: children require care that partly displaces the self. In part, as the resentment of ex-children such as Beloved testifies, nurturers wield power precisely by claims to self-effacing sacrifice. As the more adult and equal relationships we seek are shaped by a (familial) past of power and dependence, so the ideal of nurture can repeat the forms of power and self-denial in the history it would repair.

In the name of beloved community as a (familial) refuge that redeems past wounds, we can be wed to the past, injury, and one another in ways that drown the present, devalue separation, and sanction resentful vindication. In *Beloved*, therefore, moral superiority does not derive from oppression, or innocence from love. Redemptive countercommunity, built on these terms by ex-slaves, can veil a self-imposed captivity, which Morrison "rips" for the sake of their freedom.

Of course, masters create domination in seeking redemption from dependence as captivity, while ex-slaves would redeem the wounds inflicted by domination. Thus Sethe's family does embody an alternative to slavery, patriarchy, and capitalism. Yet masters and ex-slaves both make family a model of politics, and redemption its purpose. Indeed, Sethe's relation to Beloved signifies the American dream, made flesh, of the "more perfect union" that redeems the crimes, and thus the divisions, haunting us. Since the prophets, this dream has been emplotted in a narrative of captivity and deliverance, which *Beloved* depicts as a tragic, inevitably imprisoning attempt to make community a home that redeems its members and the past. How, then, should the final moment in Morrison's captivity story be understood?

In my reading thus far, freedom in America has been joined to the pursuit of redemption, the promise that we can make good—render worthy and justified—both a self defined by lack or flaw and a past defined by wound or crime. This promise does empower, but in a way that can bind autonomy to domination, nurture to self-denial, and agency to repetition. Thus do Sethe's neighbors intervene, to exorcise a ghostly "invasion" by the past, for the sake of life and change in the present. As the "voices of women" formed a "sound that broke the back of words," Sethe "trembled like the baptized in its wash." Yet her rebirth, and Beloved's departure, also seem to depend upon her reliving her primal terror and redoing her primal deed, a second chance, as Tom Paine said, to begin the world over again.

Is this not the redemptive American dream, and possible only in fiction? In part. But Morrison's fiction suggests the transformative capacity of humans who are free because, or to the extent that, they can begin to act rather than react, by changing inherited patterns. Sethe cannot change the past, and her life is still conditioned by bodily need and human bonds, by poverty, patriarchy, and white power. That she attacks the man rather than the child, though, signifies how choices can be made differently, in part to direct rage against its proper targets.

The ghost disappears; Sethe is delivered by the voices of women and her own action. Yet she had willed its presence, and now feels loss, not liberation; her act is pregnant with a change she does not intend, but laments. Without her beloved other and "best thing," her identity is no longer bound to a nightmarish past, or to her bloody choices in the name of love. But who is she without the effort to redeem them? Her guilt and sense of worthlessness have led her to think that she requires redemption; since no one and no past *can* be redeemed, however—not by any sacrifice or creation—she has lodged in such acts an impossible and imprisoning burden.[21]

Since the Garden of Eden, freedom has been a gift experienced as loss. The loss of Beloved is that painful gift if Sethe can relinquish an identity that feels the need to redeem itself and its past. Freed from this captivity, which had made her life meaningful, she could enter the present and will not suffering and self-denial but a future. Facing her separateness, she could become her own "best thing," defined by the accident of birth, childrearing, and circumstances, but also by her re-creation of herself over time, servitude, sins, and all.

She did not create the horrible wounds on her back, but as the white girl, Amy, describes them as a broad tree, and as Sethe communicates this to Paul D., we witness the act of transfiguring the markings inflicted by history. In a parable of renaming that crosses racial and gendered lines, we become our own "best thing" in relation to scars we cannot efface or redeem, but whose beauty we can help one another affirm. This is an act of love, and art: as Paul D.'s friend said of his lover, "[T]he pieces I am, she gathers them and give them back to me in all the right order" (p. 272). We re-member by means of stories no one authors alone; community, Paul suggests, is laying our stories "next" to each other. But transfiguration by love and art is not transcendence: the novel's last word is "Beloved" because the plea, be-loved, cannot escape or redeem the pain, loss, and longing that name also speaks.

CONCLUSION

Morrison uses the genre of slave narrative to subvert the nationalist jeremiad, in which good sons escape captivity by redeeming a legacy of freedom, but also to subvert the genre she uses, which endows redemptive promise in the suffering of a captive countercommunity. Confronting the power of this story, however, depends on a retelling that takes it seriously, to reveal the motives and consequences of its framing of identity, community, and history.

Beloved solicits, makes visible, and then defeats the desire (and mental framework) of readers who identify with a protagonist seeking not only emancipation from servitude but also redemption of the self and the past. The novel ruptures patterns of repetition because readers who witness the vicissitudes in (their own) dreams of deliverance gain a (second) chance to think and act differently. Thus does *Beloved* retell a captivity narrative to dramatize and then relinquish the dream of redemption at its core, precisely for the sake of the freedom the narrative also has promised.

Indeed, since a transformed relationship to the past, the self, and others, and thus a language of captivity and rebirth, is central to the imagination of freedom in America, *Beloved* is a work of political education indebted to the legacies and stories it illuminates and moves beyond. To clarify its repetition with a difference, hence its view of freedom, and thereby its political resonance, consider how the language and action within the novel is related to the world beyond it.

Most obviously, the novel shows how freedom depends on naming captivity. *Beloved* reveals a society constituted by profound divisions, historically embedded, psychologically charged, and socially sedimented in practices of labor and nurture. Sethe bespeaks the particular and the general in the fact that she is legally free—but bound to a mortal and desiring body, and implicated in bonds of love and power, rooted in an unchangeable past, conditioned by inherently problematic but changeable forms of labor, and situated in contingent but recalcitrant relations of race and gender, and invested in a powerful but constructed narrative of redemption.

By naming such conditions as a legacy confronted in the world and the self, *Beloved* represents a struggle to *become* free. It involves an effort to achieve a right relationship to the past, but also to distinguish in the present which kinds of servitude are inescapable, coerced, or self-imposed. As characters deliberate about their suffering, bonds, and choices, they exemplify Nietzsche's "digestion," by which a worldly legacy taken into the self becomes not only an "illness" of repetition and reaction, but a "pregnancy." As Sethe arrives in all ambivalence at a generative moment once precluded, so the novel has digested an all-too-present past, to foster the power to originate that is buried in what Emerson called the sepulchers of the fathers.

That power, to create not a child but new stories to pass on, bespeaks the intimate bond between narration and freedom that is exemplified by *Beloved*'s characters, and the novel as a whole. For naming captivity and suffering, digesting the past, testing the limits it has imposed, and exercising the value-bestowing power in defining, desiring, and laboring, are accomplishments and activities tied to the poetics of narratives. One bridge between *Beloved* and the world, then, is the act and art of narration that it makes central to freedom and thus to politics, which appears as a struggle—

through stories—about which stories to let go, and how to tell the ones we pass on.

A second bridge, therefore, is *how* the novel relates stories and our (political) life together, for it is dialogic: Sethe's interior life is a conversation; other characters reinterpret her choices, each narrating the history that binds them and the responses that distinguish them. *Beloved* thereby creates a space in which plural voices engage in an ongoing practice of making sense because, in reverence for particularity and the richness of language, it lays stories "next" to one another. In that space, authority lies not in origins, revealed truth, or even consensus, but in experience, and in the language by which the characters voice, confirm, and contest it, thus deepening, reconceiving, and changing it.

In a space created by a captivity story whose form is stories, the past, experience, and choices are endowed with a meaning that is not self-evident, authored singly, or produced once and for all. By way of its form, then, a novel about the effort to redeem the past defeats longings for redemption as narrative closure. In turn, as narration opens a space in which characters confront their history, their struggle for freedom, and their dreams of redemption, *Beloved* engages its post-Reconstruction context.

On the one hand, the novel enters a culture haunted by a history of servitude. Facing that history seems impossible: the ideology of self-making warrants denial, fantasies of escape, and resentment toward those signifying failed self-determination. But insisting on historical wrong also risks intensifying the resentment that weds identities to denial and guilt, injury and retribution. The novel enacts political education, then, by showing the necessity of confronting the past, but also the difficulty of moving beyond it rather than drowning in it. Like Sethe, *Beloved* rejects the dream of escaping the past, but raises the dead and lives with them; unlike Sethe, it relives the past to relinquish the dream of redeeming the suffering and crimes that make it haunting. Thus, the novel does not use the past to prove guilt or innocence, or recover a model for life. Unlike such stories, *Beloved* dramatizes the need to vindicate a past it does not heroize or demonize, to elicit the grieving for irreparable loss that, by changing both anger and hope, releases energy to will a future.

By this achievement, on the other hand, a revised captivity narrative emplots the internal and worldly dimensions of democratic possibility. For *Beloved*'s textual spaces are an experiment—through language, with others, and on the self—in carving out of past and present servitude not a promise of redemption but self-government in its personal and political senses. By going behind liberal origins, below contractual surfaces, and outside redemptive symmetries, *Beloved* represents the language and spaces by which a haunted people could confront the history and servitude, suffering, resentment, and stories that hold them captive, to achieve neither solace nor unity, but a new kind of authority as authors and citizens.

As memory is used to separate from the past, and anger to contest rather than pass on its legacy, the present appears as if for the first time, in its profound difficulty and divisions, but ripe with possibilities once foreclosed by resentful energies and redemptive dreams. Surely, poetry is not politics. But some such retelling of the story of captivity and redemption seems crucial to moving the American experiment in democracy beyond its current stalemate.

NOTES

This essay is indebted to conversations with Lynnette Taylor and Victoria Hattam, and to the editorial suggestions of Tracy Strong and, especially, Mark Rhinehart.

1. Sacvan Bercovitch, *The American Jeremiad* (Madison: University of Wisconsin Press, 1978).

2. America is a "Puritan and trading nation" because of faith in self-determination, and thus commitment to rights, propertied individualism, and popular sovereignty, secured by a "Puritan" investment in moral self-control and rational self-possession, and underwritten by a providential view of history. These terms create the charged cultural horizon that defines who can bear rights, while endowing their exercise with meaning. *Ibid.*

3. *Ibid.*, p. 79.

4. At issue is the *self-limitation* generated by identities defined through a narrative of revolutionary origins, and thus committed (in principle) to the unprecedented.

5. Bercovitch puts the idea of self-making at the core of national identity, arguing that elsewhere, "to be independent was to challenge society," whereas here, "independence became the norm for representative selfhood" and "a model of consensus." "Rites of Assent," in *The American Self*, ed. Sam Girgus (Albuquerque: University of New Mexico Press, 1981), pp. 13, 20.

6. His own use of "must" is central to controversy about his view of power and contestation in American culture. See, for example, the exchange between David Harlan and Bercovitch in *The Journal of American History*, December 1991, pp. 949–987.

7. Cf. D. H. Lawrence, *Studies in Classic American Literature* (reprint, New York: Viking Press, 1961); William Carlos Williams, *In the American Grain* (New York: New Directions, 1933); Winthrop Jordan, *White over Black* (New York: W. W. Norton, 1968); Richard Slotkin, *Regeneration through Violence* (Middletown, Conn.: Wesleyan University Press, 1973); Slotkin, *Fatal Environment* (Middletown, Conn.: Wesleyan University Press, 1985); Michael Rogin, *Fathers and Children* (New York: Knopf, 1975); Rogin, *Subversive Genealogy* (New York: Knopf, 1983); Rogin, *Ronald Reagan, the Movie* (Berkeley: University of California Press, 1987); Paul Boyer, *Urban Masses and Moral Order in America* (Cambridge: Harvard University Press, 1978); David Roediger, *The Wages of Whiteness* (London: Verso, 1991); Toni Morrison, *Playing in the Dark* (New York: Vintage, 1993).

8. Antebellum southern men invoked rights, but made plantations a household

and redemptive alternative to mercenary relations in the capitalist North. Northern men exposed the despotism in this idealization, and defended propertied individualism, but also lamented a "house divided" and called Isaacs to sacrifices that would redeem its sins. Facing industrial capitalism, Progressives read city and nation as both a business and a moral household. In each case, households were seen as endangered by people and activities figured as antifamilial, and derived their allegorical power from sites of racial and female subordination. Not coincidentally, female reformers and black nationalists have used familial imagery to signify and form alternative communities.

9. Cf. Christine Stansell, *City of Women* (New York: Knopf, 1986); Nick Salvatore, *Eugene V. Debs: Citizen and Socialist* (Urbana: University of Illinois Press, 1992); Eldon Eisenach, *The Lost Promise of Progressivism* (Lawrence: University of Kansas Press, 1994); Keith David Miller, *Voice of Deliverance: The Language of Martin Luther King and Its Sources* (New York: Free Press, 1992).

10. Cf. Anne Norton, "Engendering Another America," in *Rhetorical Republic*, ed. Frederick Dolan and Thomas Dumm (Amherst: University of Massachusetts Press, 1993), who criticizes liberal exclusion by invoking an "America" whose promise exceeds any limitation.

11. Cf. Richard Sennett and Jonathan Cobb, *The Hidden Injuries of Class* (New York: Vintage, 1973); Norman Jacobson, "New World Passional," unpublished; William Connolly, "Appearance and Reality in Politics," in *Interpreting Politics*, ed. Michael Gibbons (New York: New York University Press, 1988); Stanley Cavell, "Ending the Waiting Game," in Cavell, *Must We Mean What We Say?* (Cambridge: Cambridge University Press, 1976).

12. An identity politics plotted by contrasting narratives of innocent captivity emerges from the vicissitudes of postwar liberalism. For while cold war liberals had projected evil onto sites outside an innocent nation, they also were forced to face the historical guilt of unreconstructed racial relations. Seeking a cross-class and interracial coalition, their jeremiads linked combat on new frontiers and social reform, to redeem the purpose and suffering of ancestors. But this "beautiful revolution," as Marx put it, foundered on "the social question." Middle-class students, feminists, and black power advocates, confronting the limits of liberal reform, began to reject the symbolism of America; working-class people, invested in the story of sacrifice that redeems suffering and dignifies labor, felt their lives (and America) betrayed, robbed of meaning. For contrasting accounts, cf. Wendy Brown, "Wounded Attachments," *Political Theory* 21, no. 3 (August 1993): 390–410, and Paul Gilroy, *The Black Atlantic* (Cambridge: Harvard University Press, 1993).

13. See, for example, the writings of Christopher Lasch, John Patrick Diggins, and Cornell West, who revise a prophetic Calvinism.

14. Readings of the novel focus, first, on the history of the middle passage and slavery that haunts African Americans; second, on power exercised on black and female bodies, and in these terms on labor, nurture, and the power of and over language; third, on the familial dynamics of the pre-Oedipal mother-child bond, as a paradigm of tensions between authority and autonomy, and between memory and agency; and fourth, on the multiple voices in the text, which disclose Sethe's story but also the impossibility of knowing it definitively. See Susan Bowers, "*Beloved* and the New Apocalypse," *Journal of Ethnic Studies* 18, no. 1 (Spring 1990: 59–77; Emily Miller Budick, "Absence, Loss, and the Space of History in Toni Morrison's *Beloved*," *Arizona Quarterly* 48, no. 2 (Summer 1992): 117–138; Anne E. Goldman,

"'I Made the Ink': (Literary) Production and Reproduction in *Dessa Rose* and *Beloved*," *Feminist Studies* 16 no. 2 (Summer 1990): 313–330; Mae G. Henderson, "Toni Morrison's *Beloved*: Re-membering the Body as Historical Text," in *Comparative American Identities*, ed. Hortense Spillers (New York: Routledge, 1991), pp. 62–86; David Lawrence, "Fleshly Ghosts and Ghostly Flesh: The Word and the Body in *Beloved*," *Studies in American Fiction* 19, no. 2 (Autumn 1991): 189–201; Andrew Levy, "Telling *Beloved*," *Texas Studies in Literature and Language* 33, no. 1 (Spring 1991): 114–123; Barbara Offutt Mathieson, "Memory and Mother Love in Morrison's *Beloved*," *American Imago* 47, no. 1 (Spring 1990): 1–21; Helene Moglen, "Redeeming History: Toni Morrison's *Beloved*," *Cultural Critique*, Spring 1993, pp. 17–40; Ashraf Rushdy, "Daughters Signifyin(g) History: The Example of Toni Morrison's *Beloved*," *American Literature* 64, no. 3 (September 1992): 567–597; Barbara Shapiro, "The Bonds of Love and the Boundaries of Self in Toni Morrison's *Beloved*," *Contemporary Literature* 32, no. 2 (Summer 1991): 194–209.

15. For Morrison's account, see Gloria Naylor and Toni Morrison, "A Conversation," *Southern Review* 21 (1985): 567–593. For the Douglas quote, see Rushdy, "Daughters," p. 573. In turn, I focus on Sethe's story, and only note the other story lines, which involve the black men of Sweet Home, the role of the black community in the north, Sethe's grandmother, Baby Suggs, and her surviving daughter, Denver.

16. Toni Morrison, "Site of Memory," in *Inventing the Truth: The Art and Craft of Memoir*, ed. William Zinser (Boston: Houghton Mifflin, 1987), pp. 109–110; and Morrison, "Living Memory," in *Small Acts*, ed. Paul Gilroy (London: Serpent's Tail, 1993), pp. 175–182.

17. On the veil, cf. W.E.B. Dubois, *The Souls of Black Folk* (reprint, New York: Signet, 1982); on romance, see Morrison, *Playing in the Dark*; on forgetting the past see Morrison, "Living Memory."

18. Cf. Gilroy, *Black Atlantic*, p. 221.

19. Henderson, "Toni Morrison's *Beloved*," p. 82–83. Making the same assumption about suffering and redemption, Stanley Crouch viciously attacks *Beloved* for canonizing victims: "Above all else it is a blackface holocaust novel." Crouch, quoted in Gilroy, *Black Atlantic*, p. 217.

20. Beloved in many ways is not only Sethe's daughter, but also the ghost of Sethe's own murdered mother; the symmetry in their bond, then, involves two child-women coming to terms with the meaning of maternity (and abandonment) under slavery. The result is a tragic view of love, for, as Morrison says about Margaret Garner, by loving "something other than herself so much," and placing "all the value of her life in something outside herself," she demonstrated how "the best thing in us is also the thing that makes us sabotage ourselves." Naylor and Morrison, "A Conversation." Thus, the familial story is a political parable about what Emily Budick describes as the "desperate and ultimately doomed effort to resurrect, compensate for, or replace an irrevocably lost past." Budick, "Absence, Loss," p. 129.

21. "Memory of the past must include the idea of loss: that what the past has taken from us no present or future reality can restore." Budick, "Absence, Loss," p. 135.

PART FOUR

Democratic Individuality and

Civic Action

Democracy and Its Discontents

AMY GUTMANN

A REPRESENTATIVE DEMOCRACY will work well, morally speaking, only if it succeeds in cultivating the independence of spirit that George Kateb so eloquently defends. Such a democracy will also cultivate controversy over matters of social justice.[1] A commitment to individuality, to freedom of thought and speech in particular, therefore poses a formidable challenge for democratic theory and practice. Does representative democracy in any form deal fairly with disagreements about matters of social justice that are bound to arise among a free citizenry? Neither procedural nor constitutional democracy as commonly conceived, I argue in this essay, offers an adequate response to our moral disagreements. Only a more deliberative conception of democracy encourages the eternal vigilance that is necessary to guard against abuses of political power.[2]

At its best, representative democracy peacefully expresses and provisionally resolves political disagreements. It encourages ordinary people to manifest their discontents about politically relevant issues (and many issues are politically relevant). Democracy also makes many people uneasy about its tendency to cultivate disagreement and discontent. Democracy cannot guard against injustice without also encouraging disagreements over what constitutes justice. These disagreements pit morally motivated people against each other.

Democratic citizens disagree on *moral* grounds over many political issues, but people on different sides of an issue such as abortion often do not respect their opponents. We have a tendency to impugn our opponents' motives, dismissing even respectable arguments as rationalizations for hostility toward the freedom of women, if we are pro-choice advocates, or toward human life itself, in its most innocent form, if we are pro-life advocates. The practice of treating one's political opponents as immoral (and often hypocritical as well) threatens to undermine the promise of democratic politics. When we think of our opponents as immoralists or hypocrites, we are more likely to turn to violence, and less likely to learn from the partial truths in our opponents' perspective.

Moral issues that divide citizens with respectable points of view are wide ranging. They include the use of violence and deception in pursuit of humanitarian goals, the constitutionality of capital punishment, the nature of just health care reform (what services to cover, for whom, and how), the freedom to publish violent pornography, the freedom to use commercial surrogacy and other unorthodox means to create a family, the justice of various school choice plans and curricular reform programs in public education, and the legalization of abortion and its subsidization for poor women. This is just a sampling, but it should do for illustrative purposes. Some of the conflicting responses to these issues reflect serious divisions of moral opinion in our society, not merely immorality or foolishness on one side's part. There may be psychological security to be gained by viewing ourselves as fighting a Manichean battle against evil over some or all of these issues, but democracy cannot withstand the widespread perception that our political opponents are immoralists. Nor does this perception involve an adequate appreciation of the conflicting values at stake in such controversies.

In recognizing the existence of respectable moral disagreements on many issues in democratic politics, we need not deny that some of our disagreements are attributable to self-interest, stupidity, ignorance, or even bad will. Democracy can also play an important role in resolving disagreements that pit good against bad, reason against ignorance or stupidity. By making public officials electorally accountable to an inclusive citizenry, by protecting basic human liberties, and by educating citizens to stand up for their own interests and their understanding of the public good, democracy can decrease the damage that might otherwise be done by ruthless, irresponsible, ignorant, or stupid people. In this sense, democracy is indeed the worst form of government except for all the others.

But the ideal of democracy is something more than the least bad alternative. We may expect more than damage control from democracies, and more than mere toleration among democratic citizens. We also may expect morally serious responses to moral disagreements, and respect among citizens and public officials who offer such responses when something morally significant is at stake on opposing sides. Respectable responses from a public perspective are not morally definitive, but they merit more than mere toleration, an attitude of live and let live. They merit a positive regard for the people who are willing and able to offer good reasons, even if not definitive reasons, for why a public policy should be resolved one way or the other. There will also be respectable disagreements about what constitutes a respectable disagreement, but we cannot do without some sense of the difference between responses to moral disagreements in public life that are worthy of respect and those that must merely be tolerated.

Here is one working understanding of three characteristics that respectable responses from a public perspective share: (1) They presuppose a moral perspective, rather than a merely self-interested or group-interested point of view. (2) To the extent that the responses rest upon empirical claims or logical inferences, these are open to challenge by the most adequate methods of public inquiry that are available. (3) To the extent that the responses rest on premises for which empirical evidence or logical inference is not appropriate, these premises are not implausible.[3]

Respectable responses take seriously the moral goods and bads that are at stake in a political conflict. And the way they take morality seriously is accessible to as many citizens as possible. The public accessibility of responses is important because the issues at stake in such controversies are political, and the responses call for policies that are publicly binding. Both the pro-choice and the pro-life positions on abortion, for example, call for publicly binding policies. The pro-life position would prevent women from obtaining abortions under most circumstances. The pro-choice position would permit women to obtain abortions under most circumstances and prevent states from protecting fetuses. Neither policy is morally neutral among the alternatives, and both bind citizens in practice. The public defense of an abortion policy therefore should satisfy some public standard of respectability. The standards of respectability outlined above may not be precisely the right ones, but a democracy needs some such standards if citizens are to respect their moral disagreements rather than resort to power politics, which reduces democratic decisionmaking to an indefensible position of might makes right.

One attempt to defend democracy without relying on any (even provisional) standards of public respectability is to remove all morally controversial issues from the political agenda, leaving individuals free to make controversial moral decisions (about conceptions of the good life) in private, or at least out of politics. This is the strategy of preclusion. According to this strategy, a liberal government avoids resting any public policies on any particular conception of the good life. The paradigmatic use of this strategy is thought to be the liberal argument for religious toleration; religious toleration flows from the state's commitment to neutrality among competing (religious and secular) conceptions of the good life. The liberal state does not enforce secularity among citizens; it simply precludes deciding any *public* issues on religious grounds.

This principle of preclusion is acceptable to most (although not all) religions, since it coincides with the principle of not forcing anyone's faith. Whatever the merits of this defense of religious toleration, philosophers have yet to succeed in finding analogous principles of preclusion that would resolve many other moral controversies in public life, most of which (like abortion) concern conceptions of justice, not only conceptions of the good life. Both pro-life and pro-choice positions in the abortion controversy can be defended on grounds of justice; they need not rely on religious conceptions of the good life. (Respect for life or liberty cannot be called a conception of the good life, even though many conceptions of the good life entail such respect. If moral values such as respect for life are put into the category of conceptions of the good life, then most major moral arguments turn out to be precluded from democratic politics, making the strategy of preclusion unworkable and indefensible.)

Another attempt to deny the distinction between respectable and merely tolerable disagreements in public life is to insist that the only relevant standard of decisionmaking is for citizens and the state to do the right thing. Why worry about democratic citizens *respecting* one another's responses to controversial political issues when only one response, at most, can be morally right? On this view, a conception of democracy should focus exclusively on the need to enact the right response, or at least the best one, and not worry about how citizens or public officials treat the views of their opponents. Citizens and public officials must, of course, tolerate opposing points of view, whether or not those views are respectable, but why worry about their respecting differences of political opinion?

The answer to this question points us in the direction of deliberative democracy, which supports more than mere toleration among citizens. Toleration is a version of live and let live. It does not expect anyone to pay close attention to the content of other people's beliefs, let alone to value or respect them. As long as the speeches and writings of the American Nazi Party or the Ku Klux Klan do not threaten or libel individuals, we can, and should, tolerate them. But we certainly should not value or respect anti-Semitic and racist beliefs. They do not live up to a publicly defensible standard of respectability. But we owe something more than mere toleration to the strongest pro-life and pro-choice views on abortion. These views, unlike those of the Nazi Party or the Ku Klux Klan, make some substantive claims on public policy that are eminently worthy of our serious consideration. Whether we believe that a fetus is a potential human being or an actual one for constitutional purposes, we can recognize the plausibility of the opposing premise, and the reasonableness of concern for protecting both fetal life and the basic freedom of women. The best available responses to many political controversies are contestable, and therefore citizens who close their minds to disagreement, who merely tolerate but refuse to respect opposing points of view, often claim too much certainty, more than can be publicly justified, for their own positions.

The three criteria of respecting opposing points of view that I outlined above suggest three reasons why some degree of openness to disagreement, as reflected in respect for points of view that we oppose, is often democratically desirable. First, the competing values at stake (fetal life and women's liberty in the case of abortion) are often difficult to weigh against each other. Alternative ways of weighing may therefore have something morally significant to be said for them. Secondly, the relevant evidence (such as whether nonviolent means are adequate to stop international aggression) may be hard to assess by the most adequate methods of inquiry. Differing interpretations of the evidence may therefore alert us to risks to shared values, such as life and liberty, that we would otherwise be prone to overlook. Third, some morally relevant premises (such as whether a fetus is or is not a human being with rights) are plausible but controversial, and some morally relevant concepts (a human right, human dignity, basic liberty) admit of several plausible interpretations with conflicting practical implications. By paying attention to conflicting interpretations that are plausible, we may find ways of improving our own interpretations. Or we may at least recognize that our own interpretations are not as firmly grounded as we would otherwise be prone to believe.

The distinction I am drawing between the rightness and the respectability of a political response highlights a sense of moral indeterminacy that is inescapable in a democracy, and can serve good political purposes if citizens respect positions that they nonetheless (and for good reasons) oppose. Moral indeterminacy should not be confused with moral skepticism or relativism; "it is rather the belief that within a frame of settled commitments, a number of contrasting and competing responses or answers to morally tinged questions are to be expected and welcomed."[4] I have suggested both a negative reason and a positive one—the negative one stemming from the limits of our certainty about justice and the positive one from the illumination provided by alternative perspectives—for why democracies might not only expect disagreements but welcome them, even about matters of justice.

These two reasons are, of course, incomplete. They presuppose that democracy is a moral conception of politics designed to deal with moral disagreements, and not merely a matter of majority rule. But what kind of moral conception is democracy? There are two dominant conceptions of democracy, procedural and constitutionalist, each of which offers an importantly incomplete answer to the question of how democracies can best deal with moral disagreement. The answers are incomplete because each conception poses only one of two equally relevant questions. The procedural conception poses the question, By what processes should we be governed? The constitutional conception poses the question, What principles should govern outcomes?

We can build a more complete conception, a version of deliberative democracy, on the strengths of these two conceptions, constructively responding to their weakness. The two distinctive strengths of deliberative democracy are that (1) it addresses both questions, of process and principle, and (2) in so doing, it also addresses moral disagreements on their own terms. Deliberative democracy does not try to reduce or otherwise transform moral disagreements into something they are not. Deliberative democracy subjects our moral disagreements, which include disagreements about the very principles of democracy, to the give-and-take of substantive (as well as procedural) argument in a public forum. In criticizing the responses to moral disagreements of procedural and constitutional democracy, I suggest why democratic standards should include a commitment by citizens and public officials to deliberating over our disagreements, and creating political institutions that support public deliberation.

PROCEDURAL DEMOCRACY

Procedural democracy considers democracy first and foremost a political procedure that answers the question of contested authority. Who should govern when people cannot completely agree on the principles by which they should be governed, or on the practical implications of those principles? The answer of procedural democracy is that the people should rule themselves rather than being ruled by an external power or a self-selected minority. The value of democracy is, in short, popular rather than unpopular rule. Majorities should rule unless there are good publicly defensible reasons to the contrary. To presume otherwise is to count some people's opinions politically more than others, and therefore to believe that some people have a greater than equal right to participate in making the laws and policies that bind everyone. If good reasons cannot be publicly offered against majority rule, then constraints or qualifications on it are unjustified by democratic standards.

Procedural democrats recognize that good reasons sometimes can be publicly offered to constrain majority rule. The value of majority rule is consistent with, indeed, requires, constraining majorities for the sake of democracy itself, and therefore in its name. The constraints typically include free political speech, press, and association, the rule of law, formal voting equality, and universal adult suffrage, all of which must be preserved over time. These constraints are democratic because they help ensure (to the extent possible) that democratic decisions genuinely reflect popular will and preserve it over time. Although these are constraints on majority rule, they are ideally self-constraints, which the majority places upon itself as it goes about governing. If a majority does not constrain itself, and (for example) restricts freedom of political speech or refuses to support universal suffrage, then it ceases to be democratic and to this extent loses its right to rule.

To be justified on democratic grounds, the popular will, as revealed by the outcome of majoritarian procedures, must represent the unmanipulated will of the majority of all adults. A procedural democracy must preserve popular rule and the conditions of popular rule over time. In any actual society, the majority of citizens or the public officials representing them sometimes cannot be counted upon to constrain their political decisions by democratic standards. If a minority can be relied upon to uphold any of these constraints and a majority cannot, then procedural democracy sides with the minority here, and looks for nonmajoritarian ways to constrain the majority for the sake of upholding the preconditions of procedural democracy. On those political disagreements that do not call the preconditions into question, the majority simply rules, and justifiably so, on procedural grounds.

Notice that, so conceived, political disagreements turn out to be relatively easy to resolve. Disagreements over the preconditions, involving restrictions on political speech or the enfranchisement of women, for example, are conflicts between democratic principles (necessary to create the conditions of popular will) and an undemocratic will (either a popular will that seeks to destroy the conditions of democracy or an unpopular will that attempts to usurp democratic authority). These disagreements call for the procedure that is most likely to resolve them consistently with the preconditions of popular rule.

By contrast, disagreements that do not threaten the preconditions of proceduralism, such as conflicts over tax and environmental policy or health care reform, are resolvable by majority rule, because majority rule reflects the right of free and equal citizens to make political decisions that are consistent with the preconditions of proceduralism (its procedural framework, which is a kind of constitution). The body politic must move one way or the other when its members disagree, and procedural democracy justifies the way that commands agreement of the greatest number provided that the agreement is consistent with the procedural framework. The views of all citizens or their representatives are counted equally, and the greatest number rules.

Are there really no moral disagreements that should be treated as genuine moral disagreements, rather than as disputes over the procedural preconditions or as matters of majority will? What about all those situations in which majorities cannot be relied upon to uphold democratic standards and the reliability of minorities is also uncertain? Procedural democracy has too little to say about how to resolve genuinely moral conflicts where to say that the majority should decide is to say far too little. It lacks substantive principles beyond those we have already discussed. Its silence suggests that all the political disagreements that arise within the procedural framework can be treated as conflicts among individual preferences, simply to be settled by popular rule. It does not distinguish between political conflicts in which integrity, dignity, primary goods, or basic human interests—all values that go beyond the value of popular rule per se—are at stake and those where they are not.

Proceduralism defends majority rule whenever the procedural framework is not at stake, but this response is surely too simple and dangerous to democracy understood as a moral system of government. By majoritarian standards, popularly elected representatives may vote on issues as serious as health care policy without any deliberation, publicizing only the results of their votes. Public officials need not give reasons for their actions or disclose the influences on them. Without any requirements of deliberation or disclosure, legislative action will be poorly informed by the views of citizens and tell us very little about the merits of policy decisions in the public realm.

Even if majority rule is the best way to settle some moral conflicts, we need to supplement majoritarianism with a set of deliberative standards that recognize the moral significance of what is often at stake in political decisionmaking. When human values as basic as life, liberty, and opportunity are at stake, citizens are owed an accounting of what policies their representatives support and why they support them. Reasons are relevant to whether citizens support a policy or a politician. By itself, even within a procedural framework that helps ensure that the popular will prevails, majority rule falls short as a democratic procedure. Majority rule can adequately express the democratic ideal of popular rule only if political processes also encourage citizens and public officials to deliberate before deciding.

CONSTITUTIONAL DEMOCRACY

Constitutional democracy suggests that popular rule constrained by its own preconditions is not sufficient to resolve moral disagreements in politics, and maybe not even necessary. Majority rule is an inappropriate response to many moral conflicts, including those where all sides respect the preconditions of popular rule. A democratic society needs a more robust set of constitutional principles by which to be governed. Democratic procedures, even deliberative ones, are at best an imperfect means to just ends. At worst, they distort decisionmaking. The decisions of public officials who are accountable to their constituents are likely to be governed by political considerations (such as winning reelection) that are irrelevant to the substantive moral requirements of constitutionalism. In resolving principled disagreements, public officials should be bound to follow the substantively correct principles of justice, but they will often follow the electoral returns instead.

Constitutional democracy highlights the role of substantive principles in resolving moral disagreements. It affirms the status of citizens as free and equal persons by constitutionalizing certain basic liberties, among them, freedom of speech (and not only political speech), religion, and association, due process of law, and the rule of law. Constitutional democracy also may support fair equality of opportunity and therefore constitutionalize certain welfare rights, including a right to education, health care, housing, productive work, and a minimum income.

What, then, becomes of popular rule as a response to moral disagreement in a constitutional democracy? The constitutional essentials of constitutional democracy include the right to vote and participate in politics, freedom of political speech and association, and the rule of law, all of which are also preconditions of popular rule. Whereas procedural democracy defends certain substantive principles (such as the right to free political speech) as the preconditions of a fair political procedure (the ability to speak one's mind as a citizen), constitutional democracy defends certain procedural principles as a means of achieving the morally best outcomes of public policy, quite apart from the role that these principles may play in making popular rule possible. Although the right to vote and participate in politics are said to be basic liberties, majoritarian procedures for determining outcomes are not. Majority rule, as John Rawls notes, "has a subordinate place as a procedural device."[5] Why? Because it cannot ensure either the basic liberties or fair equality of opportunity. As Rawls rightly emphasizes, what the majority wills is not necessarily what is right.

We should not therefore conclude that deliberative decisionmaking has a subordinate place in a theory of justice, even if the process of majority rule does. There are ways of respecting the political equality of individuals and their equal status as citizens other than majority rule. (The unanimity rule for jury trials is an example of a nonmajoritarian process that respects the political equality of jurors.) Rawls's more recent work rightly points in the direction of deliberative democracy.[6]

One virtue of constitutional democracy, which deliberative democracy adopts, is its recognition that majority rule, even after due deliberation, may yield unjust outcomes. Even deliberative decisionmaking does not determine justice. But we still need to ask what a more adequate political response to moral disagreements would entail. Constitutional democracy focuses on principles rather than procedures because all procedures, including deliberative ones, are imperfect. The right response to moral disagreements, by constitutional democratic standards, is to pick the procedure that is most likely to secure the principles of justice.

This response avoids the problem of moral disagreement in democracy rather than resolving it. Constitutional democracy rightly suggests that substantive principles should supplement political procedures, by guiding the judgment of decisionmakers. But how is it possible to pick procedures that are most likely to realize justice when, on so many matters, justice itself is reasonably contested? Who is to do the picking? Every political procedure, including deliberative majoritarianism, is imperfect from the standpoint of achieving substantively just decisions. It does not follow, however, that procedures have a subordinate place to substantive principles of justice. The rights of all citizens to vote and to participate in politics are procedural rights, which constitutional democracy recognizes to be basic. Even though any voting and participatory procedure will be imperfect, constitutional democrats deem the existence of some such procedure to be a matter of justice. Procedures that give every individual a voice in political decisionmaking and that encourage deliberation are no less matters of justice than are various freedoms of speech and association. At any given time, these rights are imperfectly specified, but such imperfection does not undermine the moral importance of political procedures any more than it undermines that of free speech and association. Imperfections in all these rights, as presently constituted, underline our incomplete moral understanding.

When citizens respectfully disagree about how much and what kind of health care should be universally provided, substantive principles of justice alone cannot definitively resolve our disagreement. Not only do substantive principles conflict; most are indeterminate at this level of policy. Philosophers along with ordinary citizens hold conflicting views about what is right. Most of us are probably wrong, assuming a single standard of rightness exists but is beyond our grasp. Even if one of us is right, there is no superlegislator, no Platonic philosopher-king or -queen, to appoint the knowing authority. No one stands above the philosophical and political fray to do the choosing. We therefore evade the problem of moral disagreement in democracy rather than resolve it if our response is to advocate a just and legitimate authority who will best defend the right substantive principles of justice. This response leaves democratic societies without just or legitimate authorities even when we respectfully disagree over the right response to political conflicts.

DELIBERATIVE DEMOCRACY

To value respectful disagreement when agreement is not possible does not entail any moral skepticism, as some critics of deliberative democracy suggest. Just as our self-respect as citizens and our protection against political tyranny depend on our having the right to vote and to participate in politics, so, too, does mutual respect among citizens depend on a deliberative politics that takes our moral disagreements seriously, and does not assume that open-mindedness in search of provisionally justified policies is a form of moral or political weakness. Respect for morally serious citizens with whom we disagree is a virtue, both a good in itself and a way of arriving at morally better understandings than any of us has at the moment. We respect others when we deliberate with them.

What is deliberation? It is the give-and-take of reasoned argument in a public forum that aims at justifying a mutually binding decision. The deliberators are not impartial spectators or philosophers who imagine what hypothetical people would decide were they ideally motivated and situated. They are people acting in their public capacity. Because they are acting in their public capacity, they are accountable, either directly or indirectly, to other citizens and noncitizens whose lives they significantly affect by their actions. Accountability does not necessarily entail elections, but it does mean that the decisionmakers must try to justify their decisions to the people who are seriously affected by them, offering reasons and addressing opposing positions.

What is the forum for deliberation? The forums are public and serve the purposes of political decisionmaking. The forums may be legislative, judicial, or bureaucratic, but they must be directly or indirectly subject to public accountability. The reason-giving also must be public, as are both court opinions and congressional records. The decisionmakers must be open to public criticism as well as praise.

What is the authority of the deliberative outcomes? The authority is not that of either truth or the sheer power of numbers. Democratic decisions at their best are, as far as we can tell, provisionally justifiable. They possess political legitimacy provided they were deliberatively determined and do not violate anyone's rights. Deliberative decisions bind no one's conscience, nor do they substitute for philosophical reflection or further moral inquiry into their justification. The outcome of deliberative decisionmaking that respects everyone's rights is binding. Such decisions are legitimate as long as they respect constitutional constraints, as best we can know them at any given time. Legitimate decisions are open to criticism by citizens, public officials, and philosophers and reevaluation in future deliberative forums.

The constitutional constraints on legitimate deliberative decisions are ideally considered self-constraints, which deliberative bodies accept as principled constraints on their own decisionmaking. These constraints typically do not dictate singular policy outcomes, but they do have a special status of mutually agreed-upon principles within deliberative forums. They not only aid the deliberators in their attempt to develop justified decisions but also allow citizens standing outside of the deliberative forum to judge the justifiability of outcomes by something other than the quality of the deliberative process itself.

A critic might ask, Why, then, are the deliberative procedures themselves a matter of justice? Why not simply judge the justice of democratic decisions by their substance? Deliberation then becomes a mere means to the end of achieving just decisions. This is too narrow a notion of justice. It neglects both noninstrumental and instrumental reasons for thinking that deliberative decisionmaking is a matter of justice.

Consider first the noninstrumental reasons, which are also common to constitutional democracy. Two different procedures for determining whether someone is innocent or guilty of a crime—one accurately characterized as "due process," the other as "arbitrary" or "ad hoc"—may yield similar results, but this does not mean they are equally justifiable to the people who are to be bound by them. Similarly, a scheme of unequal voting rights, one that denies women equal voting power, for example, may yield results similar to those of a scheme of equal voting rights, which gives women equal voting power. Constitutional democrats do not conclude that unequal voting rights and equal ones are equally justifiable. Because citizens reasonably disagree about what constitutes substantively just results and because we also care about being equally represented in decisionmaking processes that determine those results, democratic societies need to rely upon some procedural principles that can be justified independently of their realization of substantively just results. The value of deliberation is similar in this sense to the value of equal voting rights. Deliberation is a manifestation of mutual respect that is appropriate among people who reasonably disagree with one another. Mutual respect is entailed by the democratic ideal of free and equal persons. Equal voting rights are less defensible if we do not also value mutual respect among citizens.

Deliberation is also instrumentally valuable, and in ways that constitutional democrats can also appreciate on their own terms. It encourages reasonable people to change their minds in light of unanswerable objections to their present positions. Even when deliberation falls short of finding the singularly correct policy, it can create the broadest justifiable consensus across a range of reasonable but conflicting concepts of justice.

It is reasonable to think that on matters concerning constitutional essentials, deliberative decisionmaking is more likely than its alternatives to yield justifiable results. This is not to say that political procedures, however deliberative, are sufficient responses to moral disagreements. Deliberative democracy recognizes that some values, such as those basic liberties that support the integrity of individuals, must be respected by deliberative democratic forums if the decisions of such forums are to be binding. No amount of deliberation can justify decisions that violate the basic liberties (or basic opportunities) of individuals. Democratically authorized and accountable groups of public officials can deliberate and arrive at unjust decisions, just as philosophers can defend unjust theories. Deliberative democracy therefore asks deliberators to constrain themselves by substantive principles, such as respect for the basic liberties of individuals. But we may have no better way of understanding and specifying the content of those liberties than through some kind of deliberative process.

Deliberative decisionmaking is not merely procedural. It is guided by substantive principles that supply the conditions of ongoing deliberative decisionmaking and that support the basic liberties and opportunities of individuals, whose value is independent of democracy itself. A deliberative body that fails to constrain itself by substantive principles is falling short of the standards of deliberative democracy. Substantive principles are also open to deliberative disagreement, and subject to improvement by ongoing deliberation. On this conception of deliberative democracy, substance and procedure interact in ways that make it impossible to assign priority to either.

What has happened to majority rule, a procedural democrat may ask? I have suggested that majority rule is an insufficient response to principled moral disagreements in politics, but it does not therefore become subordinate to substantive principles of justice. Proceduralists are correct in concluding that majority rule may be independently valuable and, in at least some situations, an important expression of democratic equality. Rawls himself recognizes that majority rule is not like any other procedure in at least one important sense. It "possesses a certain naturalness; for if minority rule is allowed, there is no obvious criterion to select which one is to decide and equality [of persons] is violated."[7]

•

I have argued that whereas procedural democracy, as commonly understood, offers a response to moral disagreements that is deficient in substantive principles, constitutional democracy, as commonly understood, offers a substantive response that is insufficiently appreciative of the value of procedural principles. Faced with a moral disagreement among citizens, procedural democracy tells us that a majority should decide but not how they should decide or what they should decide. Constitutional democracy, by contrast, tells us what should be decided but not by whom or how. To some theorists, the constitutional response seems more adequate—once we determine what should be decided, they argue, we need only look for the agents who will make the right decision. But I have argued that this strategy evades the problem of political authority rather than resolving it. To those who value popular participation in politics, procedural democracy may seem more adequate because it faces up to the fact that most substantive principles are reasonably disputed, even by philosophers. In cases of reasonable disagreement, a decision should be justified to the people who are being bound by it, and one way of so justifying the decision (proceduralists argue) is to let the majority decide.

Deliberative democracy suggests that both constitutionalists and proceduralists are partly right, that substantive and procedural principles are both necessary parts of an adequate conception of democracy. But neither is sufficient or morally prior to the other, and the two are not as distinct in either theory or practice as both common conceptions of democracy suggest. The two sets of principles, as proceduralism and constitutionalism conceive them, cannot simply be put together, because their claims (let the majority decide, or leave legislatures free to make policy while courts decide matters of principle) leave too little room for responding to moral disagreements on their own terms in daily democratic politics. We need a conception of democracy that recognizes the importance of our engaging in an ongoing effort to develop provisionally justifiable resolutions to unsettled conflicts about social justice in the day-to-day workings of democratic politics.

On this deliberative conception of democracy, we should expect democracy continuously to generate discontent with political outcomes because the moral understanding of human beings is inadequate to the task of determining what is just once and for all. We should therefore expect widespread discontent even with legitimate or provisionally justifiable democratic decisions. This discontent is most productive when it motivates more public deliberation, which is the best means we have for improving on our past decisions and designing fair compromises among respectable positions whenever fully justifiable decisions are still beyond our reach.

Democratic citizens should be eternally vigilant about the use of political power by representatives who act in their name.[8] By deliberating together with mutual respect, yet without ever expecting to come to final agreement, we can make a virtue out of our discontent.

NOTES

1. George Kateb, *In The Inner Ocean: Individualism and Democratic Culture* (Ithaca, N.Y.: Cornell University Press, 1992).

2. This essay draws on the theoretical conception of deliberative democracy and some of the arguments found in Amy Gutmann and Dennis Thompson, *Democracy and Disagreement* (Cambridge: Belknap Press of Harvard University Press, 1996).

3. For more on these criteria and mutual respect among citizens, see Amy

Gutmann and Dennis Thompson, "Moral Conflict and Political Consensus," *Ethics* 101 (October 1990): 64–88.

4. Kateb, *Inner Ocean*, p. 40.

5. John Rawls, *A Theory of Justice* (Cambridge: Harvard University Press, 1971), p. 356.

6. See John Rawls, *Political Liberalism* (New York: Columbia University Press, 1993); and Rawls, "Reply to Habermas," *Journal of Philosophy*, 92, no. 3 (March 1995): 132–180.

7. Rawls, *Theory of Justice*, p. 356.

8. On eternal vigilance, see Kateb, *Inner Ocean*.

Juries and Local Justice

JEFFREY ABRAMSON

CONSIDER TWO PORTRAITS of the ideal juror. The first and more familiar one highlights the impartiality of the juror and the ignorance that, ironically, makes impartial judgment possible. In this view, the primary qualification of good jurors is that they themselves know nothing beforehand about the case they are about to judge. Precisely because they bring no personal knowledge or opinions to the case, they can judge it with the distance and dispassion that marks impartial justice. These jurors can with integrity swear the sacred oath to decide the case solely "upon the evidence developed at the trial."[1] Their great virtue is that their minds "should be as white Paper, and know neither Plaintiff nor Defendant, but judge the Issue merely as an abstract Proposition, upon the Evidence produced" in open court.[2] As a federal judge once described this tabula rasa of the impartial juror:

> The entire effort of our [trial] procedure is to secure . . . jurors who do not know and are not in a position to know anything of either [the] character [of the parties] or events [on trial]. . . . The zeal displayed in this effort to empty the minds of the jurors . . . [is a sign] that the jury, . . . like the court itself, is an impartial organ of justice.[3]

In contrast, the second portrait of the ideal juror emphasizes the closeness of the juror to the case on trial: the juror as peer and neighbor. As neighbor, the juror will likely have heard of the case prior to trial and may even know the parties or witnesses or at least know of their reputations. "What is meant by [the defendant's] peers?" asked Patrick Henry. He answered that they were "those who reside near him, his neighbors, and who are well-acquainted with his character and situation in life."[4] This so-called local knowledge of the neighborhood qualifies the juror to understand the facts of the case and to pass judgment in ways that a stranger to the community could not. Local jurors more accurately get at what happened because they are familiar with, say, the grade crossing where a certain railroad accident occurred.[5] In addition, such jurors can *judge* cases better than strangers because they know the conscience of the community and can apply the law in ways that resonate with the community's moral values and common sense.

Of course, there is considerable tension between these two portraits. The local knowledge that gives competence to the juror as neighbor and peer destroys the impartiality of the juror as neutral arbiter of events. Indeed, what qualifies a person to serve as a juror in one model (an understanding of the conscience of the community) disqualifies the person in the other model (an embodiment of the prejudices of the community).

Moreover, the different qualities we want in a juror lead to different geographies for justice. If we want impartial jurors who know nothing of the case beforehand, then we should import them from a great distance—the greater the distance, the more likely the jurors will never have heard of the case. But if we want jurors who can represent the conscience of the community and judge a case according to local standards, then we should seek jurors close at hand—the closer the juror, the better the inside knowledge.

One of the central dilemmas of modern jury selection is how to reconcile these competing visions of the jury. How can we impanel a jury that has enough knowledge to be competent but enough ignorance to be impartial? To express the dilemma another way, how can the jury be at one and the same time an instrument of justice (with all the *insulation* from popular pressure and local gossip that doing the "just thing" often requires) and an instrument of democracy (with all the *exposure* to public opinion that doing the "democratic thing" often requires)? The jury immediately inspires but confuses us because it wants matters both ways: to insulate justice from popular prejudice and yet to leave justice in the hands of the populace.

Two brief examples will illustrate the way this tension plays out in real cases. In 1987, Eddie Crawford went on trial for his life before a jury in Spalding County, Georgia. In fact, as many in the county knew, this was Crawford's second trial for the same crime. A prior jury had already found Crawford guilty of murder and sentenced him to death. However, the state supreme court set aside that conviction and ordered a new trial, on the ground that the jury might have convicted Crawford not of murder but of felony murder, a crime not charged in the indictment.[6]

Prior to the start of the second trial, Crawford's lawyers moved for a change of venue, arguing that an impartial jury could no longer be found in a county where so many persons knew the results of Crawford's first trial. The motion was denied, and jury selection commenced with a pool of ninety persons. Fifty-seven acknowledged that they were aware of the prior proceedings, fifty indicated that they knew Crawford had been convicted, and thirty-two said they knew that Crawford had been sentenced to death. Of the twelve jurors finally selected, eight knew generally about the prior trial, five knew Crawford had been convicted, and three knew that he had been sentenced to death. This second jury likewise convicted Crawford of murder and sentenced him to death. The U.S. Supreme Court denied Crawford's petition for review, and in early 1996 he was still awaiting execution.[7]

Crawford's case seems a clear instance where failure to grant a change of venue resulted in an extreme denial of impartial justice. It is particularly difficult to believe that Crawford's jurors could grant him his presumption of innocence, knowing that their fellow citizens had once sentenced him to die for the same crime. In the circumstances of this case, holding the trial locally was dramatically at odds with the most elemental notions of blind justice.

In many jury trials, the opposite problem occurs: granting a change of venue blinds justice by relying on strangers to view events from afar that people in the community would have put in clearer perspective. The first trial in 1992 of the four Los Angeles police officers accused of beating Rodney King provides a compelling example of this complaint. In the name of protecting the defendants' right to an impartial jury, a California appeals court ordered the trial judge to move the trial out of Los Angeles County. Press accounts mistakenly reported that the change of venue was ordered to find impartial jurors who had not seen the notorious, incriminating videotape of the alleged beating made by a bystander and shown repeatedly on television prior to trial. But the court understood that there was no place it could move the trial where the videotape had not been aired. What, then, could be accomplished by a change of venue? Since only Los Angeles jurors were likely to treat this as a political trial, a virtual referendum on forcing out Police Commissioner Daryl Gates and reforming the entire Los Angeles Police Department (LAPD), the appeals court hoped to insulate the jury from matters of electoral politics by moving the trial.[8]

So directed by the appeals court, the trial judge chose Ventura County as the new place of trial—geographic neighbor to Los Angeles but demographic stranger. In a case involving white officers and a black victim, it was significant that African Americans constituted a far smaller percentage of the Ventura County population than of the Los Angeles County population.[9] No African Americans made it onto the jury of ten whites, one Asian American, and one Hispanic American that acquitted the officers of virtually all charges (the jury was hung on one charge against the officers).[10]

In the aftermath of the verdict, there was near-unanimous agreement that the Ventura County jurors were not well situated to judge the events accurately or democratically.[11] King's confrontation with the officers had taken place in a context far removed from the conditions in which the mostly suburban Ventura County jurors lived. They no doubt judged the events partly in light of their knowledge about police work and police treatment of minorities in their own area, but this was the wrong local knowledge. Rodney King and the LAPD officers met elsewhere, in a different racial climate and prepared by a different set of expectations and prior events in the neighborhood. A Los Angeles jury would have better understood the specific, concrete background against which the confrontation took place. This is true not only because the jury would have been more likely to have had African Americans on it to compare Rodney King's experience with their own personal knowledge of police behavior toward blacks but also because even the

Anglos- and Hispanic Americans on the Los Angeles jury would have been more likely to have been conversant with and concerned about local conditions. By comparison, the Ventura County jurors suffered from having to view the events out of context and from a distance.[12]

The cases of Eddie Crawford and Rodney King show that the tensions between impartial justice and local justice are deep and abiding. In this essay I trace how the tension is gradually being resolved in U.S. history in favor of the impartial stranger ideal. I will focus on the criminal jury, although a similar shift has affected civil jury trials as well.

To go back in the history of juries in the United States is to see that insistence on disqualifying prospective jurors for knowing or caring too much about a case prior to trial was not always typical of jury selection. Although the decline of communal-based justice dates from before the American Revolution, still the jury that was given protection by the Bill of Rights was the local jury: knowing about a case and about the community asked to judge it qualified rather than disqualified a person for jury duty. In the United States, the eventual shift away from the local knowledge model of the jury has been dramatic. The shift brings the jury in line with prevailing notions that distance puts justice in perspective, but it also contributes to a growing crisis of confidence in the competence of juries.

Too often, especially in highly publicized cases, the search for impartial jurors leads to the elimination of all persons who are normally attentive to and hence knowledgeable about the happenings around them. A remarkable level of inattention and apathy becomes the necessary condition for impartiality as a juror.[13] For example, before New York subway vigilante Bernhard Goetz could be tried, a special prescreening of three hundred persons took place in the judge's chambers for over three months prior to trial; only those who had not followed the case closely in the media were kept in the pool of eligible jurors.[14] In 1986, this kind of spectacle was carried to a high-water mark in the trial of Lieutenant Colonel Oliver North on charges arising from the Iran-contra scandal. Any resident of the nation's capital who had been enough of a concerned citizen to follow the lead story of the day or to have watched some of North's own televised testimony before the Senate was automatically disqualified.[15] The only persons whose impartiality was intact were those rare individuals who could say that they "saw North on television but it was just like watching the Three Stooges or something" or that all they remembered was that "it was about something overseas."[16]

A similar tension between impartial jurors and knowledgeable jurors surfaced during jury selection in the 1990 obscenity trial of a Cincinnati art museum and its director, charged with showing the provocative photographs of Robert Mapplethorpe. The trial judge dismissed the only potential juror "who had seen the Mapplethorpe exhibit, the only one who said she attended museums regularly." Her "knowledge of the entire exhibition," and not just the particular photographs alleged to be obscene, was thought to put "an unnecessary burden" on her. Among those who survived challenges was a panel member who "never went to museums."[17]

When impartiality gets defined as ignorance, the gnawing question is this: Why should anyone believe that juries are capable of rendering accurate verdicts? It becomes a paradox, with the search for impartial jurors setting off in a different direction from the search for competent jurors. This predicament justifies our revisiting the local knowledge model of the jury. A visit to the jury's past is fascinating in its own regard, but I go to retrieve a vision of jury deliberation enriched by the ability of local jurors to know the context in which events on trial took place.

THE LOCAL JURY AT THE TIME OF THE CONSTITUTION'S RATIFICATION

When the U.S. Constitution was sent to the thirteen states for ratification in 1787, a remarkable debate ensued about the kind of criminal jury system the new nation was to have. Crucial to the debate was the question of whether local juries were an asset or a hindrance to impartial justice. As originally drafted, the Constitution guaranteed trial by jury in all federal criminal felony trials (except those involving impeachment) but left the federal government free to hold those trials anywhere in the state where the crime occurred.[18] Anti-Federalist opponents of the Constitution pointed out that the common law had long required a narrower, more local geography for justice.[19] Juries were to be selected from the "vicinage" where the crime occurred—a term that jurist Sir William Blackstone interpreted in the 1760s to require jurors to be "of the county where the fact is committed."[20] "To the safety of life, it is indispensably necessary the trial of crimes should be in the vicinity; and the vicinity is construed to mean county," remarked an opponent of ratification in Massachusetts.[21] "[The] idea which I call a true vicinage is, that a man shall be tried by his neighbors," echoed a delegate to the Virginia convention.[22]

Patrick Henry charged that by adopting the more "extensive provision" of holding a trial anywhere in the state where the crime occurred, the proposed Constitution perverted trial by jury from a protection for the accused into an instrument for tyranny.[23] Just as the British government made an end run around the purpose of jury trials by bringing colonists across the Atlantic to be tried by hostile jurors in England, so, too, the new federal government possessed the power to "shop" for a jury of its liking anywhere in the state, to carry an accused "from one extremity of the state to another," and try the accused before a jury that might have been biased against him or her. Another anti-Federalist in Virginia concurred: "They can hang any one they please, by having a jury to suit their purpose."[24] Juries "from the vicinage being not secured, this right is in reality sacrificed," Patrick Henry concluded; it would have been better that "trial by jury were struck out altogether."[25] Anti-Federalist pamphlet after pamphlet measured out the miles, the distances, the inconveniences, and the disadvantages that an accused would suffer when the federal government had free choice of both venue and jury anywhere within a state.[26]

The anti-Federalist case for preserving local juries grew directly from colonial experience in using juries to resist the crown. During the Stamp Act crisis of 1765–1766, the great complaint (alongside "No taxation without representation") was that trials would be held without juries in admiralty courts for those accused of failing to pay the new taxes. Likewise, in 1774, George Mason of Virginia drafted the Fairfax County resolves, protesting the "taking away our Trials by Jurys, the ordering Persons upon Criminal Accusations, to be tried in another Country than that in which the Fact is charged to have been committed."[27] By 1776, Virginia (which up until 1750 had displayed only a weak commitment to jury trials) responded to the home country's threats to local trials before local jurors by including the right to "Trial by an impartial jury of his Vicinage" among the criminal defendant's rights guaranteed by the Virginia Declaration of Rights.[28] So, too, did the Declaration of Independence highlight threats to local trials and local juries among the list of grievances sparking revolution ("For transporting us beyond Seas to be tried for pretended offenses [and for] depriving us in many cases, of the benefits of Trial by Jury").

Perhaps more than in any other colony, Massachusetts juries functioned as resistance bodies in high-profile cases.[29] Town meetings controlled jury selection and used that power openly to select jurors hostile to local enforcement of English customs laws.[30] By 1765, "a Bostonian could boast that the Whigs 'would always be sure of Eleven jury men in Twelve.'"[31] In 1769, during a charge to a Suffolk County jury, the royal chief justice, Thomas Hutchinson, lamented that town meetings were sending jurors who were willing to convict ordinary criminals but who "connive at and pass over in Silence and entirely smother other Crimes of an alarming Nature."[32] Hutchinson might well have had in mind the many cases involving the merchant and suspected smuggler John Hancock, in which local juries effectively outranked Parliament when it came to announcing what the law was in Massachusetts. As historian John Phillip Reid points out, local control over grand juries "meant that it was impossible for the king's officials to obtain indictments against persons accused of . . . violating imperial statutes such as the revenue laws."

In 1768, Hancock refused to permit a customs official to go below deck to inspect a discharge of cargo from his brigantine, the *Lydia*. The applicable statute gave customs officials the right "freely to go and remain on Board until the Vessel is discharged of the Lading." Sensing the futility of seeking a grand jury willing to indict Hancock, the customs officials prodded the attorney general to proceed by the alternative method called filing an "information." But the attorney general refused, as well. Practically speaking, the inability to proceed against Hancock through either the grand jury or the filing of an information operated as a veto of the inspection statute in Boston Harbor.[33]

Hancock profited from other methods of jury defiance. Royal authorities seized one of his ships for importing more goods than had been declared during loading at a Scottish customs port. Because the case involved enforcement of laws on the high seas, British procedure entitled officials to prosecute Hancock in admiralty court without a jury. The admiralty court decreed the seizure lawful and ordered the vessel and its cargo to be condemned and turned over to customs agents. But Hancock then turned the tables and sued the customs officers for trespassing on his vessel—a lawsuit that entitled him to a jury trial. At trial, the jury was dutifully instructed that the decree of the admiralty court could not be "traversed," or challenged, in this way. But the jury ignored the instructions and rendered a verdict for Hancock, ordering the customs agents personally to bear the costs of repaying Hancock for the value of his ship and cargo. When the customs officials appealed to the king in council, Hancock withdrew his lawsuit. But the political point had been made: customs officials enforced the trade acts in Massachusetts at peril of being found by local juries to be guilty of trespass. Even if such jury verdicts would ultimately be overturned, the customs agents would be out of pocket the personal expenses involved in defending at the jury trial. "A few actions of this type," notes Reid, "and Hancock and his fellow merchants could expect the customsmen to proceed more cautiously in the future."[34]

The Hancock trials became part of jury lore for the colonists. Hancock's jurors took their place among other jury heroes who resisted tyrannical laws, such as those who struck a blow for freedom of the press in 1735 by refusing to imprison New York printer John Peter Zenger simply for publishing criticisms of the crown.[35] The most famous jury of all was in London in 1670—it refused to convict William Penn of unlawful assembly simply for preaching Quaker doctrine on the street, even though the court instructed the jury that such preaching did violate the law.[36] These legendary cases cannot be regarded as typical, but they demonstrate the way jury trials gave local residents, in moments of crisis, the last say on what the law was in their communities.

Juries had this raw, democratic power over the law only so long as the crown could not decide where to try the likes of a Hancock or who the jurors would be. The power of the jury to defend against tyranny depended vitally on the principle that a central government would have to leave enforcement of its laws in the hands of the local population—a principle that the anti-Federalists found sorely lacking in the proposed Constitution of 1787.

Federalists, as defenders of the Constitution, denied any conspiratorial motive in not specifically protecting the "jury of the vicinage" in the Constitution. The reason for the absence of such protection, maintained Governor Samuel Johnston at the North Carolina ratification convention, was far more mundane. If "vicinage" simply referred to the vicinity where the crime occurred, then the term was impossibly vague to use in a written constitution. The vagueness was insurmountable because state practice had never achieved a consensus on what the term meant.[37] From early colonial days, diversity was the rule. At one extreme of localism, the seventeenth-century Fundamental Laws of West Jersey required all trials to be decided by the verdict of "twelve honest men of the neighborhood."[38] At the other extreme, early colonial Virginia for a time tried all cases involving loss of life and limb in one location (Jamestown), summoning jurors from court bystanders.[39] Even at the time of the ratification debates, Virginia procedure still called for trying cases with loss of life or limb in the state capital, with jurors summoned from the county where the crime occurred.[40]

Citing such examples, the Federalists explained the practical difficulties that stood in the way of specifying in the Constitution an exact locale for federal jury trials. But at times the Federalists went beyond reciting practical difficulties to challenging the very ideal of local justice. In Massachusetts, delegate Christopher Gore put the case against neighborhood juries elegantly and succinctly:

> The idea that the jury coming from the neighborhood, and knowing the character and circumstances of the party in trial, is promotive of justice, on reflection will appear not founded in truth. If the jury judge from any other circumstances but what are part of the cause in question, they are not impartial. The great object is to determine on the real merits of the cause, uninfluenced by any personal considerations; if, therefore, the jury could be perfectly ignorant of the person in trial, a just decision would be more probable.[41]

Capturing the Federalist preference for enlarging the geography of justice, this passage is remarkable because it anticipated modern views on impartiality and the benefits of finding jurors "perfectly ignorant of the person on trial." But this was not an isolated example of the Federalists' preference. In North Carolina, Governor Johnston responded to critics of the Constitution's jury provisions who said that

> this clause is defective, because the trial is not to be by a jury of the vicinage. . . . We may expect less partiality when the trial is by strangers; and were I to be tried for my property or life, I would rather be tried by disinterested men, who were not biased, than by men who were perhaps intimate friends of my opponent.[42]

Taken together, the Gore and Johnston remarks show that the debate over the Constitution's criminal jury provisions was at times explicitly about the inherent tensions between doing justice impartially and doing justice locally. James Madison, the Constitution's preeminent architect, was grappling with this tension when he pointed out during the Virginia ratification debates that there was no "safe" way to honor the tradition of local jury trials. Forces of disunion and rebellion still existed in the country; the new federal government would be hamstrung if it had to try alleged rebels in the home base of their rebellions:

> It might so happen that a trial would be impracticable in the country. Suppose a rebellion in a whole district; would it not be impossible to get a jury? . . . This is a complete and satisfactory answer.[43]

Madison had legitimate reason to fear disunion (recall Shay's Rebellion in 1786 in western Massachusetts). The logic of the Federalist argument for preferring the impartiality of strangers to the intimacies of neighbors when it came to jury trials was strong. But it is remarkable that the anti-Federalists won, or at least partly won, this debate. In four different states, demands were made for amending the Constitution to protect the jury of the vicinage.[44] In time, those demands bore partial fruit in the adoption of a Sixth Amendment that required criminal juries to be selected from the "district" within the state where the crime occurred (I will discuss shortly what it meant to require juries to be drawn from the district of the crime.) The Anti-Federalist success in forcing amendment of the Constitution, shrinking the geography of jury justice to some area smaller than the state, shows the vitality of the local jury ideal in 1789.

Anti-Federalist arguments in favor of local juries were of two kinds. One argument centered on the fact-finding mission of juries, a mission that local jurors with personal knowledge of the case could accomplish more accurately. "In all criminal prosecutions, the verification of facts, in the vicinity where they happen, is one of the greatest securities of the life, liberty and property of the citizens," read the Massachusetts Declaration of Rights of 1780; similar language appeared in the Maryland Constitution of 1776 and the New Hampshire Constitution of 1784. The advantage of local jurors, said Patrick Henry, was that they were "neighbors . . . acquainted with [the defendants'] characters, their good or bad conduct in life, to judge of the unfortunate man who may be thus exposed to the rigors of government."[45]

By contrast, jurors from afar did not know whether the accused was "habitually a good or bad man," said James Winthrop, the anti-Federalist who wrote under the pseudonym Agrippa. Agrippa offered the specific example of a trial where the defendant's guilt turned on whether his acts were done "maliciously or accidentally."[46] Local jurors had a decided leg up on strangers in making such a judgment about an acquaintance.[47]

In Virginia, Edmund Pendleton, a supporter of the Constitution, arose to correct Agrippa's assumption that juries of the vicinage would have personal knowledge of the accused's character. That might be true in cases where defendants commit crimes in their own neighborhoods, but when outsiders commit the crimes, the juries that try them come from the neighborhoods of the crime, not from the defendants' home neighborhoods. Hence the knowledge that a jury of the vicinage brings to a case is a "knowledge of the fact, and acquaintance with the witnesses who will come from the neighborhood," and not always a knowledge of the accused.[48]

Knowledge of the witnesses and their reputations, Pendleton agreed, is a great asset in the search for the truth. British statesman Edmund Burke once remarked, in another context, that such knowledge makes jurors the best at distinguishing perjured from truthful testimony. And as James Wilson, another supporter of the Constitution, put it at the Pennsylvania ratification convention:

> When jurors can be acquainted with the characters of the parties and the witnesses . . . they not only hear the words, but they see and mark the features of the countenance; they can judge of weight due to such testimony. . . .[49]

In the final analysis, however, the anti-Federalist defense of the local jury was not primarily a brief for its superior fact-finding ability. The most sophisticated defense of the local jury began with this concession:

> When I speak of the jury trial of the vicinage, or the trial of the fact in the neighbourhood,—I do not lay so much stress upon the circumstance of our being tried by our neighbours: in this enlightened country men may be probably impartially tried by those who do not live very near them.[50]

Instead, another point of view "made local juries "essential in every free country." The jury served freedom not only by getting the facts right, but also by getting the people right. Local citizens were empowered to control the actual administration of justice—thus the jury was our best assurance that law and justice accurately reflected the morals, values, and common sense of the people asked to obey the law. Functioning as the conscience of the community, the jury, according to the anti-Federalists, was as much a "political" institution as it was a judicial body; it brought democracy alive, made it possible for "common people . . . [to] have a part and share of influence, in the judicial as well as in the legislative department."[51]

The democratizing features of local jury service were likely to grow in importance under the proposed Constitution, where avenues for direct participation in the federal government were limited for the citizen. Theoretically, under the new Constitution, all offices of government were open to the people. But this could not "answer any valuable purposes for [the person who was] not in a situation to be brought forward and to fill those offices; these and most other offices of any considerable importance, will be occupied by the few."[52]

Nor would election of representatives secure to the people a real voice in government. The anti-Federalists constantly pointed out that the proposed republic was too large and the number of representatives too small to provide genuine dialogue between most citizens and their representatives.[53] As the colonial historian Gordon Wood writes, the anti-Federalists recognized by 1787 that diversity of interests in the republic required giving ordinary persons more actual representation than they were likely to receive in the executive and legislative branches of the new national government.[54]

In the "extensive empire" of the new Constitution, Congress and its laws would dependably reflect the voices and interests of "the few, the well-born." By contrast, trial by jury could remain an oasis of genuine democracy, if practiced on a scale small enough to "secure to the people at large, their just and rightful controul in the judicial department."[55]

Anti-Federalists were impeccable localists. But which local citizens did the jury empower? Colonial practices were more restrictive than anti-Federalist references to the people at large serving on juries implied. Not only was jury eligibility limited to white males, but, as in England, property and religious qualifications kept large numbers of the adult white male population from voting or serving on colonial juries.[56] In his study of Plymouth, Massachusetts, historian William Nelson found that about 28 percent of the adult male population served on juries between 1748 and 1774; only 3 percent of jurors serving in the county between 1748 and 1774 could be identified as ever belonging to a dissenting congregation.[57]

The prevailing view throughout the colonial period was that property gave persons a stake in society and thus made their decisions more responsible.[58] Restricting jury service to the propertied was also seen as a way of securing the jury against temptations of bribery and other forms of corruption.[59]

I have not found any evidence that the anti-Federalists objected to prevailing restrictions on jury service. Nor did they argue, in 1787, for broadening the suffrage.[60] But even though they were not perfect populists, the anti-Federalists stood against traditional notions of elite politics; they saw in the jury an embodiment of local people representing local values. However limited their own vision of who "the people" were, they were farsighted enough to appreciate that juries gave more voice to the common freeholder than did other institutions of government. Anti-Federalists agreed with Jefferson when he wrote, "Were I called upon to decide, whether the people had best be omitted in the legislative or judiciary department, I would say it is better to leave them out of the legislative. The execution of the laws is more important than the making of them."[61]

Although they differed on the issue of the jury's geography, both Federalists and anti-Federalists agreed on the jury's overall importance. Here, however, we must note that the jury they extolled was one that enjoyed the right to decide questions of law as well as of fact. Today, the absence of the familiar division of labor between jury and judge (juries decide the facts, judges decide the law) seems odd, but throughout the eighteenth century, the prevailing view remained that jurors "could ignore judges' instructions on the law and decide the law by themselves in both civil and criminal cases."[62] In Massachusetts, at that time, there was no practical alternative to permitting juries to decide questions of law, because virtually all cases were tried before a panel of at least three judges, each of whom delivered separate and often contradictory instructions. Add to this the privilege of opposing counsel to argue the law, and the jury heard up to five different versions of the law.[63] By default if not design, the jurors had to decide the law.

In 1771, John Adams wrote in his diary about the right of Massachusetts juries to disobey judicial instructions. "Every intelligent Man," Adams began, "will confess that cases frequently occur, in which it would be very difficult for a jury to determine the Questions of Law." Still, what should a juror do if the judge's statement of the law runs counter to fundamental principles of the British Constitution? Must the juror abide by the instructions?

> Every Man, of any feeling or Conscience, will answer, no. It is not only his right, but his Duty, in that case to find the Verdict according to his own best Understanding, Judgment, and Conscience, tho in Direct opposition to the Direction of the Court. . . . The English Law obliges no Man . . . to pin his faith on the sleve of any mere Man.[64]

That juries decided questions of law meant that "the law applied in the towns . . . on a day-to-day basis was not the product of the will of some distant sovereign."[65] In his study of Massachusetts law at the close of the eighteenth century, William Nelson concluded that "the representatives of local communities assembled as jurors generally had effective power to control the content of the province's substantive law."[66] An in-depth study of the civil jury in seventeenth-century Connecticut found that jurors decided legal issues by reference to "community norms" and to "a template of common beliefs and expectations as to how neighbors should treat one another."[67] Indeed, historian Bruce Mann found "no indication that [Connecticut] judges instructed juries on the law" at all until the end of the seventeenth century. To be sure, Mann documented Connecticut juries' losing their lawmaking authority considerably earlier than did Massachusetts juries, a fact that helps illumine why the anti-Federalists were fighting for a lost ideal of local justice. But early Connecticut juries still embodied that communal ideal when they "decided for themselves how the law should apply—a process that is inextricably linked with, and at times indistinguishable from, deciding what the law is."[68]

In Rhode Island, a 1677 code directed the charging of jurors, but as the eighteenth century was about to dawn, a contemporary report noted that judges "give no directions to the jury."[69] The situation was similar in New Hampshire and Vermont, where a large percentage of the judges were laymen, "lacking the professional qualifications which would have made their instructions convincing."[70] As Nelson summarized the Massachusetts situation through the eighteenth century, juries possessed an "ultimate power" that enabled the colony to achieve a substantial degree of self-governance, rendering judgments "on a day-to-day basis [that] were a reflection [less] of law set out in statute books and in English judicial precedents [than] of the custom of local communities."[71] Historian J. R. Pole goes so far as to conclude that, practically speaking, in several colonies the court and jury outranked legislative and executive institutions when it came to "settl[ing] many of the issues that affected the life of town and county."[72] For those who qualified for jury duty, jury service became what Jefferson called the "school by which [the] people learn the exercise of civic duties as well as rights."[73]

With this colonial legacy of decentralized justice in mind, the Anti-Federalists made the case at several ratification conventions that only local trials could preserve the jury as a "democratic institution of self-governance." Far from being troubled by the prospect of different juries' applying different laws, the anti-Federalists embraced the fracture of unity: "The body of the people, principally, bear the burdens of the community; they of right ought to have a controul in its important concerns, both in making and executing the laws, otherwise they may, in a short time, be ruined."[74]

Uniform justice was no friend of impartial justice, in the anti-Federalist view, if the uniformity was achieved by empowering an elite judicial class to dictate the law to the people. Such an arrangement promised objectivity but in fact invited "secret and arbitrary proceedings."[75] The black robes merely masked "severe and arbitrary" conduct by judges and left abuse of the law unchecked by any popular authority.

In fact, if bribery was the mortal enemy of impartiality, then a network of local juries rotating anonymous persons through its ranks was far more bribery-proof than standing panels of known judges ever could be. As one anti-Federalist put it, "Judges once influenced, soon become inclined to yield to temptations, and to decree for him who will pay the most for their partiality."[76] By contrast, jurors were bribery-proof by reasons of character as well as opportunity. In terms of opportunity, "it is not, generally, known till the hour the cause comes on for trial, what persons are to form the jury." In terms of character, jurors possess the "honest characters of the common freemen of a country, . . . untaught in . . . affairs [of corruption]."[77]

The anti-Federalists conceded that citizens will not come to the jury with "minute skill . . . in the laws, . . . [but] they have common sense in its purity, which seldom or never errs in making and applying laws to the condition of the people."[78] Here, once again, local knowledge of the conditions of the people compensated for the lack of formal legal training. Not only was formal legal training unnecessary, but jurors did not even need to rely on a judge's instructions to know the common law of the land, rooted as it was in fundamental principles of natural justice. Even John Adams, no populist, noted:

> The general Rules of Law and common Regulations of Society, under which ordinary Transactions arrange themselves, . . . [are] well enough known to ordinary Jurors.[79]

Thus, members of a Massachusetts grand jury in 1759 were told that they "need no Explanation" as to most legal matters because "your Good Sence & understanding will Direct ye as to them."[80]

Moreover, the anti-Federalists continued, those who argued that people of the neighborhood were too ignorant to do justice missed the crucial civic education and moral transformation jury service worked on the ordinary citizen. Jury duty was a crucial "means by which the people are let into the knowledge of public affairs—are enabled to stand as the guardians of each others [*sic*] rights."[81] Said another anti-Federalist on the theme of civic education: "Their situation, as jurors and representatives, enables them to acquire information and knowledge in the affairs and government of the society."[82] Or, as an anti-Federalist who wrote under the pen name Maryland Farmer put it:

> Why shall we rob the Commons of the only remaining power they have been able to preserve. . . . I know it . . . will be said . . . that they are too ignorant— that they cannot distinguish between right and wrong—that decisions on property are submitted to chance; and that the last word, commonly determines the cause:—There is some truth in these allegations—-but whence comes it—The Commons are much degraded in the powers of the mind:—They were deprived of the use of understanding, when they were robbed of the power of employing it.—Men no longer cultivate, what is no longer useful. . . . *Give them power and they will find understanding to use it.*[83]

In retort, the Federalists accused those who wanted to maintain the local jury of fighting old battles. Prior to the Revolution, the colonies had to obey laws passed by a distant parliament that did not represent them. In that situation, local juries provided the best available avenues for community control over the law's application. But the proposed relationship between Congress and the states according to the Constitution did not recreate the relationship between colony and empire, argued the Federalists. Congress was to be composed directly of representatives chosen by the people or by the state legislatures. The representation of local views would be accomplished democratically in the legislature, undercutting both the need for and the legitimacy of jury interpretations of the law.

THE LOCAL JURY AND THE BILL OF RIGHTS

At the end of the ratification process, six states were specifically on record as concerned, even alarmed, about the absence of constitutional protection for local criminal jury trials. Virginia and North Carolina passed twin resolutions calling for a Bill of Rights that would specifically recognize "trial by an impartial Jury of his [that is, the defendant's] vicinage."[84] New York called for an amendment guaranteeing "an impartial Jury of the County where the crime was committed." Rhode Island, the last of the original thirteen colonies to ratify, made a similar proposal, but only after Congress had sent the first ten amendments to the states for ratification. Massachusetts and Pennsylvania debated the issue but took no specific action.[85]

Given the nature of the ratification debates, it was clear to the first Congress that it was wise policy, as well as wise politics to amend the Constitution to include a Bill of Rights. In the House, Madison took the lead in resolving the vicinage problem by suggesting that the body of the Constitution itself be amended to guarantee, in Article 3, that the "trial of all crimes . . . shall be by an impartial jury of freeholders of the vicinage." The only exception would be that "in cases of crimes committed within any county which may be in possession of an enemy, or in which a general insurrection may prevail, the trial may by law be authorized in some other county of the same State, as near as may be to the seat of the offence."[86] During July of 1789, Madison's proposals were submitted to the Committee of Eleven—a select committee composed of one representative from each of the eleven states that had by then ratified the Constitution. The Committee of Eleven kept intact the general guarantee that trials would be local. It dealt with trials in areas of rebellion by amending Madison's language to permit removal of the case to "some other place within the same State" and not necessarily to a place "as near" as possible to the seat of the offense.[87]

In August of 1789, the House made the decision to collect and submit to the Senate its proposed changes to the Constitution in the form of a Bill of Rights.[88] The language concerning "juries of the vicinage" became part of a proposed Ninth Amendment, later to be what we now know as the Sixth Amendment of the Bill of Rights. In that form, it was submitted to the Senate in August of 1789 for action.[89]

Unlike the House, the Federalist-controlled Senate proved hostile to the idea of local juries. In a letter dated September 23, 1789, Madison noted:

> They are equally inflexible in opposing a definition of the *locality* of Juries. The vicinage they contend is either too vague or too strict a term, too vague if depending on limits to be fixed by the pleasure of the law, too strict if limited to the County.[90]

By "too vague," the Senate apparently meant that "vicinage" had no precise legal meaning and meant different things in different states. By "too strict," it no doubt was echoing Madison's fear of local juries' promoting disunion by shielding local rebels from federal prosecution. For these reasons, the Senate voted to delete the House language regarding vicinage from the Bill of Rights.[91]

When the House received the Senate revision of the proposed amendments, it ultimately voted to accept all but three of the Senate changes. One point of resistance was renewed House insistence on the importance of local juries to the scheme of justice.[92] But given Senate stubbornness against the term "vicinage," the House sought compromise language. From the House's point of view, the body of the Constitution dangerously empowered the central government to pick and choose trial locations and juries from anywhere within the state where the crime occurred. According to the Senate point of view, requiring federal trials to be held in the county where the crime occurred was too strict, an invitation to disunion. On September 24, the House proposed that the language of the future Sixth Amendment be changed to the following:

> In all criminal prosecutions, the accused shall enjoy the right to a speedy and public trial, by an impartial jury of the State and district wherein the crime shall have been committed, which district shall have been previously ascertained by law.[93]

Available records do not tell us who proposed the new language or why. But the language about districts most probably refers to the Judiciary Act of 1789, which Congress was debating simultaneously with the proposed Bill of Rights. The Judiciary Act created federal courts inferior to the Supreme Court and mapped out judicial districts over which these courts would have jurisdiction.[94]

The language of the Sixth Amendment requiring criminal trials to be tried before a jury that hailed not only from the state where the crime occurred but also from the district within the state was a genuine compromise that both supporters and opponents of local juries could accept. To opponents, the important thing, no doubt, was that the districts actually created by the Judiciary Act were exactly synonymous with the boundaries of the states. As originally drafted, the Judiciary Act created eleven judicial districts—one each for the eleven ratifying states. Prior to the act's passage, the number was enlarged to thirteen—a twelfth district was added in the part of Virginia that became the state of Kentucky, and a thirteenth was added in the part of Massachusetts that later became Maine.[95] Thus, the language in the Sixth Amendment regarding districts had virtually no immediate practical significance. Because the boundaries of the districts "ascertained by law" were the same as those of the states, the federal government still had the right to hold trials and draw jurors from anywhere within those boundaries.

For supporters of the tradition of local juries, the compromise could also be counted as a partial victory. First, the Constitution itself had been amended to recognize the principle that juries had to be drawn from discrete districts within a state. Congress retained authority to ascertain by law what these districts were, but any time it legislated new districts that were smaller than a state's boundaries, the Sixth Amendment kicked in to shrink the geography of justice.

In the Judiciary Act itself, the ideal of local juries received more immediate, practical vindication. Although attempts to require all federal juries to "be drawn from the county in which the offense was committed" were defeated,[96] the act was successfully amended on the floor of the Senate to require that

> in cases punishable with death the trial shall be had in the County where the offence was committed, or where that cannot be done without great inconvenience, Twelve petit Jurors at least, shall be summoned from thence.[97]

Here the local jury, expressly defined as coming from the county where the crime occurred, received protection in arguably the most important kind of cases: those in which a jury must pass on the life of the accused. To be sure, "great inconvenience" would justify removing the *venue* of trial from the county. But, remarkably, even then the law required at least twelve jurors to be summoned from the county where the crime occurred to the place of trial.

THE DECLINE OF THE LOCAL JURY AND THE RISE OF THE IMPARTIAL JUSTICE IDEAL

Local juries never again enjoyed the reputation for doing justice that they held during the country's founding. Within a generation of the Constitution's ratification, two lines of cases combined to sap the historical powers of the local jury. The first solidified an ideal of impartiality that presumed bias in local jurors who were familiar with the facts, parties, or witnesses in a case. The second stripped the local jury of its historical right to decide questions of law as well as of facts.

The presumption of bias in persons who knew about a case prior to trial was not new at the beginning of the nineteenth century—it had been part of the jury's previous evolution from a self-informing body to a neutral body that listened to witnesses. However, the banishment of local knowledge from the jury room continued over the next two centuries, and today the ban stands history on its head—disqualifying jurors for having precisely the acquaintances or information that once qualified them to judge their community's events in context. One wonders why trials should be held locally anymore, when we go to such lengths to eliminate local knowledge from the jury box.

The second line of cases (depriving the jury of its lawmaking function) led to a steep decline in jury power. In contrast to the Revolutionary period, by the end of the nineteenth century, jurors were presumed to be ignorant of the law and obligated to abide mechanically by the court's instructions on legal matters. This decline did not take place overnight or without a struggle.[98] Jacksonian democracy brought with it the era of the "common man" and concepts of egalitarianism that supported a broad role for the lay jury. But the before-and-after pictures are clear. The jury entered the nineteenth century as a body authorized to resolve contested points of law on its own and even to refuse to enforce laws it considered unjust.[99] The jury exited the century duty-bound to follow judicial instructions and to enforce the laws whether it agreed with them or not.[100]

Together, the two lines of cases rationalized the juror's function at trial, separating it both from that of a witness to the facts and from that of a judge of the law. But though these changes brought the jury in line with emerging notions of impartial justice, uniformly and blindly dispensed, they also produced unwelcome consequences. An ideal of jury impartiality that can be practiced only by disqualifying the best-informed members of the community does not inspire confidence in the accuracy of jury verdicts. It naively defines an impartial mind as an empty mind. Confidence in jury verdicts is further sapped by treating jurors as so ignorant of the law that they must mechanically obey the judge's instructions to the letter. In the remainder of this essay, I will trace the way that the local knowledge model of the jury gradually gave way to the impartial juror ideal.

The Impartial Juror at the Beginning of the Nineteenth Century: The Trial of Aaron Burr

In 1807, former vice president of the United States Aaron Burr was arrested on suspicion of treason against his country. The specific acts constituting the treason were said to have taken place in 1806 on Blennerhassett's Island in the County of Wood, Virginia.[101] Here, Burr supposedly arranged for roughly thirty armed men to set out in nine boats down the Ohio and Mississippi rivers to seize New Orleans. Even prior to Burr's arrest, Thomas Jefferson issued a presidential proclamation warning of rebellion, Congress debated whether the danger warranted a suspension of the writ of habeas corpus, and the partisan Republican newspapers in Virginia saturated the state with details of Burr's planned insurrection and his grandiose plans to invade Mexico, detach the Southwest from the United States, and form an empire stretching from the Mississippi Valley to Mexico City. Key depositions and documents even found their way into the pages of the *Alexandria Expositor* and other papers.[102]

In such an atmosphere, a federal grand jury convened in Richmond in 1807 to consider indicting Burr. The difficulty of getting a fair hearing in a local hotbed of partisan Republican passions must have been immediately apparent to Burr from the names of the twenty-four freeholders summoned for grand jury duty. They included Senator William Giles, Jefferson's floor leader in the Senate, and Colonel William Cary Nicholas, the president's choice for floor leader in the House.[103] Jefferson's personal hostility toward Burr was well known, born of Burr's cooperation with the Federalists who threw the election of 1800 into the House, almost making Burr president. The presence of Jefferson's political allies on the grand jury hardly seemed accidental. To add to the suspicions, the federal marshal who summoned the grand jury had acted illegally by choosing substitutes at his own discretion for any persons excused; the proper procedure for making up any shortfall in the original panel was to choose from among the bystanders at court. The presiding judge—none other than Chief Justice John Marshall, sitting as a circuit judge, himself no friend of Jefferson—agreed with Burr that the federal marshal's procedure smacked of handpicking the grand jury. He ordered the substitutes removed and replaced from among the bystanders.[104]

Burr proceeded to make the novel argument that he had a right to challenge individual *grand* jurors for bias or "favor."[105] This is a right that American law does not often recognize even to this day,[106] and it was certainly unheard of at common law. As one reporter of Burr's trial noted at the time, "At most the authority goes no further than this: that a grand juror may be challenged for incompetency, or for being irregularly or improperly returned. This is a very different thing from a general right to challenge for 'favor.' "[107] But Burr saw no reason why his right to impartial justice should not include the privilege of challenging biased grand jurors. His objection to Senator Giles was especially significant in this regard. Burr went out of his way to make clear that he did not think Giles was biased or prejudiced in the sense of bearing him any ill will. In fact, Burr conceded that Giles's mind was "as pure and unbiased" as possible in the circumstances. But absence of ill will was not enough to secure impartiality. "It would be an effort above human nature for this gentleman to divest himself of all prepossessions."[108] The problem was not personal animus but personal knowledge. After all, Giles was so impressed by the information Jefferson sent to Congress that he advocated suspension of the writ of habeas corpus because of threats to public safety. Having essentially prejudged the matter as a senator, Giles could not possibly still have an open mind about whether Burr deserved to be indicted.

The reactions of Giles, the prosecutor, and Marshall to Burr's challenge provide a revealing look at the emerging understanding of impartial justice. Despite having precedent on his side, the prosecutor only briefly resisted Burr's challenge, and in fact urged that "every one who has made declarations expressive of a decisive opinion should be withdrawn from the [grand] jury."[109] No doubt, the government had a political motive for wanting to seem indifferent to "whether A, B and C, or D, E and F composed a part" of the grand jury. But there was also genuine confusion about how to make grand jury practice fit the new constitutional language guaranteeing impartial juries. Once the government acquiesced to Burr's claimed right to challenge grand jurors, Marshall was spared the necessity of making a ruling and simply endorsed the suggestion "that if any gentleman has made up and declared his mind it would be best to withdraw."[110] Only Giles himself resisted. Although "it was by no means agreeable to [him] to have been summoned on this grand jury,"[111] it was even more disagreeable to be branded as biased. Giles judged himself fully capable of appreciating the difference between judicial evidence and the kind of information he had as a senator. Eventually, however, he agreed to withdraw, as did Nicholas, and the dispute was over.

In the end, sixteen grand jurors were impaneled. Keeping score on the sidelines, Jefferson counted "2 Fed[eralists], 4 Quid, and 10 Republicans."[112] He privately complained that this did "not seem a fair representation of the state of Virginia." Others put the number of Republican grand jurors at fourteen.[113] Whatever the exact figure, those keeping track of juror backgrounds clearly expected local politics and local justice to rub elbows during the grand jury sessions.

The grand jury indicted Burr for treason and lesser offenses on June 24, 1807, specifying only one "overt act" of rebellion: the gathering of armed men on Blennerhassett's Island. Now charged with a capital crime, Burr was entitled, under Section 29 of the Judiciary Act, either to be tried in Wood County, where the acts on Blennerhassett's Island allegedly occurred, or, if great inconvenience prevented trial in that location, to have at least twelve jurors summoned from there. Reports of the case do not make clear whether Burr ever sought trial in Wood Country rather than Richmond or whether the required certification of great inconvenience was ever made. But Marshall did postpone the start of trial in Richmond until the marshal could summon forty-eight potential jurors from the county where the crime occurred.[114]

When jury selection commenced on August 3, the arguments about impartiality that were rehearsed at the grand jury stage now broke out in full. Burr and his lawyers argued that the "public mind has been so filled with prejudice against him that there was some difficulty in finding impartial jurors."[115] Indeed, of the forty-eight persons examined during the first day, only four could be immediately seated.[116] Virtually everyone else admitted to reading and being influenced by the newspapers. James G. Laidly was a typical member of the venire. He stated

> that he had formed and expressed some opinion unfavorable to Colonel Burr; . . . that he had principally taken his opinions from newspaper statements; and that he had not, as far as he recollected, expressed an opinion that Colonel Burr deserved hanging; but that his impression was, that he was guilty.[117]

Laidly and persons of similar mind were struck from the jury without much dispute. The controversy centered on those members of the jury pool who expressed an opinion, based on what they had read in the newspapers, that Burr had *intended* treason but were not certain whether he had ever *acted* on his designs, at least as he was charged with having done on Blennerhassett's Island.

Nathaniel Selden was typical of the jurors whom Burr wished to strike as having their minds "made up on one half of the guilt." Selden stated that he "had formed an opinion . . . that the intentions of the prisoner were hostile to the United States," but had seen no evidence to satisfy him that Burr had been guilty of an overt act.[118]

According to precedents, persons such as Selden were acceptably impartial. This had been laid down, not without controversy, only seven years earlier in the famous trial of James Callender, accused of seditiously libeling President Adams in a pamphlet entitled "The Prospect Before Us." Jurors who had read the pamphlet and were convinced it was libelous were nonetheless found qualified to serve as jurors so long as they had not concluded that Callender was the author of the pamphlet.[119]

The prosecution urged Marshall to apply the same logic to the Burr case and strike only those jurors who had decided the entire issue of guilt or innocence. If Burr were permitted to strike potential jurors who merely had opinions on some aspects of the case, then the prosecutor

> would venture to predict that there could not be a jury selected in the state of Virginia, because . . . there was [not] a single man in the state, qualified to become a juryman, who had not, in some form or other, made up, and declared an opinion on the conduct of the prisoner.[120]

This particular legal dispute called forth an opinion from Marshall interpreting the Sixth Amendment guarantee of trial before an "impartial" jury. Marshall resolved the dispute in favor of Burr. If a person had expressed a decisive opinion on any "essential" element of the crime (such as intent), then he was disqualified. However, Marshall was careful not to go too far, noting that persons with a good deal of information and opinions on the case would be welcome on the jury so long as they fell short of prejudging any essential element of the charge:

> It would seem to the court that to say that any man who had formed an opinion on any fact conducive to the final decision of the case would therefore be considered as disqualified from serving on the jury, would exclude intelligent and observing men, whose minds were really in a situation to decide upon the whole case according to the testimony, and would perhaps be applying the letter of the rule requiring an impartial jury with a strictness which is not necessary for the preservation of the rule itself.[121]

The immediate upshot of Marshall's ruling was to enlarge vastly the number of potential jurors Burr could challenge. The defendant proceeded to do so successfully over a two-week period, exhausting the first panel and requiring a second venire to be summoned.[122]

But the specifics of jury selection in Burr's case are of far less historical significance than the general principles laid down for defining the meaning of impartial justice. It is here that Marshall sounded the death knell of the local knowledge model and outlined the portrait of the impartial juror we still try to sketch today. Yet Marshall's vision of impartiality was markedly different from the tabula rasa version that triumphed only later.

In interpreting what the framers of the Constitution meant by an impartial jury, Marshall referred to the work of the great eighteenth-century codifier of common law, William Hawkins. Hawkins noted that good grounds for challenging a juror were "that he has declared his opinion beforehand that the party is guilty, or will be hanged or the like. Yet it hath been adjudged, that if it shall appear that the juror made such declaration from his knowledge of the cause, and not out of any ill will to the party, it is no cause of challenge."[123]

Here, in one of the last hurrahs for the local knowledge model of the jury, Hawkins sharply distinguished between the knowledgeable juror and the spiteful juror. Opinions spiked by personal hatred of the defendant served to prejudice the mind and destroy impartiality. But opinions born of personal knowledge of a defendant for whom a prospective juror bore no animosity were entirely consistent with bringing an open and informed mind to court.

Marshall was not prepared to reject outright Hawkins's reconciliation of pretrial knowledge and impartiality. The episode with Senator Giles at the grand jury stage indicated that Marshall had already moved beyond the common-law notion that only an ill-willed juror could be a biased juror. But still, Marshall puzzled carefully over the circumstances in which pretrial knowledge should be equated with pretrial bias. He adopted a new approach, reflecting the shifting sources of local knowledge in modern society:

> Without determining whether the case put by Hawk . . . be law or not, it is sufficient to observe that this case is totally different. The opinion which is there declared to constitute no cause of challenge is one formed by the juror on his own knowledge; in this case the opinion is formed on report and newspaper publications.[124]

A juror whose opinions stemmed from firsthand knowledge of events in his neighborhood was arguably of assistance in giving accurate verdicts. But Marshall cast a jaundiced eye on those who made up their minds prior to trial simply on the basis of newspaper accounts. If this was the kind of local knowledge a prospective juror brought, then it was far more likely to be expressive of prejudice and rumor than of truth. What did it say about the virtues of the potential juror, asked Marshall, if that juror conceded that he knew nothing directly about the case and yet had made up his mind on an important part of it simply from what he read in the papers? Such behavior "manifests a bias that completely disqualifies himself from the functions of a juror."[125]

In this way, the problem of pretrial knowledge became the problem of pretrial publicity. But Marshall was careful to stress that people did not lose the ability to be an impartial juror simply because they had read the papers. Bias was not some kind of contagious disease people caught from reading inflammatory articles. Each juror had to be questioned individually to determine whether he had crossed the line from having "light impressions which may fairly be supposed to yield to the testimony that may be offered" to expressing "those strong and deep impressions which will close the mind against the testimony."[126] In other words, the focus of the voir dire must not be on the nature of the newspaper articles but on the nature of the opinions expressed by the would-be juror prior to trial. Here, Marshall accepted the common-law principle, reflective of small-town life, that a juror could be disqualified for bias only if he had expressed his opinions and bandied them about town. Until it was publicly aired, an opinion was neither decisive nor conclusive.

The gist of Marshall's reasoning is that having pretrial information does not disqualify a juror, but a predisposition against considering the facts undermines impartiality.[127] It is thus the task of the judge during the voir dire to separate those whose minds are opened by attending to the newspaper accounts from those whose minds are closed and enslaved by what they read.

When Marshall applied these standards to Burr's case, the results were consistent with neither the local knowledge jury of the past nor the tabula rasa jury that was to come. Contrary to the common law, Marshall permitted Burr to challenge not only ill-willed jurors but also well-informed jurors who expressed conclusive opinions about any essential element of the case. In contrast to our contemporary standards, however, Marshall seated a number of informed jurors who admitted to having formed generally unfavorable opinions about Burr's character after reading of his intrigues in the newspapers. For instance, Richard Parker "had, like every other person, formed an opinion . . . on newspaper statements . . . [and he had] declared that if these newspaper statements were true, Colonel Burr had been guilty of some design contrary to the interest and laws of the United States." Edward Carrington "had formed an unfavorable opinion of the views of Colonel Burr, but these opinions were not definitive." Likewise, Hugh Mercer confessed that "an opinion which he had for some time past entertained of the character of Colonel Burr was unfriendly to a strictly impartial inquiry into his case."[128] All three were seated on the jury.

In the end, twelve men were found sufficiently impartial to try Burr. They acquitted him of treason, virtually compelled to reach a not-guilty verdict after Marshall granted Burr's motion to exclude most of the evidence that the government wished to present. The government conceded that Burr was in Kentucky on the day he was charged in the indictment with fomenting rebellion hundreds of miles away, on Blennerhassett's Island. For this reason, Marshall ruled that most of the government's proposed evidence against Burr was irrelevant to proving the only overt act of treason alleged against Burr.[129]

From a contemporary point of view, the lesson of Burr's case lies not in the result but in the procedures articulated for selecting jurors in highly publicized cases. During a time of legal transition, Marshall expressed a preference for jurors who knew less rather than more about the case. He astutely understood that small-town justice, with jurors contributing firsthand knowledge to deliberations, was no longer characteristic of Virginia society. Burr's potential jurors knew about him secondhand, their information funneled through the newspapers. Already in 1807, Marshall approached such secondhand knowledge with suspicion. The classic arguments about jurors' pretrial knowledge being a boon to informed deliberation no longer worked; newspaper coverage was as likely to inflame as to inform.

Hence, Marshall set American law along the course it has been following ever since—searching for jurors who are as free as possible from local information, which came to be better described as local prejudice. Marshall himself did not define impartiality in ways that disqualified all persons whose opinions were influenced by the press. He thought a sensible line could be drawn between "light" and "strong" impressions, eliminating only those persons whose opinions on a crucial issue affecting guilt or innocence had become "fixed." We now need to see how well Marshall's approach to reconciling jurors' impartiality with some amount of pretrial knowledge has held up over time.

The Impartial Juror Today: The Problem of Pretrial Publicity

Mark Twain was no authority on the law, but sixty-five years after Burr's trial, his satirical talents made him among the first to ridicule the relentless progress of jury selection toward identifying ignorance with impartiality. In 1871, Twain reported that a "noted desperado killed Mr. B, a good citizen, in the most wanton and cold-blooded way." Not surprisingly, "the papers were full of it, and all men capable of reading read about it. And of course all men not deaf and dumb and idiotic talked about it." The odd lot that did not talk and did not read—the "fools and rascals" who neither read nor talked about the case—were sworn in as the jury. Twain recounted the relentless way "the system rigidly excludes honest men and men of brains":

> A minister, intelligent, esteemed, and greatly respected; a merchant of high character and known probity; a mining superintendent of intelligence and unblemished reputation; a quartz-mill owner of excellent standing, were all questioned in the same way, and all set aside. Each said the public talk and the newspaper reports had not so biased his mind but that sworn testimony would ... enable him to render a verdict without prejudice and in accordance with the facts. But of course such men could not be trusted with the case. Ignoramuses alone could mete out unsullied justice.[130]

A century later, we are still selecting jurors in the manner that Twain mocked. A study by two ommunications lawyers and scholars, Newton Minow and Fred Cate, estimated that during the 1980s at least 3,100 defendants claimed that pretrial publicity made it impossible to impanel an impartial jury locally.[131] Defendants throughout that decade and into the 1990s, from mobsters, such as Gennaro Anguilo and Samuel Granito, to big-time tax evaders, such as hotel magnate Leona Helmsley,[132] complained about the corruption of public opinion through the sheer barrage of sensational and inflammatory articles in local media bent on creating a circuslike atmosphere in the vicinity.[133]

Some pointed to damaging revelations about their prior criminal records; others, to reports of their suppressed confessions—all information legally inadmissible at their trial and yet sneaking through the back door straight into the jury room.[134] When local media create a firestorm over a cause célèbre, how can impartial jurors still be found locally? Marshall previewed this dilemma, but in an age of electronic media, the sheer saturation possibilities are beyond anything he ever encountered.

Trial judges remain reluctant to grant changes of venue as a way of escaping local prejudices and local publicity.[135] But the justifications for keeping trials local reveal just how weak the old ideals of community justice are today. Judges seldom defend their refusal to move a trial by identifying the positive advantages of convening a local jury to decide the case. They simply limit contamination that comes from holding trials locally, using strategies such as continuing the case until the community loses interest in it or sequestering the jury during the voir dire and weeding out persons whose impartiality is destroyed by having knowledge of the case and being prejudiced.

In theory, judges do the weeding by applying Marshall's distinction between "light" and "fixed" opinions.[136] In practice, however, judges find it difficult to mark the degree to which a potential juror's opinions are fixed.[137] Moreover, Marshall's seating of jurors who were "lightly" predisposed to finding Burr guilty no longer seems reconcilable with the presumption of innocence. Thus, the federal district judge John G. Davies greeted prospective jurors in the federal civil rights trial of the four police officers accused of beating Rodney King by "remind[ing] them of their obligation to set aside *any* impressions they had of the case or of the four officers" (emphasis added).[138] Nothing less accorded with the presumption of innocence, Judge Davies warned, despite the Herculean effort it would have taken for Angelenos to clear their minds of all preconceptions formed during the first King trial or subsequent riots.

Beyond these problems, the *Burr* standard more or less required judges to take jurors at their word. But, as one federal district judge wryly put it, it is hard to treat as meaningful a juror's promise that, for example, he or she can lay aside an opinion, gained from reading the papers, that "the high school teacher brutally killed one of his students."[139]

Moving beyond *Burr*, contemporary law has added the concept of inherent, or presumed, bias as a way of disqualifying potential jurors. Media coverage occasionally reaches such levels of revelation and inflammation that bias may simply be presumed in anyone exposed to it; there is no need to uncover particular evidence of prejudice through voir dire questions. Rather, as the Supreme Court put it, "[A]dverse pretrial publicity can create such a presumption of prejudice in a community that the jurors' claims that they can be impartial should not be believed."[140]

The notion of presumed bias has given the Supreme Court a great deal of trouble over the years. The concept came into the law in the early 1960s as an apparent reaction to fears about television's power to control local opinion. In 1961, a television station in a small Louisiana parish (population 150,000) obtained and aired a film made by police of a defendant's murder confession. The station ran the film on three consecutive nights, to audiences of twenty-four thousand, fifty-three thousand, and twenty-nine thousand, respectively. For this case, *Rideau v. Louisiana*, the Court ruled that pervasive bias could be presumed in the jury venire as a whole and that the defendant's motion for a change of venue should have been granted. There was no need to produce evidence of actual prejudice in particular jurors, because it was believed that there was no way a person could witness the television confession and still keep an open mind for trial. In fact, the Court noted, the spectacle of a defendant confessing on television reduced the actual trial to a "hollow formality."[141]

Rideau was a decision compelled by the facts; presuming bias in jurors who see a defendant confess on television was easy. Left undecided by *Rideau* was the question of what else persons could learn from the media without losing their capacity to serve as impartial jurors. In a case preceding *Rideau*, the Court had "given little weight" to jurors' affirmations of their own impartiality, after they had been exposed to media reports that the defendant had confessed to six murders and twenty-four burglaries and had offered to plead guilty.[142] In two subsequent cases in the mid-1960s, the Court carried forward the message that media coverage could reduce local courts to local carnivals, so entirely undermining the "solemnity and sobriety" of trials as to degrade jury verdicts into a "verdict of the mob."[143]

By the end of the 1960s, the oft-repeated comparison of local trials to circuses and carnivals showed how tarnished was the once-proud reputation of the jury of the vicinage as an informed and deliberative body. According to the doctrine of presumed bias, jury selection standards mapped the uphill battle judges needed to wage against the negative consequences of local jury trials. In particular, jury selection became wed to a flawed understanding of impartiality in jurors—as if the only open minds were empty minds. An impartial jury is supposed to represent all segments of the community. But, as a former U.S. attorney for the District of Columbia, Jay B. Stephens, complained, the categorical elimination of "people . . . who have read something, heard something, watched something, seen something, or talked to somebody" does not produce impartial juries. Such exclusionary standards "prejudice . . . the case against the government at the start" by disqualifying the very persons "who are an integral part of the community, who participate in the community, who are aware of what is going on in the community and who stay informed."[144]

Within a decade of its leading decisions on pretrial publicity and inherent bias, the Supreme Court began to have second thoughts. In a 1977 decision, the Court repudiated any proposition "that juror exposure to information about a state defendant's prior convictions or to news accounts of the crime with which he is charged alone presumptively deprives the defendant of due process."[145] In a 1984 case, the Court refused to find that jurors were necessarily prejudiced by media accounts prior to retrial of the defendant's conviction, confession, and plea of insanity at the first trial.[146] And in a 1991 case, the Court found no inherent bias in jurors even though there was massive publicity about the defendant's alleged confession to killing a woman after escaping from a prison work detail.[147]

In part, these cases reflect a simple, political shift in a conservative Supreme Court's reluctance to reverse criminal convictions. But the change from presuming bias in news-following members of the public also speaks to a widely shared sense that prior cases had pushed the demands for impartiality in jurors to an absurd point, where only the most inattentive citizens could readily qualify for jury service. Ignorance was becoming a virtue in jurors, and knowledge was becoming a vice.

Although recent Supreme Court cases suggest a retreat from the selection standards Mark Twain once lampooned, in practice trial procedures indicate that there is still a preference for jurors with empty minds. I turn to detailed accounts of two recent trials—one famous, the other not—to illustrate the problematic understanding of impartiality that drives jury selection today.

THE TRIAL OF OLIVER NORTH

Like Aaron Burr, Oliver North was a colonel charged with high crimes against the federal government. The scandal known as Iran-contra cast North in the leading role of diverting funds from illegal weapons sales to Iran to aid for the so-called contra forces fighting the Sandinista regime in Nicaragua. At the time, Congress had cut off funding for the contras. North went to trial in 1989 on a dozen charges of obstructing Congress, making false statements, destroying documents, conspiring to defraud the government, and receiving illegal gratuities and traveler's checks.[148]

Jury selection for North's case was particularly problematic because a national television audience had seen him testify before the Senate, which had granted him immunity for his testimony (meaning that it could not be used against him in a court of law). For this reason, the presiding trial judge, Gerhard Gesell, understandably eliminated jury panel members who retained intimate recall of the immunized testimony. But Judge Gesell went considerably further in purging pretrial knowledge from the jury.[149] First, a written questionnaire was used to prescreen the initial pool of 235 persons. The 156 venire members who acknowledged seeing or reading about North's testimony were automatically eliminated, without being individually questioned at all about their level of exposure or reactions. Next, during the voir dire, the trial judge dismissed another 56 for having "rudimentary prior knowledge" of North's Senate testimony.[150] The judge even excused a venire member who said she only listened to the hearings "with one ear."[151]

Those making the first cut included the eventual forewoman of the jury, who told the court, during jury selection, "I don't like the news. I don't like to watch it. It's depressing."[152] Also eligible were jurors who "never read the newspapers except to see the comics and horoscope," who recalled only that North was a "head of soldiers, or something like that," and who "didn't understand . . . whatever I heard about this case."[153]

Judge Gesell was in a terrible quandary. Who were these jurors who knew next to nothing about North's appearance before the Senate, and why should he entrust the conscience of the community and the hard work of justice to them? Such an "extreme application of the impartiality requirement," one commentator lamented, was "in direct conflict with the notion of a trial by a representative panel of one's peers."[154] It skewed jury selection "toward the disaffected and disinterested." Lost was the idea that some knowledge of Iran-contra, some concern for the doings of government during those years, might be helpful to the jury's task. Instead, as had happened in Watergate-related trials more than a decade earlier, "a well informed student of public affairs [was], for that very reason, disqualified from sitting on a jury in matters of public moment."[155] To anyone following the jury selection, the integrity of the jury was itself drawn into question.

In the end, the twelve chosen jurors performed their task admirably, as almost all jurors do. But the jury was lenient toward North, acquitting him of all nine charges of lying to either Congress or federal investigators and convicting him on only three charges. The verdicts arguably reflected the jury's agreement with defense suggestions that all politicians lie and that North was a scapegoat for his superiors.[156] We can never know whether there was any connection between the verdicts (with their implicit mistrust of government) and the elimination of engaged citizens from the jury. But the possibility is there.[157]

A CHILD SEXUAL ABUSE TRIAL

In 1986, Gerald Amirault went to trial on charges of sexually abusing and raping dozens of children at his mother's day care center in Malden, Massachusetts.[158] For months prior to the trial, local and Boston newspapers and television and radio stations had blanketed the community with graphic coverage of alleged abuse in the basement of the center, where Amirault, playing "Tookey the Clown," had allegedly taken the children.

A third of the initial jury pool was immediately disqualified when these panel member said they had formed impressions of the case from the media and would find it difficult to lay them aside. Subsequently, the judge's voir dire examination focused on those persons who thought they could be impartial, despite having followed the case in the news. One prospective juror thought he could be fair but remembered reading press accounts of statements made by the defendant to the police. These statements were not admissible at trial, and the judge considered it unlikely that the person, if seated, could put his knowledge of the statements out of his mind.

In contrast, the judge was more likely to certify as impartial those persons who could remember virtually nothing of what they read. Typical of the surviving candidates was a woman who said she did not read the local paper, and if she saw anything about the case at all in the Boston papers, didn't pay any attention to it. Another panel member was deemed impartial because she said she remembered reading something about the day care center, but "it was so long ago I don't remember what I read."

The voir dire also attempted to detect general attitudes about sexual crimes. An alarming number of prospective jurors apparently confided that they or people close to them had been the victims of sexual abuse as children. The judge excused all such persons from serving, on the ground that they could hardly be expected to be disinterested in a case of this sort.

A number of parents and grandparents also confessed to having certain "feelings" at the start of the case, because their children or grandchildren were roughly the same age as the alleged victims; these people were likely to be dismissed. A grandfather of six, including two at day care centers, confessed to thinking of his own grandchildren when he first heard of the case. Still, he thought he could listen objectively to the evidence. But the judge dismissed him when he conceded that it would be hard to put his grandchildren "a hundred percent" out of his thoughts.

The judge's greatest concern during jury selection was with prospective jurors who hailed from Malden itself. The list of scheduled witnesses included several of the city's doctors, social workers, and police officers. To know any of them cast a shadow of suspicion over a person's qualifications for jury duty. For example, several prospective Malden jurors had sent their own children to a pediatrician who was scheduled to testify. The judge thought that these jurors would be biased in favor of believing whatever the doctor said because they already trusted him enough to place their children in his care.

The contrasting fates of two local Malden residents sum up the way jury selection worked to eliminate pretrial knowledge. Disqualified was a longtime resident who thought he could be impartial but had come into contact with a number of persons on the witness list through his job at the Malden YMCA. The contact was infrequent and involved merely the recreational facilities. Nevertheless, the judge thought it wiser to excuse anyone "tainted" by personal knowledge of trial witnesses. Qualified as an impartial juror was a person who had lived in Malden only two years, who never read the local paper, and who did not even know her neighbor across the hall, let alone the names on the witness list.

At the end of the voir dire, the search for impartial jurors had substantially altered the composition of the jury pool. The remaining panel contained a smaller percentage of Malden residents and no one who had personal knowledge of the witnesses or parties to the case. The average age of jurors was older than that of the venire group, and they were less likely to have children currently at a day care center. The percentage of college-educated jurors had dropped dramatically.

It seems plausible that there was another major difference between the excused jurors and those that remained. Massachusetts law strikingly uses the word "indifferent" to describe the mental posture of the impartial juror. But it is odd to demand indifference in a child rape case. A juror of Asian background was excused for saying that his culture did not tolerate behavior of this sort. The judge explained that Massachusetts law did not tolerate it either, and that the question for trial was whether the defendant did the reprehensible things charged. The prospective juror seemed to understand the point, but the judge excused him anyway, because his remarks betrayed a moral passion at odds with the indifference welcomed as a sign of objectivity.

•

Together, the North and Malden day care cases illustrate what we might call a process of deselecting well-informed citizens, as if civic engagement, concern for the issues on trial, and interest in reading the papers were enemies of fair-mindedness. The Malden case in particular shows just how far we have come from colonial times, when having local knowledge brought a juror praise and being informed made one an ally of justice.

When jury selection works overtime to eliminate persons who follow events closely in the news, judges are assuming that the media have power over people's opinions. Fortunately, recent jury verdicts have called this assumption into question. In 1984 the CBS program "60 Minutes" broadcast an FBI videotape of John DeLorean in a hotel room with a convicted cocaine smuggler and a suitcase full of drugs.[159] In 1991 there was the surefire incriminating videotape of four officers delivering eighty-odd blows to a prostrate Rodney King.[160] In 1990 District of Columbia mayor Marion Barry was captured on tape using cocaine in the Vista Hotel.[161] Finally, there were the riveting television pictures of truck driver Reginald Denny being beaten in the riot that followed the first King verdicts.[162]

In all these instances, virtually everyone forecast convictions. Yet the juries acquitted DeLorean, acquitted or deadlocked on the King police officers during the first trial, convicted Barry of only one minor misdemeanor drug charge and deadlocked on twelve other charges (including the one based on the Vista Hotel tape), and acquitted the Denny defendants of the most serious charges against them. Whatever one thinks of these verdicts, they certainly explode the myth that pretrial publicity—even of a dramatic sort—makes it impossible for defendants to get a fair trial locally.[163]

CONCLUSION: THE PRACTICAL DILEMMAS OF JUDGING

Practically speaking, what are judges to do in cases generating high levels of pretrial publicity? I acknowledge that they will not find the history of local jury traditions reviewed in this chapter immediately useful. Our contemporary notions of impartiality make it a foregone conclusion that judges will have to select juries gingerly whenever a crime touches a community's raw nerve.

Every once and a while a case comes along where the defense prefers to keep the trial local, despite massive publicity. Susan Smith's lawyers understood that she would appear most human to hometown jurors who knew something about her other than that she had drowned her two children. Marion Barry also gained a kind of home field advantage by being tried in the District of Columbia. But these are the exceptions; in most cases, the defense cites pretrial publicity as a reason to move the trial. Any judge who routinely denied motions for changes of venue would therefore soon be accused of being biased against the defendants. This helps explain why the judge in the Oklahoma City bombing case moved the trial to Colorado, after finding that press coverage made it difficult for the defendants to receive a fair trial anywhere in the state of Oklahoma. Likewise, in California, the trial judge had no alternative but to move the trial of Richard Allen Davis, a convicted felon charged with kidnaping and killing a twelve-year-old girl in rural Sonoma County, to another county.

It would be nice if the press developed habits of self-restraint and problems of pretrial publicity simply faded away. But this is unlikely. The Canadian model, where draconian legal restrictions muzzle the press, is also unacceptable in a democracy where the people have important interests in knowing about arrests, indictments, and pretrial hearings. The best that judges in the United States can do, therefore, is to search for ways to avoid changes of venue or wholesale disqualifications of local persons if they deny the venue motion. Certainly judges should use their powers to gag lawyers and litigants: there is especially no reason to tolerate deliberate leaks to the press from government sources. Judges can also grant continuances and postpone a trial's start, in hopes that passions born of publicity will fade. But, unless the defendant waives the right to a speedy trial, the judge's authority to delay a trial is quite limited.

Given the paucity of alternatives, the judge's choice often comes down to granting a change of venue or keeping the trial local but sequestering the jury to combat continuing publicity. Neither choice is satisfactory. Sequestered juries are notoriously unrepresentative, because so many persons can claim hardship on account of their jobs, child care responsibilities, or health. Sequestration also strains relations among jurors and places the group under pressures that grow with the length of the trial. Besides, sequestration probably does not work well to keep the news away from jurors (for instance, how are sheriff's deputies to monitor what gets said during conjugal visits?). For all these reasons, many judges prefer to grant a change of venue, in hopes of finding a new locale where light publicity will make sequestration unnecessary. The problem is that when a trial is moved, many state laws require the judge to move it to the neighboring county. The distance may prove too short to lower the intensity of news coverage. Moreover, as happened in the first trial of the Los Angeles police officers accused of beating Rodney King, the neighboring county may have a dramatically different demographic profile than the county where the crime took place. Changing the venue may thus trade one form of bias (sensationalized news coverage) for another (impaneling a jury that does not represent a cross section of the community affected by the crime). In the aftermath of the King trials, bills were introduced in many state legislatures requiring a judge to consider not only proximity but also demography in choosing a new trial venue. But seeking a venue that is a demographic match to the community where the crime took place creates nightmares of its own. In the Florida trial of William Lozano, a Hispanic police officer who shot and killed a black motorcyclist in Miami, the trial venue shifted five times, as various judges weighed whether the "right" match had been found to Miami's Hispanic/black ratio.[164]

The problems created by changes of venue do not mean a judge should turn a deaf ear to a litigant's complaint about bias in a local jury pool. But candid acknowledgment that even jurors in some distant community will not be perfectly impartial (in the sense of coming to the trial without values or preconceptions rooted in demography) should make us redouble our efforts to keep trials at home. No doubt, robust voir dires will then be necessary to smoke out those persons whose minds are closed by what they have read, heard, or seen in the media. But judges can also be creative during the voir dire, seizing the opportunity to rehabilitate potential jurors, inspire them with a sense of fairness, and appeal to their better instincts.

Many potential jurors will still need to be disqualified. But judges should cease striking persons simply because of their exposure to the media. The voir dire should establish, not just assume, that such exposure prejudices the mind. If we can at least stop "deselecting" news-following jurors so automatically, then we can start closing the often maddening gap between the ideal of the impartial juror and the ideal of the knowledgeable juror.

NOTES

1. *Irvin v. Dowd*, 366 U.S. 717, 722 (1961). ("The theory of our system is that the conclusions to be reached in a case will be induced only by evidence and argument in open court, and not by any outside influence, whether of private talk or public print"). See also *Patterson v. Colorado*, 205 U.S. 454, 462 (1907).

2. *Mylock v. Saladine*, 1 Wm. Blackstone Rep. 480, 481 (1781).

3. *United States v. Parker*, 19 F.Supp. 450, 458 (D.N.J. 1937), *aff'd*, 103 F.2d 857 (3d Cir. 1939), *cert. denied*, 307 U.S. 642 (1939).

4. Jonathan Elliot, *The Debates in the Several State Conventions on the Adoption of the Federal Constitution* (New York: Burt Franklin, 1888), vol. 3, p. 579.

5. *Flannelly v. Delaware & Hudson Co.*, 225 U.S. 597 (1912). For other

examples of cases where local jurors used knowledge of local conditions to resolve factual questions, see Dale W. Broeder, "The Impact of the Vicinage Requirement: An Empirical Look," *Nebraska Law Review* 45 (1966): 99–118.

6. *Crawford v. Georgia*, 489 U.S. 1040 (1989), *reh'g denied*, 490 U.S. 1042 (Marshall, J., dissenting from denial of *cert.*).

7. *Ibid.*, p. 1041. See also *Swindler v. Lockhart*, 495 U.S. 911 (1990) (Marshall, J., dissenting from denial of *cert.*), in which the defendant was granted a change of venue on retrial, but only to a neighboring county, where jury members knew that he had been previously convicted of murder and sentenced to death.

8. *Powell v. Superior Court*, 232 Cal. App. 3d 785, 789, 283 Cal. Rptr. 777, 779 (Cal. Ct. App. 1991). See also Barry Scheck, "Following Orders," *New Republic*, May 25, 1992, p. 17.

9. According to the 1990 U.S. census, 11.2 percent of the Los Angeles County population was black, compared with 2.3 percent of the population in Ventura County. Bureau of the Census, U.S. Department of Commerce, *1990 Census of Population and Housing: Summary Population and Housing Characteristics, California* (Washington, D.C.: U. S. Government Printing Office, 1991), p. 60.

10. Seth Mydans, "The Police Verdict: Los Angeles Policemen Acquitted in Taped Beating," *New York Times*, April 30, 1992, p. A1; Linda Deutsch, "Police Officer Acquitted in King Beating," *Philadelphia Inquirer*, April 30, 1992, p. A1; Andrew Kull, "Racial Justice," *New Republic*, November 30, 1992, p. 17.

11. See, for example, David Margolick, "As Venues Are Changed, Many Ask How Important a Role Race Should Play," *New York Times*, May 23, 1992, p. 7 (Margolick quoted a defense lawyer for one officer as saying, "I wouldn't say the case was won at that point, but if [the change of venue] hadn't been granted, the case would have been lost, no question"); "Out of the Frying Pan or into the Fire? Race and Choice of Venue After Rodney King," *Harvard Law Review* 106 (1993): 705–722; S. Herman, "Justice Sees Through a Glass, Darkly," *Newsday*, May 4, 1992, p. 37.

12. On August 5, 1992, a federal grand jury returned new indictments against the four officers, charging them with violation of Rodney King's civil rights through the use of unreasonable force during arrest. Trial was held this time in the federal judicial district for Los Angeles County, and on April 17, 1993, a racially mixed jury, including two black jurors and one Hispanic juror, convicted two officers and acquitted the other two. Seth Mydans, "2 of 4 Officers Found Guilty in Los Angeles Beating," *New York Times*, April 18, 1993, sec. 1, p. 8.

13. See Newton N. Minow and Fred H. Cate, "Who Is an Impartial Juror in an Age of Mass Media?" *American University Law Review* 40 (1991): 631–664; and Joseph M. Hassett, "A Jury's Pre-Trial Knowledge in Historical Perspective: The Distinction between Pre-Trial Information and "Prejudicial' Publicity," *Law and Contemporary Problems* 43 (1980): 155–168.

14. George Fletcher, *A Crime of Self-Defense: Bernhard Goetz and the Law on Trial* (Chicago: University of Chicago Press, 1988), pp. 6, 85–90.

15. *United States v. North*, 713 F. Supp. 1444, 1445 (D.D.C. 1989), *vacated*, 910 F.2d 843 (1990), *modified* and *reh'g denied*, 920 F.2d 940 (1990), *cert. denied*, 500 U.S. 941 (1991). For a detailed account of the North jury selection, see text accompanying notes 137–147.

16. Michael Wines, "Selection of Jury Begins for North," *New York Times*, February 1, 1989, p. A12.

17. Stephen Salisbury, "Graphic Questions: Potential Mapplethorpe Jurors Are Asked about Their Beliefs," *Philadelphia Inquirer*, September 26, 1990, p. C1.

18. U. S. Constitution, art. III, sec. 2, clause 3.

19. When the Norman kings first invaded England, they were in need of some administrative device for discovering the traditional properties and privileges of the monarchy. They found what they were looking for in the Frankish Empire's practice of holding an inquest or inquisition on the local level and interrogating neighborhood notables for the desired information. From this sworn royal inquest, modern jury trial arose in the twelfth century. To enforce its authority and to bring matters within the jurisdiction of itinerant royal courts, the crown relied on men of the neighborhood (originally the small local area of the vil, or the hundred) to function first as a kind of grand jury making presentments about crimes in the neighborhood and those suspected of a crime. Here, the jurors functioned more like neighbor-witnesses than like impartial judges, "presumed to know before they come into court the facts about which they are to testify." Frederic W. Maitland and Francis C. Montague, *A Sketch of English Legal History* (New York and London: G. P. Putnam's Sons and Knickerbocker Press, 1915), pp. 45–60; Roger D. Groot, "The Jury of Presentment before 1215," *American Journal of Legal History* 26 (1982): 1–24.

Prior to 1215, those "presented" on suspicion of crime still customarily faced trial by ordeal. But in that year the Fourth Lateran Council forbade clergy from participating in the ordeal, thereby withdrawing its divine credentials. In the vacuum created by the loss of trial by ordeal, the presenting jury evolved into the trial jury. Theodore F. T. Plucknett, *A Concise History of the Common Law*, 4th ed. (London: Butterworth, 1948), pp. 104–121; John Marshall Mitnick, "From Neighbor-Witness to Judge of Proofs: The Transformation of the English Civil Juror," *American Journal of Legal History* 32 (1988): 201–235.

20. Sir William Blackstone, *Commentaries on the Laws of England* (Oxford: Clarendon Press, 1769), vol. 4, p. 344. The terms "venue" and "vicinage" should be, but are not always, distinguished. "Venue" refers to the place of trial; "vicinage," to the place where the jury comes from. Usually, the place of jurors and the place of trial will be the same, but it is possible to hold trial in one venue while summoning jurors from another vicinage. This was true in colonial Virginia, where serious cases were tried at the capital but jurors were summoned from the vicinage or county where the crime occurred. See Drew Kershen, "Vicinage," *Oklahoma Law Review* 29 (1976): 801, 831; William Wirt Blume, "The Place of Trial of Criminal Cases: Constitutional Vicinage and Venue," *Michigan Law Review* 43 (1944): 59–60.

21. Elliot, *Debates in Several State Conventions*, vol. 3, p. 112 (Gore quoting Holmes).

22. *Ibid.*, p. 569.

23. *Ibid.*, pp. 541–542.

24. *Ibid.*, p. 569.

25. *Ibid.*, pp. 545, 542, 541.

26. *Ibid.*, p. 578 ("Your juries may be collected five hundred miles from where the party resides"); see also Herbert J. Storing, *The Complete Anti-Federalist* (Chicago: University of Chicago Press, 1981), vol. 2, p. 231, vol. 3, p. 61.

27. John M. Murrin and A. G. Roeber, "Trial by Jury: The Virginia Paradox," in *The Bill of Rights: A Lively Heritage*, ed. John Kukla (Richmond, Va.: Virginia State Library and Archives, 1987), pp. 110, 126.

28. Virginia Declaration of Rights, art. 8 (1776). For a detailed analysis of Vir-

ginia's commitment to jury trials in the seventeenth and eighteenth centuries, see Murrin and Roeber, "Trial by Jury," pp. 109–129. As late as 1750, juries held a less conspicuous position in Virginia than in any other mainland jurisdiction, mattering mostly in capital trials. *Ibid.*

29. The romantic defense of the jury given by the colonies on the eve of the American Revolution was not true to the history of every colony. In his study of early Connecticut, historian Bruce Mann documented a precipitous decline of the civil jury after 1700. At the beginning of the century, civil juries still decided most contested civil cases; by 1745, juries decided 20 percent or fewer cases, depending on the county. Mann connected the civil jury's decline to a general shift from communal ideals for law (where neighbors still judged one another on the basis of shared values) to a formal model for law (where technical rules aimed at predictable and uniform decisions). Bruce H. Mann, *Neighbors and Strangers: Law and Community in Early Connecticut* (Chapel Hill: University of North Carolina Press, 1987), pp. 75–81; Mann, "The Evolutionary Revolution in American Law: A Comment on J. R. Pole's 'Reflections,'" *William and Mary Quarterly*, 3d ser., 50 (1993): p. 171.

In his study of seventeenth-century New England juries, historian John Murrin also found great contrasts. At one extreme were pro-jury colonies established without strong leadership from magisterial elites (e.g., Rhode Island). At the other extreme were anti-jury colonies dominated by powerful magistrates (e.g., New Haven Colony, which abolished juries, even for capital cases). John M. Murrin, "Magistrates, Sinners and a Precarious Liberty: Trial by Jury in Seventeenth-Century New England," in *Saints and Revolutionaries: Essays in Early American History*, ed. David D. Hall, John M. Murrin, and Thad W. Tate (New York: W. W. Norton, 1984), pp. 152–206.

30. William E. Nelson, *Dispute and Conflict Resolution in Plymouth County, Massachusetts, 1725–1825* (Chapel Hill: University of North Carolina Press, 1981), pp. 23–25.

31. John Phillip Reid, *In a Defiant Stance: The Conditions of Law in Massachusetts Bay, The Irish Comparison, and the Coming of the American Revolution* (University Park: The Pennsylvania State University Press, 1977), pp. 28–29.

32. *Ibid.*, p. 29.

33. *Ibid.*, pp. 45, 50–51.

34. *Ibid.*, p. 32.

35. James Alexander, *A Brief Narrative of the Case and Trial of John Peter Zenger*, ed. Stanley Katz (Cambridge: Harvard University Press, 1963).

36. *Penn and Mead's Case*, 6 Howell's State Trials 951 (1670).

37. See, for example, Elliot, *Debates in Several State Conventions*, vol. 2, p. 112, vol. 4, pp. 150, 165; Francis H. Heller, *The Sixth Amendment* (Lawrence: University of Kansas Press, 1951) pp. 1, 27.

38. Heller, *Sixth Amendment*, p. 17.

39. *Ibid.*, p. 20.

40. Kershen, "Vicinage," p. 831; Elliot, *Debates in Several State Conventions*, vol. 4, pp. 150, 467. That there was no uniformity in the colonies in regard to holding trials in the county where the crime occurred can be seen by comparing provisions in the early constitutions adopted by the original thirteen colonies. Maryland (1776), Massachusetts (1780), and New Hampshire (1784) required "the trial of facts where they arise." Virginia (1776) specified a jury of "his [the accused's] vicinage." Pennsylvania (1776) required trial in the "country," changing "country" to

"vicinage" in 1790. Georgia specified trial in the county. But none of the other colonies specified a venue in their early state constitutions. Blume, "Place of Trial," pp. 67–78.

41. Elliot, *Debates in Several State Conventions*, vol. 2, pp. 112–113.

42. *Ibid.*, vol. 4, p. 150.

43. *Ibid.*, vol. 3, p. 537.

44. Kershen, "Vicinage," pp. 816–818 (Virginia, North Carolina, New York, and Rhode Island).

45. Blume, "Place of Trial," p. 68 (legislative language); Elliot, *Debates in Several State Conventions*, vol. 3, pp. 578–579 (Patrick Henry quote).

46. Storing, *Complete Anti-Federalist*, vol. 4, p. 78.

47. An interesting example of the neighbor versus stranger issue is recorded for the year 1694 in the colony of West Jersey, when Janet Monroe went on trial for her life, charged with infanticide. Given an opportunity to challenge the jurors, Monroe noted that they "are strangers to her." Her preference, she said, would have been for jurors who knew her and could vouch for her decency. Larry D. Eldridge, *A Distant Heritage: The Growth of Free Speech in Early America* (New York: New York University Press, 1994), pp. 81–82. In his study of one Puritan county in Massachusetts during the 1600s, historian David Konig also described an early system of local community justice, where arbitrators chosen to settle disputes "were well-acquainted with the facts of the problem, and great efforts were made to find those who were familiar with the dispute." David Thomas Konig, *Law and Society in Puritan Massachusetts: Essex County, 1629–1692* (Chapel Hill: University of North Carolina Press, 1979), p. 109.

48. Elliot, *Debates in Several State Conventions*, vol. 3, p. 547.

49. *Ibid.*, vol. 2, p. 516.

50. Storing, *Complete Anti-Federalist*, vol. 2, p. 249.

51. *Ibid.*

52. *Ibid.*

53. *Ibid.*, pp. 142, 250.

54. Gordon S. Wood, *The Radicalism of the American Revolution* (New York: Alfred A. Knopf, 1992), pp. 258–259.

55. Storing, *Complete Anti-Federalist*, vol. 2, pp. 249, 320.

56. Heller, *Sixth Amendment*, pp. 16–24; Mann, *Neighbors and Strangers*, p. 78 (1715 compilation of long-standing practice that jurors were to own freehold worth forty shillings a year or have personal estate in the county of fifty pounds); Murrin and Roeber, "Trial by Jury," pp. 120–124 (between 1705 and 1748 statutes required jurors in Williamsburg to possess "visible real and personal estate" of one hundred pounds sterling and county jurors to possess estates valued at fifty pounds or more). As the Revolution approached and in its aftermath, several colonies or states lowered property qualifications for voters and jurors, by requiring that a man had only to be a taxpayer. See Willi Paul Adams, *The First American Constitutions: Republican Ideology and the Making of the State Constitutions in the Revolutionary Era*, trans. Rita Kimber and Robert Kimber (Chapel Hill: University of North Carolina Press, 1980), pp. 196–207 and tables at pp. 293–311; Chilton Williamson, *American Suffrage: From Property to Democracy, 1760–1860* (Princeton: Princeton University Press, 1960), pp. 92–137; Merrill Jensen, *The New Nation: A History of the United States during the Confederation, 1781–1789* (New York: Alfred A. Knopf, 1950), p. 128. But in 1787 only the territory of Vermont had abolished taxpaying or property-owning qualifications for voters entirely. Adams, *First American Constitu-*

tions, p. 196; Gordon S. Wood, *The Creation of the American Republic, 1776–1787* (Chapel Hill: University of North Carolina Press, 1969), p. 168.

57. Nelson, *Dispute and Conflict Resolution*, pp. 25–26.

58. Adams, *First American Constitutions*, pp. 207–217.

59. Murrin and Roeber, "Trial by Jury," p. 120; Albert W. Alschuler, "The Supreme Court and the Jury: Voir Dire, Peremptory Challenges and the Review of Judgments," *University of Chicago Law Review* 56 (1989): 153, 164.

60. See Cecilia M. Kenyon, "Men of Little Faith: The Anti-Federalists on the Nature of Representative Government," *William and Mary Quarterly* 12 (1955): 3, 43.

61. Letter of Jefferson to the Abbe Arnoux, July 19, 1789, in *The Papers of Thomas Jefferson*, ed. Julian P. Boyd (Princeton: Princeton University Press, 1958), vol. 15, p. 283.

62. William E. Nelson, *Americanization of the Common Law: The Impact of Legal Change On Massachusetts Society, 1760–1830* (Cambridge: Harvard University Press, 1975), p. 3.

63. *Ibid.*

64. *Diary and Autobiography of John Adams*, ed. L. H. Butterfield (Cambridge: Harvard University Press, 1961), vol. 2, p. 5.

65. Nelson, *Americanization of the Common Law*, p. 3.

66. *Ibid.*, p. 29.

67. Mann, *Neighbors and Strangers*, pp. 75, 71.

68. *Ibid.*, p. 74.

69. Amasa M. Eaton, "The Development of the Judicial System in Rhode Island," *Yale Law Journal* 14 (1905): 148, 153. This source came to my attention through Shannon C. Stimson, *The American Revolution in the Law: Anglo-American Jurisprudence before John Marshall* (Princeton: Princeton University Press, 1990), p. 49.

70. Mark DeWolfe Howe, "Juries as Judges of Criminal Law," *Harvard Law Review* 52 (1939): 582, 591.

71. Nelson, *Americanization of the Common Law*, p. 29; J. R. Pole, "Forum: Reflections on American Law and the American Revolution," *William and Mary Quarterly*, 3d ser., 50 (1993): 123, 126–127, 130–132; Reid, *In a Defiant Stance*, pp. 27–64.

72. J. R. Pole, "Reflections on American Law and the American Revolution," *William and Mary Quarterly*, 3d ser., 50 (1993): 136. Pole also found the jury's role to be more political and representative than judicial. *Ibid.*, p. 128. His conclusions have been criticized for exaggerating the jury's importance in shaping law. See Mann, "The Evolutionary Revolution," pp. 168–175; Peter Charles Hoffer, "Custom as Law: A Comment on J. R. Pole's 'Reflections'"; and James A. Henretta and James D. Rice, "Law as Litigation: An Agenda for Research," *William and Mary Quarterly*, 3d ser., 50 (1993): 160–167; 176–180.

73. Quoted in Stimson, *The American Revolution in the Law*, p. 88.

74. Storing, *Complete Anti-Federalist*, vol. 2, p. 320.

75. *Ibid.*

76. *Ibid.*, p. 321.

77. *Ibid.*

78. *Ibid.*, p. 320.

79. *Diary and Autobiography of John Adams*, vol. 2, p. 5; Nelson, *Americanization of the Common Law*, p. 26.

80. *Ibid.*

81. Storing, *Complete Anti-Federalist*, vol. 2, p. 320.

82. *Ibid.*, p. 250.

83. *Ibid.*, vol. 5, p. 39 (emphasis in original).

84. Edward Dumbauld, *The Bill of Rights and What It Means Today* (Norman: University of Oklahoma Press, 1957), p. 183 (Virginia), p. 200 (North Carolina).

85. Kershen, "Vicinage," p. 817; Dumbauld, *The Bill of Rights*, pp. 31–32 (Rhode Island), 175–177 (Massachusetts), 173–175 (Pennsylvania minority), 190 (New York).

86. Kershen, "Vicinage," p. 818, quoting *Annals of Congress*, 1st Cong., 1st sess., vol. 1, p. 435; Heller, *Sixth Amendment*, p. 30.

87. Kershen, "Vicinage," pp. 820–821; Dumbauld, *The Bill of Rights*, p. 215.

88. Dumbauld, *The Bill of Rights*, pp. 213–216.

89. Kershen, "Vicinage," p. 822; Dumbauld, *The Bill of Rights*, p. 214.

90. *The Papers of James Madison*, ed. Charles F. Hobson and Robert A. Rutland (Charlottesville: University of Virginia Press, 1979), vol. 12, p. 419.

91. Kershen, "Vicinage," p. 822.

92. *Ibid.*, p. 825.

93. *Annals of Congress*, vol. 1, p. 913.

94. Blume, "Place of Trial," p. 66.

95. Maeva Marcus, ed., *The Documentary History of the Supreme Court of the United States, 1789–1800* (New York: Columbia University Press, 1992), vol. 4, p. 29.

96. *Ibid.*, pp. 91–92; Charles Warren, "New Light on the History of the Federal Judiciary Act of 1789," *Harvard Law Review* 37 (1923): 49, 105–106.

97. Marcus, *Documentary History of Supreme Court*, vol. 4, p. 92.

98. Compare *United States v. Hutchings*, 26 Fed. Cas. 440, 442 (C.C.D. Va. 1817) (No. 15,429) (Marshall, J., instructing criminal jury that they were not bound to accept his opinion of the law), with *United States v. Battiste*, 24 Fed. Cas. 1042 (C.C.D. Mass. 1835) (No. 14,545) (Story, J., denying that jury has any right to decide contested points of law). For a fuller discussion of the jury's loss of lawmaking and law-nullifying authority, see Jeffrey Abramson, *We, the Jury: The Jury System and the Ideal of Democracy* (New York: Basic Books, 1994), ch. 2.

99. *Georgia v. Brailsford*, 3 U.S. (3 Dall.) 1, 4 (1794).

100. *Sparf and Hansen v. United States*, 156 U.S. 51 (1895).

101. *United States v. Burr*, 25 Fed. Cas. 55, 87–88 (C.C.D. Va. 1807) (No. 14,693); Albert J. Beveridge, *The Life of John Marshall* (Boston: Houghton Mifflin, 1919), vol. 3, pp. 274–387.

102. *United States v. Burr*, 25 Fed. Cas. 49 (C.C.D. Va. 1807) (No. 14,692g).

103. Paul S. Clarkson and R. Samuel Jett, *Luther Martin of Maryland* (Baltimore: Johns Hopkins Press, 1970), p. 247 n. 6.

104. 25 Fed. Cas. at 55–56, 59.

105. *Ibid.*, p. 56 n. 2.

106. On June 24, 1994, a California state judge took the highly unusual step of dismissing a grand jury that was considering whether to indict O. J. Simpson for the murder of his ex-wife and Ronald Goldman. The judge acted after both the prosecution and defense expressed concern that the grand jurors had been exposed to prejudicial pretrial publicity—most notably the release of tapes of 911 calls made by Nicole Brown Simpson after her former husband broke down the back door to her house. Seth Mydans, "Citing News Deluge, Simpson Judge Excuses Grand Jury," *New York Times*, June 25, 1994, p. 1.

For federal courts, Fed. R. Crim. P. 6b(1) provides that a defendant may challenge "the array of jurors on the ground that the grand jury was not selected, drawn or summoned in accordance with law, and may challenge an individual juror on the ground that the juror is not legally qualified." An earlier draft of the rule did allow challenges for bias or prejudice, but this permission was omitted in the final draft. *Estes v. United States*, 335 F.2d 609, 613 n. 7 (5th cir. 1964), *cert. denied*, 379 U.S. 964 (1965). See also Lester B. Orfield, *Orfield's Criminal Procedure under the Federal Rules* (Rochester and San Franciso: Lawyers Cooperative and Bancroft-Whitney, 1985), vol. 1, pp. 263–334; vol. 4, p. 44 (challenge for bias, "however appropriate in the selection of trial jurors, is wholly irrelevant and improvident in the case of members of the grand jury which prefers the charge and which of course should be scrupulously fair but not necessarily uninformed or impartial").

107. 25 Fed. Cas. at 56 n. 3.

108. *Ibid.*, p. 57.

109. *Ibid.*

110. *Ibid.*

111. *Ibid.*

112. Clarkson and Jett, *Luther Martin*, p. 247 n. 7.

113. Beveridge, *Life of John Marshall*, vol. 3, p. 413, n. 1.

114. *Ibid.*, p. 475.

115. 25 Fed. Cas. 49.

116. Beveridge, *Life of John Marshall*, vol. 3, p. 482.

117. 25 Fed. Cas. at 77.

118. *Ibid.*, p. 80.

119. *United States* v. *Callender*, 25 Fed. Cas. 239, 244–245 (C.C.D. Va. 1800) (No. 14,709). See also *Burr*, 25 Fed. Cas. at 77. For an excellent discussion of the *Callendar* case, see Kathryn Preyer, "United States v. Callendar: Judge and Jury in Republican Society," in *Essays on the Judiciary Act of 1989*, ed. Maeva Marcus (New York: Oxford University Press, 1992), pp. 173–195.

120. 25 Fed. Cas. at 76.

121. *Ibid.*, p. 51.

122. *Ibid.*, pp. 84–85.

123. Hawkins, quoted in Hassett, "A Jury's Pre-Trial Knowledge," p. 162; *Burr*, 25 Fed. Cas. at 52. I am indebted to Hassett for the point made in the text about Hawkins and Marshall.

124. 25 Fed. Cas. at 52.

125. *Ibid.*, p. 77.

126. *Ibid.*, p. 51.

127. Hassett, "A Jury's Pre-Trial Knowledge," pp. 162–163.

128. 25 Fed. Cas. at 81.

129. *The Papers of John Marshall*, ed. Charles F. Hobson (Chapel Hill: University of North Carolina Press, 1993), vol. 7, pp. 5, 8–9, 74–119.

130. Mark Twain, *Roughing It* (Hartford: American Publishing, 1903), vol. 2, p. 75.

131. Minow and Cate, "Who Is an Impartial Juror," pp. 631, 636 n. 22.

132. *United States* v. *Anguilo*, 897 F.2d 1169, 1180–1183 (1st Cir. 1990), *cert. denied*, 498 U.S. 845 (1990); *United States v. Helmsley*, 726 F. Supp. 929 (S.D.N.Y. 1989), *cert. denied*, 502 U.S. 1091 (1992); Paul Craig Roberts, "Leona May Be Guilty, But Not as Charged," *Wall Street Journal*, April 19, 1992, p. A14.

133. Typical of the complaints about local juries and pretrial publicity were those

made by Pamela Smart in her celebrated 1991 New Hampshire trial for conspiring with her high school students to murder her husband. In arguing unsuccessfully for a change of venue, Smart stressed the sheer number of articles about her in the print media (nearly twelve hundred), in addition to blanket radio and television coverage. She derided the inflammatory nature of newspaper headlines, such as "Smart Wanted Key Witness Killed, Police Say." She objected to the "circus-like" atmosphere surrounding the court during jury selection that was created by the "overpowering physical presence" of reporters, equipment, satellite trucks, and the like. The combined effect of the media barrage reduced the trial process to a "Roman circus" acted out in the "white heat glare of media scrutiny." *State of New Hampshire v. Pamela Smart*, 136 N.H. 639 (1993).

134. *Mu'Min v. Virginia*, 500 U.S. 420–422 (1991) (details of alleged confession); *Patton v. Yount*, 467 U.S. 1025 (1984) (defendant objected to media reports of suppressed confession inadmissible on retrial); *Murphy v. Florida*, 421 U.S. 794, 798–799 (1975) (media barrage about defendant's prior convictions and notoriety as Star of India jewel thief).

135. Minow and Cate, "Who Is an Impartial Juror," pp. 646–647.

136. The Supreme Court has reiterated that "mere familiarity with the petitioner or his past" is not disqualifying; there must be an "actual predisposition against him." *Murphy v. Florida*, 421 U.S. 794, 800–801 n. 4 (1975). The relevant question, the Court noted in 1984, "is not whether the community remembered the case, but whether the jurors . . . had such fixed opinions that they could not judge impartially the guilt of the defendant." *Patton v. Yount*, 467 U.S. 1025, 1035 (1984). See also *Irvin v. Dowd*, 366 U.S. 717, 722–723 (1961); *Holt v. United States*, 218 U.S. 245 (1901); *Spies v. Illinois*, 123 U.S. 131 (1887); *Reynolds v. United States*, 98 U.S. 145, 156–157 (1878); *Yount v. Patton*, 710 F.2d 956, 972 (3d Cir. 1983) (Stern, J., concurring) (*Burr* has been standard for 175 years), *rev'd*, 467 U.S. 1025 (1984).

137. *Yount v. Patton*, 710 F.2d 956, 972 (3d Cir. 1983) (Stern, J., concurring), *rev'd*, 467 U.S. 1025 (1984).

138. Jim Newton, "Prospective King Jurors Get Bias Questionnaire," *Los Angeles Times*, Feb. 4, 1993, p. A1.

139. *Yount v. Patton*, 710 F.2d. at 972.

140. *Patton v. Yount*, 467 U.S. at 1031 (referring to *Irvin v. Dowd*, 366 U.S. 717, 725). See also *State v. Laaman*, 114 N.H. 794, 798, 331 A.2d 354, 357 (1974), *cert. denied*, 423 U.S. 854 (1975) ("inherent prejudice . . . exists when the publicity by its nature has so tainted the trial atmosphere that it will necessarily result in lack of due process").

141. *Rideau v. Louisiana*, 373 U.S. 723, 726–727 (1963).

142. *Irvin v. Dowd*, 366 U.S. at 725–728. In a 1977 case, the Court rejected any suggestion that its decision in *Irvin* rested on "presuming" bias. Instead, the Court emphasized that *Irvin* turned on evidence of "actual bias" in eight of the twelve persons selected as jurors. See *Murphy v. Florida*, 421 U.S. 794, 798 (1977).

143. *Sheppard v. Maxwell*, 384 U.S. 333, 358 (1966); *Estes v. Texas*, 381 U.S. 532 (1965).

144. "Must Ignorance Be a Virtue in Our Search for Justice? Panel Two. Current Judicial Practice, Legal Issues, and Existing Remedies," *American University Law Review* 40 (1991): 573, 581.

145. *Murphy v. Florida*, 421 U.S. 794, 799 (1977) (no presumption of prejudice from pervasive reporting of famous jewel thief's prior convictions).

146. *Patton v. Yount*, 467 U.S. 1025 (1984).

147. *Mu'Min v. Virginia*, 500 U.S. 415, 422 (1991). The defendant complained that the publicity was especially prejudicial, because it compared his crime with that of Willie Horton, made famous during the 1988 presidential election.

148. David Johnston, "North Guilty on 3 of 12 Counts; Vows to Fight Til 'Vindicated,'; Bush Denies a Contra Aid Deal," *New York Times*, May 5, 1989, p. A1.

149. Richard Moran and Peter d'Errico, "An Impartial Jury or an Ignorant One?" *Boston Globe*, Feb. 12, 1989, p. A18.

150. *United States v. North*, 713 F. Supp. 1444, 1445 (D.D.C. 1989), *Vacated*, 910 F.2d 843 (1990), *Modified and reh'g denied*, 920 F.2d 940 (1990), *cert. denied*, 500 U.S. 941 (1991).

151. Dennis Bell, "North Jury Selection Begins; Effect of Iran-contra Hearings at Issue," *Newsday*, Feb. 1, 1989, p. 7.

152. Fred Kaplan, "North Jurors Won Seats with Blissful Ignorance," *Boston Globe*, April 22, 1989, p. 3.

153. Bell, "North Jury Selection Begins," p. 7; Kenneth Winkler, "A Verdict on the Jurors," *Newsday*, March 21, 1989, p. 56.

154. Winkler, "Verdict on Jurors," p. 56.

155. Hassett, "A Jury's Pre-Trial Knowledge," p. 156. See also Bruce Fein, "Face-Off: Picking the Oliver North Jury," *USA Today*, Feb. 9, 1989, p. 8A.

156. Johnston, "North Guilty," p. A1; David E. Rosenbaum, "Jurors See North as a Scapegoat for His Superiors," *New York Times*, May 6, 1989, p. A1.

157. In an epilogue that underscored the tension between impartiality and knowledge in the *North* case, the U.S. court of appeals vacated even the three convictions against North, and remanded the case to the district court for a hearing to ensure that the government made no use of North's immunized testimony. North was never retried. *United States v. North*, 910 F.2d 843, *modified* and *reh'g denied* 920 F.2d 940 (1990). The difficulty of finding impartial jurors in highly publicized cases was front-page news again in 1993, when Erik and Lyle Menendez came to trial on charges of killing their wealthy parents. The story made for sensational news because the state alleged that the brothers killed for the inheritance, whereas the brothers claimed fear of a sexually abusive father. Jury selection started in June with a phenomenal 1,017 persons—larger than usual not only because of pretrial publicity but because separate juries were needed for the brothers. By July 7, only 180 jurors remained eligible. Struck for cause was a juror who said media reports made him think of the defendants as "wealthy, spoiled kids." Acceptable was the person who read "only *Cosmopolitan* and *Water Ski Magazine.*" After five months of trial testimony, both juries deadlocked. Alan Abrahamson, "Menendez Brothers' Murder Trial Opens," *Los Angeles Times*, June 15, 1993, p. B3; Abrahamson, "Lyle Menendez Case Ends in Mistrial; D.A. to Retry Brothers," *Los Angeles Times*, January 29, 1994, p. A1.

158. The accounts of jury selection come from my own observations of the process.

159. Steven Brill, *Trial by Jury* (New York: American Lawyers Books/Touchstone, 1989), p. 230.

160. Seth Mydans, "The Police Verdict: Los Angeles Policemen Acquitted in Taped Beating," *New York Times*, April 30, 1992, p. A1.

161. William Raspberry, "The Verdict for Barry and a Verdict for the City," *Washington Post*, Aug. 11, 1990, p. C1.

162. Seth Mydans, "Jury Acquits 2 on Most Charges in Beatings in Los Angeles Riots," *New York Times*, Oct. 19, 1993, p. A1.

163. Minow and Cate point out that "regular exposure to media" may be preferable in jurors, because it inculcates the same habits of "evaluating the barrage of . . . rhetoric" that are necessary in the jury room. Minow and Cate, "Who Is an Impartial Juror," p. 658. They quote former CBS law correspondent Fred Graham to similar effect: "I was assigned by CBS to cover a series of some of the most sensational trials of the century [Watergate, Hinckley, Connelly, DeLorean]. It became absolutely clear to me that *jurors were absolutely unphased* [sic] by all of that broadcasting that my colleagues and I had been doing on television. . . . As citizens, [jurors] were given responsibility over the high and the mighty. They were not going to let someone like me tell them what to think because I had been on television two and a half minutes on a few nights when they had sat through six weeks of trial; it was so clear to me that we were not affecting that process." *Ibid.*, p. 659.

164. Larry Rohter, "Florida Trial Odyssey Ends for an Officer Charged in 2 Killings," *New York Times*, May 9, 1993, sec. 1, p. 16.

Doing Death: Violence, Responsibility, and the Role of the Jury in Capital Trials

AUSTIN SARAT

Let's do it.

—*Gary Gilmore*

Let's get on with it.

—*William Rehnquist*

"CAPITAL PUNISHMENT," George Kateb notes with unqualified directness, "is evil."[1] It is a particular evil in a constitutional democracy because, as Kateb puts it, "the institution of capital punishment strengthens the sentiment that the state owns the lives of the people."[2] The death penalty is dangerous, if not deadly, to constitutional democracy because of its insidious impact on our political lives, our lives as citizens. Yet everyday citizens are put to death in and through legal rituals that enlist other citizens as authorizing agents.

In spite of the enthusiasms of persons as seemingly different as Gary Gilmore and William Rehnquist, and the substantial public support that the death penalty continues to garner, it is nonetheless unsettling that the United States clings tenaciously to such a policy long after almost all other democratic nations have abandoned it.[3] It is unsettling because the conscious, deliberate taking of life as an instrument of state policy is always an evil, but never more so than in a constitutional democracy. The conscious, deliberate taking of life as an instrument of state policy "strains an unspoken premise of the democratic state."[4] That premise may variously be named respect for the equal moral worth or equal dignity of all persons.[5] Democratically administered capital punishment, punishment in which citizens act in an official capacity to approve the deliberate killing of other citizens, contradicts and diminishes the respect for the worth or dignity of all persons that is the enlivening value of democratic politics.[6] And a death penalty democratically administered, a death penalty that enlists citizens to do the work of dealing death to other citizens, implicates us all as agents of law's violence.

In this chapter I want to explore how citizens, in their roles as jurors, allow themselves to participate in the capital punishment process. I take up this question through an investigation of the way jurors read and interpret the discourse and representational practices of capital trials in order to enable them to authorize and lend themselves to the project of using lethal violence, the violence Kateb calls "evil," as an aspect of state policy. Writing about the continuing place of the death penalty in our apparatus of criminal justice, Justice Stevens noted the essential role of the jury in both administering and legitimizing that punishment. "If the State wishes to execute a citizen," Stevens wrote,

> it must persuade a jury of his peers that death is an appropriate punishment for his offense. . . . If the prosecutor cannot convince a jury that the defendant deserves to die, there is an unjustifiable risk that the imposition of that punishment will not reflect the community's sense of the defendant's "moral guilt." . . . *Furman* and its progeny provide no warrant for—indeed do not tolerate— the exclusion from the capital sentencing process of the jury and the critical contribution only it can make toward linking the administration of capital punishment to community values.[7]

By highlighting the jury's place in the administration of capital punishment, Stevens called attention to something that is widely taken for granted but is nonetheless quite remarkable, namely, the fact that ordinary citizens are regularly enlisted as authorizing agents for law's own lethal brand of violence, for the "evil" that the state perpetrates in their and our name. This kind of democratically administered death penalty is a reminder of a venerable, yet enduring problem in social life, namely, the question of how people come to participate in projects of violence, of how cultural inhibitions against the infliction of pain can be turned into cultural enthusiasms in the acts of otherwise decent persons.[8]

Along with the right to make war,[9] the death penalty is the ultimate measure of sovereignty and the ultimate test of political power. "Political power," John Locke wrote, ". . . [is] the right of making laws with penalties of death."[10] But for Kateb, such penalties manifest a wish and desire that have no place in our politics; as he puts it, "[T]he state's power deliberately to destroy innocuous (though guilty) life is a manifestation of the hidden wish that the state be allowed to do anything it pleases with life."[11]

The right to dispose of human life through sovereign acts was traditionally thought to be a direct extension of the personal power of kings.[12] With the transition from monarchical to democratic regimes, some theorists argued that the maintenance of capital punishment was essential to the demonstration that sovereignty could reside in the people. For such theorists, if the sovereignty of the people was to be genuine, it had to ape the sovereign power and prerogatives of monarchy. Rather than seeing the true task of democracy as the transformation of sovereignty and its prerogatives in the hope of reconciling them with a commitment to respecting the dignity of all persons, the death penalty was miraculously transformed from an instrument of political terror used by "them" against "us," to our own instrument wielded consensually by some of us against others.[13] Thus punishment became a key to understanding modern mechanisms of consent.[14]

And if the death penalty is, on this account, the ultimate measure of popular sovereignty, capital trials are the moment when that sovereignty is most vividly on display. Indeed, capital trials have displaced execution itself as the venue for the display of sovereignty, since, in regard to the death penalty, "[p]unishment . . . (has) become the most hidden part of the penal process."[15] As Foucault argues,

> This has several consequences: . . . [punishment] leaves the domain of more or less everyday perception and enters that of abstract consciousness; its effectiveness is seen as resulting from its inevitability, not from its visible intensity; it is the certainty of being punished and not the horrifying spectacle of public punishment that must discourage crime. . . . As a result, justice no longer takes public responsibility for the violence that is bound up with its practice.[16]

But, to use Foucault's phrase, justice, by which he really means law, cannot completely or fully severe its responsibility for violence.

To take but one particularly striking recent example, the much-publicized execution of Robert Alton Harris in 1992 is a telling reminder of the continuing linkage of law and violence.[17] During the twelve-hour period immediately preceding Harris's execution, no less than four separate stays were issued by the Court of Appeals for the Ninth Circuit.[18] Ultimately, in an exasperated and unusually dramatic response to the seemingly endless appeals in capital cases—"Let's get on with it"—the Supreme Court took the virtually unprecedented, and seemingly illegal, step of ordering that "no further stays shall be entered . . . except upon order of this court."[19] With this order, the Court stopped the talking and took upon itself the responsibility for Harris's execution.

Contra Foucault, seldom has the law's own role as a doer of death been so visible. Yet just as the law's role was rendered unusually visible, Harris's death was, as Foucault would have it, rendered invisible. His execution was carried out, as is the modern custom, behind penitentiary walls, beyond public view.[20] In this way the penalty of death is linked to the privilege of viewing.[21]

Silencing the condemned and limiting the visibility of lawfully imposed death is part of the modern bureaucratization of capital punishment,[22] and part of the strategy for transforming execution from an arousing public spectacle of vengeance to a soothing matter of mere administration.[23] In Foucault's words, "[I]t . . . (was) as if this rite that 'concluded the crime' was suspected of being in some undesirable way linked with it. It was as if the punishment was thought to equal, if not exceed, in savagery the crime itself . . . to make the executioner resemble a criminal, judges murderers."[24] The ferocity of death at the hands of the law as well as its premeditated quality arouse anxiety and fear; they suggest that law's violence bears substantial traces of the violence it is designed to deter and punish.[25] The bloodletting that such acts signal strains against and ultimately disrupts all efforts to normalize or routinize them and cover their tracks.

While execution itself is effectively hidden from public view, the spectacle of law's dealings in death is (re)located and made visible in capital trials.[26] The formality, complexity, and ritual of capital trials displace, at least symbolically and analogically, execution itself as the site of law's violent majesty. Such trials provide one striking example of what Robert Cover called the "field of pain and death"[27] on which law acts. While that formality, complexity, and ritual seek to allay fear of law's violence by exemplifying the way law differs from mere slaughter, in capital trials the violence of law is inscribed in struggles to put violence into discourse and to control its discursive representation.[28] In capital trials we focus on the case rather than the body of the condemned.[29]

As a result, the Supreme Court has invested enormous effort in regulating the conduct of capital trials, insisting almost two decades ago that because "death is different,"[30] capital trials must be conducted according to procedures designed to ensure their special reliability.[31] In these procedures the jury plays a special role.[32] It provides the mechanism through which the death penalty is made an instrument of popular sovereignty;[33] it provides the mechanism through which citizens are enlisted to authorize the ferocious, life-ending violence of law. It helps do the complex deed of differentiating the violence of law from the violence to which law is opposed.[34] A jury's decision to impose a death sentence expresses public condemnation for the violence that exists just beyond law's boundary while muting the violence of law, shading and toning it down, and rendering it acceptable, thus making the act of the executioner a kind violence which can be approved and rationally dispensed.

THE CENTRALITY OF THE JURY IN THE JURISPRUDENCE OF DEATH

In capital trials the force of law is represented as serving common purposes and advancing common aims, as against the anomic or sectarian savagery beyond law's boundaries.[35] Capital trials are thus both the field of pain and death on which law plays and the field of its discursive representation. And, as Robert Weisberg argues, such trials provide "a representational medium that . . . serves as a grammar of social symbols. . . . The criminal trial is a 'miracle play' of government in which we carry out our inarticulate beliefs about crime and criminals within the reassuring formal structure of disinterested due process."[36]

The "we" to whom Weisberg refers is, in the instance of capital trials, made literal in and through the central role assigned to the jury in contemporary death penalty jurisprudence. It is the jury that represents, in the context of the death penalty, the fullest actualization of popular sovereignty, of the right of the people to exercise power over life and death.[37] As Judge Patrick Higginbotham put it, "[T]he history of the death penalty and the history of juries are entangled."[38] "This," Higginbotham contends,

> should not be a surprise. The choice between a sentence of life or death is uniquely laden with expressions of anger and retribution. . . . By its nature it is a decision that we instinctively believe is best made by a group of citizens, because a group of citizens better represents community values and because responsibility for such a decision is best shared. Equally the ultimate call is visceral. The decision must occur past the point to which legalistic reasoning can carry; it necessarily reflects a gut-level hunch as to what is just.[39]

The jury, in Higginbotham's view, both stands in for and re-presents the vengeful anger of the democratic community,[40] which is the truest expression of community values.[41] The jury's justice is itself a kind of violent transgression of both reason and law. Because of the gravity and uniqueness of a decision to sentence someone to death, the juror voting on whether to authorize a killing by the state, on Higginbotham's account, knows no law.[42] As Justice Stevens has observed, "[I]n the final analysis, capital punishment rests not on a legal but on an ethical judgment. . . . [T]he decision that capital punishment is the appropriate sanction in the extreme cases is justified because it expresses the community's moral sensibility—its demand that a given affront to humanity requires retribution. . . ."[43]

Because jurors give voice to the community's instincts, they help to diffuse responsibility for the punishment of death when it is authorized. Here, then, is an important reformulation of the problematic of popular sovereignty and the death penalty. On the one hand, the juror speaks in the powerful, angry, retributive tones of a sovereign assaulted; on the other hand, the juror speaks in the muted, timid tones of someone whose sovereignty exists as an act of displaced blame.

Beginning with *McGautha v. California*,[44] the Supreme Court has struggled to come to terms with this contradictory image of the jury in capital cases. Since the mid-1970s, the Court has alternated between expressing expansive faith in and support for the jury as a reliable, trustworthy repository of the sovereign right over the lives of citizens and expressing doubt and concern about the jury's capacity to exercise that power responsibly.[45] Throughout, the Court has labored to define the jury's role as the crucial decisionmaker in the capital punishment process.[46]

McGautha provided the framing conception for the constitutional struggle that was to follow. In that case, the defendant alleged that a California statute that left the "decision whether the defendant should live or die . . . to the absolute discretion of the jury" violated due process of law.[47] This claim evoked two very different responses: one, from Justice Harlan, embraced the California scheme, and with it, expansive power for the jury in capital cases, while the other, from Justice Brennan, rejected that scheme in the hope of encouraging legislatures to provide standards or guidelines to limit jury power.[48] Both Harlan and Brennan, however, used the language of sovereignty and consent to speak about the jury's role in capital cases, and both recognized the jury, not the legislature, as the locus of law's death-dealing power.

For Harlan, the comparison between legislature and jury was distinctly favorable to the latter. In capital cases, for the final decision to be acceptable, it has to be based on a highly individualized assessment of a myriad of factors peculiar to each crime and criminal. This detailed judgment was, in Harlan's view, precisely the kind that legislative assemblies were incapable of making. Unbridled jury discretion to choose who shall die from among all those who commit capital offenses was both just and necessary given what Harlan saw as legislative disability. As he put it,

> Those who have come to terms with the hard task of actually attempting to draft means of channeling capital sentencing discretion have confirmed. . . . [that] [t]o identify before the fact those characteristics of criminal homicides and their perpetrators which call for the death penalty, and to express these characteristics in language which can be fairly understood and applied by the sentencing authority appear to be tasks which are beyond present human ability.[49]

In Harlan's view, words are unable to contain and convey the authorizing requisites for capital punishment. Language fails. It is made impossible in the face of death. As a result, legal authority must respond to linguistic inadequacy. If legislatures are unable to speak about the pain and death that the law dispenses, there is no choice but to legitimate the de facto discretion of the jury.

But the impossibility of specifying, in advance, standards to determine the particular criminals who should be executed was, for Harlan, not enough to justify a sovereign role for the jury. What was needed, in addition, was an image of how the jury would use its sovereign power. Here, the best Harlan could do was to engage in a Tocquevillian imagining of the jury ennobled by the responsibility given to it.[50] In this imagining,

> jurors confronted with the truly awesome responsibility of decreeing death for a fellow human will act with due regard for the consequences of their decision and will consider a variety of factors. . . . For a court to attempt to catalog the appropriate factors in this elusive area could inhibit rather than expand the scope of consideration. . . . The infinite variety of cases and facets to each case would make general standards either meaningless "boiler-plate" or a statement of the obvious that no jury would need.[51]

In Brennan's view, there was neither persuasive evidence of legislative inability to provide structuring guidelines nor reason to assume that unbridled discretion would not, like all exercises of such unfettered power, produce arbitrariness and discrimination rather than reason and responsibility. Brennan countered Harlan's theory of linguistic failure by surveying a variety of means and mechanisms that legislatures might employ to communicate with the jury and to guide it in its interpretive task.[52] "A legislature," Brennan argued,

> that has determined that the State should kill some but not all of the persons whom it has convicted of certain crimes must inevitably determine how the State is to distinguish those who are to be killed from those who are not. Depending ultimately on the legislature's notion of wise penological policy, that distinction may be hard or easy to make. But capital sentencing is not the only difficult question which legislatures have ever faced.[53]

In addition, Brennan rejected Harlan's Tocquevillian optimism regarding jury sovereignty and substituted a hardheaded kind of due process realism. The power and responsibility that Harlan saw as ennobling, Brennan believed to be fraught with the danger of abuse. As he put it, "[T]he Due Process Clause of the Fourteenth Amendment is fundamentally inconsistent with capital sentencing procedures that are purposely constructed to allow the maximum possible variation from one case to the next, and provide no mechanism to prevent that consciously maximized variation from reflecting merely random or arbitrary choice."[54] Brennan suggested that Harlan would ask us to choose between "the rule of law and the power of the states to kill" and to resolve the conflict "in favor of the State's power to kill."[55]

Two years after *McGautha*, this choice was repudiated and undone by the Court's decision in *Furman v. Georgia*.[56] In *Furman*, the Court held that the unbridled discretion Harlan had embraced in *McGautha* was, as Brennan suggested it should be, constitutionally unacceptable. Yet in *Furman*, the Justices continued to wrestle with the problem of defining the jury's proper role in capital trials. Like Brennan, Justice Douglas feared that leaving juries with the untrammeled discretion to decide who should live and who should die would ensure "selective and irregular use" of the death penalty and allow the punishment of death to be reserved for "minorities whose numbers are few, who are outcasts of society, and who are unpopular, but whom society is willing to see suffer."[57] Instead of Tocquevillian responsibility, Douglas suggested that jury sovereignty meant that "[p]eople live or die, dependent on the whim of one man or of 12."[58]

Against Douglas's doubt, Chief Justice Burger took up Harlan's defense of jury sovereignty in capital cases. Burger suggested that "trust in lay jurors . . . [is] the cornerstone of our system of criminal justice"[59] and that juries, as the " 'conscience of the community,' " are properly "entrusted to determine in individual cases that the ultimate punishment is warranted."[60] Jurors in capital cases, facing the awesome decision about whether one of their fellow citizens should live or die are, on Burger's account, "meticulous" in their decisions,[61] and "cautious and discriminating [in their] reservation of . . . [the death] penalty for the most extreme cases."[62]

The Harlan/Burger advocacy of complete jury sovereignty was finally put to rest by the Court in *Gregg v. Georgia*,[63] when it upheld a Georgia statute whose purpose was to provide guidance to jurors in selecting those who should actually receive the death penalty from among the class of convicted capital murderers. Justice Stewart, writing for the majority, held that jury discretion "on a matter so grave as the determination of whether a human life should be taken or spared . . . must be suitably directed and limited so as to minimize the risk of arbitrary and capricious action."[64] Absent such direction, he claimed, "juries imposed the death sentence in a way that could only be called freakish."[65]

Stewart, finally completing the work begun by Brennan in *McGautha*, rejected Harlan's arguments about the linguistic impossibility of formulating standards to provide such direction by saying that "while some have suggested that standards to guide a capital jury's sentencing deliberation are impossible to formulate, the fact is that such standards have been developed."[66] He argued that it was particularly important to provide such standards for a jury because "members of a jury will have had little, if any, previous experience in sentencing."[67] Standards that direct the jury's attention to the specific circumstances of the crime and of the person who committed the crime would, in Stewart's view, be sufficient to "produce non-discriminatory application" of the death penalty.[68]

Yet despite Stewart's apparent confidence in the efficacy of legislative standards in ensuring the rationality of life-and-death decisions made by ordinary citizens, how those decisions are made—how jurors interpret the issues of violence and responsibility that are present in capital trials, as well as how they understand their own responsibility and the violence they are asked to authorize—remains, in the jurisprudence of death, a mystery.[69] "Individual jurors," Justice Powell has written, "bring to their deliberations qualities of human nature and varieties of human experience, the range of which is unknown and perhaps unknowable. The capital sentencing decision requires the individual jurors to focus their collective judgment on the unique characteristics of a particular criminal defendant. It is not surprising that such collective judgments often are difficult to explain."[70]

From the perspective of someone interested in understanding the relationship of law and violence as well as the relationship of democracy and the death penalty, how ordinary citizens, in their roles as jurors, could allow themselves to use their sovereign power to authorize death is almost inexplicable. This is because "to any person endowed with the normal inhibitions against the imposition of pain and death, the deed of capital punishment entails a special measure of reluctance and abhorrence."[71] However, some insight into both the nature of that reluctance and how it is overcome is provided by the work of Robert Cover.

Cover noted that while for most people "evolutionary, psychological, cultural and moral considerations inhibit the infliction of pain on other people . . . in almost all people social cues may overcome or suppress the revulsion to violence under certain circumstances."[72] Providing such cues is, Cover contended, the peculiar work of law. Thus Cover called attention to features of the "organization of the legal system [itself that] operate . . . to facilitate overcoming inhibitions against . . . violence."[73]

Two features of that organization have special relevance for understanding how ordinary citizens become the authorizing agents of law's violence in capital trials. First, those who authorize violence, in this case the death penalty, do not themselves carry out the deed which their words authorize. The juror is asked only to say the words that will activate a process that at some considerable remove may lead to death.[74] The juror's act is purely linguistic. Were jurors required to pull the switch on those they condemn to death, the ability of law to engage their authorizing decisions would be radically diminished.[75] As Cover puts it, "The most elementary understanding of our social practice of violence ensures that a judge know that she herself cannot actually pull the switch. This is not a trivial convention. For it means that someone else will have the duty and opportunity to pass upon what the judge has done."[76] What Cover says about the judge is surely no less true of jurors.

The second feature of law's social organization that helps overcome inhibitions against doing violence is, in fact, suggested by the first, namely, that jury decisions are subject to review on appeal. This means that the judge or juror who initially authorizes execution is able to transfer responsibility for his or her authorizing act, and, in so doing, to deny the very authority of that act. As Cover put it, "Persons who act within social organizations that exercise authority act violently without experiencing the normal degree of inhibition which regulates the behavior of those who act autonomously."[77]

The consequences of this ability to transfer responsibility have been well understood in the jurisprudence of death. They are, in fact, detailed by the Supreme Court's opinion in *Caldwell v. Mississippi*.[78] In *Caldwell*, the question was whether comments by a prosecutor to the effect that a jury should not view itself as finally determining whether the defendant should die because a death sentence would automatically be reviewed by the state supreme court violated the Eighth Amendment. Reviewing those comments in light of its prior holdings, the Court found that it is constitutionally impermissible to rest a death sentence on a determination made by a sentencer who has been led to believe that the responsibility for determining the appropriateness of the defendant's death rests elsewhere.[79]

Justice Marshall, writing for the majority in *Caldwell*, explained that

> this Court's Eighth Amendment jurisprudence has taken it as a given that capital sentencers would view their task as the serious one of determining whether a specific human being should die at the hands of the State. . . . Belief in the truth of the assumption that sentencers treat their power to determine the appropriateness of death as an "awesome responsibility" has allowed this Court

to view sentencer discretion as consistent with—and indeed indispensable to—the Eighth Amendment's "need for reliability in the determination that death is the appropriate punishment in a specific case."[80]

The question of how juries sentence, is, in Marshall's view, central to the question of whether they may constitutionally exercise the sovereign power to make life-and-death decisions.

Marshall then went on to paint a picture of the capital sentencing jury as

> made up of individuals placed in a very unfamiliar situation and called on to make a very difficult and uncomfortable choice. They are confronted with evidence and argument on the issue of whether another should die, and they are asked to decide that issue on behalf of the community. Moreover, they are given only partial guidance as to how their judgment should be exercised, leaving them with substantial discretion. . . . Given such a situation, the uncorrected suggestion that the responsibility for any ultimate determination of death will rest with others presents an intolerable danger that the jury will in fact choose to minimize the importance of its role.[81]

Marshall, echoing the insights of Cover, suggested that anything that encouraged the sentencing jury to believe that it was not responsible for authorizing death would encourage juries to provide such authorization. A jury thus unburdened might use a death sentence even when it is "unconvinced that death is the appropriate punishment" to "'send a message' of extreme disapproval for the defendant's acts."[82]

From Marshall's opinion in *Caldwell* we can glean the suggestion that the less responsible a jury feels for the actual decision to execute, the more likely it is to authorize death as a punishment. Yet the mystery of how jurors are enlisted as agents of state violence remains. This mystery is, as I have already suggested, in one sense a problem of popular sovereignty and in another sense a problem of understanding the way humans relate to the imposition of pain and violence on other humans. It is a mystery that can be explored only by carefully attending to what jurors actually do in, and say about, capital trials.

VIOLENCE, REPRESENTATION, AND RESPONSIBILITY IN THE CASE OF JOHN HENRY CONNORS

Convenience stores are, despite their reassuring, welcoming name, some of the most dangerous places in America. Late at night, such stores provide, as much as anything else, convenient settings for robbery and murder. This is as true in small towns, such as Bowling, Georgia,[83] as in big cities throughout the United States. The case of John Henry Connors is an apt illustration.

At 10:30 P.M. on July 23, 1986, John Henry Connors was picked up by two friends from his modest home on the outskirts of Bowling. Connors, twenty-six years old, worked in a local auto body shop. He had been married for seven years but was now having serious marital problems. He frequently sought the company of his friends to escape his troubled domesticity. On the night of July 23, Connors and his friends spent several hours driving around, smoking marijuana, and drinking. Each of them had a gun with him.

There was, however, nothing unusual in any of this. It had become a regular leisure activity for these men to drive along backcountry roads, get high, and fire shots into the night until they got bored, or sick, or sleepy. And there was nothing on the night of July 23 to suggest that anything would be different that night.

However, three hours after they first went out, Connors and his friends stopped at the local convenience store—The Jiffy Store—to buy one of Jiffy's advertised "Do-It-Yourself Microwave Meals" and some beer. The two friends went to the back of the store, while John Henry waited for them near the counter, where Andy Donaldson was working at his job as a cashier. After Donaldson finished ringing up the friends' purchases and opened the cash register to make change, Connors suddenly pulled out the .357 Magnum pistol that he had brought with him and shot Donaldson in the chest.

Connors's friends, who would later be granted immunity from prosecution in return for their testimony against him, were, by their own account, taken totally by surprise. At the sound of the shot they ducked, and then ran for the door. In the meantime, Donaldson had fallen to the floor in a bloody heap, moaning and writhing in pain, while Connors took ten one-dollar bills and some food stamps from the register. Connors then leaned over the counter and fired a second shot, which hit Donaldson above the left eye. After firing the second shot, he joined his friends in their car and escaped into the night.

However, eight days later, Connors was arrested when his two friends turned themselves in to the police. At the time of his arrest, the gun that killed Andy Donaldson was found in his home, along with the food stamps and nine of the dollar bills he had taken from the Jiffy Store.[84] Connors was charged with, and subsequently convicted of, robbery and malice murder in the death of Andy Donaldson. He was eventually sentenced to death.

I will recount what the jurors in the Connors case said about that case, and explore how they lent themselves to the decision that John Henry Connors should be sentenced to die.[85]

Imagining Violence

One of the crucial tasks of the prosecution in a capital case is to answer two questions: who did what to whom, and why does the killer deserve to die? To answer these questions the prosecutor has to portray, in a vivid and compelling way, the circumstances and nature of the killing. He or she has to make what is for most people quite unreal—namely, a scene of violent death—become real. He or she has to put violence and pain into discourse.[86] However, the problems confronted in putting violence into discourse would seem, at first glance, to be the opposite of those confronted in representing pain.

Violence is visible and vivid. It speaks loudly; it arouses indignation; and as a result, its representation threatens to overwhelm reason. Thus the problem of representing violence would seem to be one of taming and disciplining its seemingly unruly representations. Pain, on the other hand, is invisible.[87] It defies language and representation, and is, as a result, a largely silent and unshareable part of our lives.

Yet violence and its linguistic representation are inseparable from pain and its representation. We know the full measure of violence only through the pain it inflicts; the indignation which we experience in the presence of violence is, in large part, a function of our imaginings of the hurt it inflicts. In this sense, the problem of putting violence and pain into discourse is one problem rather than two.

It is the business of law in general and capital trials in particular to make violence and pain knowable, and to find the means of overcoming their differing resistances to language and representation. Elaine Scarry suggests that the courtroom and the discourse of the trial provide one particularly important site to observe the way violence and pain "enter language."[88] In that discourse the problem of putting violence and pain into language is compounded by the fact that

> it is not immediately apparent in exactly what way the verbal act of expressing pain . . . helps to eliminate the physical fact of pain. Furthermore, built into the very structure of the case is a dispute about the correspondence between language and material reality: the accuracy of the descriptions of suffering given by the plaintiff's lawyer may be contested by the defendant's lawyer. . . . For the moment it is enough to notice that, whatever else is true, . . . (a trial) provides a situation that once again requires that the impediments to expressing pain be overcome. Under the pressure of this requirement, the lawyer too, becomes an inventor of language, one who speaks on behalf of another person . . . and attempts to communicate the reality of that person's physical pain to people who are not themselves in pain (the jurors).[89]

Scarry invites us to consider the way jurors interpret and imagine the violence and pain they are called upon to judge. However, she suggests that in law, as elsewhere, the languages that can be invented to facilitate that imagining are quite limited.[90] "As physical pain is monolithically consistent in its assault on language," Scarry writes, "so the verbal strategies for overcoming the assault are very small in number and reappear consistently as one looks at the words of the patient, physician, Amnesty worker, lawyer, artist."[91] Those verbal strategies, Scarry suggests, "revolve (first) around the verbal sign of the weapon."[92] Here, we know violence and pain through its instrumentalities. Second, Scarry continues, we know them through their effects. Here, violence and pain are represented in the "wound," that is, "the bodily damage that is pictured as accompanying pain."[93]

As the jurors in the Connors case talked about that case, weapons and wounds, instrumentalities and effects, loomed large in what were vivid recollections of the scene of death and the violence that surrounded it. This is the payoff of the enormous effort that is put into the graphic presentation and re-presentation of the murder, as well as the technique used to bring about death, and its consequences. Words and photographs were in the Connors case, as in most other capital trials, used to bring to life the violence outside law,[94] It is important to note, however, that there was no comparable effort made to enable jurors to imagine the scene of the violence and death that they were being asked to authorize. Jurors were presented with no images of the scene of the prospective execution, of the violence of electrocution. No such images were admissible or available for any jurors eager to understand what they were being asked to authorize.

In the Connors case, weapons and wounds made the violence Connors had visited on Donaldson real and pressing. As Joseph Rane, one of jurors, put it,

> Connors shot the man—I don't remember the man's name, I can see his face, I don't remember his name—he shot him. If I'm not mistaken it went into his chest and came out by his shoulder blade with a .357 Magnum, if I remember correctly. He leaned over, got some money out of the cash register. The clerk of the store was laying on the ground, moaning and moving around from . . . you figure a maximum of three feet with a high-powered weapon like that. It had knocked him against the back . . . he was on the floor bleeding. And he reached over the counter as he was retrieving the money and shot him again. It went in, if I'm not mistaken, over his eye and out behind his ear on the opposite side.

Like other jurors, Rane was able to speak in a detailed way about the murder weapon as well as about the entry and exit wounds that it caused, and about its ballistics and bullet trajectories. When asked if there was anything specific about the case that stood out in his mind, Rane, a twenty-eight-year-old salesman, said,

> What I remember is seeing the pictures of the man laying behind the counter, laying in a puddle of blood probably bigger than this table. And the pictures— the other jurors and I had to . . . It was difficult for some of them to look at the pictures. They'd take them up so close and they'd show the clear shots and all. Then we handled the weapon and a lot of them really didn't want to do that.
>
> Q: Do you still think about those pictures and the gun?
>
> Surely.

Another juror in the Connors case, a seventy-three-year-old, retired grandmother, Belle Givens, recalled the violence that Connors had done in terms of "a big gun. Right that's it. He used a big gun." On her own account, confronting the instrument of death was a horrifying, rather than a pleasurable, experience. In fact, she confronted it unwillingly. She described herself as an unwilling victim of a process that would not respect her squeamishness in the face of violence: "Reason I say big gun is because they passed it around and made me look at it and touch it, and I didn't want to. They made me look at it and touch it." The image of the violence done by the "big gun" "followed us into the jury room and it bothered me very much."

For her, like Joseph Rane, the image of violence was fixed in the photographic evidence of the crime scene. "[T]hese photographs," Luc Sante argues, "lack the functions that are usually attached to images of death. They do not memorialize, or ennoble, or declare trimuph, or cry for vengeance. As evidence they are mere affectless records, concerned with details, as they themselves become details in the wider scope of police philosophy, which is far less concerned with the value of life than with the value of order. They are bookeeping entries, with no transfixing mission, and so serve death up raw and unmediated."[95]

Belle Givens was a reluctant viewer of death served up "raw and unmediated." However, once seen, the image was deeply imprinted on her:

> But what did this idiot do. As the guy fell down behind the counter he hit the shelves right in back of him, and John Henry took the gun and leaned over the counter, put the gun behind the guy's ear—bam—and another shot killed him. And they showed a picture of the man to the jury. I didn't want to look. They insisted I had to look. If I don't look, what they decide, well. I didn't want not to look and then have to have another trial. So I had to look, and that's still following me into that deliberating room.

In the system of capital punishment, the execution is hidden, the violence jurors are asked to authorize has no image, and no one can claim an entitlement to see the state's deadly deed[96]—but viewing the violence to which the jurors are asked to respond is made compulsory. The law compels the juror to view such graphic representations and to grasp the death-producing instrumentalities, which are given special evidentiary value in the state's case against the accused. To refuse to participate in the spectacle of seeing and touching those representations and instrumentalities is, in essence, to refuse to consider all the evidence and is thus to defy one's oath as a juror. Because the gaze cannot be legitimately averted, the juror becomes a victim of viewing.

Images and instrumentalities, in their evidentiary guise, engender a vivid and immediate confrontation with illegal violence and its consequences. They focus attention by their own particularized focus. As another juror, Charlotte Howles, explained, "The only thing we saw were pictures they had taken of the scene and they were just from the head up. You know, of where the gunshot wounds were at. That's all we saw of him." The victim is presented only in the violent images of the wounds which ended his or her life. And no one has a right to refuse to see those images.

Being forced to confront those images has dramatic consequences in enlisting jurors to authorize execution. The images mean that the victim will often be remembered as nothing other than the wounds that ended his or her life. As Sante says, "If photographs are supposed to freeze time, these crystallize what is already frozen, the aftermath of violence, like a voice-print of a scream. If photographs extend life, in memory and imagination, these extend death, not as a permanent condition the way tombstones do, but as a stage, an active moment of inactivity. Their subjects are constantly in the process of moving toward oblivion."[97]

Kristin Bumiller has argued, referring to similar evidence in a rape trial, that the principle that ensures that the images of violence have such an effect is one of "maximum visifiability."[98] This principle, Bumiller argues,

> is applied by using the techniques of close-ups and editing made possible by staged film production to orient the spectator in the most ideal position for viewing pleasure. In the courtroom, the prosecutor and expert master . . . [the] body as technique rather than art; they make use of photographs . . . to stage repetitive viewings of parts of . . . [the] body. This technique fetishizes the wound.[99]

Indeed, so powerful are those images that Charlotte Howles, when asked if she could remember what Donaldson looked like, said, "No, because to be honest I didn't look directly at the picture of his face because we were looking at where the bullets went in and came out. I didn't really look in his face." As Ms. Givens put it,

> Normally I consider myself a liberal easterner transplanted here to Georgia and against capital punishment—always was—but after I saw that picture of that man, something popped. I saw the pictures of him slumped down behind the counter and he was shot at somewhere around here and behind the ear, that was terrible. . . . I think about it even now and it bothers me very much.

Assigning Responsibility and Explaining Motivation

But the juxtaposition of images of murder made vivid and the virtual invisibility of law's own violence does not, in itself, explain how jurors read the discourse and representational practices of capital trials in ways that allow them to be enlisted as authorizing agents of capital punishment. The recollections of the jurors who convicted Connors suggest that two other factors are crucially in play. The first of those factors is what I call the "compulsion" to assign responsibility and explain motivation.

The origin and force of this "compulsion" in the case of John Henry Connors can perhaps be appreciated if we first understand that the story of his killing of Andy Donaldson is a garden-variety episode of what Robin West has called "post-modern murders."[100] Such murders, West argues, are

> chance encounter[s] between strangers, in which what . . . (was) casually exchanged happens to be death. . . . The radical disjunction, or discontinuity, between the immeasurably great value of what is being destroyed . . . and the minuscule, trivial, "perceived gain" that prompted the murder . . . leaves . . . a palpable, profound and almost physical need to reestablish sense and meaning in the universe. . . . [Such murders] strip the natural world of its hierarchy of

values—life, love, nurture, work, care, play, sorrow, grief—and they do so for no reason, not even to satisfy the misguided pseudo-Nietzschean desire of a Loeb or Leopold to effectuate precisely that deconstruction. They are meaningless murders.[101]

Events such as the killing of Andy Donaldson in the context of a ten-dollar robbery produce an intense effort to restore meaning, to answer the kind of question put by juror Howles when she asked, "Why? Why did he do it? Why, for such a small amount of money? I would love to have confronted him, face-to-face, and asked him why he committed such a senseless, stupid to me to take another human life." Howles's questions express "a simple primal fear that our collective attempt to reassert meaning and value in a world deconstructed by random violence . . . will be . . . fleeting and unsuccessful. . . . [The juror] is swamped by a physical as well as psychic need not to succumb, not to be drawn, not to be sucked under, not to be seduced by the meaninglessness of such murders, into the falsely sophisticated, David Lynch-ian belief in the meaninglessness of the particular lives ended."[102] The response, West suggests, is a virtually overwhelming desire to "assign personal responsibility for the murder and its consequences—including the arrest, trial and its outcome—imposition of the death penalty—squarely and irrevocably on the defendant."[103]

The Connors jurors responded quite as West would have predicted when they voiced a strong desire to fix personal responsibility on the defendant, to make him a moral agent capable of being held to account for what otherwise seemed unaccountable actions. For each of those jurors, the capital trial was, in fact, a drama, in which the question of Connors's agency was at the fore. As Ranes said, "There really wasn't much of a question about Connors' guilt. He was there. He never denied that. His gun fired the shot; he never denied that. There was just a lot of talk as if, you know, the fact he was drinking, as if the bottle left Connors behind, got out of the car, went into the Jiffy, and fired the shots." As Howles explained,

> They [the defense] said that alcohol had taken hold of his mind at the moment and that, if he had not been under the influence of alcohol, he wouldn't have been where he was at. They were blaming it on the alcohol because that's when they were questioning us as jurors . . . that was the one question they asked us, did we think that alcohol could make you do things that you normally wouldn't do. It was one of the questions that the defense asked when they were selecting the jurors.

Another juror, Sylvia Mann, a forty-nine-year-old high school social studies teacher, rejected the argument that alcohol could provide a sufficient explanation of why Connors killed Donaldson or that it should somehow diminish his responsibility:

> It did come up that he was under the influence of alcohol and drugs even though they told us from the beginning that that was not a defense. I felt that the defense really pushed it a lot. They kept talking about it a lot even though they said it was

not a defense. When we deliberated it was brought up fairly often that the person was under the influence. But so what? I mean a lot of people get drunk, but they don't take guns and go shoot up the Jiffy Store. I don't think anybody really ever felt it was much of a defense. . . . He shot someone because he wanted money. Like lots of people want money but they don't kill other people to get it. And he knew what he was doing. Because he'd already shot the man and the man was on the floor and unconscious and there was no need to shoot him a second time. Apparently he intentionally intended for the man to die.

For this juror, Connors was, despite his alcohol problems, still a moral agent, fully capable of knowing what he was about, one whose actions suggest an inexcusable intention to kill.[104] "Bottles," she continued, "don't kill people. Only people, people like Connors, kill people." By insisting that Connors was both legally guilty and morally responsible for the murder of Donaldson, this juror and her colleagues refused to accept the picture of a social world governed by causes beyond human control; instead, they constructed a moral world of free agents making choices for which they could be held to account.[105]

As Joseph Rane saw it, "there is a simple explanation for why he [Connors] did it":

He made a really bad choice. He valued human life for $10. And whether he was under the influence of alcohol or drugs or whatever, he's still responsible for what he does and that's something that was brought out. . . . He wanted money though if you are familiar with convenience stores you know that after eleven o'clock they don't even carry twenties in the drawer. And being under the influence of drugs and alcohol, there's no telling what it'll make you do. But you still do it. I think he just saw an opportunity to get some money to go get whatever and he just took that opportunity. . . . There was no reason in the world why somebody under the influence of alcohol or drugs should take anybody else's life. Why should he be any different from the rest of us?

In these narratives, we see jurors confronting what Ranes himself called "just one of them whimsical things" and needing to "reassert responsibility and human agency for a momentous act and momentous deprivation; so that we can again feel in control of destiny."[106] Connors seemed to the jurors to be enough like them that he could be justly subject to their judgment. Yet, at the same time, he was different enough so that his "cold-blooded," "vicious" act could be seen as deserving the most severe, and thus unusual, punishment.

But as the jurors in the Connors case contemplated the question of whether to authorize such a punishment, another question of responsibility arose. This time what was in question was their own status as agents and their own responsibility as jurors. As West argues,

The juror's responsibility for his fellow citizen, and responsibility to reach the morally right decision, is precisely what defines the juror as citizen. . . . That capacity gives the juror a stake in the affairs of others and makes him care about the consequences of his decision. The juror's capacity for doing so, his duty to engage this capacity, and his responsibility for the outcome are all necessary contributions . . . to the vitality of a liberal, participatory, and non-apathetic society.[107]

If Marshall's speculations in *Caldwell* are correct, jurors who see themselves as directly and personally responsible for the execution their decision might authorize would be less likely to lend themselves to the project of law's violence, whereas those who can convince themselves that the responsibility lies elsewhere would be less likely to do so. Three jurors in the Connors case conform to Marshall's expectation; even as they insisted on Connors' agency, they refused to see themselves in a similar light.

Jurors Mann, Givens, and Rane each talked about their decision to condemn Connors to death as if that decision were somehow made elsewhere, as if they were not really making choices or authorizing anything. Each of them echoed an argument made by Herbert Morris, namely, that the person who is truly responsible for the punishment is the defendant himself.[108] In this view, the murderer, by his or her own acts, actually determines the death sentence. Thus the juror who votes for such a punishment is merely the agent of the defendant.

However, the efforts of Mann, Givens, and Rane to avoid responsibility for their authorizing act of violence did not end there. Each of them was acutely aware of a point made by Cover, namely, that "the social organization of legal violence . . . [ensures that] responsibility for the violence must be shared." Law, Cover noted, "manifests itself in the secondary rules and principles which generally ensure that no single mind and no single will can generate the violent outcomes that follow from interpretive commitments. No single individual can render any interpretation operative as law—as authority for the violent act."[109] Thus is, of course, readily apparent from the group character of jury decisionmaking, but it is also apparent to jurors from the hierarchical nature of law's social organization.

Each of the four Connors jurors quoted above knew, or believed, that their decision was not the last word. Each knew or believed that it would be reviewed by the judge who presided over the trial and/or by an appellate court. All four thought that the appeals courts were as likely to reject the death penalty imposed on Connors as they were to accept it, and Mann, Givens, and Rane each said that the fact that the death sentence would be reviewed by other actors in the legal process meant that should Connors actually be executed, they would not have his death on their consciences. For them, the very structure of "super due process," and of extended review and appeal, which had been put in place to ensure heightened reliability in capital cases, made it easier to impose the death penalty.[110]

Only Charlotte Howles saw herself as directly and personally responsible for the death sentence for which she voted. As she put it,

> I was really surprised when I could go in and vote for death because really and truly, before I was on this jury I had never given it a lot of thought. And I didn't

have any strong convictions one way or the other. It is a big responsibility, and hard to accept, but I think that's why they have juries so people like me have to make those hard decisions. I felt from the beginning that it would be my call, and I thought that if the facts are there and for certain things I would have no problem going in and finding somebody guilty and giving them the death penalty. I think that if it's a heinous thing and if it warrants it, then I would certainly vote again for the death penalty. . . . My opinion was that, hey, I'm not going to let this guy [Connors] out. I would feel the same way if he was guilty, electrocuted later on, and they found him innocent. I'd feel bad, but not as bad as if I didn't give him the death penalty and he somehow got out and killed again. For me, my job was to make sure that that didn't happen again.

The responsibility that Howles felt most acutely was one where the death penalty seemed to be the morally responsible answer to a social crisis engendered by the kind of random, valueless violence perpetrated by people like Connors. In contrast to the meaningless act for which Howles was prepared to hold Connors responsible, Howles saw law's violence, and her participation in the authorization of death itself, as meaningful and purposive, as being necessary to protect innocent others from him.

When "Life Doesn't Mean Life" and "Death Doesn't Mean Death," Yes Means Maybe, But Probably Not

When people like Charlotte Howles step up to the plate and accept responsibility for imposing the death penalty, what is the meaning of the penalty they are voting to impose? When jurors lend their voices and votes to capital punishment how do they understand the act they are authorizing? Here, conversations with the jurors in the Connors case suggest that substantive inadequacies in the arsenal of criminal punishment as well as the processes of review and appeal that automatically are entailed by a death sentence combined to push them to authorize such a sentence when most were, in fact, neither deeply enthusiastic about their decision nor convinced that Connors would ever be executed.

Those inadequacies and those processes make the violence of the death penalty seem both a necessary and, at the same time, a highly improbable event. The former make a death sentence more immediate, while the latter make execution all the more remote. Those inadequacies and those processes allowed jurors in the Connors case to decide one thing, namely, that Connors should be sentenced to death, as a way of achieving something else, namely, that he should spend the rest of his life in jail. While Connors's violent act could not be gainsaid, their violent gesture would likely be a gesture whose efficacy would not reside in its being taken literally.

The jurors in the Connors case were overwhelmingly concerned with incapacitation as a goal of criminal punishment.[111] None of them believed that executions served as a deterrent to others, and none embraced a retributivist rationale for capital punishment.[112] Each of them was, however, deeply concerned with the possibility that Connors might someday be back on the streets of Bowling. Each seemed sure that Connors's vicious, bloody acts qualified him to die under the laws of Georgia, yet each believed that what was necessary to achieve justice was something less than his death at the hands of the state.

Because Georgia law does not provide for a sentence of life without parole,[113] each was persuaded that unless they voted for death, John Henry Connors would soon be out of prison, posing a threat to innocent others. For these jurors, then, sentencing someone to die was the only way of ensuring that he would live the rest of his life in prison. As juror Howles explained,

> If he had not been found guilty of capital murder he would have gotten life. But that doesn't mean that he would have served a life term. It means he would have gotten out in however many years it is you have to serve before you get out on parole. Isn't it something like seven years? I think I'm just going by what I hear on TV, you know.

Like the other jurors, Howles embraced death as a punishment as insurance against the possibility that "if we didn't give him the death penalty, if he did get back out into society, he would hurt someone else. And I really didn't want that."

Rane and Mann stated that they would have preferred an alternative to the stark choice of death or a life sentence that did not really mean life in prison. Both said that they would have preferred it if they could have voted for a sentence of life in prison without the possibility of parole. Both suggested that they chose death because this alternative was not available to them. In fact, Rane reported that a substantial part of the jury's initial deliberations about Connors's fate focused on the meaning of life in prison:

> We were concerned that if he got life in prison he would serve only a few years and then be turned loose. There was one woman who was particularly adamant that she didn't want that, only problem was she said that she couldn't vote for death. So that's when the question of life in prison without the possibility of parole came up and that's when we sent a note to the judge asking if we could give that. And he called us back out and had us in the jury box again and he read the question and then told us that we couldn't, that that was not one of the options given. It would either be the death penalty or life in prison which means he would have a possibility of parole.

This turned out to be a decisive moment in the Connors case. As Sylvia Mann said,

> I was truly amazed because many of the people that were on the jury did not really seem to understand that life does not mean life. And I was astonished that a good number did not realize that when they started it. Those of us who did understand that, it took us to explain it to them because they really did not

understand that. A lot of them would have liked to have given John Henry Connors life if it had really meant life, you know, that he was going to go to jail and stay there forever. When the judge told us it was either life that didn't mean life or death that changed things for most of us. But there were still a couple who didn't want Connors to die. . . . That meant that we had to talk about the fact that this, just for the reason that we voted for death, did not necessarily mean that Connors would die at the hands of the state. And I think we talked a good bit about the fact that this would go to the Georgia Supreme Court and it would be reviewed and that if anything was out of the ordinary then it would be thrown out, and that even after then the man would have many opportunities to appeal. And I think that probably that discussion helped more than anything to persuade the two that was reluctant. Just because we voted death didn't mean he would die.

Life that doesn't mean life and death that doesn't mean death—given these alternatives, jurors in the Connors case struggled to find a way to express what seems to have been the consensual view that the appropriate response to the killing of Donaldson would be to put Connors away and throw away the proverbial key. Indeed, no one—not Howles, Mann, Givens, or Rane—believed that execution was a likely result of a death sentence. As Howles put it, "We all pretty much knew that when you vote for death you don't necessarily or even usually get death. Ninety-nine percent of the time they don't put you to death. You sit on death row and get old."

In Georgia where capital punishment is concerned, saying yes does not necessarily mean yes. To the jurors in the Connors case, saying yes to the death penalty meant both more and less than it seemed. It was a way of expressing their moral horror and revulsion at the violent and "whimsical" killing of Andy Donaldson and of ensuring, as best they were able, that Connors would himself never be an agent of such violence again.

CONCLUSION

Jurors in capital trials are asked to participate in a set of complex rituals through which law seeks to gain the right to exercise the ultimate power of sovereignty, namely, the power over life itself. They are asked to cast the weight of citizenship on the side of law's violence. It is, as I have said, a remarkable and troubling aspect of democratic politics that jurors so regularly do so. The Connors case helps us understand how and why this happens.

In the Connors case, and in most other capital trials, the representation of violence is as difficult and as uncertain as it is anywhere else. Yet the representational practices of capital trials make some kinds of violence vivid and visible while effectively hiding others and rendering them invisible.[114] The violence made visible is the murderous violence of people such as John

Henry Connors, whose acts are graphically displayed and the consequences of whose acts are eagerly implanted in the consciousness of jurors. While great efforts are made to persuade jurors that such violence is unnecessary, irrational, indiscriminant, gruesome, and useless, law's violence, the violence of the death penalty, is described, when it is spoken about at all, as rational, purposive, and controlled through values, norms, and procedures external to violence itself. In capital trials, the force of law is represented as serving common purposes and aims, as against the anomic savagery lurking just beyond law's boundaries.[115]

Yet in all capital trials the juxtaposition of two different representations of violence is disquieting, if not destabilizing. This is especially true of the juxtaposition of the narratives of violence outside law with the linguistic representation, or nonrepresentation, of law's own violence. In these moments, putting law's violence into discourse threatens to expose law as essentially similar to the antisocial violence it is supposed to deter and punish. Benjamin argues that "in the exercise of violence over life and death more than in any other legal act, law reaffirms itself." "But," he continues, "in this very violence something rotten in law is revealed, above all to a finer sensibility, because the latter knows itself to be infinitely remote from conditions in which fate might imperiously have shown itself in such a sentence."[116] As a result,

> Anglo-American law has traditionally suffered a serious identity crisis over its awkward relation to violence. . . . Our system assumes that law is to hold a monopoly on violence, but this is a monopoly viewed as both necessary and discomforting. It is necessary because it is viewed as the alternative to something worse—unrestrained private vengeance—and it is discomforting because those who make and enforce the law would like us to believe that, though they may be required to use force, force is somehow categorically distinguishable from violence. . . . [T]he efforts of modern jurisprudence to finesse or deny the role of violence have not ceased.[117]

These efforts put enormous pressures on such events as the capital trial to demonstrate and affirm the difference between the violence of law and the violence that law condemns. The jury's verdict, the spoken truth of the community, as it embraces capital punishment is the ultimate affirmation of the meaningfulness of that difference. Thus death sentences, some might assume, speak for themselves. They convey the authority and the desire that someone should be put to death by the state. They represent the ultimate public embrace of law's special brand of violence.

But in the Connors case, while the death sentence did authorize the state to extinguish the life of John Henry Connors, it is by no means clear that such a result was, for the jurors who authorized it, the desired result. In this case, and I think in many others, the death sentence was not simply a linguistic command whose integrity depended on the materialization of punishment on the body of the condemned. In this case, and I think many others, the death sentence pronounced was, at best, plural, if not indeterminate, in its meanings. It was at one and the same time a powerful condemnation of Connors for his vicious crime, an expression of frustration at the incompleteness of a sentencing system that did not provide for life without parole, and a way of ensuring that Connors would be incapacitated for life.

Finally, the law, with its elaborate structure of rules, reviews, and appeals in capital cases, diffuses responsibility for the violence that jurors are asked to authorize.[118] In this sense it makes it easier for citizens to participate in the doing of the evil that is capital punishment. Here, paradoxically, the greater the protections for defendants in capital cases, the greater this diffusion of responsibility will typically be. And in the case of the Connors jurors, this greater diffusion of responsibility itself invited a death verdict.

Law may prize juror sovereignty in capital cases, but jurors themselves do not seem eager to claim their sovereign prerogative. This suggests an interesting possibility, namely, that the greater the protections afforded capital defendants and those convicted of capital crimes, and the fewer the resulting executions, the more willing jurors may be to lend their authorizing voice to the death penalty. However, as protections are stripped away by a Supreme Court ever-intent on accommodating the state's appetite to own and control its citizens, an appetite George Kateb has vigorously and vividly exposed and demounced,[119] as law's eager impatience to get on with the business of turning death sentences into executions is revealed, and as the frequency of execution increases, law may find itself less well able to enlist ordinary citizens in the project of authorizing its life-destroying violence.[120] In this way the law's eager appetite to respond to violence with violence may evoke the disciplining scrupulousness of its citizen sovereigns.

NOTES

1. George Kateb, *The Inner Ocean: Individualism and Democratic Culture* (Ithaca, N.Y.: Cornell University Press, 1992), p. 200.

2. *Ibid.*, 191–192.

3. Franklin Zimring and Gordon Hawkins, *Capital Punishment and the American Agenda* (Cambridge: Cambridge University Press, 1986).

4. Terry Aladjem, "Revenge and Consent: The Death Penalty and Lockean Principals of Democracy" (unpublished manuscript, 1990), p. 2. Robert Burt has recently suggested that "[t]he retaliatory force justified by the criminal law . . . has the same place in democratic theory as majority rule. Each is a form of coercion and neither is legitimate as such. Criminal law penalties and majority rule are both rough equivalents, tolerably consistent with the democratic equality principle only if all disputants (but most particularly, the dominant party) see their application of defensive coercion as a limited waystation working ultimately toward the goal of a consensual relationship among acknowledged equals." Burt, "Democracy, Equality and the Death Penalty," in *The Rule of Law*, Nomos 36 (New York: New York University Press, 1994), pp. 80, 89.

5. See A. I. Meldren, "Dignity, Worth, and Rights," in *The Constitution of Rights*, ed. Michael Meyer and William Parent (Ithaca, N.Y.: Cornell University Press, 1992). See also Jordan Paust, "Human Dignity as a Constitutional Right: A Jurisprudentially Based Inquiry into Criteria and Content," *Howard Law Journal* 27 (1984): 150.

6. See *Furman v. Georgia*, 408 U.S. 238, 270 (1972) (Brennan, J., concurring); and Hugo Adam Bedau, "The Eighth Amendment, Dignity, and the Death Penalty," in Meyer and Parent, *The Constitution of Rights*.

7. *Spaziano v. Florida*, 468 U.S. 447, 490 and 489 (1984).

8. See Stanley Milgram, *Obedience to Authority: An Experimental View* (New York: Harper and Row, 1974). See also Hannah Arendt, *Eichman in Jerusalem: A Report on the Banality of Evil* (New York: Viking, 1963).

9. See Elaine Scarry, "The Declaration of War: Constitutional and Unconstitutional Violence," in *Law's Violence*, ed. Austin Sarat and Thomas R. Kearns (Ann Arbor: University of Michigan Press, 1992).

10. John Locke, *The Second Treatise of Government* (Indianapolis: Bobbs-Merrill, 1952), ch. 1, sec. 2, p. 4.

11. Kateb, *The Inner Ocean*, p. 192.

12. Michel Foucault, *Discipline and Punish*, trans. Alan Sheridan (New York: Random House, 1977), p. 9.

13. Locke, *Second Treatise*.

14. Aladjem, "Revenge and Consent." See also Thomas L. Dumm, *Democracy and Punishment: Disciplinary Origins of the United States* (Madison: University of Wisconsin Press, 1987).

15. Foucault, *Discipline and Punish*, p. 9.

16. *Ibid.*

17. See Judge Stephen Reinhardt, "The Supreme Court, The Death Penalty, and the *Harris* Case," *Yale Law Journal* 102 (1992): 205. See also Evan Camiker and Erwin Chemerinsky, "The Lawless Execution of Robert Alton Harris," *Yale Law Journal* 102 (1992): 225.

18. Beneath the headline "After Night of Court Battles, a California Execution," the April 22, 1992, edition of the *New York Times* reported the tangled maze of last-minute legal maneuvers that immediately preceded the death in California's gas chamber of Robert Alton Harris, the 169th person to be executed since the Supreme Court restored capital punishment in 1976. As in many previous executions, the hope for clemency or the possibility of a stay of execution was in Harris's case pursued until the last minute.

19. The Court scolded Harris's lawyers for "abusive delay which has been compounded by last minute attempts to manipulate the judicial process" (*New York Times*, April 22, 1992, p. 22). In so doing, it displaced Harris as the soon-to-be victim of law, and portrayed law itself as the victim of Harris and his manipulative lawyers. To defend the virtue of law required an assertion of the Court's supremacy against both the vexatious sympathies of other courts and the efforts of Harris and his lawyers to keep alive a dialogue about death.

20. The *New York Times* reported, "In a last macabre twist, the A.C.L.U., which opposes capital punishment in all cases, received last-minute permission . . . to videotape (Harris's) execution" (April 22, 1992, p. 22). See also Jef Richards and R. Bruce Easter, "Televising Executions: The High-Tech Alternative to Public Hangings," *U.C.L.A. Law Review* 40 (1992): 381.

21. While executions have to be witnessed to be lawful, witnessing is carefully monitored. Who will be allowed to see what is for most of us unseeable is an important question in every execution. See Robert Johnson, *Death Work: A Study of the Modern Execution Process* (Pacific Grove, Calif.: Brooks/Cole, 1990), pp. 103–104. Thus capital punishment is a hidden reality; what we know about the way law does death comes in the most highly mediated way as a rumor, a report, an account of the voiceless expression of the body of the condemned. "According to several witnesses Mr. Harris appeared to loose consciousness after about one and one-half minutes although his body continued a series of convulsive movements and his head jerked backward several times." *New York Times,* April 22, 1992, p. 22.

22. The association of law and violence, though rendered invisible in the bureaucratization of capital punishment, is sometimes made visible elsewhere, for example, in the use of lethal force by police. It is, moreover, linguistically present in the ease and comfort with which we speak about enforcing the law. " 'Applicability,' 'enforceability' is not," as Derrida puts it, "an exterior or secondary possibility that may or may not be added as a supplement to law. . . . The word 'enforceability' reminds us that there is no such thing as law that doesn't imply in itself, *a priori,* . . . the possibility of being 'enforced,' applied by force. There are, to be sure, laws that are not enforced, but there is no law without enforceability, and no applicability or enforceability of the law without force, whether this force be direct or indirect, physical or symbolic. . . ." Jacques Derrida "Force of Law: The 'Mystical Foundation of Authority,' " *Cardozo Law Review* 11 (1990): 925.

23. Foucault, *Discipline and Punish,* ch. 1.

24. *Ibid.,* p. 9.

25. See Thomas L. Dumm, "Fear of Law," *Studies in Law, Politics and Society* 10 (1990): 29, 44–49. As Dumm puts it, "In the face of the law that makes people persons, people need to fear. Yet people also need law to protect them. . . . Hence fear is a political value that is valuable because it is critical of value, a way of establishing difference that enables uncertainty in the face of danger" (p. 54).

26. See Austin Sarat, "Speaking of Death: Narratives of Violence in Capital Trials," *Law and Society Review* 27 (1993): 19.

27. Robert Cover, "Violence and the Word," *Yale Law Journal* 95 (1986): 1601.

28. See Sarat, "Speaking of Death."

29. Foucault suggests that "publicity has shifted to the trial, and to the sentence; the execution itself is like an additional shame that justice is ashamed to impose on the condemned man." *Discipline and Punish,* p. 9.

30. As Justice Stewart said in *Woodson v. North Carolina,* 428 U.S. 280, 303–304 (1976), "[D]eath is a punishment different from all other sanctions in kind rather than degree." See also Margaret Jane Radin, "Cruel Punishment and Super Due Process for Death," in *Punishment and Rehabilitation,* ed. Jeffrie Murphy (Belmont, Calif.: Wadsworth, 1985).

31. Recent Supreme Court decisions have retreated significantly from this effort. See, for example, *Blystone v. Pennsylvania,* 494 U.S. 299 (1990); and *Walton v. Arizona,* 497 U.S. 639 (1990).

32. In *Witherspoon v. Illinois,* 391 U.S. 510, 519 (1968), the Supreme Court held that the basic question of whether the death penalty is excessive in any particular crime must be answered by the decisionmaker that is best able to "express the conscience of the community on the ultimate question of life or death." But see *Spaziano v. Florida,* 468 U.S. 447 (1984).

33. As Tocqueville put it, "The institution of the jury . . . invests the people . . . with the direction of society." See *Democracy in America*, trans. Henry Reeve (Boston: John Allyn, 1876), p. 361.

34. Some, of course, suggest that there is no difference between capital punishment and murder. See Albert Camus, "Reflections on the Guillotine," in Albert Camus and Arthur Koestler, *Reflexions sur la peine capitale* (Paris: Calmann-Levy, 1957).

35. See Susan Jacoby, *Wild Justice: The Evolution of Revenge* (New York: Harper and Row, 1983). See also Jonathan Rieder, "The Social Organization of Vengeance," in *Toward A General Theory of Social Control*, ed. Donald Black (New York: Academic Press, 1984).

36. Robert Weisberg, "Deregulating Death," *Supreme Court Review* 8 (1983): 385.

37. See *Witherspoon*, 391 U.S. 510. As Justice Stevens argues in his dissent in *Spaziano*, "[T]he jury is central to the link between capital punishment and the standards of decency contained in the Eighth Amendment. . . ." 468 U.S. at 483.

38. Patrick Higginbotham, "Juries and the Death Penalty," *Case Western Reserve Law Review* 41 (1991): 1048–1049. Justice Stevens argues in *Spaziano* that "[t]he authors of our federal and state constitutional guarantees recognized the special function of the jury in any exercise of plenary power over the life and liberty of the citizen." 468 U.S. at 481. See also Stephen Gillers, "Deciding Who Dies," *University of Pennsylvania Law Review* 129 (1980): 1.

39. Higginbotham, "Juries," p. 1051.

40. As Justice Blackmun put it in *Spaziano*, "The imposition of the death penalty . . . is an expression of community outrage." 468 U.S. at 461.

41. This view of the jury as itself a representative body, imagines sovereignty to lie in the community. As the Supreme Court suggested in *Witherspoon*, "[A] jury that must choose between life imprisonment and capital punishment can do little more— and must do nothing less—than express the conscience of the community on the ultimate question of life or death." 468 U.S. at 519.

42. As Justice Stewart noted in *Woodson*, 428 U.S. at 293, ". . . American jurors have, with some regularity, disregarded their oaths and refused to convict defendants where a death sentence was the automatic consequence of a guilty verdict."

43. See *Spaziano*, 468 U.S. at 480 and 490. Justice Stevens, dissenting in *Spaziano*, argued that because of the uniqueness of the death penalty, "it is the one punishment that cannot be prescribed by a rule of law as judges normally understand such rules" (p. 469).

44. See *McGautha v. California*, 402 U.S. 183 (1970).

45. See Vivian Berger, " 'Black Box Decisions' on Life or Death—If They're Arbitrary, Don't Blame the Jury: A Reply to Judge Patrick Higginbotham," *Case Western Reserve Law Review* 41 (1991): 1067.

46. In *Spaziano* the Court rejected a due process claim that defendants were constitutionally entitled to have a jury make sentencing determinations in capital cases. However, thirty of thirty-seven states with capital punishment now leave the life-or-death decision exclusively to the jury.

47. See *McGautha*, 402 U.S. at 185.

48. These two different responses have been a persistent feature of the Supreme Court's death penalty decisions. For a critique of the Court's inability to definitively choose between them see Justice Scalia's concurrence in *Walton*, 110 S. Cr. 3047.

49. See *McGautha*, 402 U.S. at 204.

50. See Tocqueville, *Democracy in America*, p. 364.

51. *McGautha*, 402 U.S. at 208.

52. See *ibid.*, pp. 250–251.

53. *Ibid.*, p. 271.

54. *Ibid.*, p. 248.

55. *Ibid.*, p. 249. Brennan was, I think, prophetic in framing the debate about capital punishment as a debate about the rule of law itself. For an elaboration of his prophecy, see Justice Marshall's dissent in *Payne v. Tennessee*, 501 U.S. 808, 844 (1991).

56. *Furman v. Georgia*, 408 U.S. 238 (1972).

57. *Ibid.*, p. 245.

58. *Ibid.*, p. 253.

59. *Ibid.*, p. 402.

60. *Ibid.*, p. 388.

61. *Ibid.*

62. *Ibid.*

63. See *Gregg v. Georgia*, 428 U.S. 153 (1976).

64. *Ibid.*, p. 189.

65. *Ibid.*, p. 206.

66. *Ibid.*, p. 193.

67. *Ibid.*, p. 192.

68. *Ibid.*, p. 198.

69. As Robin West put it in her discussion of recent death penalty cases dealing with the responsibility of jurors, "What is missing . . . is a robust discussion of the nature of the responsibility the juror ought to possess, to which the defendant should be constitutionally entitled: what it means for a juror to engage in morally responsible decision making. . . ." West, "Taking Freedom Seriously," *Harvard Law Review* 104 (1989): 87.

70. See *McCleskey v. Kemp*, 481 U.S. 279, 311.

71. Cover, "Violence and the Word," p. 1622.

72. *Ibid.*, p. 1613.

73. *Ibid.*, p. 1614.

74. Johnson, *Death Work*.

75. But see Milgram, *Obedience to Authority*.

76. Cover, "Violence and the Word," p. 1626.

77. *Ibid.*, p. 1615.

78. *Caldwell v. Mississippi*, 472 U.S. 320 (1985).

79. See *ibid.* But in *Sawyer v. Smith*, 497 U.S. 227. (1990), the Court upheld a death sentence although the jury had been told explicitly that it was not ultimately responsible for the sentence it imposed.

80. *Caldwell*, 472 U.S. at 330.

81. *Ibid.*, p. 333.

82. *Ibid.*, p. 331.

83. This is a pseudonym. In what follows I have also used pseudonyms for the case I describe and for the jurors whose views I discuss.

84. One of the jurors in the Connors case explained how the police were able to link the money to the defendant: "In convenience stores they have several different kinds of detection devices that let them know that they're being robbed or going to

be robbed or are in the process of being robbed. They have . . . I call it a panic button, a red button. You mash it and all these sirens go off. Some of them are silent, some of them send a signal directly to the police. In some they have the cash drawer arranged with ones, fives, tens, and they have a spot for what they call, not fake money, but mad money. They reach in and may grab this mad money. It is marked so they know when it is recovered. It's got a little sensor on the bottom and when the mad money is taken off it that goes off automatically signalling the police."

85. The Connors case is one of thirty Georgia cases that I am studying as part of a national study of jurors and the death penalty. One object of that study is to understand how jurors interpret the discourse and representational practices of capital trials and how they come to be effectively enlisted as agents of law's violence. In each of the Georgia cases four jurors are randomly selected and interviewed about the case; interviews last between two and five hours.

86. See Sarat, "Speaking of Death."

87. As Elaine Scarry argues, "Physical pain has no voice. . . . When one hears about another's physical pain, the events happening within the interior of that person's body may seem to have the remote character of some deep subterranean fact, belonging to an invisible geography that, however portentous, has no reality because it has not yet manifested itself on the visible surface of the earth." Pain is, according to Scarry, "Vaguely alarming yet unreal, laden with consequence yet evaporating before the mind because not available to sensory confirmation, unseeable classes of objects such as subterranean plates, Seyfert galaxies, and the pains occurring in other people's bodies flicker before the mind, then disappear. . . . [Pain] achieves . . . its aversiveness in part by bringing about, even within the radius of several feet, this absolute split between one's sense of one's own reality and the reality of other persons. . . . Whatever pain achieves, it achieves in part through its unsharability, and it ensures this unsharability through its resistance to language." Scarry, *The Body in Pain* (New York: Oxford, 1985), pp. 3–4.

88. *Ibid.*, p. 10.

89. *Ibid.*

90. *Ibid.*, p. 13.

91. *Ibid.*

92. *Ibid.*

93. *Ibid.*, p. 15. As violence and pain are put into language, we may be tempted to forget that their metaphorical representation as weapons and wounds cannot truly capture the meaning of violence and pain themselves. And, in the process of putting those things into language, some kinds of violence and pain—those engendered by particular weapons and those that leave visible marks on the body—may be more easily available to us (see Kristin Bumiller, "Real Violence/Body Fictions" (unpublished manuscript, 1991); Sara Cobb, "The Domestication of Violence in Mediation: The Social Construction of Disciplinary Power in Law" (unpublished manuscript, 1992), whereas more diffuse, systemic violence, which leaves no visible marks or scars—the violence of racism, poverty, and despair—will be less easily represented and so less easily understood as violence and pain. "A great deal is at stake," Scarry herself suggests, "in the attempt to invent linguistic structures that will reach and accommodate this area of experience normally so inaccessible to language." *The Body in Pain*, p. 6.

94. For a comparable analysis in another context, see Bumiller, "Real Violence/ Body Fictions." Luc Sante argues that photographic evidence of crime scenes is used

"to prove that the crime was committed in the county or municipality where the body was found and the trial scheduled; to give proof of the corpus delicti . . . and its venue; to help establish a motive, by means, for example of the position of the body . . .; and to clarify the relationship of the body to the weapon and other properties." Sante, *Evidence* (New York: Farrar, Straus and Giroux, 1992), p. 90.

95. Sante, *Evidence*, p. 60.

96. See *Garett v. Estelle*, 556 F.2d 1274 (5th Cir. 1974), *cert. denied*, 438 U.S. 914 (1978). See also *KQED v. Vasquez*, No. c-90–1383 RHS (N.D. Cal. 1991).

97. Sante, *Evidence*, p. 60.

98. Bumiller, "Real Violence/Body Fictions," p 9.

99. *Ibid.*

100. *Ibid.*

101. See Robin West, "Narrative, Responsibility and Death: A Comment on the Death Penalty Cases from the 1989 Term," *Maryland Journal of Contemporary Legal Issues* 1 (1990): 1, 11.

102. *Ibid.*

103. *Ibid.*, p. 12.

104. See Herbert Morris, "Persons and Punishment," in *Human Rights*, ed. A. I. Meldren (Belmont, Calif.: Wadsworth, 1970).

105. *Ibid.*

106. West, "Narrative, Responsibility and Death," p. 12.

107. West, "Taking Freedom Seriously," p. 91.

108. See Morris, "Persons and Punishment."

109. Cover, "Violence and the Word," p. 1628.

110. Radin, "Cruel Punishment and Super Due Process for Death."

111. For a discussion of the nature and meaning of incapacitation in criminal sentences, see Andrew Von Hirsch, *Doing Justice: The Choice of Punishments* (New York: Hill and Wang, 1976).

112. Contra *Witherspoon*, 391 U.S. 5100.

113. For a discussion of the meaning and significance of life without parole, see Note, "'The Meaning of Life' for Virginia Jurors and Its Effect on Reliability in Capital Sentencing," *Virginia Law Review* 75 (1989): 1605. See also Note, "Life without Parole: An Alternative to Death or Not Much Life at All," *Vanderbilt Law Review* 43 (1990): 529.

114. Sarat, "Speaking of Death."

115. As Justice Stewart put it in his concurring opinion in *Furman*, 408 U.S. at 309, "The instinct for retribution is part of the nature of man and channelling that instinct in the administration of criminal justice serves an important purpose in promoting the stability of a society governed by law."

116. Walter Benjamin, "Critique of Violence," in *Reflections*, trans. Edmund Jepchott (New York: Harcourt, Brace, 1978), p. 286.

117. See Robert Weisberg, "Private Violence as Moral Action," in *Law's Violence*, ed. Austin Sarat and Thomas Kearns (Ann Arbor: University of Michigan Press, 1992), pp. 175–176.

118. See Cover, "Violence and the Word."

119. See Kateb, *The Inner Ocean*, ch. 4.

120. A similar possibility is suggested by Samuel Gross, "The Romance of Revenge: Capital Punishment in the United States," *Studies in Law, Politics and Society* 13 (1993): 71.